If Texas Were Chile

Other Sequoia Seminar Publications
available from ICS Press

Policy Reform and Equity

Beyond the Informal Sector

Development With Trade

More Taxing Than Taxes?

Capital Markets and Development

*Promoting Democracy and Free Markets
in Eastern Europe*

IF TEXAS
WERE CHILE
A PRIMER
ON BANKING REFORM

A Sequoia Seminar

Edited by
Philip L. Brock

 PRESS

Institute for Contemporary Studies
San Francisco, California

If Texas Were Chile

Inquiries, book orders, and catalog requests should be addressed to ICS Press, 243 Kearny Street, San Francisco, California 94108. (415) 981-5353; Fax: (415) 986-4878; book orders within the contiguous United States: **(800) 326-0263**.

The cover was designed by Irene Imfeld.

The index was compiled by Julia Petrakis.

This book is derived from the proceedings of one of the seminars in a series conducted by the Sequoia Institute. Both the seminar series and this publication were funded by the United States Agency for International Development.

PDC-0092-A-00-6050-00

U.S.A.I.D.

Library of Congress Cataloging-in-Publication Data

If Texas were Chile : a primer on banking reform / edited by Philip L.
  Brock.
      p.   cm.—(A Sequoia seminar)
    Includes bibliographical references and index.
    ISBN 1-55815-206-7 — ISBN 1-55815-207-5 (pbk.)
    1. Banks and banking—State supervision—Congresses.   2. Banks and
banking—Chile—State supervision—Congresses.   3. Banking law—
Chile—Congresses.   4. Banks and Banking—Texas—State supervision—
Congresses.   5. Agricultural prices—United States—History—20th
century—Congresses.   6. Deposit insurance—United States—
Congresses.   I. Brock, Philip Lawton.   II. Series.
    HG1725.I3   1992
    332.1'09766—dc20   92-6658
                                                                          CIP

Contents

List of Figures

List of Tables

Preface

The central message of *If Texas Were Chile: A Primer on Banking Reform* is that government shielding of banks from the hazards, and thereby the influence, of the free market fosters unsound, crisis-prone banking systems.

Almost anywhere in the world, insolvent and mismanaged banks are allowed to go out of business only at the discretion of government supervisors. Banks are often maintained in business for so long that their afflictions spread throughout a regional or national economy: a situation that has yielded catastrophe for entire financial systems. Historically, efforts to mandate government monitoring of financial institutions and state-directed closing of insolvent banks do not adequately take account of bureaucratic inertia and the failure—for whatever reason—of supervisors to enforce such guidelines.

Chile's 1986 banking law is a focal point of this volume. This law makes banking operations transparent to the public and permits bank monitors a minimum of discretion in either the recapitalization or the closing of failing firms—thus increasing the regulatory atmosphere's resemblance to a free market. This law has had profound effect on the Chilean financial community and on the thinking of innovative economists there and elsewhere.

As was the case with an earlier volume in the Sequoia series— *Capital Markets and Development*, edited by Steve H. Hanke and Alan A. Walters (ICS Press, 1991)—we are reminded that properly functioning, advanced financial infrastructures are needed for all countries, be they of the third world or of the first. Although faulty banking systems certainly do plague developed economies—hence this volume's attention to the Texas crisis of the 1980s—their effects can be even more oppressive in less developed economies. The concentration of *If Texas Were Chile* on primary commodity-exporting economies lends it special pertinence in this regard.

It is our hope at the Institute for Contemporary Studies that the ideas and evidence found in this volume will have an important and enduring influence on the restructuring of banking systems. In advancing the self-governance of banks and bankers relative to the discretion of central governments, this book both reflects the principles of ICS's Center for Self-Governance and introduces a key ingredient in the self-governance recipe for economic prosperity— a program that can apply wherever governments allow it and citizens adopt it.

Robert B. Hawkins, Jr.
President and CEO
Institute for Contemporary Studies

San Francisco, California
April, 1992

Foreword

If Texas Were Chile publicizes a paradox: When a bank goes out of business, financial uncertainty and instability are increased, but when poorly performing, money-losing banks are *prevented* from going out of business those problems are *compounded*.

Rather than attempt either to evade or to solve this paradox, this volume wisely accepts it as being as inescapable as any other catch-22. It also recognizes that banks that should go out of business are always allowed to do so eventually, albeit at greater financial, economic, and social cost than would have been incurred had closure not been delayed. In consequence, this volume explores the means by which bank closures that should occur, will occur—at the earliest possible date, and with the least possible damage.

Early identification of banks that should be closed was a paramount concern of those who authored and enacted a new banking law for Chile in 1986. Approximately one-fourth of the law's text is devoted to the precise specification of several alternative closure and recapitalization mechanisms for banks that permit a minimum amount of discretion on the part of government supervisors. The

law has already influenced financial reforms in Mexico and elsewhere in Latin America; now, with its initial publication in the
English language, in this volume, it may affect future reforms in
many other countries.

"We call this volume a primer on banking reform," Philip L.
Brock advises in the book's opening chapter, "because it combines
the elements of sound historical studies of financial crises, dialogue
among distinguished discussants on the meaning of the studies for
financial reform today, and the text, analysis, and discussion of a
significant banking law." Then he expresses the hope "that the
combination has produced a treatment of banking reform that is
elementary in the most sophisticated sense of the word." His hope
has been realized.

In consequence, my own hope is that all those who influence
banking legislation, regulation, and supervision will adopt the
reading of this primer as one of their responsibilities. They will learn
that primary commodity-exporting economies like those of Chile
and Texas are the classrooms in which the universal lessons of
financial stability are most apparent and abundant.

Readers of this volume will also learn of an array of banking
calamities in a variety of economies at different times in history;
some of these, such as the financial breakdown of 1837–1839 in the
United States, have the added utility of representing the history of
financial collapses occurring in the complete absence of government deposit insurance.

The earlier the identification of near-bankrupt banks, the greater
the likelihood that additional infusions of private capital will enable
some to stay in business. With respect to banks that are unable to
attract private recapitalization, it may be impossible to read this
book carefully without coming to view their earliest possible closure
as one of the best things that can happen, both for the banks that
remain and for the more general economy.

Sponsorship by the United States Agency for International Development (AID) of the Sequoia series of seminars—of which the one
represented here, convened in October 1989, was the seventh—is

an outgrowth of the agency's policy endeavors for more than a decade. The primary objectives of the series are:

(1) to shed new light on critical issues of third world development and its assistance
(2) to serve as a catalyst for a new generation of thinkers and ideas that will accelerate the inclusion of *all* people in the process of individual and social development

Support for these seminars sustains a commitment by the agency to encourage the reexamination of established precepts and practices, pursuant to the formulation of more effective development policies. In accordance with this purpose, the series strives to enlarge the supply of talent and ideas that are dedicated to development issues. One component of this effort is the publication and dissemination of each seminar's proceedings. Another is to bring together, within each of the seminars, several promising scholars who are relatively new to the international development field, by virtue of their youth or the concentration of their previous scholarship on other subject matter, to interact with established development scholars and practitioners.

No seminar in the series more completely illustrates the fulfillment of the series' objectives than the ones represented in this volume. Indeed, the origins of *If Texas Were Chile* date to the very first seminar in the series, in May 1987; especially to the contributions of one of its select scholar participants, Professor Brock (who had been nominated for participation by Anne O. Krueger). The nascent idea largely took on its present form in the aftermath of the series' fourth seminar, in June 1988, when the talents of Professor Brock were reengaged on the topic of capital markets and development.

In addition to the support of the administrator of the agency, Ronald W. Roskens, and assistant administrators Richard E. Bissell and Reginald J. Brown, the cooperation of numerous AID personnel has been instrumental in the success of the seminar series. Especially important are the contributions of several AID project officers: Edwin L. Hullander, Warren Weinstein, Neal S. Zank, Fred Kirschstein, and, from the agency's Bureau for Private Enterprise, Catherine R. Gordon.

Peter Hayes and Janet Mowery of ICS Press also warrant special mention for their customary diligence and skill in bringing this manuscript to press.

The opinions expressed in the volumes of this series are not necessarily shared by either Sequoia Institute or the Agency for International Development. Nonetheless, it is anticipated that the diversity and strength of the ideas and evidence found in these pages will reward all those who attend to them.

Jerry Jenkins
Series Director/Editor

April 1992

1 *Philip L. Brock*

Introduction

In the decade of the 1980s, a sustained decline in world commodity prices and a prolonged rise in world real interest rates produced severe financial pressures on the banking systems of many primary commodity-exporting economies, including those of Argentina, Brazil, Chile, Colombia, Costa Rica, Ecuador, Malaysia, Mexico, Norway, Peru, Venezuela, and Texas and the U.S. Farm Belt states. This volume focuses on the episodes of financial collapse of two of those economies, Chile and Texas, as well as on a period of financial distress for the U.S. Farm Belt states during the 1920s.

Although the financial collapses of both Texas and Chile have been well publicized, the extent of financial collapse in the 1980s elsewhere is not generally appreciated. The first section of this introduction offers an overview of the financial problems in Latin America as a way of putting the experiences of Chile and Texas into a broader hemispheric perspective. The second section discusses the way in which this volume is designed to serve as a primer on banking reform. The third section contains a brief summary of the volume's chapters.

Financial Distress in Latin America during the 1980s

Financial collapse or distress characterized most Latin American economies in the 1980s. In the wake of government bailouts of many small and large banks, a number of countries revised their banking legislation, but others saw proposals for reform tied up in political struggles. The following short summaries indicate the widespread nature of banking problems in the region.[1]

Argentina. Argentina was the first country to undergo a large-scale bank collapse, when 20 percent of its banks were liquidated during the 1980–1982 banking crisis. In July 1983 the economic reform team of José Dagnino Pastore and Domingo Cavallo began to reduce the internal debt burden by engineering a hyperinflation with deposit controls that imposed a capital levy on depositors through highly negative real deposit rates. Between June 1982 and February 1983 the real value of deposits in the banking system fell by 58 percent. Even with the capital levy, the third largest bank (Banco de Italia) failed in May 1985, and half a dozen other banks failed in September and October 1986. In 1987 a new banking law was passed that attempted to tighten controls over the banking sector.

Brazil. Although Brazil had a number of minor financial problems during 1980–1983, the first major problem was the collapse of the five largest independent savings companies in April and May 1984. The system's supervisory agency was left with the clean-up of a massive default on mortgages made by the savings companies. In 1985 the government intervened in Comind, Banco Sul-Brasileiro, and Banco Auxiliar, the eighth, thirteenth, and fifteenth largest banks. In May 1988 Brazil approved a new banking law that bans the use of public funds for bailouts of failed banks and establishes a special reserve fund for banks.

Chile. Between 1981 and 1983 the government took over many banks, including the two largest, altogether accounting for over 50 percent of the financial system's assets. Between 1983 and 1986 the government engaged in two global reschedulings of private sector debt, purchased large quantities of uncollectable loans from banks at face value, provided large subsidies to dollar debtors, and oversaw the bankruptcy and restructuring of some of the largest firms in the country. In September 1986 the government approved a new banking law designed to prevent future government rescues of the financial system. The law was amended in May 1988 and August 1989 in an attempt to limit fiscal discretion in circumventing the law.

Colombia. Between June 1982 and October 1984 the government intervened in twenty-two financial entities. In 1986 the government created a deposit insurance fund. By late 1987 the deposit insurance fund had been forced to intervene in a number of large banks. By early 1988 the government, through the deposit insurance fund, controlled the operation of 80 percent of the nation's financial institutions.

Costa Rica. At the beginning of 1987 estimated financial losses of both public and private banks constituted a large percentage (perhaps greater than 100 percent) of bank capital and reserves. Between the second quarter of 1987 and the first quarter of 1988 the central bank found itself in the middle of a banking crisis that began with the failure of a number of small, nonregulated financial institutions and eventually included the failure of one of the largest nonregulated finance companies in January 1988. Although the central bank maintained that depositors at these institutions should have been aware of the risks they were assuming, the spread of the panic to banks and brokerage firms finally forced the central bank to intervene in late January 1988. During 1989 and 1990 the Costa Rican government attempted to restructure the banking system.

Mexico. After two large devaluations of the peso in 1982, President José López Portillo nationalized the Mexican banking system on September 1 of that year. The nationalization imposed exchange controls and capital losses on holders of dollar deposits. Although the size of the system's uncollectable loans is not known with much certainty, it is estimated in the neighborhood of at least 15 percent of total loans. Much of the period following 1982 was spent in a discussion of the reprivatization of the banks, a process that finally began in 1987.

Peru. In November 1981 the government of Peru intervened in the operation of Banco de la Industria de la Construcción, the flagship bank of a conglomerate that invested heavily in property development. In late 1982 the government liquidated the third largest private commercial bank, Banco Comercial, after having found U.S. $100 million of irrecoverable loans on the bank's portfolio. In April 1983 the seventh largest private commercial bank was liquidated. In July 1984 the Banco Popular, Peru's second largest commercial bank and one of the three banks owned by the state, was forced to stop lending when 12 percent of its loans were classified as irrecoverable by the Superintendency of Banks. In July 1987 President Alan García announced the nationalization of the banking system but was forced to retreat on the issue during 1988.

Uruguay. During 1981 and 1982 several large banks failed in Uruguay. The central bank repurchased a large part of the uncollectable loan portfolio of the banks, some of which were subsidiaries of foreign banks. By 1983 the central bank's portfolio of uncollectable loans was about 15 percent of gross domestic product.

Venezuela. In November 1982 the Superintendency of Banks took over the management of the country's largest bank, the Banco de los Trabajadores de Venezuela, because of the bank's inability to meet clearinghouse payments. In December 1982 three of the four largest banks received an injection of U.S. $2.3 billion provided by the issuing of domestic bonds, which were purchased in large part by the state-owned oil company. In 1985 several other large banks were taken over by the government, including Banco de Comercio. In May

1985 the government set up a deposit guarantee fund. During 1986–1988, legislation to overhaul the regulation of the banking system was mired in a political battle.

A Primer on Banking Reform

Whether in Latin America or elsewhere, the aftermath of a banking collapse has inevitably produced proposals to restructure the banking system and to reform banking legislation. The process of reforming banking legislation and regulatory practice is, however, very rarely simple. Economic theory provides insights that can aid policy makers engaged in financial reforms, but even very good theoretical work on financial intermediation—such as Williamson (1987), Bernanke and Gertler (1989), Townsend (1990), and Calomiris and Kahn (1991)—does not attempt to model governmental financial regulation. For example, in existing theoretical models of banks, bank closure occurs as part of efficient private sector monitoring arrangements. In a world with government insurance of depositors, in contrast, bank closure never occurs automatically but rather takes place at the discretion of the government.

In the absence of explicit models of governmental bank regulation, proposals for banking reform are often closely linked to a set of prudential financial standards that go by the acronym CAMEL (referring to bank capital, assets, management, earnings, and liquidity). Prudential financial standards, however, are often diluted or not enforced by governments at precisely those times when financial institutions come under stress. Inattention to the possible unwillingness of the government to enforce banking legislation is a shortcoming of many financial reforms that appear on paper to encourage safe and sound banking practices.

The failure to monitor banks carefully and to close insolvent banks, even though financial legislation mandates such monitoring and closure, is an example of time-inconsistent behavior by a government. Time inconsistency refers to the tendency of a government not to self-enforce policies that the government had previously adopted. Neither theoretical models of financial intermediaries nor general discussions of the principles of financial regulation can accurately portray the political pressures and discretionary fiscal behavior that may lead to the breakdown of prudential regulatory practices.

Understanding breakdowns in the enforcement of prudential financial legislation ultimately requires historical studies of banking crises. Historical studies generally concentrate on a single episode, making it difficult to separate the idiosyncratic aspects of an episode from more general aspects that are relevant for the design of banking legislation. The three studies we have chosen for this volume avoid the limitations of single case studies by examining financial crises in economies that share the common characteristic of a high dependence on primary commodity exports. Such economies have historically been particularly vulnerable to banking crises, and unlike larger, more diversified economies, face observable shocks (such as export price declines) that precipitate banking crises. The comparison of financial crises across these three studies consequently proves indispensable for investigating whether banking legislation and regulation can be crafted to create a credible and nondiscretionary set of monitoring and closure processes for financial institutions.

In planning this volume we recognized that there are two types of banking crisis history. One is the written economic history. The studies in this volume exemplify the best characteristics of good economic histories: they are rich in detail, they make judicious use of economic theory, and they carefully weigh alternative viewpoints on the crises. The other type of history is the informal one created for the policy maker who faces the task of reforming banking legislation. The policy maker must make decisions expeditiously and can only with some difficulty take into account the complexity of causes and the ambiguities of interpretation that emerge from careful analyses of financial crises. Because the policy maker's interpretation of history is the one that ultimately affects the outcome of financial reforms, we attempt to create an accessible policymaking history by weaving into the volume the dialogue of the participants at the conference that gave rise to this volume. The spirited debate that took place among the authors, lead commentators, and other participants at the conference makes the dialogue on policy reform an integral part of the volume.

From the outset of planning for this volume, we believed that a thorough treatment of financial reform had to contain an analysis of a substantive piece of financial legislation to focus discussion onto the details of translating ideas for banking reform into workable law. We chose Chile's 1986 banking law to anchor this volume. The distinctive feature of the Chilean banking law is its attention to the time-consistency problem as it relates to bank monitoring and closure rules. The Chilean banking law includes size-based and maturity-based deposit insurance, risk-adjusted capital requirements, market-value accounting of banks' assets, and rules regarding disclosure of bank information to private risk-rating firms. Approximately one-fourth of the text of the banking law is devoted to the precise specification of several alternative closure and recapitalization mechanisms for banks that permit a minimum amount of discretion on the part of the government.

Seminal banking legislation in one country has always had an influence on policy reform in other countries. For example, Chile's 1860 banking legislation was influenced by free-banking legislation in the United States while Japan's 1872 banking law was modeled after the 1863 National Bank Act of the United States.[2] The 1986 Chilean banking law has already influenced financial reforms in Mexico and elsewhere in Latin America, and for that reason alone merits serious attention.

We call this volume a primer on banking reform because it combines the elements of sound historical studies of financial crises, dialogue among distinguished discussants on the meaning of the studies for financial reform today, and the text, analysis, and discussion of a significant banking law. We hope that the combination has produced a treatment of banking reform that is elementary in the most sophisticated sense of the word.[3]

An Overview of the Studies

Chapters 2 and 3 provide microeconomic analyses of the incentives created by financial regulations in Chile and Texas before their financial collapses in the early 1980s. In Chapter 2, Sergio de la Cuadra and Salvador Valdés present a comprehensive study of the events leading from the liberalization of the Chilean financial system in 1974 to the system's collapse in 1983. The authors' academic training and experience (de la Cuadra was vice president of the central bank, president of the central bank, and finance minister between 1977 and 1982; Valdés wrote his 1986 dissertation at the Massachusetts Institute of Technology on financial regulation) permit a rare, analytically focused, inside view of the events leading to the 1983 collapse.

In Chapter 3, Paul Horvitz undertakes a similar analysis of the Texas bank collapse. In addition to having credentials as former head of the research department at the Federal Deposit Insurance Corporation (FDIC) (1967–1977) and as the coauthor of *Perspectives on Safe and Sound Banking* (MIT Press, 1986), Horvitz was also well placed at the University of Houston to observe the events he analyzes.

These two studies provide an intellectual background of specific examples, comparisons, and contrasts of regulatory and bank behavior that are of critical importance for anyone who wishes to understand the issues of banking reform. De la Cuadra and Valdés provide, among other contributions, an analysis of the problems financial regulators encounter in effectively supervising the risk-taking propensities of bank holding companies. They also document the internal policy-making struggle in Chile during 1976–1983 between three factions in the government (the free-banking, state-supervision, and financial-repression factions). Horvitz discusses four contrasting strategies followed by Texas banks to regain profitability after 1981, and the role of deposit insurance in permitting those strategies. He also provides a detailed look at supervisory problems in the Texas bank collapse.

Chapter 4 focuses on the 1986 revision of the Chilean banking law. The analysis of the antecedents and debate leading to the 1986 banking legislation is written by Guillermo Ramírez (superintendent of banks in Chile at the time of the seminar) and Francisco Rosende (head of the Studies Department at the central bank at the time of the seminar), both of whom were active participants in the process leading to the new law.[4] Appendices I and II present an English translation (made for the volume) of the new legislation.

In Chapter 5, Charles Calomiris shows that before the adoption of federal deposit insurance in 1933, the United States was a rich source of information on the performance of alternative financial structures in commodity-exporting economies. Calomiris demonstrates that different state financial regulations explain a large part of the differences among the "farm crisis" states in limiting the disruption of their financial systems caused by the prolonged downturn in agricultural prices during the 1920s. Drawing on an extensive data base, Calomiris makes a thirty-eight-state comparison of the relative performance of national banks and state banks, banks in states with and without branch banking, and banks with and without deposit insurance.

Chapters 2, 3, 4, and 5 are each followed by the transcript of the discussion that took place during the day of the seminar. The lead commentators for the chapters—Gary Gorton (the Wharton School), Peter Diamond (MIT), Kenneth Scott (Stanford Law School), and Richard Webb (president, Central Bank of Peru, 1980–1985)[5]—are all distinguished researchers on various aspects of financial markets.

Chapter 6 was written in response to a theme that emerged during the seminar regarding the importance of prompt closure mechanisms for insolvent banks to eliminate loan-loss rollovers. Chapter 6 analyzes the macroeconomic consequences of loan-loss rollovers in an analytical model to interpret certain aspects of the financial collapses that occurred in Chile (1981–1983), Texas (1986–1988), and the United States (1837–1839). Chapter 7 concludes the volume with a discussion of alternative approaches to bank regulation in the aftermath of a financial collapse.

2 *Sergio de la Cuadra and Salvador Valdés*

Myths and Facts about Financial Liberalization in Chile: 1974–1983

Chile's financial liberalization of 1974–1983 has claimed the attention of numerous analysts hoping to extract lessons from it. This chapter provides detailed evidence and analyses of the main episodes in this experience, and, having concluded that the prudential regulation of banks is critical for the success of financial liberalization, explores this issue in particular depth.

A number of analysts have singled out regulatory failures in the financial system as an important cause of the 1982–1983 recession in Chile. Most of these analysts, however, take a macroeconomic approach and do not investigate the precise reasons for failure within the financial sector. This inattention to detail has led some analysts to express wholesale doubts about the appropriateness of financial liberalization (as in Arellano, 1983).[1] In contrast, the aim of this chapter is to provide more discrete and precise conclusions. Such conclusions are required for the design of financial liberalizations that may not preclude temporary setbacks but do preclude the pessimism that would engender a return to financial repression.

Following this introduction, the first section in this chapter reviews the dynamics of the real interest rate in the Chilean financial liberalization, excluding issues of prudential regulation. The second section provides a conceptual framework for analyzing issues of prudential regulation. The third section covers the Chilean experience with prudential regulation during the years 1976–1982 and includes subsections addressing the Chilean experience with contingent government subsidies, moral hazard, the rollover of unrealized loan losses, and the problems raised by intragroup lending by business groups that controlled banks. Finally, the fourth section draws lessons for both financial liberalization and prudential regulation.

The Dynamics of the Real Interest Rate

In this section we offer an explanation for the high level that the real interest rate reached during Chile's financial liberalization in 1974–1980. The approach is basically microeconomic, in the sense that it emphasizes the behavior over time of the suppliers and the borrowers of funds and the production costs of financial services. We begin with a brief description of the liberalization process, stressing events in the banking industry. We then discuss in some detail the timing and sequencing of the deregulation of different controls because these factors are relevant to the two hypotheses that we propose on the dynamics of the real interest rate: (1) investors' portfolios adjust slowly to liberalization, and this delay causes the interest rate to overshoot at the beginning of the liberalization; (2) after many years of financial repression the banking industry loses its capacity to act as an efficient intermediary for funds, and hence when deregulated it behaves like an infant industry in which costs decline through time.

The high interest rate in Chile during the first stage of financial liberalization was also the result of macroeconomic factors, primarily a perception that the 1975–1976 recession was a transitory real income shock.

The empirical evidence is consistent with our two hypotheses for the 1974–1980 period. It cannot, however, fully explain the sharp rise of the real interest rate in 1981. This issue is discussed in the second section of this chapter, which presents a framework for the analysis of prudential regulation.

The financial liberalization, step by step. Financial liberalization in Chile comprised two policy areas: deregulation of the banking industry and development of a securities market. Deregulation focused primarily on phasing out a battery of credit controls, including credit ceilings, maximum interest rates, reserve requirements, and a ceiling on foreign borrowing by banks. This policy area also involved the standardization of operations and regulations among three types of institutions—commercial banks, development banks, and *financieras*, or finance companies—as well as some operations of credit and saving cooperatives.

As a basic principle this process regulated specific operations without distinction among institutions, so the difference between commercial and development banks disappeared. *Financieras*, however, were excluded from the checking account market and foreign trade financing (the idea was to induce them to become banks). In this sense, the Chilean bank deregulation policy included a shift toward multiproduct banking.

The second policy area was intended to establish the basis for developing a securities market by the modernization of the legal framework and the creation of new financial institutions. Important changes were made in several laws regulating corporations and public offerings of commercial paper and long-term debt (bonds and debentures). New institutions were introduced to the market, such as *agencias de valores* (market makers for securities), mutual funds, and private pension funds. The stock exchange and the insurance industry were among the other traditional institutions boosted by the financial liberalization.

Because this chapter deals mainly with the banking industry, our description of the liberalization process concentrates on this sector, identifying the types of restrictions present at the outset of liberalization and the timing of their elimination.

Credit ceilings. The credit ceiling is a common tool for monetary control in countries where the central bank is the main source of financing for public sector deficits. This was the case in Chile from the creation of its central bank in 1925 until April 1976. Under President Salvador Allende's socialist government, the public sector deficit increased to 14 percent of gross domestic product with heavy reliance on the printing press for deficit financing. By the end of 1973, when the military government came into power, inflation had reached an annualized monthly rate of 1,000 percent. A deep fiscal reform in 1975 eliminated the deficit by 1976, when the ceilings were abandoned.

During the two years before the credit liberalization, there were four distinguishable stages of credit ceilings. From January 1974 to September 1974 global limits for the banking system were established. During this initial period, sectoral sublimits on credit for agricultural, nonagricultural, and capital goods simplified the previous tangle of credit controls to manageable levels. From October 1974 to December 1974 credit ceilings were completely lifted. From January 1975 to July 1975 ceilings were reestablished, but banks were allowed to increase their loans by the increment in time deposits over the outstanding amount as of September 1974. From August 1975 to March 1976 the credit ceiling was made equal to the outstanding loans as of July 1975. In April 1976 the authority abandoned this tool of monetary control.

The attempt to liberalize credit in October 1974, before the required fiscal adjustment, was abandoned after only one quarter because the elimination of credit ceilings, which are equivalent to a 100 percent marginal reserve requirement, reduces the base against which the inflation tax is levied. Credit ceilings were reestablished in January 1975 and became more stringent in October to ensure fiscal equilibrium. Once the fiscal reform succeeded, a sustained liberalization was possible.

Interest rate controls. The pegging of maximum interest rates substantially below market-clearing levels was defended by Chilean politicians for many years on two grounds: first as a way of subsidizing specific groups of borrowers and second as a way of "fighting inflation"—similar to the argument given for fixing the prices of goods. Because the nominal interest rate ceilings were generally much lower than the ongoing inflation rate, the ceilings imposed a high tax on time deposits. During the three decades before 1975 time deposits were, consequently, never significant in relation to gross domestic product (see Table 2.1).

Until June 1974 maximum interest rates were fixed for both time deposits and loans. The lending rate was 20 percentage points above the deposit rate. The deposit rate was liberalized first, while a ceiling was maintained on the rate of loans. The rate on thirty-day loans was 115 percent (on an annualized basis) during a period when inflation was over 400 percent. In May 1975 the lending rate was also liberalized and immediately went up to impressive levels of 1,300 percent nominal and 246 percent real. This experience was short-lived; in October of the same year interest rates for deposits and

TABLE 2.1
Monetary Aggregates, Ratios, 1940–1980 (percentages)

	$\dfrac{M1}{GDP}$	$\dfrac{\text{Time deposits}}{GDP}$	$\dfrac{\text{Time deposits}}{M1}$
1940	12.0	1.9	15.8
1950	10.5	0.4	3.8
1960	9.0	1.9	21.1
1970	10.2	0.8	7.8
1973	22.2	0.1	0.5
1975	8.7	2.5	28.7
1980	7.3	12.0	164.4

NOTE: M1 consists of currency held by the nonbank public, demand deposits, other checkable deposits at all depository institutions, and traveler's checks.
SOURCE: Banco Central de Chile, *Indicadores económicos y sociales 1960–1982* (Santiago, 1983).

loans were fixed again. In January of 1976 interest rates were again allowed to be freely determined in the market. This policy was maintained until December 1982, when the central bank began to intervene in the market by "suggesting" a deposit rate to the banks.

Another important event in this process was a parliamentary act of May 1974 (Decree Law No. 455), by which interest was defined as "the amount received by the creditor in excess of the principal adequately adjusted by inflation." This legislation can be singled out as the institutionalization of indexation in the Chilean financial system; a corresponding monetary correction was incorporated into the tax system in 1975. Indexation was initially allowed only for operations a term of one year or more; in July 1976 this restriction was reduced to ninety days. In September 1977 commercial banks were allowed to make contracts using a unit of account indexed to the consumer price index (CPI),[2] a practice previously employed only by mortgage and development banks.

The 1974 act also established that interest rates should be freely determined in the market, but that commercial banks, the state bank, and savings and loans were exempted from this scheme. These institutions were subject to a different timing of interest rate controls, as previously described.

Reserve requirements and interest. In the Chilean context of very high inflation, legal reserves on bank deposits were intensively used by the central bank as a way of raising funds to finance its own loans; the commercial banks were only intermediaries between depositors and the central bank.

The policy adopted in April 1976 established a clear break between financial repression and financial liberalization. In that month credit ceilings were abolished and a program for phasing out high reserve requirements was begun.

There had been previous attempts to reduce reserve requirements. In October 1974 reserve requirements on thirty- to eighty-nine-day deposits and ninety-day to one-year deposits were reduced from 40 percent to 8 percent. In July 1975 reserve requirements on demand deposits were also reduced to a uniform rate of 80 percent.

Before the reduction there had been a base rate of 100 percent and a marginal rate of 80 percent. In August 1975, however, this policy was reversed, and thirty- to eighty-nine-day time deposits were subject to a high technical reserve (95 percent in August, 90 percent in September, and 80 percent thereafter) to be fulfilled by a mandatory investment in Treasury bills. The reduction of reserve requirements took place in five stages, summarized in Table 2.2.

The general idea of the monetary authorities was to unify the reserve requirement rates on time deposits and to proceed faster in the reduction of reserve requirements on longer-term deposits. The initial targets were the minimum rates authorized by the law at that time: 20 percent on demand deposits and 8 percent on time deposits. A subsequent amendment to the law reduced these minimum rates to 10 percent and 4 percent, respectively.

When the liberalization program began in May 1976, the reserve

TABLE 2.2
Reserve Requirements, 1976–1980 (percentage)

	Demand deposits	30- to 89-day time deposits	90 day–1 year time deposits
First stage			
(May 1976–December 1977)			
Initial rates	85	55	55
Final rates	59	20	8
Second stage			
(January 1978–July 1978)			
Initial rates	59	20	8
Final rates	42	20	8
Third stage			
(August 1978–March 1979)		(no changes)	
Fourth stage			
(April 1979–December 1979)			
Initial rates	42	19	8
Final rates	42	8	8
Fifth stage			
(January 1980–December 1980)			
Initial rates	21	7	7
Final rates	10	4	4

SOURCE: Banco Central de Chile, *Boletín mensual*, various issues (June 1976–January 1984).

requirement rates were calculated in such a way that the lending capacity of the banks in that month was equal to the credit ceiling being eliminated.

The gradual reduction of the reserve requirements through 1976–1980 was managed according to a credit program that established targets for credit expansion and reduction of central bank lending through the substitution of commercial bank credit for central bank credit. The minimum rates reached in December 1980 have been maintained since then. (On average they are not binding; in that sense they are quite similar to voluntary reserves.)

Reserve requirements were reduced slowly to avoid a steep rise in the money multiplier, which would have jeopardized the parallel process of reducing the inflation rate. High reserve requirements, however, imposed a heavy tax on funds for which banks and other financial institutions acted as intermediaries. To alleviate this situation the central bank decided to pay interest on reserve requirements on time deposits. The rate at which this interest was paid changed over time. Specifically, the interest rate on reserves was equal to

- The short-term Treasury bill rate (May 1976–October 1976)

- 70 percent of the rate paid on time deposits (November 1976– December 1976)

- 90 percent of the rate paid on time deposits (January 1977–April 1977)

- The rate paid on time deposits (May 1977–April 1979)

- 50 percent of the rate paid on time deposits (May 1979–August 1979)

- Zero (since September 1979)

With regard to reserve requirements on foreign currency liabilities, a distinction was made between two types of liabilities: foreign currency deposits and foreign borrowing by banks, firms, and individuals. Until December 1979 the reserve requirement rates on foreign currency deposits were 20 percent for demand deposits and 8 percent for time deposits. These rates were reduced to 10 and 4 percent in January 1980.

Reserve requirements on foreign borrowing were established in April 1978 as part of a policy to restrict this kind of indebtedness. Loans with an average maturity of two years or less were forbidden; for longer terms the required reserves were:

Average maturity less than thirty-six months: 25 percent

Average maturity from thirty-six to forty-seven months: 15 percent

Average maturity from forty-eight to sixty-five months: 10 percent

Average maturity of sixty-six or more months: 0 percent

No interest was paid on these reserves, since the idea was to tax this source of finance in a way that promoted longer-term borrowing. This objective was achieved successfully, since most borrowing was done in the longer terms, favoring what was, for the central bank, a more manageable structure of the foreign debt.

Ceilings on foreign liabilities. Foreign borrowing by banks was legally restricted to a small multiple of their capital and reserves. Until January 1978 foreign borrowing was authorized only for the financing of loans related to foreign trade. After January 1978 commercial banks were allowed to extend loans for any other purpose but were not permitted to assume foreign exchange risk directly because of the requirement that their foreign borrowing be used for the sole purpose of funding foreign currency loans. The evolution of limits on foreign borrowing by commercial banks is shown in Table 2.3.

Authorized foreign currency loans were also limited to 25 percent of banks' capital and reserves, and this sublimit was included in the global limit, shown in Table 2.3. (The remainder of foreign borrowing was restricted to trade financing.) Additional limits for foreign currency loans with average maturities of over thirty-six months were instituted in April 1978.

Foreign currency loans were also limited in flow. There was a

TABLE 2.3
Ceiling on Foreign Borrowing by Banks, 1974–1979 (percentage of capital and reserves)

	Global	Extra
January 1974	200	0
January 1975	100	0
June 1976	150	0
March 1978	160	0
April 1978	160	20
December 1978	180	35
April 1979	180	45
June 1979	free	free

NOTE: There was no limit on foreign indebtedness for nonbank corporations.
SOURCE: Sergio de la Cuadra and Dominique Hachette, *The Timing and Sequencing of a Trade Liberalization Policy: The Case of Chile*, Vol. 2 (Santiago: Pontificia Universidad Católica de Chile, Instituto de Economía, 1985).

maximum amount that each bank could lend in any month. For the months listed below, these amounts were:

January 1978:	5 percent of capital and reserves
November 1978:	the larger of 5 percent of capital and reserves or U.S. $2 million
July 1979:	the larger of 5 percent of capital and reserves or U.S. $1 million
February 1980:	the larger of 5 percent of capital and reserves or U.S. $2 million
April 1980:	unrestricted (limited only by the bank's legal maximum debt/equity ratio of 20)

The policy of the central bank was to manage the growth of foreign debt attributable to foreign borrowing by domestic banks. The principal argument in support of this policy was that it would minimize the instability introduced by volatile capital flows. The supply of foreign capital to the country had proven remarkably unstable in the past, and the central bank authorities were attempting to smooth the fluctuations of the capital account.

The business community, in general, and some academic economists strongly attacked the central bank's policy. The business community blamed the policy for delaying a decline in the interest rate and for discriminating among borrowers, since those better connected to banks had access to cheaper financing. The dissenting academic economists did not agree with the hypothesis of instability in supply, although a few suggested that a small tax on foreign borrowing could be justified if there were an upward-sloping supply schedule of foreign capital to the economy.

Finding little support for its stance, the monetary authority eventually opened the capital account without restrictions—except for the prohibition of foreign loans with an average maturity of less than two years and the imposition of reserve requirements on foreign loans with maturities of between twenty-four and sixty-five months. This opening of the capital account occurred in April 1980 and was followed by large capital inflows during the remainder of the year and during 1981.

The dynamics of financial liberalization. The Chilean experience highlights interesting issues related to the microeconomic dynamics of a financial liberalization, which have not been dealt with in the literature in spite of their importance for the successful implementation of such a policy.

Chile's financial liberalization encompassed an overshooting of the interest rate, a costly market development process that took about five years, and a delayed reaction by the supervisory authority to the introduction of prudential regulations. We discuss these experiences in the following sections, while omitting any discussion of the macroeconomic effects on the interest rate of the severe recession in 1975–1976.

Asymmetric costs of portfolio adjustment. Interest rate controls ensure that nominal interest rates are set below market-clearing rates. With inflation, these controls often produce interest rates that are negative in real terms. Negative real interest rates had been the norm in Chile since 1940, becoming most negative during the hyperinflation of the early 1970s.

Following the removal of interest rate controls, it seems likely that a slow and inelastic adjustment in the flow supply of credit, in tandem with a fast and elastic flow demand for credit, will produce an asymmetry in the financial market's adjustment to the interest rate liberalization.

The cause of this asymmetry is simple: It will generally take time for households to become able and willing to invest in the new financial assets offered by banks. The ability of households to adjust quickly is limited because it is expensive and difficult to mortgage physical assets in order to generate funds to invest in deposits, especially when the loan-arranging capacity of banks is in its infancy. The willingness to invest is also limited in an environment where the risk of inflation is very high and there is a fresh experience of government-imposed losses on depositors (such as those produced by the failure of the Chilean savings and loan system in June 1975). On the other hand, the large number of firms and individuals that had no access to the credit market during the repressed period is likely to adjust very rapidly, because a firm can easily increase a leverage that is initially zero. The capacity limit here is located on the lending side, that is, the banks.

Asymmetric adjustment costs imply that where interest rate ceilings are the only initial distortion, the freeing of interest rates will cause the real interest rates to overshoot their long-run level. This adjustment, shown in Figure 2.1, helps to explain the Chilean experience of high but falling real interest rates.

Table 2.4 displays the interest rate on short-term loans (thirty to eighty-nine days) in commercial banks, from 1974 (the last year of the financial repression before the initial liberalization attempts in 1975) until the final year of the deep recession of 1982–1983.

During the first six quarters, real interest rates were highly negative; at this time nominal interest rates were fixed by the central bank. Inflation was 376 percent in 1974 and 341 percent in 1975. By the end of the second quarter of 1975, interest rate controls were eliminated and the real rate skyrocketed, reaching 246 percent during the third quarter. This episode accords with the hypothesis that after liberalization the demand for credit adjusts much faster than the supply. In this case the pace of the adjustment was magnified

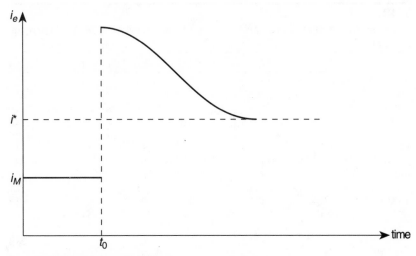

i_M = maximum interest rate.
i^* = long-term equilibrium rate.
i_e = short-term equilibrium rate.

Figure 2.1 Interest Rate on Short-term Loans, 1974–1983

by the existence of credit ceilings (maintained until March 1976). The unexpected overshooting of the rate alarmed the authorities, who returned to fixed interest rates in October of the same year. The new maximum rates were, however, much higher, allowing a real rate of 48 percent during the last quarter of 1975, almost the same as the market-clearing rate that prevailed in 1976.

On January 2, 1976, interest rates were completely liberalized and were not fixed again until late 1982. The market-determined rate found a very high equilibrium, which was sustained over the next three years. The real lending rate fluctuated in a range of 105 percent to 24 percent, with an average rate of 49 percent in 1976, 57 percent in 1977, and 46 percent in 1978. The stubbornly high real rate subsided only in the second quarter of 1979 when the rate fell to 14 percent before continuing to decline to its lowest level of negative 2.4 percent in the fourth quarter of 1980.

This evidence suggests that portfolio adjustment by asset holders

TABLE 2.4

Real Rate of Interest on Thirty-Day Loans, by Year and Quarter, 1974–1983 (percentage, annualized)

	%	%		%	%
1974	−48.0		1979	19.6	
I		−74.3	I		40.9
II		−54.8	II		14.0
III		−21.5	III		6.2
IV		−19.6	IV		18.2
1975	0.0		1980	11.4	
I		−37.2	I		29.8
II		−69.0	II		8.7
III		246.1	III		12.7
IV		47.6	IV		−2.4
1976	49.4		1981	34.5	
I		54.6	I		21.0
II		36.1	II		28.3
III		37.7	III		47.6
IV		75.5	IV		42.6
1977	56.5		1982	31.4	
I		105.8	I		49.4
II		58.3	II		45.9
III		32.9	III		31.4
IV		36.1	IV		2.4
1978	45.9		1983	8.7	
I		88.0	I		29.8
II		23.9	II		1.2
III		25.3	III		1.2
IV		52.9	IV		4.9

NOTE: Commercial banks' lending rate, for thirty-to-eighty-nine-day loans, deflated by the CPI.
SOURCE: Banco Central de Chile, *Boletín mensual*, various issues (May 1977–January 1984).

may exhibit a lag of three years when the financial market is liberalized after a long period of financial repression. The length of the lag, however, is likely to be affected by the timing of particular steps in the overall liberalization program. Thus, the downward pressure on interest rates after the third year (evident in Table 2.4) may be caused in part by the partial opening of the economy to international capital flows beginning in 1978 (and evident in Table 2.3).

Table 2.5 indicates that the annual percentage increase in the

TABLE 2.5
Time Deposits, 1974–1983

	Billions of 1983 pesos	Percentage change
1974	19.3	1.6
1975	23.5	21.8
1976	38.9	65.5
1977	72.3	85.9
1978	152.6	111.1
1979	168.0	10.1
1980	197.0	17.3
1981	362.0	83.8
1982	383.3	5.8
1983	298.0	−22.2

NOTE: Includes passbook accounts.
SOURCE: Banco Central de Chile, *Indicadores económicos y sociales 1960–1982* (Santiago, 1983).

outstanding amount of interest-bearing deposits issued by commercial banks exceeded the percentage increase of the preceding year through 1978. The table reflects slow adjustment during the initial year of liberalization, followed by more sizable increases in each succeeding year.

Market development. Our hypothesis is that at the moment a repressed financial system is liberalized, the banks will be unable to supply intermediation services efficiently because they lack expertise, qualified human resources, and adequate technology. These elements require high intermediation costs represented by a large spread (or difference) between interest rates charged (to borrowers) and paid (to depositors). For the same reason, one should expect banks' portfolios to become more risky as a consequence of an inadequate ability to evaluate the riskiness of loans and higher interest rates.

The same limitations faced by the banks were present in the supervisory agency, the Superintendency of Banks. Before liberalization, the main functions of the bank regulators were to enforce the interest rate and credit controls dictated by the monetary authority.

Their role was confined to seeing that requirements were fulfilled; paying attention to the quality of the banks' assets was not required. There was as a result virtually no capacity to control risks assumed by banks, and prudential regulations were almost absent from the regulatory body of rules. As with official regulators, so with the general public. Never having been exposed to bank risk, the public could scarcely be expected to be helpful in controlling such risk in the newly liberalized banking system. We return to this topic in greater detail in the next section of this chapter.

Bank liberalization after many years of financial repression displays many of the characteristics of an infant industry: Costs can only be reduced through time by a process of learning by doing. In Chile, bank modernization was expensive. Banco de Chile, for example, spent over U.S. $1.5 million in 1978 alone in consulting fees for a reorganization plan bought from Booz, Allen & Hamilton.

In summary, we hypothesize that a liberalized banking industry will initially experience high intermediation costs that decline through time. This decline implies that for a given constant interest rate on deposits over the same period of time, an initially high real lending rate will also decline.

Table 2.6 estimates intermediation costs in Chile over the 1976–1983 period by the spread between the lending and the deposit interest rates on short-term operations, net of the cost of required reserves.

Table 2.6 shows a declining trend from 1977 to 1980—from a very high level (17.4 percent) to a more typical one (5.2 percent). This evidence looks similar to the cost function of an infant industry, supporting the hypothesis that financial repression destroys productive capacity in the banking industry. This consideration acquires great importance for the design of a financial liberalization because in the learning process the banks can take on excessive portfolio risk that may be difficult for a supervisory authority to detect.

We can observe that during the first year of free interest rates in Chile, the net spread did not go up immediately. Because the net

TABLE 2.6

Administration Costs and Spreads in Thirty-Day Operations, by Year and Quarter, 1976–1983 (percentage, annualized)

	Administration cost[a]	Net spreads[b]			Administration cost[a]	Net spreads[b]	
1976	6.9	8.1		1980	4.9	5.2	
I			1.2	I			3.8
II			6.7	II			6.8
III			14.3	III			5.7
IV			10.7	IV			4.4
1977	5.9	17.4		1981	4.4	6.3	
I			26.8	I			3.4
II			19.3	II			5.3
III			14.3	III			7.2
IV			9.8	IV			9.5
1978	5.7	10.7		1982	3.6	9.6	
I			15.9	I			10.0
II			11.2	II			11.0
III			8.1	III			9.3
IV			7.8	IV			8.0
1979	5.1	7.3		1983	2.8	11.0	
I			11.9	I			12.4
II			5.5	II			11.2
III			6.8	III			10.8
IV			5.3	IV			9.8

[a]Administration cost is defined as nonfinancial operating cost as a percentage of total assets.
[b]Net spread is defined as NS $= i_L - i_D - C$; where i_L is the loan rate, i_D is the deposit rate, and C is the interest cost of the legal reserves.
SOURCE: For net spread, Banco Central de Chile, *Boletín mensual*, various issues (January 1976–January 1984). For administration costs, Held (1989, Table I-9).

spread required four quarters to reach a peak, its gradual increase may be largely explained by the inexperience of bank managers in pricing new products.

The increase in the net spread during 1981 may have reflected a growing risk premium and therefore the growing intermediation costs associated with higher domestic and world interest rates. The crisis that had started to develop in Chile during 1981 is consistent with this view.

Coordination failures in financial liberalization: The bankruptcy of the savings and loan system. This subsection will show that financial liberalization is fraught with coordination failures, thus illustrating the need for the utmost care in the detailed design of financial liberalizations.

At the start of 1975 the financial intermediaries in Chile included (1) the commercial banks, all of which continued under government control after Allende's nationalization; (2) the National System of Savings and Loans (SINAP), which was regulated by the government, but most of whose members were controlled by the private sector; (3) the large commercial and development state bank (Banco del Estado de Chile); (4) the formal *financieras*, created during the second half of 1974, which were privately owned, free to set interest rates, and, in the main, unregulated; (5) the informal *financieras*, which had been inadvertently permitted by a 1974 statute that gave the already overworked Superintendency of Banks the task of policing the intermediation of credit by nonbanks; and (6) a few growing and unregulated financial cooperatives that operated like formal *financieras*.

SINAP, which was required by statute to invest only in new buildings, tended to accumulate reserves during any downturn in construction activity. These reserves were held at the central bank and indexed to the CPI. During 1972 and 1973 SINAP accumulated very large reserves at the central bank because few construction companies were willing to risk increasingly common wildcat strikes and their usual outcome—a government decree that designated an administrator and effectively expropriated the buildings under construction. In addition, the government delayed making cost-of-living adjustments to the maximum price SINAP members could charge for new housing.

At the same time, SINAP's long-term loan dividends were adjusted only once a year to past changes in the price level. In the face of 400 percent annual inflation, this lagged indexation process implied that SINAP lost most of its real income from mortgages in those years, while its expenses on sixty-day deposits were adjusted much faster. Therefore, savings and loan members had little true capital left by mid-1974.[3]

At this juncture a large additional element of risk emerged. In early 1974 the new government began to announce that interest rates would be freed. By mid-1974, liberalization measures had allowed *financieras* to set their interest rates freely, and the resulting real rates had been much higher than the real rate of 7 percent on most SINAP long-term loans. Both regulators and private managers of the members of SINAP could therefore easily foresee (indeed, early in the year the issue was being discussed in the press) that if they invested their reserves in long-term loans at fixed real rates and the high short-term rates persisted, failure was inevitable. On the other hand, if free real interest rates were to fall quickly, SINAP would survive to recover its capital base over time.

A key ingredient for the construction boom that took place during the second half of 1974 was a government deposit guarantee for SINAP. Though a guarantee was never given in any statute, depositors had every reason to believe that they would be bailed out. First, heavy regulation by the government—in the tradition of financial repression rather than solvency regulation—justified that belief. Second, a high government official had made the following declaration in a seminar at the central bank in April 1974:

> Foreseeing that the free real interest rate might be high, and that SINAP has a large volume of loans at low fixed real interest rates, the government will subsidize SINAP directly to make up the differ-ence, preventing its bankruptcy. (Undurraga, 1974)[4]

One might expect the private managers of the savings and loans to have turned the moral hazard potential of this commitment into reality as soon as the central bank allowed them to recover their reserves. The government body that regulated SINAP had, however, limited the investment portfolio of savings and loans to mortgage loans and working capital loans, and good information was available. This means that moral hazard cannot explain the failure of SINAP. Why then did SINAP invest so heavily in mortgage loans at fixed real rates during the second half of 1974? Two considerations help to explain the ultimate insolvency of SINAP.

First, SINAP was undoubtedly exposed excessively to interest rate risk. Its assets were long-term mortgages earning a fixed CPI-adjusted interest rate, whereas its liabilities were sixty-day deposits earning a CPI-adjusted interest rate. While interest rates were regulated, the authorities made sure that an appropriate spread was maintained. Later, when the authorities planned an interest rate liberalization in 1974, they realized that SINAP would fail and announced operating subsidies to cover the shortfall. In this sense there was no coordination failure in this area of liberalization.

After liberalization and government support were announced, however, a coordination failure within the government did apparently produce the very rapid growth SINAP exhibited during the second half of 1974. The coordination failure happened as follows: The savings and loans were unable to do anything but increase mortgage lending when the central bank decided to return SINAP's excess reserves in 1974. Because deregulation had just started, there was no short-term instrument that offered CPI indexing in the market, apart from the one issued by SINAP itself and the savings passbooks at Banco del Estado. In addition, the only short-term instruments yielding free nominal interest rates were the liabilities issued by the newly created *financieras*, which were much smaller than SINAP and which exposed SINAP to inflation risk. Even more important, SINAP was not allowed to invest in money market instruments or savings passbooks at Banco del Estado, because only mortgages and loans to construction companies were permitted by its statute; only too late (March 26, 1975) was SINAP allowed to invest in the short term for nonhousing purposes. Finally, individual savings and loans were unable to return to depositors the funds they could not use safely by, say, reducing deposit interest rates, because those rates were fixed by the board of regulators. Thus, even though mortgage lending was a risky use of the excess reserves returned to SINAP by the central bank, there was no alternative available to SINAP that would have provided protection against interest rate risk.

This episode, then, provides a good example of what financial liberalization might mean when it is not designed properly: the failure of the long-term mortgage intermediaries. It also shows that the biggest peril at the outset of a financial liberalization is not moral hazard but the strains of an incomplete and uncoordinated liberalization.

In the case of SINAP, the political economy of poor coordination was founded in the conflict of objectives between the board of senior regulators of SINAP, which was heavily committed to increasing the supply of housing, and the authorities that pushed liberalization. The latter did not realize that SINAP could have been saved if the central bank had issued a CPI-adjusted, fixed interest rate long-term bond to mop up the excess reserves of SINAP.

The crisis developed as follows. In mid-1974 SINAP started to draw on its excess reserves and to invest feverishly in new housing, first financing construction companies and then lending to the buyers at long term. Housing starts by the private sector increased 50 percent during the second half of 1974, as compared to the three previous semesters. Because SINAP's deposits were exempt from reserve requirements, the banking multiplier allowed it to grow 100 percent in real terms during 1974. Starting August 1, 1974, SINAP's regulators attempted to limit bankruptcy risk by requiring a minimum maturity of 180 days in order for deposits to be eligible for indexing. This was three times the traditional sixty days. Although this new decree made the liabilities of *financieras* even more attractive, depositors continued increasing their deposits at SINAP. We assign this fact to the effect of the banking multiplier, operating in a semirepressed market, effecting a huge increase in total investible financial wealth.

The end of the game occurred in January 1975, when depositors began to withdraw. The detonator was an exogenous event, beginning in October 1974: the steep fall in the world price of copper, Chile's main export and the government's main source of revenue. This phenomenon had two major effects: First, a severe recession began, and many depositors withdrew funds to finance growing inventories; second, the fiscal shock put in doubt the government's resolve to honor its guarantee.[5]

But the end of the game was not truly the end; the way SINAP's crisis was handled set precedents for the future. In June 1975, after many depositors had fled SINAP and only those who believed official promises of the deposit guarantee remained, the government decided to freeze the most popular type of SINAP deposit. In the next months the holders of these sixty-day deposits were authorized to withdraw the equivalent of U.S. $100 per month per account but to exchange the remainder only for long-term bonds whose price in the secondary market fluctuated between 80 percent and 60 percent of face value. It is amazing that holders of other types of SINAP liabilities, even liquid ones, were not touched; the basic rules of precedence in a bankruptcy were thereby not respected, signaling that the authorities considered themselves entitled to redistribute wealth according to political priorities in the insolvencies of financial intermediaries.

A side effect of the SINAP failure was the loss of credibility of government guarantees on deposits: The military government had clearly shown its willingness to force depositors to pay for bank losses. For the next eighteen months this termination of the implicit guarantee of bank deposits helped to create an episode of free banking in Chile.

A Framework for the Analysis of Prudential Regulation

This section dissects the issues in prudential regulation to show the distinct types of problems that must be addressed. In order to elucidate (and apply to) the problems posed by deposit insurance as currently practiced around the world (see McCarthy, 1980), our framework assumes that free banking is not a feasible alternative for governments (regardless of its feasibility otherwise). Although government regulation of banks takes myriad forms, it is always conducted in an environment where the government guarantees most bank deposits, either explicitly or implicitly. Deposit guarantees obviate the incentives that depositors would otherwise have to consider the solvency risks of banks when allocating their funds. This lack of incentives increases the likelihood that deposit guarantees will have to be employed in fact. Thus, the guarantor has the clearest interest in controlling the use of its guarantee by the banks.

The problem of banking regulation can take many forms. We posit that problems involving bank regulators are different from those involving asymmetry in information or contingent government subsidies, to which most analyses have been confined. This distinction is intensified if we take into account the effect of the main complicating factors recognized in Table 2.7.

Table 2.7 specifies the necessary conditions for each of three regulatory problems. In practice, these three problems—structural contingent subsidies, moral hazard, and rollover of unrealized loan losses—tend to occur in combination. The result is that most real regulatory problems must be attacked simultaneously on several fronts. In addition, the Chilean experience abundantly demonstrates

---

TABLE 2.7

Necessary Conditions for the Existence of Bank Regulatory Problems

	Regulatory problem		
Necessary conditions	Structural contingent subsidies	Moral hazard	Rollover of unrealized loan losses
1. Exogenous uncertainty	X	X	
2. Asymmetric information		X	X
3. Inability to assess risks related to government policy	X		
4. Inability to denounce own regulatory errors			X

NOTE: Simple incompetence of bank regulators was excluded because the solution for it, restructuring, is obvious, though difficult to put into practice. Other complicating factors may include intragroup lending of business groups, incompetence of private bankers, and self-selection favoring fraud-prone bankers.

the substantial importance of the complicating factors listed in the table.

The ultimate causes of the main regulatory problems include the state of existing technology and of the economic environment (the first two conditions in Table 2.7) and the institutional setting in which bank regulation is conducted (conditions 3 and 4 in Table 2.7). In the following sections we explain in detail each of these causes and sketch the likely result of each regulatory problem.

Structural contingent subsidies. The issue in this section concerns the incentive effects of giving away a deposit guarantee, given that all agents have symmetric access to the same imperfect information about the future. Exogenous uncertainty is a requirement for the guarantee to be valuable in the market.

As is well understood from modern finance theory (Mayer, 1965; Merton, 1977; Marcus, 1984), a valuable government guarantee provided at less than a market price is in fact a contingent subsidy, and the receiving economic agents have an incentive to seek more of it. The profit earned by an individual bank is an arbitrage profit in the sense that expansion of the bank's liabilities raises the amount of contingent subsidy provided by the government.

A deposit insurance subsidy induces individual competitive banks that are risk-neutral to grow more than is socially optimal, because the banks become a vehicle for arbitrage that exploits the difference between the market value of the government guarantee and the price that banks paid for the guarantee. Of course, decreasing returns to scale in the aggregate eventually limit the expansion of competitive banks. Banks that earn other rents, monopolistic or otherwise, weigh the benefits of getting more of the free guarantee against the risk of losing their other rents and conceivably going out of business.

The obvious solution to the problem of contingent subsidies is for the government to charge banks the market value of the guarantee it provides. Alternatively, by a device such as risk-weighted capital requirements the government could drive the value of the guarantee to zero by limiting the banks' risk of failure through regulation while still providing the guarantee.

Charging banks the market price for the deposit guarantee may not work in some cases, even if a government is able perfectly to observe risk. For example, above some risk level a bank may be forced to reduce the expected return to lending if it wishes to increase the variance of returns. As Herring and Vankudre (1985) have shown, when a government attempts to limit risk taking in such a situation by raising the charge for the guarantee, the banks' best reaction is to extend riskier loans, even though this action reduces the expected return on lending. Obviously, a government is unable to compensate for this last effect by raising the charge, so an optimal schedule of risk-rated guarantee charges simply does not exist over the whole range of bank choices.

To manage this situation, governments have most frequently employed a combination of risk-rated capital requirements or risk-rated loan-loss provisioning requirements, which include maximum individual quotas of risk. Conceptually, this strategy is a sufficient solution if the market value of the guarantee is basically reduced to zero. This regulatory problem might therefore appear to be solved. A solution to the problem of structural contingent subsidies requires, however, that regulators be able to assess risks created by one or more government policies, and certain structural elements in the regulatory process prevent regulators from correctly evaluating these risks. For example, regulators may be unable to implement a policy of risk-rated capital requirements with regard to some risks when other government policies would thereby be affected. A well-documented example is the failure of the U.S. government to limit exposure of its international banks to country risk in the late 1970s (Meigs, 1984). In that case Treasury officials wanted to avoid interference with the recycling of petrodollars, and State Department officials wanted to avoid souring relations with debtor countries. We would also argue that in the late 1980s Federal Reserve regulators were unable to promote capital requirements proportional to interest rate risk for U.S. savings and loans because the Federal Reserve itself can decisively affect the outcome of that risk. We suggest that the Chilean government suffered a similar problem in 1981, when the finance minister upheld his previous decision of fixing the exchange rate, even though many expected that this policy could not be sustained. Had Chilean bank regulators forced banks to provision more (foreign currency reserves) when debtors were more exposed to currency risks, they would have undermined the finance minister's exchange rate policy—and that was unthinkable.

We therefore posit that contingent government subsidies continue to exist in banking because government regulators are unable to assess risks whose outcome is driven by their superiors' actions or omissions. The problem becomes acute when the lending bank does not cooperate in the risk assessment process and the whole burden of assessment falls on regulators. This is a permanent regulatory problem, inevitable as long as bank regulators are subordinate to authorities who influence or determine the outcome of the risks that must be assessed.

It is not obvious how the existence of structural contingent government subsidies can be established empirically. The first prerequisite for such a subsidy is the existence of an explicit or implicit government guarantee on deposits. Implicit guarantees are, however, hard to document and must be inferred from the previous record of government bailouts of failed intermediaries. The second prerequisite is inadequate prudential regulation of the guaranteed intermediaries. Of course, it is easy to assert that prudential regulation was inadequate *after* guaranteed banks have failed. Indeed, the ease of such an evaluation creates a temptation to attribute too many (even all) bank failures to the existence of contingent government subsidies. It may be possible, however, to construct convincing *ex ante* evidence of structural contingent subsidies by documenting the observable institutional limitations placed on regulators' ability to assess some risks.

Moral hazard. Both moral hazard and contingent government subsidies induce debtors to take actions that will create maximum leverage—and bring them ever closer to bankruptcy. Moral hazard, however, implies a contingent subsidy that the issuer did not want to issue, whereas contingent subsidies are willingly offered. The issue of moral hazard exists as a regulatory problem because of asymmetric information in circumstances where government regulators are unable to observe the riskiness that a guaranteed bank assigns to its own choices. Even after failure, it is difficult for outsiders (including government regulators) to draw reliable inferences about a bank's actions and motivations from knowledge of its potential profit outcomes because the actual outcome of loans depends on exogenous risk as well as bank actions.

To minimize the problem of moral hazard, governments are frequently advised to adopt a series of procedures to control lending risk. This strategy, usually referred to as prudential regulation, is based on the idea that, even though the risks of bank decisions cannot be publicly observed, government can privately observe those risks much more precisely if it requires banks to adopt administrative procedures such as classification of individual loans on a risk scale. The government can then use its inside information— access to bank records—to prevent banks from taking excessive risk.

Many of the current methods of risk classification were developed by private banks in their own interest. Indeed, the process of risk classification is a necessity for competent bank owners, especially in large, modern banks characterized by a hierarchy of executives with diverse management responsibilities. If prudential regulation is understood as the participation of bank regulators in ascertaining inside information about banks, the prudential regulation therefore need not impose a substantial burden on the banks, insofar as private banks themselves already use these methods in their own interest. In this sense, moral hazard is a regulatory problem that should not present regulators with insurmountable difficulties.

Certain complicating factors can, however, make moral hazard a difficult problem in practice. The first of these complications is the incompetence of private bankers, and the second is self-selection toward fraud-prone bankers.

It is not uncommon to find private banks with no internal risk classification scheme in place. This may be the result of mere incompetence or calculated fraud. In either case the private information needed by regulators is fragmented among executives or employees. Moreover, fraud and incompetence may be linked, because the incompetence of the board or chief executive may allow fraud by one or more employees.

These complicating factors can be massive in a banking system that has only recently been liberalized after decades of financial repression (as in Chile in 1976). During the years of repression risk classification schemes had become entirely superfluous. Self-selection of fraud-prone bankers is a serious risk during financial liberalization because there is an unusual need to allow more people into banking and the potential candidates for entry are certain to include those who are most prone to fraud. Where a complicating factor makes inside information unavailable to regulators, banks cannot be reined in adequately by risk-adjusted capital requirements, and the likely consequences of moral hazard are much the same as those of contingent government subsidies, as previously described.

Empirically establishing the existence of moral hazard as an important regulatory problem requires both identifying an information asymmetry and documenting the substantial nature of such an asymmetry. In general, it should be possible to document the existence of moral hazard by ascertaining whether information on risk-taking by banks was available to the regulators and by analyzing the reaction of regulators as information became available to them.

Rollover of unrealized loan losses. The rollover of unrealized loan losses has not previously been acknowledged in the academic literature as an important feature of banking. This phenomenon becomes a regulatory problem when a bank's independent operations continue after the conditions leading to insolvency become known (at least to bank officials). It may not pose a special regulatory problem, however, if a bank's accounting net worth plus goodwill is positive: If a bank still possesses economic net worth, the rollover of unrealized loan losses may reduce profits but have no more serious effect. It is when a bank's economic net worth becomes negative (that is, when it cannot be sold to honest bankers) that the new behavioral elements are introduced.

When a bank is known to be insolvent and continues operating because bank regulators are able to avoid or postpone bankruptcy proceedings, the rollover of unrealized loan losses is most certainly a regulatory problem. The problem is conceptually different from moral hazard because it does not concern the abuse of a guarantee by assuming greater risk than would otherwise have been assumed. Indeed, the problem of rollover of unrealized losses may exist even if there is no risk in the economy after the bank's failure.

Of course, additional opportunities for risk taking become available over time. If these opportunities are acted on by insolvent intermediaries, the rollover of unrealized loan losses may combine with moral hazard to produce an explosive mixture. To highlight the independent nature of this regulatory problem and to simplify the exposition of its consequences, however, we have chosen to stress that no further risk taking is required after insolvency. This emphasis also allows us to present a solid foundation for the concept of a "false demand for credit," the mechanics of which were elaborated (Harberger, 1984; Held, 1989) to explain Chilean events in the 1970s.

The result of the rollover of unrealized losses under certainty is the same as that of a simple Ponzi game. By definition, the insolvent bank has more liabilities than assets. If the bank pays and charges market interest rates, it must incur operating losses whose present value is the unrealized loss. The access of the insolvent bank to a government guarantee on deposits, however, allows it to cover the negative net cash flow from operations with the issue of new deposits. Both the size of the deposits at the insolvent bank and the size of the effective liability of the government therefore grow geometrically.

In this circumstance, the government's liability is effective, not contingent, but it has not been realized or acknowledged. A direct implication of allowing the failed bank to continue operations is that the deposit interest rate must rise over time to attract the required additional deposits.

A complementary strategy for the bank is to direct some of its loan recoveries to finance part of the operating loss. This results in the volume of the bank's healthy outstanding loans falling over time, thereby restricting the credit it provides. By healthy loans we mean the portion of the loan portfolio that is able to service the current deposit interest rate. The rest of the loan portfolio simply consists of unrealized losses.

The effects of the situation just described are a rising deposit rate and a falling volume of healthy loans, *ceteris paribus*. The volume of deposits will rise at the rate of interest minus the rate of reduction of healthy outstanding loans.

These dynamics may be more easily understood by considering the case in which the government acknowledges the loss in the bank and bails it out by buying the bank's loan losses at face value with a long-term bond. This situation is completely equivalent to the rollover of unrealized loan losses if the government fails to adjust its primary deficit and meets the interest payments on the long-term bond by placing additional Treasury bills among investors. It then becomes clear that the government is playing a Ponzi game, because the stock of Treasury bills grows without bound, raising the market interest rate and crowding out the private sector.

If there is competition in banking and most banks are free of the unrealized loss problem, the spread between the lending and deposit interest rates may narrow down to efficient operating costs. If, however, most banks roll over unrealized losses, they will have a third source of funds to absorb their operating loss: an increase in the spread. As long as most banks roll over unrealized losses and the spread between the lending and borrowing rates can be sustained at the greater resulting margin, then banks cease to be insolvent, deposits do not need to grow geometrically, and healthy loans need not be restricted.

A large spread, however, creates an unstable situation because it enables marginal, highly risky loans to be very profitable. If high marginal reserve requirements and quantitative credit controls are then eliminated or if foreign and new domestic banks are authorized to operate (as in a financial liberalization), competition will lead market interest rates to a level at which the spread will be less than enough to allow the elimination of operating losses. The weakest banks—that is, those with the largest shares of unrecoverable loans under automatic rollover—will be the first to play the Ponzi game just described.

Viewed from another perspective, the consequences of the rollover of loan losses just described help to explain debtors' behavior. The estimate of any debtor's riskiness should be raised by high lending rates, even with no change in the debtor's behavior. With all else being constant, then, increased real lending rates increase the share of unrealized losses of loans by banks and accelerate the Ponzi game. This effect is, of course, exacerbated if debtors react to high lending rates by increasing their leverage and their operating risk. Such a reaction should be expected because it is most advantageous to the subset of debtors with negative economic net worth who are rolling over unrealized losses. They are able to participate in the Ponzi game because the creditor bank insists in rolling over those debts even if it is insolvent.

There are three main empirical requirements that make the rollover of unrealized loan losses a regulatory problem: a government guarantee on bank deposits, large unrealized losses in the loan portfolio of the banking industry, and official reluctance to take over failed banks.

Intragroup lending by business associates. Of the three complicating factors identified in Table 2.7, two have been adequately addressed in the preceding discussion of the three principal regulatory problems. The third complicating factor is addressed separately because it has been prominent enough in Chile to be considered a principal regulatory problem in its own right. In Chile, the overlap between business activities and their financing is even more extensive and intensive than in other settings because the members of a *business group*, a diversified conglomerate of business firms that includes a government-guaranteed bank, are closely held, rather than publicly traded, enterprises. Indeed, in Chile the intertwining of ownership and interests within a group is so close, and ownership of those interests is so exclusive, that a business group is commonly viewed as constituting a single entity. For this reason, lending by the banking component of a group to any of its other enterprises is frequently termed *self-lending*. In the following discussion we will analyze the consequences of self-lending under two different assumptions regarding the regulator's information on the riskiness of the group's assets.

Self-lending and symmetric information. If it were possible to evaluate the risk of a bank that is the financial component of a business group, and the government charged an appropriate fee for the guarantee, the fact that this bank is owned by a business group would be irrelevant to the regulation of banking activities. It would be as if the bank were independent and closely held. Likewise, if the independent bank were owned by many different shareholders, it would be as if the bank were part of a conglomerate with diluted ownership.

A widespread argument against self-lending is that it leads to insufficient diversification of loans so that too much is lent to an individual debtor (the business group). This argument is flawed if the debtor is a well-capitalized, diversified conglomerate that has invested in many sectors of the economy. In this case the risk would, in general, approximate that of the market. Of course, self-lending is very risky if the regulator is poorly informed about the actual risk of the conglomerate's debt or if the consolidated debt/equity ratio of the conglomerate is high.

Some authors have argued that intragroup lending is subject to less rigorous risk evaluation than lending to nongroup enterprises because such investments are evaluated only once within the business group, namely in the unit that wants to use the funds, before the loan is drawn from the group's bank. For example, the Chilean Superintendency of Banks argued in 1983 that "there was an unrestricted liaison between banks and their owners, and an unending cycle of loan renewals with interest capitalization was observed" (Acevedo and Ramirez, 1983).

Such a procedure for risk evaluation does not, however, imply that the quality of the evaluation is more relaxed than an independent bank would require. If it were, the implication would indeed be far-reaching: Investments financed with equity would be subject to a systematically biased evaluation that would invariably deem them more risky than otherwise identical investments financed by loans from independent creditors.

Investments financed with equity are not, however, equivalent to investments financed with depositors' money. When a business group draws a loan from its bank, which in turn draws on deposits from its customers, it is appropriate to ask who is evaluating the risk of that deposit on behalf of depositors. In a setting with deposit insurance and symmetrical information, the Superintendency of Banks does the evaluation, and there is no special problem with business groups.

Self-lending and asymmetric information. The practice of self-lending by business groups must be analyzed in terms of the ability of bank regulators to classify self-loans and the rollover of self-loans on a scale of risk. It is necessary to compare the superintendency's ability to monitor the risk of self-loans of a business group as compared to its capacity to monitor the risk of loans to a regular debtor, given the degree of risk-aversion of the bank owners.

As previously explained, the usual practice of prudential regulation overcomes most of the informational asymmetries by adopting a series of procedures to control lending risk and the debt-equity ratio of banks. Even though bank risk decisions are publicly unobservable, the government can privately observe those risks much more precisely when it forces a bank to provide access to its internal risk evaluation procedures.

This method largely fails, however, when the bank is part of a business group and self-lending is allowed,[6] because the business group is able to locate the risk-evaluation procedures for self-loans outside the bank without losing control over employees. In addition, the business group has access to a much larger array of legal methods to avoid presenting the true risk of a self-loan to bank regulators. The resulting inability of regulators to gain access to the private information of banks may be present *both* when the business group is closely held *and* when it is controlled by a remote risk-neutral management that responds to many different shareholders.

Chilean experience shows that the business group can avoid identifying a loan as a self-loan by dividing it into smaller pieces, lending each piece to an expressly created shell company, and finally having the shell companies relend the funds to the unit in the business group that requested them. In such a scheme the individual loans in a portfolio may fall below the limit at which classification must occur. An alternative method is to ask friends and employees to accept the loan and do the relending, which may be defined as evasion from regulatory control through vertical disintegration.

In addition the business group can drag its feet when classifying the self-loans. If the bank is unabashedly optimistic when evaluating its self-loans, the Superintendency of Banks is forced to do its own evaluation and might thereby discover insolvency too late.

Moreover, when the superintendency attempts its own risk evaluation of self-loans, it confronts severe informational asymmetries: Such an evaluation must obviously attempt to ascertain the solvency and cash flow of the business group as a whole, including all the shell companies. The problem is further complicated because noncontrolling shareholders in some of the business group's firms must be taken into account. Furthermore, since the network of holding companies is always changing and can be made to change very fast, the superintendency cannot put much faith in information that the regulated bank is ordered to gather about the financial situation of a single unit of the group. These difficulties can be compounded if the business group's administration does not keep records of its consolidated situation.[7]

The critical regulatory problem is that the supervisory powers of the superintendency reach only to the bank; it has no authority over the successive layers of holding companies that define the structure of the business group. Furthermore, as in most countries, the powers of a Chilean bank to request information from a debtor are limited by law. The superintendency is therefore subject to a loss of control through vertical disintegration, which leaves it unable to monitor for risk taking associated with moral hazard or for rollover of unrealized losses.

In conclusion, the problems caused by self-lending by business groups are not conceptually different from the problems caused by contingent subsidies, moral hazard, and rollover of unrealized losses. Implementing prudential regulation when self-lending is present is, however, more difficult by several orders of magnitude than it is with independent banks, because the informational asymmetries are much deeper and the usual regulatory tools are more easily blunted by a noncooperative business group. This is true regardless of the ownership structure of the business group.

Prudential Regulation in Chile: 1976–1982

Observers of Chile's financial evolution have asserted that until 1982 the country's system of bank regulation comprised the "worst of both worlds" in that it issued a government-subsidized guarantee and maintained lax regulation of the risks taken by the guaranteed institutions. In this section we examine this assertion in more detail in order to extract specific lessons about the experience. We find that, on the whole, the diagnosis is correct. It is also true, however, that the Superintendency of Banks took important steps toward the improvement of bank regulation during the years 1976–1982.

The first subsection addresses pure moral hazard in 1976–1979, with emphasis on the failure of Banco Osorno. The other subsections examine rollover of unrealized loan losses, structural contingent subsidies, and self-lending.

Moral hazard: The Chilean experience, 1976–1978. As previously explained, three elements must be present at any given time in order to establish that moral hazard constitutes a regulatory problem: a government guarantee on deposits, a substantial information asymmetry between banks and regulators, and extensive, market-wide participation in increasingly risky debt. In this section, we review the episode that has been singled out as critical in the literature, the failure of Banco Osorno y La Unión, and its consequences in the next three years.

Moral hazard before Banco Osorno. The privatization of the commercial banks (expropriated by Allende) occurred as interest rates were being liberalized, credit controls eliminated, and regulation standardized across intermediaries. Bids for the banks were asked just after the freezing of SINAP's short-term deposits, in July 1975. The government offered its shares in exchange for a down payment of at least 20 percent, with the remaining principal to be paid over the following two years at an interest rate of 8 percent plus CPI variation. Although the interest rate was substantially below market rates, this advantage was offset by the inflated prices that the government asked and received for the banks. Most banks were bought by local business groups, which obtained actual control by February 1976. Less than a year later (January 6, 1977), regulators took over one of the banks sold to business groups, Banco Osorno y La Unión. This was the first failure of a privately owned bank in Chile since 1926.

The takeover of Banco Osorno had been preceded, in early December 1976, by a spate of ten insolvencies of financial intermediaries. They began when the manager of an informal *financiera*, "Manuel Rodriguez," fled to Buenos Aires. The authorities declared that this was to be expected of informal (nonregulated) *financieras*.

But when Finregio (a formal *financiera*) failed a week later and its lending proved to have been concentrated in only the two companies that were its main shareholders, the public came to realize that supervision was practically nonexistent even in formal institutions. For example, Finregio grossly violated Article 5 of Resolution 26 of the Superintendency of Banks, which prohibited loans to bank owners in excess of 10 percent of bank equity.[8] In ensuing weeks the following institutions all failed: La Familia, Colocadora Central de Valores, Financiera Gain, Financiera Farema, Financiera El Sendero, Eduardo Montes (informal), Sociedad de Inversiones Décima Región, and Banco Osorno.

The government announced that Banco Osorno's deposits would be backed by the central bank. The next day the government announced the creation of an explicit guarantee for small deposits in banks, supervised *financieras*, and supervised savings and credit cooperatives. The limit on the guarantee was set in a CPI-adjustable amount[9] of approximately U.S. $2,750 per account. The government also guaranteed small deposits at the already-failed Finregio and La Familia but did not extend this benefit to depositors at the informal institutions.

Did Banco Osorno's failure stem from risk taking associated with moral hazard? The first of three empirical determinations required for an affirmative answer is a government guarantee on deposits. Apart from the failures beginning in December 1976, the only failure before Banco Osorno's was that of SINAP. In that case, the government had promised to guarantee its liabilities but, as previously discussed, did not fulfill its promise. The failure of the government to honor its guarantee in the wake of the SINAP collapse would have justified a belief on the part of the depositing public that government guarantees of deposits did not exist, despite the presence of a Superintendency of Banks. Indeed, as subsequently shown in the episode recounted below, the only opinion that anyone held on the matter was a belief in the *absence* of government deposit guarantees, not in their existence. This fact has been frequently overlooked in other analyses of the incident but is sufficient to lead to the conclusion that moral hazard cannot account for the failure of Banco Osorno. This conclusion remains, of course, even in the presence of the substantial asymmetry of information between banks and regulators that we *do* find in this episode.

Instead of moral hazard, we find a free-banking era in Chile between the February 1976 privatization of commercial banks and the failure of Banco Osorno in January 1977. This period was characterized by the absence of guarantees on bank deposits, prudential regulation that was little and lax, free entry of new banks into the financial market, and losses to depositors from the failure of financial intermediaries. We will show, however, that the failure of intermediaries was the outcome of their expectation that neither the government *nor they* would redeem the deposits of their customers if such redemption entailed forgoing loans to themselves or their ownership.

This additional expectation provides the same inducement to risky lending as a government guarantee would yield. The only difference is in the identity of the guarantor; customers acted as surrogates for government by guaranteeing their own deposits. It is not surprising, therefore, that in 1976 the third element required for moral hazard to exist as a regulatory problem was abundantly evident in the form of excessively risky lending as a marketwide phenomenon. With depositors as guarantors of their own deposits, however, the dynamics of moral hazard are fundamentally altered: Depositors can withdraw their funds and move them elsewhere.

The widespread distrust of banks by depositors, the negative vision of the financial system presented by the press at the time, and the small growth of aggregate deposits in 1976 suggest that the public considered itself susceptible to fraud.

Banking policy after the failure of Banco Osorno. At the time of Banco Osorno's failure, the Superintendency of Banks was supposed to employ up to 120 employees, but only sixty remained because of staff departures in response to low public sector wages. Of those sixty, only ten were inspectors, and they had the obviously impossible task of supervising fourteen banks and twenty-six formal *financieras*.

The central bank authorities were alerted to Banco Osorno's problems only after Banco Osorno asked for unusual amounts of emergency credit in December 1976.[10] At that point, bank regulators discovered that Banco Osorno had experienced an operating loss in November 1976. They also found that Finregio had violated the maximum debt/equity ratio of 5.0 applicable to *financieras*, had lent long term with short-term funds, and had lent without evaluating the collateral of debtors.

After Banco Osorno's takeover, the regulators found that its failure was associated with the failure of the informal *financiera* called Sociedad de Inversiones Décima Región, controlled by the same business group (Fluxá-Yaconi) in the previous month. This business group had used the bank's borrowing capacity to buy several big firms that the government was privatizing in 1976, including Fundición Libertad, Agencias Graham, Enagás, and Santiago Centro. Banco Osorno had opened off-balance-sheet credit lines to these firms and issued guarantees to others without registering them.

Banco Osorno was not abusing any government guarantee. In our view, Banco Osorno abused the depositing public's confidence in banks as responsible institutions warranting their trust. In fact, during the rapid succession of failures by intermediaries in December 1976, the depositing public's movement of funds toward the largest banks bordered on panic. This movement suggests that the public did not believe that bank deposits were guaranteed by the government. In this respect, the events preceding the Banco Osorno collapse were akin to a free-banking episode of the nineteenth century in the United States.

The analogy is confirmed by the stories published in the local press, after the failure of Finregio, and amidst rumors about the failure of other banks, that Javier Vial, the president of the Bankers' Association, was trying to form a pool of banks to bail out Finregio and avoid the loss of public confidence. This is exactly what the New York bank cartel did before the formation of the Federal Reserve (Gorton, 1985). But in New York the government did not intervene.

Several authors have singled out the Banco Osorno episode as the one that set the stage for the massive bank failures of 1982 (see, for example, Harberger, 1984). They argue that if depositors at Banco Osorno had suffered some losses, and/or if regulators had supervised banks more strictly, then domestic banks would not have engaged in excessively risky lending practices and foreign banks would have been more careful in lending to Chile in 1981. The two components of this argument—allowing some losses and maintaining stricter regulation—were both represented in the local press at the time, but rarely together. For example, a columnist who worked at the central bank asserted:

> The financial market is special because bankruptcy produces public alarm. . . . There is consensus that the Superintendency must be refurbished to be able to exercise enough control. . . . We must rethink the objective of bank regulation. At present, the objective is to make sure the norms are complied with. But by itself, this doesn't assure the ability to analyze the loan portfolio and its guarantees. (Tapia, 1977)

This statement typifies an important school of thought, which we will call the "state supervision school." Its proponents argued that the government had to guarantee bank liabilities and therefore regulate the risk of failure. One implication was that the government had acted appropriately in bailing out Banco Osorno depositors.

This view was not shared by important authorities at the Ministry of Finance and the central bank, who were unconvinced that the costs of bankruptcy in banking were different from those of any other business. They were therefore unconvinced, as well, that the bankruptcy of a bank should be treated as a special case. These authorities took note that the state supervision school failed to mention moral hazard or information asymmetry in their arguments and addressed this theoretical weakness by insisting on a free-banking view of the financial market. They were not convinced that bank failure was special and refused to accept a need for government guarantees.

When asked about future bank failures, the president of the

central bank answered, "The government will respond only up to the small-depositor guarantee, as it did in the cases of Finregio and La Familia."[11] This answer implied that only small depositors would be insured in the future, although that had been obviously untrue for Banco Osorno. The proponents of this school of thought preferred to explain the insolvencies in late 1976 and early 1977 as the result of poor management and fraud. Poor management was not the government's concern, and fraud could be dealt with by defining white-collar crimes more precisely and enabling the affected parties to protect their interests in the courts. Small depositors would be guaranteed only because they would be unable to inform themselves properly or would not find it worthwhile to sue in court. According to the free-banking school, therefore, Banco Osorno should have been allowed to fail.[12] From the viewpoint of the free-banking school's proponents, the most important lesson from the Banco Osorno failure was the extraordinary difficulty of holding Banco Osorno's executives and directors legally accountable for simple fraudulent conduct.

There was a third school of thought, represented by old-timers at the Superintendency of Banks. This group asserted that risk taking by banks could not be controlled and that the government should bail out depositors. From their perspective, therefore, the best policy was to repress the financial market; this would ensure a small size and low risks because lending would occur at negative real rates.

The outcome of bank regulation in Chile reflected some of each position advanced by the three schools; it did not represent the entire position of any one school. After the Banco Osorno episode, the free-banking school failed to prevent the government from providing deposit guarantees. Its proponents obtained legislation that defined new crimes, but they continued to distrust prudential regulation. Proponents of the state supervision school obtained some new powers for the superintendency and a government guarantee for deposits to keep the public's confidence, but they were unable to implement tight prudential regulation. The financial repression group obtained the government's guarantee for depositors and delayed the implementation of tight prudential regulation but could not return the financial market to repression. The social cost of this incoherent financial regulatory policy was substantial.

The argument in Harberger (1984) that inflicting some losses on Banco Osorno's large depositors would have avoided the creation of an implicit government guarantee and the problems suffered in 1982, is not convincing unless we also accept free banking as a good idea. We view free banking as a risky investment for a country undergoing financial liberalization because we doubt its ability to manage some externalities without fostering collusion. There is significant evidence that free banking has worked well only where it has led to the formation of a bank cartel. In Chile, such a bank cartel would have been dominated by the business groups, thereby increasing their ability to discriminate against nongroup firms.

We agree, however, with Harberger's suggestion that it would have been feasible after the failure of Banco Osorno to have introduced tight prudential regulation.

In the years after Banco Osorno's failure the free-banking school introduced legislation—Decree Law Nos. 1,638 (December 30, 1976) and 2,099 (January 13, 1978)—that defined new crimes in financial practices. A sample of these legal reforms[13] includes

1. The failure of a bank manager to record a banking operation became a crime.

2. Attempts by bank directors, managers, employees, external auditors, and agents to alter or "disfigure" balance sheets, books, mail, accounts, and other documents became a crime.

3. The crimes defined for bank managers and directors pertaining to the approval or presentation of a false balance sheet were extended to *financieras.*

4. Giving false or maliciously incomplete data for the purpose of obtaining a bank loan became a crime.

5. The balance sheets of all banks were made subject to examination by external auditors, resulting in a published audit report.

Many authors have overlooked these reforms, and others, observing that there were no instances of punishment of the newly prohibited activities until 1982, have asserted that the new laws were unimportant. These assertions have not, however, been supported by evidence of criminal activities that went unpunished and with respect to everyday loans are simply unreasonable, considering that the penalties included jail. The cases of self-loans and fraud will be taken up later.

The state supervision school obtained reforms such as the following:

1. The Superintendency of Banks was given a larger budget, and its employees obtained salaries above the public sector pay scales. In the future, a council of ministers would define the wage scale and the number of employees. In the interim, forty central bank employees were assigned to the superintendency to help as inspectors.

2. The minimum capital requirement for a formal *financiera* was raised to 75 percent of that required of a bank, in an explicit attempt to reduce the number of *financieras* and the regulatory load.

3. Informal *financieras* were banned, and formal *financieras* were prohibited from acting as brokers for commercial paper issued by companies.

4. Limits were placed on loans issued by a bank to each individual client. These limits were 5 percent of capital and reserves for loans to each person and company without guarantees and 10 percent if guarantees applied to the additional 5 percent. For stock companies and state enterprises, the limit was 10 percent without guarantees and 25 percent if guarantees applied to the additional 15 percent.

5. The acceptable collateral for a bank loan was restricted by the exclusion of bills of exchange and commercial paper.

6. The Superintendency of Banks was empowered to order the correction of the accounting value of any investment, when the superintendency established that the registered value was not realistic. This authority did not, however, extend to loans.

One interesting reform required the liquidator of a bank to be designated by the superintendent of banks. This reform bears the influence of the state supervision school, in that regular liquidators were excluded, but the need for a special bankruptcy procedure for banks, which was the natural response to the state supervision school's preoccupation with "special" bankruptcy costs,[14] was not proposed by either the free-banking or the state supervision school. It turned out to be most unfortunate that the Chilean banking law mirrored the banking laws of other countries by considering only two avenues for the management of a bank's failure: liquidation and takeover by the government.[15]

Such was the inconsistency of government actions leading to the banking reforms just outlined that they were in accord with each of the schools some of the time and none of the schools all of the time. Thus, for example, the free-banking school lamented the *ex post facto* guarantee on all deposits at Banco Osorno, but the government allowed the regular bankruptcy of several small *financieras* without intervention. The government also allowed losses to be inflicted on large depositors at Finregio and La Familia. Later in 1977, and further reflecting the influence of the free-banking school, the government allowed large depositors to lose sizable amounts in the failures of saving and credit cooperatives Crediclán, SICOOP, Copecrédito, Servicoop, Magicoop, Credibioma, Ignacio Serrano, and Credicon. The free-banking school viewed these cases as demonstrating that there was no government guarantee of deposits in Chile.

Previous authors have, however, overlooked other cases in 1977, following the government takeover of Banco Osorno, that were consistent with the Osorno case and therefore contradictory to the free-banking view. During 1977 the government also took over and refunded the cooperatives IFICOOP, SODIMAC, Creditec, and Credival, and in the process bailed out all creditors, regardless of size. The common characteristic of these institutions and Banco Osorno was that they were larger than the others, so their failure would affect many more people. The implication was that their liquidation would freeze a substantial amount of the funds of many depositors for an extended period of time and that political support for the government would suffer. In the public's mind it therefore became clear that medium-sized and larger banks were in fact guaranteed.

Given this record, it is amazing that proponents of the free-banking school continued to argue that Chile had no deposit guarantees. To be consistent, they should have acknowledged that free banking was impossible in Chile after 1977, and prudential regulation was a necessity. A free-banking approach was simply not credible after 1977.

For the public, the state supervision school was right. For example, a 1977 article titled "The Morals of Banco Osorno" asserted:

> Central Bank assistance to Banco Osorno shows that the authorities do not consider banks to be similar to other firms, so banks cannot fail. Therefore it is important to move towards professional supervision, where loans are evaluated in accordance to risk. This means that the Superintendency of Banks must have a larger budget, and salaries must be higher than in the rest of the public sector.[16]

The episode that turned the tide in favor of the state supervision school was that of Banco Español in early 1980, three years after the takeover of Banco Osorno. Since late 1978, banks had to obtain external audits of their accounts. Price Waterhouse asserted that Banco Español accounts were in order in 1978 but changed this opinion in their audit report for 1979:

> The analysis showed that, regarding a loan portfolio of 37% of total loans, there was no information that could allow the evaluation of the debtors' capacity to pay. Many of these debtors had their loans renewed repeatedly, without paying interest or CPI adjustment at the moment of renewal.

Although the loans were documented, as required by the 1978 laws, the bank had not been collecting information to evaluate their risk. Public belief (before January 1977) that the government would *not* guarantee bank deposits had so dramatically changed in the ensuing three years that a press characterization of the consequences of this audit report included the following: "When it had become widely known that Banco Español *was going towards takeover by the government*, the owners [Puig business group] sold out to Sahli and Tassara's business group."[17] (Italics added.) By 1980, everyone was convinced that depositors at a failing bank would be bailed out by the government. There was no alternative for a failed bank except government takeover.

The free-banking school was never happy to acknowledge its practical defeat and was slow to press the superintendency to improve the quality of its supervision. Conversely, the financial repression school, whose members controlled the leadership of the superintendency, was chagrined by its inability to block the financial liberalization. As a consequence of these discordant perspectives, the superintendency did not improve supervision as quickly as it could have from 1977 to mid-1980. For example, the power of the free-banking school prevented the government from taking over the failed Banco Español. Given the authorities' inaction, the Puig group sold the bank to the Sahli-Tassara group, which was not required to inject fresh capital into the bank. The state supervision school was shocked.

Reacting strongly to the Banco Español case, as the next sections will show, the state supervision school had by mid-1980 become the effective governors of bank regulatory policy in Chile. But because the state supervision school continued to base all its actions on unspecified differences between the private and social costs of the bankruptcy of banks,[18] doubts about the foundations of the new approach lingered among the free-banking authorities.

To sum up, in 1977–1980 the authorities assumed that free banking was feasible, refusing to alter this assumption even after it had been invalidated by the rescues of Banco Osorno, IFICOOP,

SODIMAC, Creditec, and Credival. Although legislation introduced prison sentences for undocumented loans and other frauds, the authorities did not acknowledge the need for prudential regulation and risk evaluation, placing their trust instead with external auditors. Their obstruction of prudential regulation was compounded, most dramatically, by their authorization of the sale of failed Banco Español to a business group without requiring that group to inject new capital into the bank.

Marketwide moral hazard after Banco Osorno. We turn now to the question of the marketwide impact of moral hazard in the period 1977–1979, when an effective government guarantee coexisted with ineffective prudential regulation. This three-year period was one of high growth in Chile's gross domestic product. Such economic growth decreases the incidence of excessively risky lending and investment behavior and, when it occurs, decreases the negative effects that might otherwise lead to large-scale insolvency of intermediaries.

As explained in the preceding section, rising real deposit interest rates and more slowly rising real lending interest rates are indicative of excessively risky lending induced by government guarantees of deposits (which we summarize as marketwide moral hazard). When other factors can lead to the same behavior of deposit and lending rates, however, it is scarcely a straightforward exercise to establish the existence of marketwide moral hazard. Thus, for example, deposit rates of interest should have risen in response to a reduction in marginal reserve requirements between 1977 and 1979. Because a reduction in marginal reserve requirements is like eliminating a tax on intermediation, it allows a reduction in loan rates and an increase in deposit rates. If moral hazard was *also* important, it could therefore be argued that real deposit rates should have risen even more rapidly and higher than they did.

Further compounding the difficulty of establishing marketwide moral hazard was the financial liberalization that was simultaneously under way in Chile, which would itself imply rising deposit interest rates and a rising volume of loans. In addition, the international

financial liberalization adopted by Chile during this period permitted an increase in the country's net capital inflow to an average of
U.S. $1.1 billion per semester by the second half of 1978. This capital
inflow would have induced a reduction in loan interest rates after
mid-1978, thereby disguising the dynamics of moral hazard had it
been operative (for relevant data, see Edwards, 1988).

In spite of these difficulties of empirical validation, we conclude
that the moral hazard hypothesis can be discarded for the following
reasons. Recall that bank actions reflecting the incentives associated
with moral hazard raise the probability of failure and the loss of
capital in economic downturns. In contrast, the banking profits and
net investment in the banking sector in Chile, presented in Table 2.8,
scarcely indicate behavior consistent with increased risk of failure;
indeed, for most years, a substantial proportion of profits was
reinvested in the banking sector. Moreover, in 1978 net investment in
banking capital was almost three times the previous year's profit.
Most important, all this happened at a time when the capital/asset
ratio was far above the minimum capital requirement (then 4.76
percent, in association with a maximum debt/equity ratio of 20).

Even though loan losses that may have been rolled over are
incorporated into the data of this table, it is doubtful that they would
have been so substantial as to change the basic story it tells. The
evidence presented in Table 2.8 is simply inconsistent with a

TABLE 2.8
Profits and Net Investment in Chilean Banking, 1976–1980 (percentage)

	1976	1977	1978	1979	1980
Pretax profit/net worth	2.6[a]	8.7[a]	18.5	23.0	23.5
Operating profit[b]/net worth	−13.8[a]	1.1[a]	13.5	17.6	22.1
Increase in net worth/net worth[c]	5.7	2.3	23.8	16.7	14.3
Increase in net worth[c]/pretax profit$_{t-1}$	40.3	86.5	274.0	90.1	62.1
Capital/asset ratio	24.8	22.2	15.1	13.2	11.9

[a]Net of taxes paid.
[b]Pretax profit minus other expenses plus nonoperating income.
[c]Adjusted for inflation.
SOURCE: Elaboration from Held (1989, Tables I-6, I-9, and A-3).

scenario of moral hazard and its most essential component: risky lending run amok. Banks enacting such a scenario would (by their own desire) keep their capital/asset ratios as low as is legally allowed. As Table 2.8 shows, the profitability of banking during 1977–1980 was independent of any government guarantee of deposits.

We believe that the figures in Table 2.8 reflect the transitory rents accompanying a financial liberalization that make the banking sector profitable for even the most cautiously managed banks. These transitory rents can be large and tend to be reinvested in the banking industry because of the temporary supernormal profits. An important implication is that a financial liberalization with entry restrictions, which themselves always produce transitory profits, has a built-in insurance against moral hazard. The problem is likely to emerge only after expansion stops, when all banks tend to experience decreased profits. In this circumstance, most banks may simply accept a reduction in profits and in fact view them as more realistic than those of the "windfall" period they have just enjoyed. Banks that do not share this perception and/or those that are more poorly capitalized, however, may be attracted to excessively risky lending practices; some may even feel "forced" to such excess. A liberalizing government therefore has only a limited period to introduce prudential regulation and absorb learning costs.

Rollover of unrealized loan losses: the Chilean experience. The first requirement for the rollover of unrealized loan losses to occur—a government guarantee of deposits—was fulfilled in 1977 by the bailout of all depositors at Banco Osorno and cooperatives IFICOOP, SODIMAC, Creditec, and Credival, convincing bank creditors that they were *de facto* guaranteed by the government.

The second requirement—bankruptcy—is not fulfilled if a bank simply delays its acknowledgment of loan losses; those losses will be reflected in lower profits of the bank. More particularly, substantial unrealized losses in the loan portfolio of the banking industry at the start of the process, in early 1977, would have been required for substantial rollover of those losses to have existed during the years 1977–1980.

Analysts sometimes forget that a bank is bankrupt only if the present value of its economic profit is negative. A bank's economic losses are permanent only if the interest it pays on deposits exceeds the interest it earns and is repaid by lenders; otherwise, unrealized loan losses are absorbed over time and the bank is not bankrupt in an economic sense.

The third requirement for the rollover of unrealized loan losses is the reluctance of government to take over failed banks. One structural reason for such reluctance is that a takeover is an acknowledgment of flawed regulation; another is that most authorities that supervise regulators are unable to obtain independent information on bank solvency.

In Chile the regulators that took over Banco Osorno and the other big intermediaries in 1977 justified their actions by deeming "previous" regulation to have been unsound. This attitude could not be sustained after the case of Banco Español in 1980. In desperation, the free-banking school decided to allow the sale of the bank to the Sahli-Tassara group, which injected no capital. A year and a half later, in November 1981, Banco Español was taken over because its losses had grown even larger. It is therefore clearly documented that the delay or absence of regulation, not the practice of regulation, characterized Chilean banking from 1978 to mid-1980, when the free-banking school was dominant.

Thus, the first and third requirements for the rollover of unrealized loan losses were fulfilled in Chile in 1978–1980. As to the second requirement, because no formal examination of bank portfolios was conducted until 1980, there is no quantitative evidence for determining whether banks were suffering economic losses and were economically insolvent. Other types of evidence must therefore be considered.

The facts, 1977–1981. In early 1977 the Chilean economy was in shambles. Following the ravages of Allende's populism, the halving of the price of copper in 1975 caused a sharp recession, with gross domestic product falling by 12.9 percent in 1975. A strong fiscal contraction, a sharp real devaluation, and very high real interest rates reduced the strength of the recovery, and the economy grew at 3.5 percent in 1976. The solvency of most business firms that had survived Allende's drive toward central planning was therefore clearly reduced in those years, and many became literally insolvent.

On the other hand, several large business firms that had been nationalized by Allende were privatized by auction during 1976 and 1977. Most of these firms had no working capital, so they urgently sought loans to finance inventories. Many of these firms also had excess manpower, but severance pay requirements of one month's salary for each year of employment meant that they sought even more bank loans.

Initially, the high real interest rates recorded in 1975 could be absorbed easily because the amount of debt that was financed was low relative to the value of equity for most business firms in late 1974. During 1976, however, the persistence of high interest rates began to affect the solvency of some business firms, as indicated by local press reports such as one, dated January 1978, a year after Banco Osorno's failure:

> In financial circles it has been asserted that, according to the Superintendency's audits, the volume of loans not serviced in time is between 10% and 15% of the banking system's portfolio. There is little hope that those debtors will be able to pay.[19]

After studying the balance sheets of many prominent companies, an economist reported in his magazine column during the same month that the country had entered a vicious circle: High real interest rates forced firms to increase their demand for credit, which in turn kept interest rates high even if the supply of funds rose (Lüders, 1978). These reports came after the record growth rate of 9.9 percent in 1977 completed Chile's recovery from the 1975 recession.

But with real growth of gross domestic product in the two succeeding years (8.2 and 8.3 percent, respectively, in 1978 and

1979), real interest rates began to fall, albeit slowly. In addition, the reforms to the banking law of early 1978 had, for the first time, required Chilean banks to publish their financial statements in newspapers of national circulation, and those statements would have to be produced by independent external auditors.

In early 1979 the four main auditing firms in Chile (Langton Clarke; Price Waterhouse; Deloitte, Haskins & Sells; and Coopers & Lybrand) certified that loan provisions on the order of 1 percent of loan portfolios were adequate for most banks.[20] At the time, the authorities of the free-banking school argued that the presence of .these auditors, who would defend their reputations, ensured that any unrealized loss problem would be discovered and solved. An alternative view, to which we subscribe, is that most of these auditors were either duped or bought off by the bankers who paid their fees. We posit that the banking policy debate was won by the state supervision school and that the superintendency switched toward direct supervision when, in 1980, it realized that external auditors would be unable to ensure adequate banking practices.

The experience of Banco Español is illustrative. Recall that in April 1980 Price Waterhouse reported that Banco Español had no information that might help to evaluate the probability of recovery of 37 percent of the loans in its portfolio. Some believed that this event showed that the external auditing process was uncovering the rotten apples in the banking system, and their confidence increased. An alternative view is that external auditors had been fooled. The fact is that in the following April, after Banco Español was bought by Mr. Tassara, Price Waterhouse declared that all the problems had been solved, but seven months later, in November 1981, the superintendency took over Banco Español to stop massive fraud.

The Superintendency of Banks was never satisfied by the claims of independent auditors and, after Banco Osorno's failure, took several steps toward reducing the likelihood of its recurrence elsewhere. The first step was to introduce new legislation, which was approved in early 1978 and has been previously described. By late 1978 the superintendency was concentrating on ensuring the completion of the first year of auditing by external auditors. In March 1979 the superintendency prohibited for the first time the accrual of interest on *delinquent* loans. In December 1979 it reduced the required general loan-loss provision from 2 percent of loans to a number independent of the actual delinquency rate but linked to "the volume of outstanding loans and the historical experience of recovery, which may be different for each bank." Of course, this last regulatory change should be described as incompetent.

In February 1980 the superintendency, for the first time, attempted to classify loans. It established an experimental system in which each bank would have to classify (on a risk scale from A to D) its thirty largest individual debtors. The superintendency required that a special folder be opened on each of them, containing the information upon which the judgment of risk was based. Initially, the system was purely informational, containing no provisions with respect to either the classifying banks or the classified debtors. The superintendency's comments on the result of this preliminary exercise were informative, to say the least:

> It was discovered that some institutions did not have the information necessary to identify their debtors. . . . In several institutions, it was verified that the loans were disbursed without knowledge of the credit needs of the borrower and with absolute ignorance about the uses to which the funds would be put.[21]

By observing the absence of documentation of some loans, the superintendency was also recording violations of the new legislation introduced in 1978. The comment, published two months after Price Waterhouse's revelations about Banco Español, with the purpose of supporting Price Waterhouse's independent finding, thus amply fulfilled its objective.

The initial results of the classification experiment spurred the superintendency to take additional actions. In June 1980 the superintendency requested that the classification be extended to the eighty largest debtors of each bank. In April 1981 it required the classification of the 300 largest debtors and introduced classification procedures for both consumer and housing mortgage loan portfolios.

Next the superintendency obtained the approval by the junta of a set of draconian reforms to the banking law (embodied in Law No. 18,022, of August 19, 1981), which took the banks by surprise. Because the superintendency did not perceive hidden losses to be the main legislative problem at that time, however, the principal purpose of the reform was not to force their realization. Instead, its main aim was to redefine the concept of individual debtor in response to the huge scale of lending within business groups (self-lending) that had been detected.

As a direct result of the loan classification experiment begun in 1980, the superintendency took over eight banks and *financieras*[22] in November 1981, the first being Banco Español. These intermediaries accounted for over 6 percent of all loans in Chile's financial system. The declared purpose of the takeovers, to end the rollover of loan losses by these institutions, demonstrated that the external auditors had been either duped or bribed during the preceding years when they had offered assurances that provisions for loan losses were reasonable for all these financial institutions.

In response to these events, the discredited free-banking school gave some evidence that it was still alive within the government by introducing Law No. 18,080 (December 16, 1981). This law, expanding the explicit government insurance of small deposits that had operated since 1977, consisted of an optional guarantee that could be purchased by each depositor up to some U.S. $3,500 in addition to the original guarantee, which was free. The optional guarantee covered no more than 75 percent of the additional loss of a depositor who purchased the option. This law is best understood as an aberration, because the takeover of eight institutions in the previous month reaffirmed the widespread belief that the government insured all bank liabilities. Indeed, this belief was reflected in the very few depositors who paid for the optional guarantee provided by the law. This anomalous episode is worth recalling, however, because it was indicative of the confusion in the minds of some of the authorities at the time and has been a source of some confusion in subsequent discussions among economists.

In December 1981 the superintendency required a general loan-loss provision at a rate of 0.75 percent of loans, this time independent of the historical experience of recovery.[23] Then, in February 1982, the superintendency requested quarterly classification of the 400 largest debtors, who on average accounted for 75 percent of the banking system's loan portfolio.

It was not until March 1982, when the Chilean economy had already entered into a steep recession, that the superintendency required provisions in relation to the classification of loans. It also, however, gave banks a generous deadline, as the required provisions would be allowed to accrue in equal amounts over the succeeding thirty-three months.

We conclude our review of the evidence by noting that the Chilean banks grew very fast during 1977–1981, a period in which the real size of loan portfolios increased 513 percent.[24] In addition, the economy exhibited strong growth up to 1981, so new loans were profitable and had the potential to dilute older, bad loans.

The evidence for unrealized loan losses, 1977–1980. The qualitative evidence just presented can be used to support either of two incompatible propositions. One proposition is that unrealized losses were not important by 1980, having been diluted by vigorous growth. This is contradicted by the other proposition: that the Superintendency of Banks was irresponsible and incompetent and unrealized losses continued to be significant (see Held, 1989, for example). We propose a third interpretation: Rollover of unrealized losses was not important as a general phenomenon until late 1981. It was, however, important in a few business groups, most notably that of Banco Español.

Two pieces of evidence may help to discriminate among these three interpretations. First, when the overall result of the classification procedure was published, it turned out that (except for the loans of the institutions that were taken over in November 1981) only 6.03 percent of loans were considered to be at risk. This percentage, as of June 1982, summarized the percentage of loans at risk in the several classifications: 1 percent of B loans; 20 percent of B− loans; 40 percent of C loans; and all the loans in the D class (Acevedo, 1983). To put this number into perspective, six years later, in May 1988, the volume of loans at risk in Chilean banks during a very good year for the economy was 5.33 percent of the total portfolio. The percentage of loans for which provisions existed had, however, increased from 1.73 percent in late 1981 to 6.08 percent in 1988.[25]

Furthermore, the volume of loans at risk was probably less in December 1981 than it was six months later at the time of the superintendent's report. In addition, 1982 was a very poor year for the economy, with gross domestic product falling 14.1 percent and banking indicators rapidly deteriorating. The percentage of delinquent loans, for example, rose from 2.34 percent in December 1981 to 6.31 percent in May 1982. We therefore believe that the volume of loans at risk, as measured by the superintendency, was below 6 percent in December 1981, after the takeover of Banco Español. Thus, *net* unrealized losses approximated 4 percent in December 1981 (after subtracting the loan-loss provision of 1.73 percent from a percentage of loans at risk of somewhat less than 6.03 percent). Additionally, capital and reserves of the banking system that were available for absorbing unrealized losses were 10.4 percent of loans in December 1981, exceeding net unrealized losses by 6.4 percent of total loans and representing the real economic capital of Chilean banks. Because Chilean banks had a loan/asset ratio of 0.774 in 1981, the overall capital/asset ratio was approximately .05 in 1981. This systemwide ratio is certainly positive and was not small by international standards.[26]

The second piece of evidence regarding the possible rollover of unrealized loan losses is the fact that the superintendency became very militant and aggressive during 1981 and took over the banks it considered to be insolvent after completing the loan classification procedure. Recall that in December 1981 the superintendency required a general loan-loss provision at a rate of 0.75 percent of loans, lower than the average provision of 1.73 percent that banks had in their books, and confirming that by late 1981, when the classification procedure was fully in place, the superintendency did not believe unrealized losses were a substantial problem. The superintendency could have requested a much higher provision without jeopardizing its position, because the mood was to mop up the troubles bred by the free-banking approach. Undoubtedly, the superintendency would have required a much higher provision had it believed unrealized loan losses to be a critical problem.

Consider now the critiques of these two sets of evidence. The first set of figures can be questioned on the grounds that the number of loans at risk in June 1982 was biased downward. It is a fact that the superintendency had not reviewed the classification of loans made by at least some important banks, and self-loans among the business groups comprising the respective banks had simply not been classified (see Held, 1989, for the example of Banco de Concepción). The second set of evidence can be challenged by the observation that the authorities did not know in November 1981 if the banks *not* taken over were solvent.

The possibility that loan losses were huge in 1980 still cannot be rejected on the basis of the foregoing evidence; additional evidence on entry, growth, and real interest rates warrants examination.

Detecting a Ponzi game. In this section we review the Chilean experience in 1977–1980 with respect to the most negative consequence of a persistent rollover of unrealized losses: a Ponzi game that creates a vicious circle, both attracting additional participants and extending the game's length.

Recall that the theoretical implications of a Ponzi game are that real interest rates rise, healthy debtors suffer a credit squeeze, the real volume of deposits and debts grow geometrically, and banks suffer economic losses in most periods. But these ramifications may also occur in the absence of a Ponzi game, making it difficult to determine from such evidence that a game is in progress. For example, a good alternative explanation for the exponential growth in deposits during 1977–1980 was available: Financial liberalization was producing its expected results.

Competition, free expansion, and new entry into banking would accelerate a Ponzi game, but they would also be expected to ensue from financial liberalization in the absence of such a game. Evidence on the entry and expansion of new banks during the period is not, in any event, indicative of a corresponding Ponzi game. As of November 1974 the Chilean government issued a decree exempting foreign investment from limitations of the Andean Pact and thereby allowed the creation of new banks and the opening of branches and subsidiaries by foreign banks. Yet Table 2.9 shows domestic banks to have been the principal entrants into the liberalized Chilean banking system, a fact that is inconsistent with a Ponzi game scenario.

Table 2.9 shows that the growth of new entrants did not prevent real growth of older banks. Indeed, the growth of the older banks, as a group, was substantial enough to allow them to grow out of much of their unrealized loan losses by diluting them with new, sound loans. Because the excessively risky loans associated with moral hazard cannot be established for this period, we assume that new loans were generally sound. Moreover, with the exception of 1980 (the year of opening to international capital flows), the growth rate of total real loans fell throughout the period, a phenomenon consistent with the bank growth resulting from financial liberalization rather than a Ponzi game.

In Table 2.10, we see that real interest rates fell over those years

TABLE 2.9

Share and Growth of New and Old Banks, 1976–1981 (real terms, end of year)

Year	1976	1977	1978	1979	1980	1981
Total real loans[a]	100	176	270	357	520	613
New banks' share		1.4%	5.5%	10.3%	19.4%	25.6%
Foreign banks		0.5%	0.6%	2.3%	3.1%	4.6%
Bank of Santiago		0.9%	4.9%	7.2%	8.4%	8.6%
Other Chilean banks		—	—	0.8%	7.9%	12.4%
Real loans of older banks[a]	100	174	255	320	419	456
Growth rate of older banks		74.0%	46.6%	25.5%	30.9%	8.8%

[a]1976 = 100.

SOURCES: Held (1989), Table I-5; and Arellano (1983), Table 8. The growth of 1980 reflects a large inflow of international bank loans to Chilean banks.

TABLE 2.10
Dynamic Simulation of Maximum Loan Losses, 1976–1981 (end of year, except interest rates)

Year	1976	1977	1978	1979	1980	1981
Total real loans[a]	· 100	176	270	357	520	613
Average real interest rate on loans						
Held (1989)		46.1%	35.9%	15.8%	11.6%	33.2%
Arellano (1983)		39.4%	35.1%	16.6%	12.2%	38.8%
Maximum share[b] of bad loans						
Older banks' portfolio		10.0%	9.3%	8.6%	7.3%	8.9%
Banking system portfolio		10.0%	8.7%	7.7%	5.9%	6.6%

[a]1976 = 100.
[b]The size of unrecoverable loans, suggested by press reports of January 1978, is assumed to be an initial 10 percent of the loan portfolio; the growth of these initially unrecoverable loans is assumed at the loan interest rate (calculated by Held) in real terms.
SOURCES: Held (1989, Table I-8); and Arellano (1983, Table 11). Arellano uses Cortazar and Marshall's corrected CPI; and elaboration from Table 2.9.

and reached normal levels by late 1980. This development supports the interpretation that a series of high-growth years eroded and diluted the original loan losses.

A simple calculation[27] presented in the footnote to Table 2.10 shows that the dynamics of loan losses favored dilution in a larger pool of loans, even though absolute loan losses were able to grow by 134 percent in 1978–1981. This means that there was no Ponzi game by rollover of unrealized loan losses in Chile until 1980 at the earliest. We have previously shown that banks were earning positive economic profits in this period, so the present value of those earnings was also positive. Moreover, in the optimistic mood of those years both banks and bank shares were traded at high positive prices.

This does not imply that the Chilean banking system was solvent in 1980 in an accounting sense, because historical accounting that acknowledged loan losses may have shown a negative accounting net worth. This net worth depends on the initial level of loan losses. An inverse calculation shows that if one wants to argue that unrealized loan losses were near 20 percent of the loan portfolio by the end of 1981, one must support the notion that initial unrealized loan losses added up to 30 percent of the loan portfolio in early 1978.

The magnitude of unrealized loan losses in early 1978 or late 1981 is unknown. Unsubstantiated estimates published in the press in early 1978 asserted that 10 to 15 percent of loans were not being serviced on time. Furthermore, delinquent loans are clearly not equivalent to unrecoverable loans. Our impression is that the substantial economic growth of 1978–1981 probably improved recoverability, while other problems, such as fraud, reduced the prospects of recovery.

Our conclusion, then, is that no Ponzi game was played in Chile in 1978–1980. This conclusion contradicts Harberger (1985), McKinnon (1988), and Held (1989), who have asserted that unrealized loan losses were so large that most of the Chilean banking system was insolvent during the entire period and that most of the "growth" was not real but the product of a Ponzi game.

In contrast, our simulation shows the beginning of a Ponzi game no earlier than 1981, a year in which real interest rates rose substantially in tandem with a decreased rate of growth in new loans. It must be acknowledged that a portion of this Ponzi game was stopped by the November 1981 takeover of Banco Español and others, but they held a small share of the total unrealized loan losses. The Ponzi game begun in 1981 continued until late 1982. That year's recession imposed huge new losses on the economy and turned even sound loans into failures.

In any case, rollover of unrealized loan losses was not the cause of the steep rise in real domestic interest rates observed in 1981. It was one more consequence that fed back into banks' demand for deposits and fueled the initial rise in interest rates. Thus, although a Ponzi game was not played over 1978–1980, unrealized loan losses increased the sensitivity of the Chilean banking system to exogenous rises in interest rates and other problems.

In this environment the superintendency reacted by introducing a loan classification scheme. In our opinion, this happened too late to reduce the fragility of the Chilean banking system. To have been effective, the loan classification scheme should have been in place in late 1977, because in that way the superintendency could have forced banks to reinvest all the profits of the good years. This was not done because of the misguided policy of the free-banking school, which ceded responsibility too late to the state supervision school in mid-1980.

Structural contingent subsidies: Chile, 1981. This section presents the Chilean experience with structural contingent subsidies. As previously explained, this concept basically refers to the inability of bank regulators to impose risk-rated provisioning requirements on banks as a result of the set of risks that are heavily influenced by the regulators' superior officers.

Risks influenced by Chilean authorities. We start with a brief macroeconomic overview of the risks that were under partial control of the Ministry of Finance. In 1981 Chile sought and obtained an extraordinary volume of foreign loans, while domestic real interest rates in peso loans rose toward an annual rate of 40 percent. Obviously, the increase in the supply of funds was overwhelmed by an increase in demand. During 1981 the domestic currency appreciated, and gross domestic product (GDP) grew by 5.5 percent. The foreign debt incurred in that year was borrowed by private domestic banks and was then re-lent to the domestic private sector. The next year, 1982, marked the end of the excess level of foreign capital inflows, the continuation of a very high real interest rate in peso loans, a large real devaluation, and a depression in which gross domestic product fell 14.1 percent and unemployment rose by 20 percentage points. The overall ratio of domestic bank loans to GDP, which was 37.6 percent in 1980, rose to 50.4 percent by the end of 1981 and to 71.2 percent by the end of 1982. By the end of 1982 most of the banking system was insolvent.

Until 1983 the Chilean debt crisis was a private sector crisis. Unlike most Latin American governments, the Chilean government did not borrow abroad in the 1977–1981 period. In 1983, however, the government took over a large portion of the banking system and guaranteed the external debt contracted by private domestic banks. By the end of 1983 the foreign debt crisis had ceased to be a private sector problem in Chile; the government was forced by the international bank cartel to extend its guarantee to commercial banks' foreign debts. From then on, Chile's debt crisis became like the crises of most Latin American countries.

Interest rate fluctuation risk. The first element to be considered in an analysis of structural contingent subsidies in Chile during 1981–1982 is Chile's reaction to the extraordinary rise in 1981 of international real interest rates. The analysis is complicated by the excessive willingness of international banks to lend to developing countries in the late 1970s and early 1980s, before the onset of the debt crisis. Table 2.11 decomposes the factors leading to Chile's debt accumulation into those that were peculiar to Chile and those that were shared with other developing countries.

In Table 2.11, the prudent trade balance is the one required to keep Chile's foreign debt from exploding in response to changes in the international real interest rate. The expected trade balance is the one that Chile would have had if the economy had behaved like the average middle-income oil-importing developing country in those years. The expected trade balance takes into account the impact of

TABLE 2.11
Actual and Expected Chilean Trade Balance, 1977–1982

	(millions of U.S. dollars)					
	1977	1978	1979	1980	1981	1982
Net external debt	5,078	5,748	6,297	7,134	11,876	14,679
Prudent trade balance	−178	−224	−296	−285	−71	308
Expected trade balance	−244	−259	−516	−728	−986	323
Actual trade balance	−170	−422	−281	−871	−3,010	33
Accumulated excess of actual over prudent trade balance	−8	189	192	801	3,852	4,774
Accumulated excess of actual over expected trade balance	−74	84	−143	−17	2,004	1,985

	(percentage)					
	1977	1978	1979	1980	1981	1982
LIBOR − change U.S. WPI	0.5	−0.6	−2.4	1.5	10.7	11.7

SOURCE: Valdés (1989). The fifth and sixth lines were accumulated at the LIBOR rate.

overlending by international banks and the average policy errors of developing countries, including their slow reaction to the rise in international interest rates. The sixth line shows that in 1981 Chile deviated strongly from the pattern of behavior exhibited by similar developing countries. The country incurred a huge excess foreign debt in 1981, which must be explained by domestic factors.

Chile did not have a normal reaction to the 9 percent rise in international real interest rates in 1981. This rise, if permanent, would have been a brutal shock to a borrower with no access to funds at long-term fixed interest rates, as was the case of most Chilean companies and investors. A real interest rate shock of the size of the international rise of 1981, even if it lasts for only two years, reduces the value of an asset with a constant cash flow by 15 percent. On the other hand, if the rise in interest rate is short-lived, the shock is much smaller. As we will see, interest rate speculation in Chile took the form of betting that the international interest rate would soon fall.

During 1981 domestic interest rates rose simultaneously with international rates. The domestic rise was much steeper, however. Real *ex post* peso lending rates increased from 12 percent in the last quarter of 1980 to 35 percent in 1981. The finance minister's policy was to maintain a gold-standard type of adjustment to the excess expenditure observed in early 1981. This excess was due not only to the changed international interest rates but also to optimistic expectations about the future and to the fall in the price of the main export, copper.

It is important then to establish the likelihood of a fast reduction in domestic interest rates, as seen from 1981. The finance minister's policy meant that the domestic money supply would be driven by the balance of payments. Such an adjustment required a monetary contraction as soon as the balance of payments came into deficit, which would raise the domestic interest rate because of imperfect capital mobility. The implication was that domestic interest rates would stay higher than the international interest rate, even if the latter fell. Consequently, many Chilean debtors began to restructure their debts by switching to U.S. dollar-denominated assets so that they would benefit if international interest rates fell.

During 1981 interest rate risk was substantial in Chile, at least for the highly indebted corporations and individuals. Although the Chilean finance minister did not control the international component of this risk, he did control the domestic component through monetary policy. In addition, the authorities controlled access to dollar-denominated funds through the exchange control law. Clearly, the minister of finance influenced both the outcome of the local interest rate fluctuation risk and access to the foreign interest rate risk.

Exchange rate risk. After successfully reducing the rate of inflation from 500 percent in 1973 to 29 percent by the end of 1978, the government became alarmed by a rise in the inflation rate to 34.6 percent in the second quarter of 1979. The government recognized that the inflation was not caused by deficit financing by the central bank, since the budget was in surplus. The government's diagnosis was that the central bank was causing the ongoing inflation by devaluing the exchange rate continuously on the basis of past inflation. This diagnosis led the government to fix the nominal exchange rate at 39 pesos/dollar in June 1979.[28] The fixed exchange rate policy seemed feasible because the 1974–1978 reduction in tariffs had substantially reduced the scope for price rises in internationally tradable goods.

The convergence of the domestic inflation rate with the international one took about two years. The local inflation rate began to fall only in the first quarter of 1981, to an 18.4 percent annual rate, and achieved the international inflation rate the next quarter. It then continued falling—to reverse the accumulated real appreciation. Convergence was slow and costly, in part because of some rigidities in the labor market, particularly the government-required full backward indexing of nominal wages to past inflation.

There had been talk about the need for a devaluation since mid-1980. The discussion centered on whether a devaluation of the local currency would correct the real appreciation that was eroding the tradable sector's competitiveness, or would merely be diluted in higher domestic inflation. The rise in the domestic real interest rate observed in the first half of 1981 was considered by some to be a seasonal effect plus a simple reflection of higher international interest rates. Others initially interpreted this rise as the effect of an inflation prediction error, with the implication that inflation had finally been eliminated and no devaluation would be necessary after all.

High real interest rates persisted, however, throughout 1981 and cast doubt on the government's claim to a successful stabilization. Even if stabilization had been successful, the large volume of external debt contracted at a floating interest rate implied a crushing debt service cost because of the sharp rise in international interest rates. The 1981 fall in the price of the country's main export, copper, also fueled expectations of devaluation.[29] Imports of durables climbed to record highs. Many thought that the way to adjust and reduce imports was to devalue. The authorities, however, insisted on the narrow view that stabilization had finally been achieved, so no devaluation was necessary. They appeared to believe that a rapid fall in international interest rates would alleviate the adjustment problems facing the economy.

Throughout 1981 the great uncertainty about the future development of the nominal exchange rate and exchange controls affected the fortunes of individual bank debtors, because reducing the cost of adjustment to the high international interest rate depended on correctly guessing the changes in exchange controls and exchange rate policy. The minister of finance directly controlled the outcome of this risk, through central bank intervention in the foreign currency market and through the central bank's power to redefine exchange controls.

Evidence of structural contingent subsidies. In a nutshell, we argue that the superintendency could not include in its loan classification procedure a truly independent assessment of the exposure of bank debtors to foreign exchange and interest rate risk because such an assessment would have interfered with official macroeconomic policies. Consequently, the institutional constraints on bank supervision allowed part of the private sector to draw on the government's deposit guarantee at a subsidized price.

Our argument assumes that bank supervisors themselves had the primary responsibility for assessing foreign exchange and interest rate risks. Most banks' assessments could not be relied on because many banks wanted to present a rosy view of their self-loans. Moreover, a bank could not classify its loans to independent debtors in proportion to exposure to exchange rate risk without classifying its self-loans in the same way. The banks preferred to insist that most debtors, independent or not, had capacity to pay given the expected course of events, which was the one espoused by the authorities: No devaluation would be forthcoming, and interest rates would fall rapidly.

Chilean bank supervisors therefore carried an unusually heavy responsibility on their shoulders in 1981: They should have claimed that both the supervised banks and their own superiors were wrong—that exchange risk and interest rate risk were substantial. If bank supervisors had taken on this responsibility, they would have had to supplement the normal guidelines for evaluating the debtors' capacity to pay with an order to calculate explicit indicators of that capacity, including exposures to exchange and interest rate risks.

The evidence suggests that the budding group of bank regulators, overburdened with the task of identifying self-loans, were willing to believe that those risks were small, as the official view proclaimed. Banks were therefore free to draw on the deposit guarantee by lending to debtors who were highly exposed to currency and interest rate risk.

Now we turn to the evidence on risk taking by the domestic private sector that drew on contingent government subsidies. First, it is clear from our analysis that the subset of the private sector that would be willing to accept a contingent subsidy had to belong to the set of corporations and individuals with little true capital to lose. Second, a significant subset of banks also had to have had little capital to lose if the bets were unsuccessful.

It is well known that by late 1980 an important set of individuals and corporations was heavily indebted. We will label this group *optimists*. They believed that the fast growth of the last three years could be sustained, so they were willing to invest with borrowed funds. This group contained small and large firms and also many consumers. We term the group holding the opposite position *conservatives*. It included many firms, of every size up to large business groups. They had been willing to sell their assets at prices they considered inflated, and some of them had moved funds out of the country.

The reaction of conservatives to the rise in international interest rates and the U.S. recession, given the large Chilean external debt, was to prepare for a devaluation by reducing their dollar debt and increasing peso debt, while simultaneously reducing expenditure. At the other extreme, the reaction of highly indebted optimists was to bet that the government would keep the exchange rate fixed, as promised. The optimists hoped that the high, 19 percent international lending rates would fall shortly. They therefore wished to change their peso debts into dollar debts in order to bet that foreign interest rates would fall shortly and that there would be no devaluation. This was the best alternative open to them, if creditors agreed, because accepting peso loans at high interest rates meant certain bankruptcy.[30]

The optimists' requests for more credit would have been met with clear opposition, however, by a healthy financial system because the increase in debt was financed by creditors whose beneficiary in expected value terms is the debtor. A healthy system would have been willing to lend more only at higher interest rates to compensate for the higher risk. Given the darkening prospects for the next few years, the best policy would probably have been not to lend more. Note that this credit policy would have been healthy only if the banks themselves were not exposed to currency or interest rate risk. It would have been appropriate for exchange risk, because the central bank had required all banks to match foreign currency asset and liabilities.

The Chilean financial system did not react like a healthy system for three reasons. First, darkened profit prospects reduced the economic value of many banks. This judgment is supported by the addition of only 8.8 percent of 1980 pretax profits to bank capital during 1981. Second, the significant portion of unrealized loan losses that would grow at the interest rate during the coming recession implied that true capital would be further eroded. Third, many banks were owned by business groups that had the ability to shift true capital out of their banks and out of the reach of the superintendency. This could happen because in 1981 the superintendency was still unable to control self-loans effectively; it did happen because the business groups found that strategy to be profitable. Most bankers rushed to offer cheaper dollar-denominated loans (financed through new external debt) to their customers, hoping that the contingent subsidy for currency risk would allow them to survive.

We must recall that a contingent subsidy is valuable only for debtors with little capital. It is hard to believe that the Chilean private sector had little capital in late 1980, even considering that in 1977 many were near insolvency: There had been three years of vigorous GDP growth. Experience showed, however, that during 1975–1977 many corporations and societies that were indebted to the banks and subject to limited liability had acquired the less-than-honest habit of shifting collateral out of the reach of their creditors.

The banks did not defend the collateral of their loans over 1978–1980 for several reasons. First, banks had limited monitoring capacity and a shortage of qualified personnel; in other words, many banks were still incompetent. Second, the Chilean court system was (and is) so slow that obtaining full redress is a very costly and lengthy process. Third, many banks were dominated by business groups that preferred to assign their limited management resources to shift the collateral of their own self-loans out of the reach of their banks. Fourth, in those years banks experienced rapid growth, so the drive to make more loans tempered considerably their interest in the design of effective collateral contracts. Fifth, because the free-banking school insisted that there were enough private incentives for banks to worry about collateral, banks received no stimulus from the superintendency to adopt loan classification schemes that provided for a careful evaluation of collateral.

In 1981 most banks saw their effective capital plummet further as soon as optimistic debtors became less willing to pay when the net worth of their corporations fell. This reluctance reinforced the previous perverse incentives to banks, so that banks became even more willing to assume credit risks derived from exchange rate and interest rate risks.

By 1981 financing decisions by Chilean firms and banks reflected a *de facto* government guarantee to the private sector for foreign exchange risk. Our analysis has identified the superintendency's lack of penalization of credit risk in its loan classification criteria as the channel for the guarantee.

The outcome of this structural contingent subsidy was that many small and medium-sized businesses got deeply into debt in 1981. Debts to banks increased during 1981 from 37.6 percent to 50.4 percent of GDP in response to the rise in real interest rates. The external counterpart was an increase in the foreign debt, because domestic deposits did not rise rapidly.

In addition, debtor-speculators were offered the easy claim on the government that they had believed in official exchange rate policy, so they should be helped if a devaluation occurred. This plausible claim further increased the value of the government's contingent subsidy for exchange risk.

Finally, many debtors that were initially honest were caught by the huge rise in domestic interest rates in 1981 and lost most of their equity. Their response was to shift collateral out of the reach of the banks, arguing that they were merely defending themselves from the finance minister's policy of allowing domestic interest rates to rise to expropriatory levels. Redistributions of wealth of this size between debtors and creditors were considered by many to be simply illegitimate.

The cost of structural contingent subsidies. Starting in 1982, unemployment rose steeply, and consumers realized that they had to stop spending. The recession deepened, and deflation became a reality. The number of employed people fell 22 percent between mid-1981 and December 1982. A substantial proportion (160,000 out of 690,000) left the labor force, and 230,000 were employed by the government in low-wage emergency employment programs.

By mid-1982 the fall in GDP was so steep that it took on the character of a depression. In June 1982 the government finally decided to devalue the exchange rate by 14 percent, followed in July by a period of free float that saw the exchange rate double in nominal terms in a few months. By the end of 1982 the losses that the devaluations had inflicted on the holders of dollar-denominated debts had created insolvency among firms of all sizes. Capital flight was rife, as the central bank scrambled to reestablish the foreign exchange controls it had lifted during the previous few years. Debtors attempted to shift their dollar debts to pesos, managing to reduce by 13.4 percent their aggregate dollar exposure in the domestic banking system during 1982.

The sorry state of most debtors caused delinquent loans to rise from 2.34 percent of loans in December 1981 to 3.83 percent in February 1982 and 6.31 percent in May. Most delinquent loans turned out to be 100 percent losses, so they reduced the net worth of banks. Moreover, a correct estimation of net worth should subtract from capital the loans at risk estimated in the loan classification procedure. Loan-loss provisions should, however, be added to net worth.

Table 2.12 shows the impact of the recession and contingent subsidies to speculation on the solvency of the banking system. It documents the dramatic reduction in the solvency of the banking system in 1982. On July 12, 1982, the central bank decided to allow banks to defer their losses over several years, so it began to buy the banks' delinquent loan portfolios at face value. The banks, however, had to promise to repurchase the portfolios at face value over time with 100 percent of their profits, so the scheme did not improve bank solvency by itself. It solved a liquidity problem but also set the stage for making good the implicit contingent subsidy that the government had offered to speculators in 1981.

In this environment the problem of rollover of unrealized loan losses naturally presented itself again. The bank debtors that had speculated insisted on obtaining a rescheduling or at least a rollover.

TABLE 2.12
Delinquent Loans and Bank Capital, 1982 (billions of Chilean pesos)

Month	Delinquent loans	Loans sold to central bank	Capital and reserves	Loan-loss provisions	Net worth[a]
December 1981	16.831	—	76.685	5.206	65.060
January 1982	21.627	—	76.685	13.359	68.698
February	27.164	—	77.484	14.456	64.776
March	31.232	—	80.256	15.294	64.318
April	41.631	—	81.993	15.294	55.621
May	42.963	—	82.760	16.565	56.362
June	45.537	—	89.692	21.000	65.155
July	45.837	8.800	89.559	18.969	53.891
August	41.816	23.895	89.626	22.330	46.245
September	45.984	28.500	91.405	21.920	38.841
October	49.643	33.860	95.800	26.654	38.951
November	45.625	40.930	96.854	27.153	37.452
December 1982	41.118	41.607	105.035	34.737	57.047

[a]Net worth is calculated from the other columns as capital plus provisions minus delinquent loans minus loans sold to the central bank. This estimate of net worth is not precise because it should also subtract the loans at risk estimated by loan classification and add the recoverable portion of delinquent loans and the economic value of intangible assets. For June 1982 the loans at risk were estimated by the superintendency to be 6.03 percent of loans (Acevedo, 1983), i.e., some 44.288 billion pesos, which puts effective net worth at 20.866 billion pesos for that date.
SOURCE: Superintendencia de Bancos e Instituciones Financieras, *Información financiera*, various issues (January 1982–January 1983).

Contrary to the situation in 1975, however, the superintendency had acquired the powers and had put the machinery in place to classify loans and question loan renewals. Nevertheless, the authorities faced difficulties in stopping an indiscriminate rollover of unrealized losses. Because insolvency was widespread, many thousands of debtors hoped that the government would announce a massive bailout package. In the meantime, they pressed for loan rollovers, and the banks accepted willingly.

The reaction of the authorities to the rollover of loan losses was to publish a circular, *Process of Definition of Bank Debtor Solvency*, in November 1982. Numerous inspectors and members of the banks' operating staffs revised the banks' evaluations of recovery of their debtors, and many debtors had to prepare a presentation to their banks to show that they were still solvent or that they deserved a rescheduling.

The publicly announced outcome of the evaluation process was as follows: A volume of 110,688 billion Chilean pesos of debt was due by "nonviable" debtors, so their guarantees would be seized and the banks would have to request their bankruptcy. In addition, the volume of debt owed by debtors defined as "in difficulty" was 315,107 billion Chilean pesos, and these debtors were made eligible for the sought-after rescheduling.

In response many debtors rushed to shift collateral out of debtor corporations. Banks, on the other hand, dragged their feet on both bankruptcy proceedings and rescheduling, forcing the authorities to think of alternative mechanisms, which will be reviewed in the next section.

Self-lending by Business Groups in Chile

As a predominantly market-oriented economy, Chile has always exhibited a number of important diversified conglomerates, most of which include a bank and therefore fall into our definition of a business group. Banks are included in most Chilean conglomerates because, during the financial repression of 1940–1973, the ownership of a bank or savings and loan secured access to scarce loans at negative real interest rates.

Unprecedented growth occurred among business groups in Chile during the 1976–1981 period. At the time, critics argued that this was the inevitable result of the shift toward free-market policies and insisted that high industrial concentration would hijack the political process.[31] Now it is clear that these prejudices were unfounded. The business groups grew unexpectedly quickly in Chile during this period not because of a bias in free-market economies but because of three specific government policies: first, privatizing banks before privatizing the industrial firms expropriated by Allende; second, privatizing banks and industrial firms through auctions to the highest bidder; and third, retaining the old set of regulations on international private capital mobility.

The policy of privatizing banks before industries allowed relatively small business groups to acquire banks.[32] The business groups were thus given access to the public's deposits, which were lent to the group itself and used to buy the industrial firms privatized by the government between 1976 and 1978. It is clear that the sequence of privatization had a profound influence on the industrial structure.

The second government policy that eased the way for business groups was the privatization of both banks and industrial firms through auctions to the highest bidder. Because of the recession of 1975, the high real interest rates for available bank loans and the complete absence of large foreign investors from post-Allende Chile, the only competitive bidders in these auctions were a few local business groups. The government made no effort to dilute ownership across tens of thousands of investors in 1976–1980.

What really gave these business groups their clout, however, were the large profits they made in 1977–1980. A substantial part of these profits was made in arbitrage operations between the high domestic interest rate and the low foreign interest rate. This type of arbitrage was possible, in part, because of the third government policy, which retained, until 1980, the old set of regulations on international private capital mobility. The other part of the profits reflected the natural advantage of any large firm that can pay lower interest rates for a large volume of loans by borrowing directly from the wholesalers of funds. Since the government decided not to use its own external borrowing capacity or that of the state enterprises to bring funds to Chile and earn arbitrage profits, only a few big industrial companies and banks, dominated by new business groups, had access to private foreign lending. Furthermore, this access was subject to individual quotas strictly enforced by the central bank. Given the high—but falling—local interest rate, the few business groups that had access to foreign loans could enjoy a large arbitrage rent in 1977–1980.

The business groups were also able to grow with the economy, independent of government policy. A substantial chunk of their equity was capital gains in property and share values, generated in part by the reduction of real interest rates over time but mostly by the expectations of permanent high growth that became believable as the economy improved over the period. On the other hand, asset prices were inflated by the new business groups' habit of continually acquiring new businesses at a higher rate than the rate of increase in aggregate real capital. In addition, two of these business groups were successful in obtaining the goodwill of smaller investors, which let them gain control of several large, loosely held corporations by purchasing a relatively small share of stock. In this way, the Vial and Cruzat-Larraín groups became partners of thousands of smaller local investors and rentiers in Banco de Chile, Cervecerías Unidas, and COPEC, among others. This partnership did not result from government policy but merely reflected exceptional appeal of these two groups among rentiers. The possible conflicts of interest between small and controlling shareholders began to be regulated somewhat late, in the 1981 reform to the securities law. Other business groups did not attempt to lure rentiers and smaller investors.

Most Chilean business groups enjoyed exceptional growth over the period for two additional reasons. First, the strong performance of the economy in 1977–1980 generated substantial operating profits in most sectors of the economy. Second, several large business groups took advantage of the opportunities opened by the reduction of tariff rates in 1976–1979. They moved rapidly to invest in the newly profitable export sectors and prepared to exploit fully the advantages that their size afforded in serving large foreign markets.[33] It is clear that these possibilities were open to many Chilean and foreign investors, and not only to local business groups. In fact, many traditional business groups, medium-sized new groups, and small investors made large profits in this period for precisely these reasons.

We do not have very precise information about the solvency of the business groups at the end of 1980. We do, however, know that the consolidated indebtedness of the two largest business groups was high, with a probable debt/equity ratio of between 2 and 3.[34] Confirming evidence is that, at the time, the managers of the largest business groups argued that high indebtedness was necessary to sustain high growth in developing countries. The largest group, Cruzat-Larraín, controlled assets of approximately U.S. $2 billion in 1981. It has been independently asserted that the controllers' equity of this group was near U.S. $300 million. If noncontrolling shareholders' equity was a similar sum, which seems likely, the solvency ratio of the group would have been in the range indicated.

These high levels of debt existed because the domestic component was short term (in that it was expected to be renewed at the interest rate that would prevail in the short-term market) while the foreign portion was based on a floating rate. As a result, Chile's two largest business groups were highly exposed to interest rate risk. A rise in interest rates would reduce the value of their fixed assets while maintaining the value of their debt. The riskiness of this exposure was not well understood at the time even within the business groups. In the Vial group, calculation of consolidated accounts began in 1981. The incompetence of private bankers extended to the business groups themselves, the natural result of fast growth and the rapid shift toward free-market policies in 1975–1980, which made many of the old habits of local businesspeople obsolete and created an acute shortage of qualified personnel. It was also the result of the failure to take advantage of the previous years to impose prudential regulation, whose principles would have forced the private sector to learn the techniques for risk evaluation.

Self-loans and loans to independent parties. This section attempts to compare self-loans of banks with loans to independent borrowers in order to examine the hypothesis that business groups had preferential access to bank borrowing. It is known that independent borrowers were able to obtain large loans during financial deepening. Arellano (1983) shows that the ratio of bank debt to sectoral GDP rose rapidly over 1977–1980 for most sectors, that the rise of this ratio was faster for the sectors known to be dominated by small and medium-sized businesses. This information is summarized in Table 2.13.

During 1981, dollar-denominated local bank loans to the local building sector (which is dominated by medium-sized firms) grew by 284 percent while the sector's peso-denominated debt rose by 13 percent. At the same time, agriculture's dollar-denominated loans grew by 48 percent while the sector's peso-denominated debt fell by 9 percent (Arellano, 1983, Tables 9A and 9B). There is also ample evidence that consumers speculated by buying imported consumer durables.

A comparison of the financial policy of the large business groups with the financial policy of smaller debtors and investors indicates that large business groups chose different strategies beginning in 1980, just as smaller investors did. The two largest business groups, Vial and Cruzat-Larraín, were optimistic about the future and very indebted. The Matte and Angelini groups, on the other hand, chose a slower growth/lower risk strategy. In fact, many analysts have concluded that the two largest groups were the largest precisely because

TABLE 2.13

Local Bank Debt/GDP Ratios, by Sector

Sector	Debt/GDP ratio		
	1977	1980	Percentage increase
1. Dominated by small firms			
Agriculture	20.1	65.6	45.5
Building	8.0	64.3	56.3
Transport	4.2	28.8	24.6
2. Dominated by large firms			
Industry	20.8	42.5	21.7
Mining	1.5	10.0	8.5
Commerce[a]	25.5	50.6	25.1

[a]Commerce is a mixed sector, with many large and small firms.
SOURCE: Arellano (1983, Table 9C).

they were willing to incur high debt/equity ratios. For this reason we will call them the speculative business groups.

A study by Gálvez and Tybout (1985) focuses on differences in the financial strategies of Chilean firms by examining the balance sheets of a sample of 177 large nonfinancial firms, of which 45 were affiliated with conglomerates (although not all the conglomerates included a bank). When analyzing indebtedness, these authors calculate a "corrected" gearing ratio, which excludes financial investments in affiliated companies from assets or equity, as the case may be. The reason for excluding financial investments is that they were in some part reciprocal, so that a standard gearing ratio would be misleading. Among large firms in 1980, the authors find similar corrected debt/equity ratios of 0.89 for independent firms and 0.92 for conglomerate-affiliated firms.

We conclude that until 1980 the two largest Chilean business groups were more indebted than the average for other businesses but that this level of indebtedness also characterized a substantial number of smaller investors and independent large firms. Because most optimists were able to incur a high debt/equity ratio independent of their size, we further conclude that the informational advantage of business groups over the Superintendency of Banks was not an important factor up to 1980.

The monitoring of business group self-loans. As shown in the theoretical section, it is much harder for the Superintendency of Banks to evaluate the riskiness of self-loans by business groups than the riskiness of ordinary loans. As noted, the problem of fiscal oversight of self-lending practices surfaced in April 1980 with Price Waterhouse's report that 37 percent of Banco Español's loan portfolio was undocumented. The superintendency was shocked and backed Price Waterhouse's findings in a June 1980 statement. Subsequent revelations indicated that the superintendency had found many of the loans for which information did not exist to be self-loans to the banks' owners. During 1980 the superintendency thought that the detection of fraud was the main problem with self-loans. Although it had begun to worry about fraud, this problem was considered to affect only a small portion of the banking system.

By early 1981 fear of the power and influence of business groups had produced a growing animosity toward them within the military government. This development reached its climax when the military discovered that the largest business groups would dominate the newly created pension fund management industry. In addition, the political opposition had been campaigning against the power of business groups since mid-1980. In this political setting, the Superintendency of Banks began to construct a map of the holding companies of all the important business groups in Chile. In addition, beginning in March 1981, the Superintendency of Securities began to force public companies to reveal all their dealings with affiliated companies.

In a surprise move on August 19, 1981, the Superintendency of Banks obtained the military's approval of an amendment to the banking law, which changed the regulatory approach to self-lending. The amendment stated:

> Failure to diversify loans away from persons and societies linked, either directly or indirectly, to a bank through ownership or management will signify that the bank is managed in a deficient way.

The amendment to the banking law gave new powers to the superintendent with respect to deficiently managed banks, such as the power to ban the extension or renewal of specific loans and the power to prevent the bank from lifting guarantees in the case of self-loans. The new law stipulated that self-lending could be stopped by the superintendency at any moment. These new powers were clearly excessive—in the sense that bankers had no way to appeal to a court—and demonstrate the backlash that a disregard for prudential regulation can generate.

The reform also introduced a diversification requirement for bank investments; it provided that a bank could not invest more than 30 percent of its capital in the securities of each issuing society.

Finally, the law forbade banks to own shares in other companies, except as a result of underwriting, and shares ceased to be acceptable guarantees. A month later, in Circular No. 1753, dated September 14, 1981, the superintendency established specific guidelines to define self-loans, which also limited drastically the maximum allowable volume of self-loans by business groups. If the scheduled limit was not met, the superintendency would declare the bank to be in a state of deficient management.

The superintendency complemented these portfolio guidelines by tightening the definition of an individual debtor. Before the new law an individual debtor was a society or person. After the reform an individual debtor included all the companies in which the debtor had more than 50 percent ownership or control, plus the prorated share of debts of companies in which the debtor had between 50 percent and 10 percent ownership. Since a bank would be able to lend at most 25 percent of its capital to any one debtor, and self-loans were at the time between two and five times capital for the largest business groups, the new law implied a drastic reduction in the quantity of permissible self-loans by business groups. For this reason, the package of reforms provided that the new limitation on self-lending would not take effect until January 1, 1982. In practice it was not until February 8, 1982, that banks were required to send a list of their affiliated debtors to the superintendency. There was no explicit timetable for adjustment at this time, so, by default, business groups were expected to divest their self-loans in just a few months.

The largest business groups reacted to the new limitations by evading them. They realized that if they had less than 10 percent ownership in a company, the company would be eligible for self-loans. They also knew that only direct ownership ties were considered in the official definition of self-loans. The first reaction, therefore, was to keep the direct participation of the group in shell companies at 9.9 percent by increasing the density of the network of shell companies.

In addition, the business groups adopted the tactic of continual creation and dissolution of shell companies, which increased the difficulty of the superintendency's task. Business groups also linked up to replace self-loans with new loans to other business groups, in exchange for reciprocal treatment by the other business group's bank.[35] Although this was criticized at the time,[36] it was inevitable given the excessive size of the self-loans. This diversification also at least allowed the superintendency to rely partially on an independent risk evaluation: the one of the other business group. In effect, a sound business group with too many self-loans would not want to engage in such linkage with an unsound business group.

The largest business groups also circumvented the new law by taking advantage of the Chilean banks' recent authorization to lend abroad. The banks would lend to a foreign enterprise, such as a Cayman Islands corporation, which would bring the money back to Chile and lend it to the other firms in the business group.

Finally, the Vial group evaded the new law by using the bank law's authorization to establish bank subsidiaries abroad: Banco de Chile and Banco Hipotecario de Chile (BHC), Vial affiliates, established subsidiaries in Panama, Uruguay, and New York. The Panamanian subsidiary drew its funds from BHC's loans and then lent directly to the other firms in Vial's business group. The Uruguayan subsidiary got loans from Banco de Chile and then lent to the Vial firms in Chile.

The evasion of regulation during 1981 allowed business groups to delay adjustment by taking on more debt. The study by Gálvez and Tybout (1985) finds that the corrected debt/equity ratio for large firms rose from 0.78 in 1980 to 0.89 in December 1981 for independent firms, while it rose from 0.92 in 1980 to 2.57 in December 1981 for firms affiliated with conglomerates.

In conclusion, although the Chilean superintendency achieved some reasonable ability to classify loans during 1982, the difficulties in supervision ran deep even during 1982. Tagle (1988), for example, states that even in 1983, one year after self-lending by the largest Chilean business groups had stopped, the superintendency continued to discover that what it had previously classified as loans to independent parties were in fact self-loans. These discoveries, which led to a 10 percent real increase in the estimated volume of self-loans in 1983, further emphasize the difficulties faced by Chilean bank regulators in overcoming the informational asymmetry in the case of self-loans by business groups.

Abuse of the informational advantage. The supervisory difficulties of the superintendency can be interpreted in two ways. The most popular interpretation is that the business groups attempted to evade prudential regulation by engaging in risky lending practices (moral hazard) and the rollover of unrealized losses. An alternative explanation is that the business groups were forced to find a way to obtain the time required to reduce the stock of self-loans without having to pay excessive prices to the new creditors or to accept low prices when selling assets. The need for a timetable for disengagement from self-loans is clear from the fact that in June 1982 the superintendency created a two-year timetable, which was extended in 1984 for six more years in acknowledgment of the fact that the 1982–1983 recession was much deeper than anticipated (see Tagle, 1988, p. xv).

It is critical to separate the analysis of 1981 from that of 1982, because in the latter year a deep recession—with GDP falling 14.1 percent—reduced the solvency of most Chilean firms, including business groups. For example, a finding that the debt/equity ratio of business groups was too large in December 1982 cannot be considered good evidence of moral hazard, because the recession may have wiped out the group's equity exogenously. One piece of evidence that would allow us to choose among these alternative hypotheses would be a risk evaluation of self-loans as compared to ordinary loans for 1981. The superintendency, however, has never published the information it had at the time, and business groups have never published their consolidated balance sheets.

An alternative way to proceed is to check what happened to investment plans in 1981 in response to very high real interest rates. Gálvez and Tybout (1985) find that both independent firms and firms affiliated with conglomerates maintained their overhead per unit sale more or less constant in 1981 and at similar levels. Independent firms, however, reduced the rate of addition to fixed capital from 7 percent in 1980 to −6 percent in 1981, while firms affiliated with conglomerates reduced the rate of fixed capital investment only from 11 percent in 1980 to 8 percent in 1981. Firms affiliated with conglomerates thus adjusted their investment plans by too little in reaction to the rise in interest rates and financed their continued expansion with additional debt. This approach suggests that business groups were unwilling to disengage from self-loans, as required, as soon as possible; if they had been willing to disengage, they would have reduced investment by much more.

We now review whether the speculative Chilean business groups had a good motive to engage in moral hazard and in the rollover of unrealized losses in 1981.

The feasibility of moral hazard. During 1981 overall indebtedness increased substantially in the Chilean private sector, from 37.6 percent to 50.4 percent of GDP, as a counterpart to the accumulation of foreign debt. If we keep equity constant, this rate of debt growth implies increases in debt/equity ratios from 2 to 2.7 or from 3 to 4. In 1981 a steep rise in real interest rates reduced equity substantially. The share price index in the Santiago Stock Exchange fell 27 percent in real terms during 1981. Assuming a conservative 15 percent reduction in asset values, we find that market-value debt/equity ratios rose from 2.7 to 6 and from 4 to 16. Clearly, after such losses have been sustained, moral hazard can become a dominant motive for behavior, given the informational advantage enjoyed by business groups.

The evidence shows that the business groups took advantage of their informational advantage over bank regulators to draw implicit government subsidies for speculating against a future devaluation, as did other speculators. Their informational advantage made the new guidelines on self-loans nonbinding during 1981.

It is misleading, however, to assert that self-lending was the main factor behind the excessive accumulation of foreign debt experienced by Chile in 1981. Self-lending by the speculative business groups merely allowed them the extra bonus of continuing their investment programs. The other result of the informational advantage was a delay in the implementation of the new regulation. This allowed the group to avoid immediately divesting self-loans and to draw on the government's contingent subsidy associated with foreign exchange and interest rate risk taking. The contingent foreign exchange and interest rate risk subsidy was offered to other investors as well, and it was this subsidy that wrecked the macroeconomic balance.

We conclude that speculative business groups engaged only marginally in behavior associated with moral hazard. The business groups did not have a good motive to engage in moral hazard in 1981, because they had a better alternative: to rely on contingent government subsidies enabling them to bet that no devaluation would occur and that interest rates would fall shortly. Both moral hazard and contingent government subsidies require the debtor to come near the brink of bankruptcy by increasing leverage. The difference between the two, as stated previously, is that in a situation of moral hazard the issuer does not want to issue a contingent subsidy, whereas in this case contingent subsidies are willingly offered. If, therefore, the speculative business groups had used their waning informational advantage to avoid a hypothetical guideline that forced provisioning for foreign exchange risk and interest rate risk, then they would probably have chosen to engage in moral hazard. This was not the case in Chile in 1981, but as we shall see, it was the case in 1982.

The feasibility of loan-loss rollover. To determine whether there was rollover of unrealized losses by abuse of the informational advantage implicit in self-loans, we must ask the following question: Given that losses were large for both small entrepreneurs and big business groups, did the latter obtain special treatment by taking advantage of their informational advantage over the superintendency?

We believe that business groups, along with all other types of investors, engaged in a generalized rollover of loan losses during 1981 and the first half of 1982. Nevertheless, most analysts believe that the ability to roll over loan losses was more widely available to companies in the business groups. In other words, we believe that the share of self-loans in banks in early 1981 was smaller than the share documented in Table 2.14 for June 1982, December 1982, and February 1983.

Table 2.14 shows that self-loans constituted a high proportion of total loans in June 1982 but that the proportion did not rise substantially in the second half of 1982. Such a result suggests that the superintendency succeeded in preventing business groups from using their informational advantage to roll over their unrealized losses in a preferential way during the second half of 1982. By June 1982 it thus appears that the superintendency had gained the ability to estimate the consolidated solvency of business groups.

Other regulatory problems. We now turn to regulatory problems related to the informational advantage of business groups in other segments of the financial system. In 1982 the Cruzat-Larraín business group began to use its control of the mutual fund industry to lend to

---

TABLE 2.14
Self-loans and Rollover of Unrealized Losses, by Business Group

		Self-loans as a percentage of total loans		
Business group	Financial institution	June 1982	December 1982	February 1983
Cruzat-Larraín	Banco de Santiago	44.1	42.3	45.8
	Banco Colocadora	23.4	23.8	24.4
	BHIF	28.2	18.5	18.9
Vial-BHC	Banco de Chile	16.1	18.6	19.7
	BHC	17.1	18.5	n.a.
	Morgan-Finansa	7.2	n.a.	6.8
Yarur	Banco Crédito e Inversiones	8.6	11.9	12.0
Errázuriz	Banco Nacional	29.1	25.7	30.1
Edwards	Banco de A. Edwards	15.9	14.9	15.4
Matte	BICE	4.0	4.0	5.5
Concepción	Banco Concepción	17.0	12.2	12.0
Sudamericano	Banco Sudamericano	13.0	14.8	16.2
Internacional	Banco Internacional	20.1	16.9	25.9

n.a. = not available
SOURCE: Superintendencia de Bancos e Instituciones Financieras, *Información financiera*, December 1982, February 1983, and July 1988.

the group's companies the funds it had obtained from thousands of small investors. The funds' shareholders (numbering 131,017 in December 1982) were kept happy by the large increases in the prices of several securities held by the mutual funds. It was soon discovered, however, that the group was manipulating the price of the securities that had been issued by the same group's firms. In addition, many of the mutual funds publicized their 1982 shift to fixed income securities, stressing the reduced risk, but shareholders failed to realize that these securities were mostly commercial paper issued by the group's largest companies, including some very indebted holding companies.

The larger firms of the group financed the rollover of unrealized losses through the sale of commercial paper[37] to medium-sized investors and to mutual funds. The use of this market raised real interest rates on commercial paper to very high levels by late 1982. The speculative business groups succeeded in fooling the public in the security markets by drawing on its confidence in well-known company names. Such deception occurred even though the 1981 reforms to the Securities Law and the Joint Stock Companies Law had restricted the scope for those practices. For example, the timely disclosure of relevant information was required of high company executives. Unfortunately, the Superintendency of Securities failed miserably in making sure that investors had access to the relevant information. For example, the superintendency never required business groups to publish their consolidated balance sheets and also failed to generate enough information about the riskiness of the commercial paper sold by holding companies to mutual funds.

The outcome: takeover by the Superintendency of Banks. We conclude our discussion on self-lending by documenting the end of the two speculative business groups. In June 1982, using the new powers obtained in 1981, the Superintendency of Banks announced a new limit on self-loans of 5 percent of total loans—that is, 100 percent of capital and reserves. All banks were forced to present "diversification plans" within forty-five days. The target would have to be met in five semesters, with the first 20 percent due by December 1982. Two weeks later the target was changed to a complete ban on self-loans to shell companies, and the limit on self-loans to productive companies was reduced to 2.5 percent of total loans.

The apparent reason for this tightening of requirements was to strengthen the superintendency in the negotiations it had opened with Vial's business group. The authorities wanted the Vial group to pay some of the debts it owed to Banco de Chile with shares in the group's productive (non-holding-company) firms. Vial did not fulfill his commitments and refused to hand over control of Banco de Chile, thereby opening a period of several months of hard bargaining. Nevertheless, Vial had lost effective control of the group, whose bankruptcy was then sealed by the devaluation of the peso during this period.

As discussed earlier, after the November 1982 solvency definition process the authorities found that banks were unwilling to reschedule loans selectively on the basis of a case-by-case analysis of debtors and preferred to roll over all loans. This practice put pressure on the authorities to stop the rollover of losses.

On January 7, 1983, a large paper-pulp firm of the Cruzat-Larraín group announced that it could not continue to service its debts. The group had been unable to survive the recession on its own, and the only question left was whether the authorities considered the group to be "nonviable" or "in difficulty." In the latter case the group would have deserved a rescheduling according to the November 1982 rules.

The authorities' answer came on January 13, 1983, when the superintendency took over the flagship banks of both speculative groups and declared the forced liquidation of another three banks. The finance minister argued that the solvency of all banks had been reviewed according to the risk classification procedure of the superintendency, including the results of the solvency definition process of November 1982. It had been found that the banks were clustered into three groups. The first group included banks whose estimated losses were less than 100 percent of capital and provisions, so that they still had a positive net worth. The second group included banks that had losses between 100 percent and 200 percent of capital and loan-loss provisions. These banks, which were taken over because they had negative net worth, were Banco de Chile (Vial group), Banco de Santiago (Cruzat-Larraín group), Banco Colocadora Nacional de Valores (Cruzat-Larraín group), Banco de Concepción (small business group), and Banco Internacional (small business group). The institutions in the third group, which had estimated losses above 200 percent of capital and provisions, were liquidated. The banks in this group were BHC (Vial), Banco Unido de Fomento (owned by a consortium of foreign banks), and Financiera Ciga.

Of course, the estimate of the solvency of these banks included an assessment of the solvency of the speculative groups. For example, Banco de Santiago's solvency depended on an estimated recovery of an amazing 45 percent of the loans it had placed with its own business group.

At this point, a different element entered the analysis: The authorities had become convinced that the existence of business groups, where banks and productive firms were managed jointly, was one important source of the excess debt burden in the Chilean private sector (see Lüders, 1985). This judgment was shared by other observers of the situation (Díaz-Alejandro, 1985, p. 13). Our analysis, on the other hand, has shown that a substantial part of the excess debt burden was caused by the implicit government subsidy to foreign exchange and interest rate risk taking during 1981. We agree, however, with the diagnosis that during 1982 the informational advantage of business groups could be countered only by takeover of the flagship banks and the main holding companies. For a short while, the business groups could roll over their losses to a larger degree than smaller debtors could, thereby causing a part of the excess debt burden.

A similar analysis of the informational advantage of business groups led the authorities to complement the takeover of the speculative business groups' flagship banks (Banco de Chile and

Banco de Santiago) with the planned acquisition of control of large companies that these business groups had controlled. In practice this control was achieved by a refusal to renew the thirty-day peso loans that these firms owed their previously affiliated banks. This refusal to renew outstanding loans forced these industrial companies into bankruptcy proceedings, and the creditors' committees came to be dominated by the representatives of the flagship banks. In this way the government took over the two speculative business groups, achieving an unexpected nationalization of a large proportion of private sector output. The intervention produced changes in the banking system's balance sheet that are represented in Table 2.15.

Lessons for Financial Liberalization and Prudential Supervision

The Chilean experience offers important lessons for both financial liberalization and bank regulation. In this concluding section we focus on lessons that are specific to the Chilean experience and on

TABLE 2.15
Delinquent Loans and Bank Capital, 1983 (billions of Chilean pesos)

Month	Delinquent loans	Loans sold to central bank	Capital and reserves	Loan-loss provision	Net worth
December 1982	41.118	41.607	105.035	34.737	57.047
January 1983	47.704	37.535	102.941	35.753	53.455
February	86.650	37.514	103.105	47.201	26.452
March	103.667	37.548	103.105	48.934	10.824
April	110.592	38.524	103.115	50.480	4.479
May	116.889	38.480	103.254	53.549	1.434
June	126.867	36.915	104.277	55.367	−4.138
July	132.781	41.662	104.793	55.394	−14.256
August	109.144	71.343	105.869	52.512	−22.106
September	108.399	85.434	106.993	56.465	−30.375
October	90.024	112.095	107.462	55.465	−38.697
November	88.724	117.695	108.289	57.528	−40.602
December 1983	92.190	109.675	127.714	61.963	−12.188

SOURCE: Superintendencia de Bancos e Instituciones Financieras, *Información financiera*, December 1982–December 1983.

those that pinpoint key areas for future research on financial liberalization and prudential regulation.

The specifics of the Chilean experience. In this chapter we have detailed the Chilean experience in a way that permits assessment of banking policy over several different episodes of bank failure and across different regulatory issues.

Dismantling the institutions of financial repression in Chile after 1973 was not a simple task. The dynamics of the transition to a liberalized financial system are complex, but liberalization apparently leads to a high initial real interest rate, which falls over time. During the transition it is difficult to coordinate reform, as the 1975 failure of the Chilean savings and loan industry shows.

A specifically Chilean problem was the internal policy struggle over the appropriate framework for the banking system after liberalization. Beginning in 1976, Chile experienced a full year of free banking because confidence in government deposit guarantees had been shattered by the government's initial unwillingness in 1975 to honor its guarantee to depositors in the failed savings and loan system. Although the failure to bail out the savings and loan system at first strengthened the position of the free-banking school with the government, an important lesson from Chile is that until significant evidence in support of free banking is accumulated over time, a realistic approach toward financial liberalization should subject a banking system to prudential regulation.

The free-banking school, however, insisted on free banking after 1977, when such a policy had lost credibility as a result of the government's support for depositors at five large financial institutions. Given this support, the only sensible regulatory route was to implement prudential supervision of the banking system, but this implementation did not occur until after the Banco Español fiasco in 1980. Thus, three years of potential learning were lost. During that three-year period the natural protection provided by transitory financial-system quasi rents against moral hazard and the rollover of unrealized loan losses was dissipated. The failure to learn during that period was paid for dearly in 1981–1982.

The first of two main culprits in the 1981–1983 bankruptcy of most of the Chilean financial system was the steepness and depth of the depression of 1982 and 1983, which by itself forced many debtors into insolvency. Moreover, the sustained rise in international real interest rates after 1980 was also a critical factor that forced many Chilean firms into bankruptcy. Other exogenous macroeconomic factors were influential too, such as the fall in the terms of trade and the overlending by international banks in 1979–1981.

Second, an important reason for the erratic behavior of the macroeconomy in 1981 and 1982 was the government's voluntary extension of guarantees on exchange rate and interest rate risk. When the private sector took advantage of those guarantees, its actions fed back into the macroeconomy, deepening the recession. These guarantees could have been withheld if bank regulators had had enough experience and if private banks had been schooled in the discipline of risk evaluation and collateral control in the period after 1977.

On the other hand, our detailed analysis suggests that several purported regulatory problems in Chile 1974–1982 did not exist. The main alleged problem—a Ponzi game through the rollover of unrealized loan losses—was probably not present in 1978–1980. The rollover of unrealized loan losses, however, became an important problem in 1981 and 1982 as a result of the other problems previously listed. In the same way, banks' risk-taking behavior, driven by moral hazard, was simply not important in 1978–1980, but such behavior became increasingly important during 1981 and 1982.

The case of self-loans by business groups is more complex. Self-lending is certainly a pernicious business practice but for different reasons than those usually mentioned. Until 1980 the speculative business groups followed a financial policy similar to that of many smaller groups and individual investors and went bankrupt along with many of them. From mid-1981 to mid-1982 the speculative business groups were able to use their informational advantage to delay the implementation of new rules that would have destroyed their access to self-loans but did not engage very much in practices linked to moral hazard. To the extent that the two largest speculative business groups used their waning informational advantage over regulators to roll over their self-loans more freely than independent debtors could, they worsened the real interest rate rise of 1981 and squeezed out more creditworthy independent debtors.

After mid-1982 moral hazard and the rollover of unrealized loan losses became important factors driving the behavior of the speculative business groups, but regulatory authorities were able to stop the groups by taking them over in January 1983. Before the January 1983 takeover, however, the speculative business groups used their informational advantage to deceive small investors in the security markets in the second half of 1982, forcing losses onto many of them.

A program for research. Much important research must still be done in the area of financial liberalization and prudential regulation. We list three of the most important research areas here.

First, the dynamics of financial liberalizations are virtually unknown. We have suggested the importance of asymmetric portfolio-adjustment costs as well as the importance of the costs of market development. The issue of coordination between the different reforms that compose a financial liberalization package is also important.

Second, the Chilean experience shows that prudential regulatory issues are much more complex and varied than generally suggested by the existing literature. We have proposed a framework for analysis that stresses the difference between structural contingent subsidies, moral hazard, and the rollover of unrealized loan losses. The dynamics of these types of behavior are virtually unexplored. Such an exploration may yield interesting insights into banking policy.

Third, the complicating factor of the initial incompetence of private bankers and regulators and the way in which bankers and regulators learn during a financial liberalization deserves special study. Learning by doing, on the part of regulators, banks, and debtors, may fundamentally affect the dynamics of macroeconomic adjustment to a financial liberalization.

Gary Gorton

Comment

Let me begin by describing a country engaging in financial liberalization. Roughly, it goes like this.

The country lifts a variety of restrictions on interest rates, credit, and reserves, and new privately owned banks are allowed to operate. The number of banks quickly grows, or the size of the banking sector quickly grows. Business conglomerates buy banks in many cases. The central bank does not have the staff or the professional expertise to monitor this enlarged banking sector. In fact, the banks themselves cannot find enough trained staff. The default rates associated with the enormous volume of new loans are unknown, and the head of the central bank announces that in principle it is resolved not to bail out insolvent banks. Now, what would be a likely outcome for this country's banking system? And what would be a desirable outcome?

The country I have just described is Indonesia. It remains to be seen what will happen there, but it seems that the Indonesian experience mirrors that of Chile prior to the collapse of its banks. In discussing this chapter, I will ask the same question posed by the authors but include an additional case. My question is, What should the Indonesian bank regulators or government in general have learned from the Chilean experience?

Before getting to that, however, I want to say that I was quite impressed by the chapter and probably agree with 99 percent of it. So I shall strive to limit my remarks to what I think are its most important elements and my points of disagreement.

Let me first make some general remarks about bank regulation. As many of you know, I am prone at times to say a lot about bank regulation. A great deal *needs* to be said on this subject, but I will confine myself on this occasion to a very few observations.

Discussions of bank regulation can be very depressing: There seems to be a consensus, at least according to perceived wisdom, that without regulation there will be big losses, yet it appears that *with* regulation, we also end up with big losses. In Chile a system of policies apparently went awry and ended up in *de facto* nationalization of the banking system. In the United States a regulatory system that appeared to work quite well for a long period of time turned out not to work very well at all. After considering these two cases, how can anyone address the subject *without* becoming depressed?

In fact, however, I think that this way of thinking about bank regulation is based on a completely false premise. Not only is there no theory underpinning it, there is an abundance of evidence contradicting it. There are banking systems that have had very good experiences over long periods of time, prone neither to collapses nor panics. It is important to distinguish the features of these systems and to ask how they might differ in design from those that have had such horrendous problems. Furthermore, once the design questions are answered, one must ask how such stable systems are implemented.

The features of trouble-free banking are not obvious; otherwise all banking would be trouble free. But one feature that appears to be very important is size. That is consistent with what we know theoretically about banks. Very large, well-diversified banks are less prone to trouble. I think that is an established fact.

Another feature is self-regulation. There is a presumption that panics and collapses are bad, that they are just unmitigated evils that ought to be avoided. (It is commonplace to cite Ben Bernanke's paper [1983] on this point. I don't think that is the principal significance of the paper, but it seems important to point out that that is not obvious.) Yet panics and collapses have served a very important function. Historically, they have motivated banks to regulate one another. And they accomplished something that regulators seem incapable of doing—closing banks when they become insolvent rather than allowing them to continue, in Ed Kane's words, as "zombie organizations." (Kane, 1989.)

In fact, a panic in the United States S&L industry would have saved billions of dollars. The undemonstrated assertion, with casual comparison to the Great Depression, that the losses would have been greater if we had had a banking panic is simply not obvious to me at all.

Whether we should allow, or design a system that allows, panics ought then to be viewed as an open question. Why don't we ever hear discussions of this? I think the reason is very important, and I think it may be the linchpin to what is going on here.

The complication is that few if any governments can credibly precommit to not rescuing large banks. Such was not always the case, but this Pandora's box appears to be open forever. Consequently, given public expectations, the collapse or the panic that would have occurred had there been no credible precommitment does not occur. Governments then appear to be in the position of delaying, or of being unable to recognize or enforce, closures. We realize *ex post facto* what went wrong, but we can then act only too late.

I think the reason is that the regulators are in an inherently untenable position, not just with respect to getting the first best outcome but in attaining the second best outcome as well.

The first of two problems is that by definition banks are firms that create nonmarketable assets. Nonmarketable assets are different from marketable assets. It doesn't matter how much discussion we have about market value accounting and information production. The fact is that these things are nonmarketable, and if they were marketable, this issue of information wouldn't be important.

In the United States it is clear that we should change the accounting rules. Is that going to have a big effect on the situation? I doubt it. There is strong evidence that the issue of market value accounting is a red herring. In the United States we know from looking at failed bank auctions what the outcomes are. If you allow banks to go in and inspect the assets of failed banks and then you look at the difference between the first and second bids at these auctions, the spread is enormous. When experts actually try to value the stuff, they have wide disagreements about it. So it is unlikely that public regulators will do a lot better than that. This disagreement among the experts makes it difficult to decide when we are supposed to close banks and so on.

The second problem seems to me to be more significant in the United States than in Chile. There seems to be a false presumption of constancy regarding the technology associated with the production of banking activities and with the larger market structure. The truth is that because of exponential changes in technology, valid answers to many fundamental questions are dramatically different from those of fifty years ago. These questions include, Which markets are open in the capital markets and which markets are closed? Are there interest rate futures? Are there options on them? Have banks substantially changed their monitoring and information production services?

By maintaining a presumption that defies and denies these changes, we act as if we knew that banks had inherent problems that always required them to be regulated, as if they were always prone to banking panics and collapse. That is simply untrue. We can imagine worlds in which we wouldn't need the regulations that the United States has had for fifty years. Other systems work fine without them. What are the differences?

The problem from the regulators' point of view is that they are in a position where they can't detect these technological changes. Let me make this a little clearer with the U. S. example. As you know, commercial banks and thrift institutions didn't fail for a long period of time, and then they started to fail. Indeed, commercial banks are now failing with increasing frequency. There are two ways of looking at this phenomenon. From one perspective, these failures are evidence that the regulators are not doing what they are supposed to do and we therefore need to equip them with more powers as well as require banks to hold more capital—in effect, we need greater financial repression.

The problem with this "solution" (apart from its incorporation of a false premise) is that it completely ignores the possibility that banks are failing because changes in technology have made old regulations inappropriate. Once this possibility is seriously entertained, a new causal proposition must be addressed. It posits that the old regulations are (in interaction with new technology) causing the very failures that they were designed to prevent.

This proposition can't be addressed by just looking out at the world and casually observing that banks are failing. It is a theoretical question, first of all, and it requires some deeper thinking. If it is valid, it explains why regulatory systems appear to work for long periods of time until everything suddenly goes completely haywire. The regulations were not designed to be flexible. Instead, the regulators must be flexible, but they would also have to recognize those technological changes that have implications for the operation of banking systems and appropriately incorporate that recognition into the regulatory process. That is one tall order—for anyone. To expect it of the regulators themselves is unreasonable. Regulators are simply too busy worrying about failures to recognize the shifts, and so not only can we get into large financial messes, but we can *expect* them, as well.

If we assume that governments cannot precommit *not* to insure deposits, it seems that the best that possibly can be expected is a painful learning process similar to the one that the chapter authors describe. The only way to deal with such situations is for governments periodically to go through them—learning about the new technology and the misdesign of bank regulations the hard way. I don't think there are any magical solutions. Realistically, it appears that this is simply the way it is going to be.

It is worth stressing that these learning processes must continually recur. If they didn't, then nothing new would happen. It is hard to imagine a world in which learning doesn't occur, and this may be simply a manifestation of that fact.

My comments on the Chilean banking case and this particular chapter may be more understandable now that my presumption regarding the obsolescence of regulations spawned by technological change has been introduced.

The chapter analyzes in great detail the situation of Chilean banking from 1976 through 1983. It has two great advantages. First, one of the authors is an active participant who contributes inside information. In addition, the authors also have great data, so they are in a position to say a lot—and they do. I can't possibly do justice to what they have done with the information, so I will emphasize a few issues. I want to focus, first of all, on the cause of the collapse.

There are a number of possible causes, but let me begin by considering what could have been going through the minds of policy makers before the liberalization actually occurred. In principle, there seem to be but two basic ways to proceed, as discussed in the chapter. One was by the route of free banking.

The authors' restrictive conception of free banking does not imply allowing competitive currencies created by banks that print their own money. Their meaning is confined, basically, to allowing free entry into banking, with no deposit insurance and few restrictions on banking practices. That some groups were in favor of this approach is apparent in the description the authors provide of the "political economy" of that time. They reject this approach out of hand, seemingly viewing it as untenable in principle. I would disagree with that. It is untenable only if a government cannot stick to a policy that disallows implicit guarantees of deposits. If a precommitment not to guarantee deposits is made credible, as Indonesia is trying to accomplish, there is nothing wrong in principle with the free-entry system. It will have costs, of course—banks will fail, and all banks will undergo a learning experience as they figure out how to respond to panics. If, as I suggested earlier, governments can no longer effectively precommit not to insure, and the precommitment is believed by depositors, one can reject the free-entry alternative because of the predictable negative consequences of that alternative in practice.

The second approach is what we have been used to in the United States. The government regulates banks and in the process creates a charter value. The government restricts entry, gives banks a license to some monopoly profits, and insures deposits. So banks have a charter value that is created and insured by government. Government, in turn, regulates the banks.

This approach seems to be the one approved by our authors as well as the one that became the dominant view of the principal Chilean authorities. This second approach may permit banks to engage in excessive risk taking. It is important to point out that this is not an inevitable result of deposit insurance. In principle, if there was positive charter value and regulation, insurance alone would not provide banks an incentive to engage in all sorts of fraud with their business groups and the rollover of unrealized loan losses. As the authors observe, Japan is one of the leading examples confirming this principle. Deposit insurance doesn't even necessarily introduce a distortion. There is no inherent defect in this second approach, therefore; its success depends on how it is designed. But it could have particular problems if the state of the banking system is bad or its members perceived it as such; if so, they are induced to engage in excessive risk taking.

When there is a confused policy toward banks in which charter values may not be positive and in which regulation monitoring is not undertaken (either because there are not enough people who know what to do or it is not clear what should be done), a confused mixture of these two systems results. Such a mixture contains elements of the free-banking system, including no positive charter value, but it also contains implicit deposit insurance. Confusion of this sort will definitely spawn problems, with banks doing all sorts of wild things.

I agree with the authors that this seems to be what happened in Chile: At crucial points the government zigzagged in its policies and finally ending up implicitly insuring everything.

The authors go on to consider a number of more detailed arguments. For example, they ask how, at various points in the process, the banks attempted to get the most value from this implicit deposit insurance. They entertain a number of possibilities. For instance, Was there rollover of unrealized loan losses? Was there a problem with self-lending by various groups?

These particular questions reflect a larger one: How does moral hazard manifest itself once participants are in a situation where it is clear that there is no charter value, there is implicit insurance, and there is not much regulation? These questions do not address the cause of moral hazard, but the various ways in which it manifests itself. In seeking to identify these manifestations, the authors focus on contingent government subsidies, which occur whenever there is a conflict of objectives between regulatory authorities and other parts of the government.

In the chapter the problem of contingent government subsidies is illustrated by the dilemma in which regulatory authorities found themselves in 1981. They couldn't force the banks to classify loans as risky when the cause of this extra risk was that the debtors were highly exposed to foreign exchange and interest rate risk that the other part of the government said didn't exist. Banks understood the risks, and had there been positive charter values, this would not have been a problem. With positive charter values, banks wouldn't necessarily have had incentives to engage in such risky loans. But in the absence of positive charter values, the only issue is what the regulators should do.

With regulators already involved in delaying the collapse, there was no way of forcing banks to price this risk in the absence of positive charter values. Regulators had already lost both the battle and the war. The only question that remained was how big the losses were going to be. Perhaps banks should be closed or at least disciplined in such circumstances, but in the embarrassing situation of contingent government subsidies (described both in the chapter and the preceding paragraph) this will not happen. Consequently, as in the United States S&L industry, the losses mount while all involved scratch their heads and try to figure out what to do when two parts of the government can't agree.

So structural contingent guarantees cannot be a cause of moral hazard; they have to be a manifestation of a cause. That is the main point I want to make on this subject. The basic points that the authors make, however, seem to me to be extremely important. First, the government did not have a clear idea of what it was doing, although individuals within the government may have known what should have been done. During this transition period they couldn't stick to a single policy.

Second, the inability of governments to stick to single policies and in particular to claim that they are not going to insure things seems basically, for reasons I don't completely understand, not to be a credible policy.

These two points seem to me to be the authors' basic lessons about Chile.

This tells me that we should expect problems in Indonesia, which has attempted to adopt basically the sort of free-banking version of financial liberalization with which Chile started. I would therefore predict a financial collapse in Indonesia. Whatever we think might be the best way of designing liberalized financial systems, it seems that a crucial element has to be the recognition that deposits will be implicitly guaranteed and regulation must therefore be an essential feature from the beginning.

Response

SERGIO DE LA CUADRA: Thank you very much for your comments, Gary. I agree 99 percent with them. I would like to know as much as you know about the subject.

I have some doubts concerning one of your points. You mentioned a disagreement with one of our propositions, the sort of arrangement where you have no deposit insurance, free entry to the market, and few regulations. Our idea is that in that system the government will end up bailing out large banks when they collapse. You say that is not necessarily the case.

When the government has to make the decision, it will take into account two types of considerations—pure economic considerations and political considerations.

The pure economic consideration is going to try to measure all the externalities to that event. If it is a large bank, it can impose huge externalities to all those that will be involved in this bank's collapse. Not only the depositors but all the parties to the transactions behind the depositors.

The economic consideration also will consider the value of those assets if the bank is kept as an ongoing operation or you close it down and create a huge difference in the value of those assets. So there will be economic considerations for favoring bailing out. The economic cost may be a hike in the inflation tax or a fiscal crisis.

On the other hand, you are always going to find political support for bailing out. The political situation that is dominant for the government is always to bail out the bank.

I would like to have a system where if there is going to be a bailout, you would at least introduce some cost to the depositors in the bailout to make it not so politically dominant as a solution for the authorities.

RICHARD SINES: How could that have been done in Chile?

SERGIO DE LA CUADRA: Today, when a bank is intervened in by the government because it has solvency problems, it is put into receivership by an administrator appointed by the government. They pay all deposits, 100 percent of deposits. And since it is paid with the central bank's money, the taxpayers don't see directly the cost of the intervention, and so they don't argue against the intervention. Politically it is very attractive. At least this has been the Chilean experience.

We proposed with Salvador that in case a bank is to be intervened in, then it will be forbidden by law to pay 100 percent of all deposits. Retain at least something, 5 percent, 10 percent, to be paid afterward if there are enough assets to pay all deposits. This would introduce a political cost to intervention.

The idea was just suggested. The government did not accept this solution.

SALVADOR VALDÉS: I would like to add a few comments. Gary's comment was very interesting and I think very good.

One way to look at the feasibility of having this almost free banking is to ask what kind of political institutions you need that will make a precommitment not to intervene credible. The usual type of institution doesn't meet that requirement. So one could rephrase what Sergio was just talking about, saying that we should have laws or constitutions that made the political process follow a path such that precommitment not to intervene became credible.

The problem is that a law is maybe not enough. Maybe you need much more than that. A law can be changed by another law, and very fast if it is needed. Representatives get scared very easily with runs and queues of angry depositors. That is the historical experience in many countries. So we are basically talking about almost a constitutional reform. That seems to be a hard thing to attain.

We also must remember that there can be huge externalities in a failure. Unless the checking accounts in banks are insured, including the money orders and that kind of thing, I think that must be taken into account. Say a given trader has a huge transaction under way, just to earn a small commission, and that huge transaction can get to be frozen if the bank collapses and for all the duration of bankruptcy proceedings. The role of bank money must be recognized.

From a purely economic point of view, these externalities must be taken into account before we can say that the free-banking approach is reasonably economical. Those losses may be huge, and bank money may lose its value. If everybody must evaluate a bank before accepting a check or before taking a money order, that introduces a large cost that must be taken into account. The alternative also has costs. We recognize that.

SERGIO DE LA CUADRA: Under our current Chilean law we have tried to approach a solution to this problem that Salvador is mentioning. It offers different types of insurance to different kinds of money. This is going to be dealt with by Mr. Ramirez this afternoon.

SALVADOR VALDÉS: I wanted to finish with a couple of smaller things. One is on Gary's proposition that bank regulation is inherently problematic. The first was that banks create nonmarketable assets and then that regulators cannot detect technological change.

Gary mentioned that regulators don't have time to recognize new technology because they are supervising and they are very busy. That doesn't seem to be very reasonable, in my view. A good regulator should have some line people managing insolvencies and keep time to develop a broad view of the market. So I would question that second point.

Finally, something on the point whether in Chile in 1981 contingent government subsidies on interest rate risk and on foreign exchange risk were a cause of the failure or were a manifestation of the fact that the banks had no positive charter value and there was little regulation. I think that is a good question.

Our view, if we could condense it in one phrase, is that banks had fragile charter value, and when the macroeconomy turned down, bank capital disappeared very fast. Suddenly they were in a very different position.

Before that, when the economy was booming, banks had very important positive charter value; banks were sold at premium prices. Those values were based more or less on the expectation that the boom would continue for several years. When it became clear that it wouldn't—and that happened more or less rapidly—then that value evaporated. Then came the risk taking that we describe. However, given that the charter value had evaporated, there would have been only modest risk taking if the government had not offered the juicy contingent subsidies we describe. In this sense, structural contingent subsidies were a separate cause of the crisis.

Discussion

CHARLES CALOMIRIS: I want to make two quick points. The first has to do with the definition of free banking. I think this is important *vis-à-vis* the point Gary made.

Free entry into banking or banking in which there is a credible commitment not to intervene by the government with a fairly laissez-faire stance toward private banks doesn't mean that banks would be prevented from coordinating their behavior or trying to find ways to resolve systemic problems. That will be one of the themes that I will return to later in the day.

The second point I wanted to make was just to link something in Phil's introductory paper with the discussion of credible nonintervention by government. I would like to generate some discussion about it if possible.

This time inconsistency or credibility problem that is being discussed now has to do with implicit insurance, or intervention in the banking system. One of the things that Phil's article raised was that the best ways to stabilize economies that are sensitive to terms-of-trade disturbances may be impossible because the government is unable to commit credibly to allow private external links.

There is an interesting parallel. An economy's banking system may be more sensitive to price shocks because of an "external" credibility problem, and insuring against these risks may be more costly because of the lack of credibility in banking policy. That leads me to think that the credibility problem is a very general one, a political problem and broader than just the intervention into deposit insurance.

PHILIP BROCK: By the external time inconsistency, you mean with respect to foreign investment?

CHARLES CALOMIRIS: You are talking about insurance markets basically, the problems of interbank relations and insurance relations across countries that really boil down in your discussion to the same kind of problem.

SERGIO DE LA CUADRA: I would like to propose a definition for free banking. It seems that there are different definitions going around. I would define free banking as a system where solvency problems in the banks are solved by the private sector. Someone is going to argue that that will encourage the formation of cartels in the system, but for me that is free banking by my definition.

PAUL HORVITZ: I think we should be clear that it is relatively easy to establish credibility for a policy of not bailing out depositors. Several years ago the FDIC started a policy of handling failures by doing what they call the modified payout, which did impose losses on uninsured depositors. They did that in a few cases.

It didn't take very many and it did generate a general expectation that failures would be handled in a way that uninsured depositors would take losses. We know that had credibility, because when there were the first rumors of difficulty at Continental Illinois a run developed that was pretty significant. That run is in itself evidence that there was credibility that uninsured depositors might well suffer a loss.

So the difficulty isn't in establishing credibility for such a policy; the difficulty is in carrying it through. Obviously the FDIC backed down on their policy in the Continental case, but I think the credibility had been established.

GARY GORTON: I don't get it. What is the distinction between credibility and not carrying out the policy? I don't understand this distinction.

PAUL HORVITZ: I am saying that if you decide you are going to carry out the policy, there is no great difficulty in convincing the market that you are going to do it. You have just got to carry it through a few times, and then that credibility is established.

GARY GORTON: But the example you gave was one in which there was exactly this inability to carry out the policy.

PAUL HORVITZ: I agree. That's the problem. But we shouldn't describe that problem in terms of the difficulty of making the policy credible if you are going to carry it out.

GARY GORTON: I think there is a problem here. I completely disagree. You can announce anything you want. If in every case you do the opposite, then it suggests that eventually people are going to learn that these are not credible even if initially they to some extent believe it.

We use the term "dynamic inconsistency" a bit too loosely, it seems to me. When I worked at the Fed some years ago, dynamic inconsistency was a popular explanation for why we systematically had high inflation or relatively high inflation in the U.S. in the 1970s. Everybody talked about constitutional amendments and redesigning the Fed. Then suddenly inflation went down, and we all forgot about this—which I think suggests that in the political economy context there is room for perhaps just out-and-out argument and convincing somebody and then they do it; they actually carry out a policy that they announce.

In some sense Paul Volcker had the courage to do it even though these loose models would have predicted that he didn't. In that sense I completely agree with what Paul is saying.

JOHN BOYD: Gary, just because you guys forgot about dynamic inconsistency doesn't mean that was necessarily the right thing to do. If I understand Salvador's and Sergio's comments, I think this whole question is important, and it is appropriate to call it "time inconsistency" or "dynamic inconsistency." Some of my associates spent a lot of time studying such issues, and we are coming to the view that this is probably the key issue in this whole area of banking regulation.

Like Salvador, I don't pretend to know the solution. But, for whatever reason, there seems to be, over time and across different kinds of economies, some set of forces that induces governments to bail out banking systems. I know Charlie Calomiris can come up with a few examples (from ancient Rome or whatever) where the governments didn't do so.

(Laughter.)

Charlie can come up with one example of laissez-faire or 100 percent reserve banking, but if one looks across many nations, it appears that there is something very common about this form of government intervention. For whatever reason, when financial systems get in trouble, governments have a very natural incentive to bail them out in one way or another. Notice what these folks have said.

I should mention, by the way, that nothing I am saying has anything to do with Fed policy. I am here as a professor from the University of Minnesota.

(Laughter.)

Now, as I was saying, it seems there is an empirical regularity here. If that is true, in some real sense you can kiss true laissez-faire banking good-bye. Regardless of how you design your deposit insurance system or how you operate your discount money, when market participants can reasonably expect that the government is going to intervene, this will produce very substantial distortions.

We have spent some time searching for examples of where organizations have successfully dealt with blatant dynamic inconsistency. The fact is, they are hard to find. One example is the Mafia's treatment of borrowers. Say you owe the Mafia a hundred bucks and you don't pay. They will still probably kill you even though it's costly to them and produces no immediate returns. In fact, they're sending a signal to other participants in the market: In the future, don't stiff us.

PHILIP BROCK: Are you suggesting that we make the central bank illegal?

JOHN BOYD: No, and I am not suggesting this treatment of borrowers is socially optimal policy, either! I just maintain this is an example of a coalition that has figured out a way to successfully deal with the time inconsistency.

Another organization which appears to deal very effectively with a time inconsistency problem is El Al, the airline, in their dealings with hijackers. If you think about it, it is exactly the same kind of a problem. You want to announce a policy of not negotiating, but of course when you actually have a hijacking, then you do. The situation is very much like the situation confronting a central bank: When one or more large private banks are failing, there are powerful incentives to do what appears to be good in the short run, even though it's clear the long-run result may be bad.

The question is, What is different about these two coalitions, and why have they been able to successfully stick with these policies? I don't know the answer.

MARVIN GOODFRIEND: I would like to take the discussion in a little more pragmatic direction. I liked the paper very much, but as I was reading it, I was struck with the following kind of tension.

This paper makes one consider how very little difference, potentially, there is between the U.S. and Chile, which I think is very good for Americans to recognize since a lot of people in this country are arrogant and think that there is a significant difference somehow between what this country's policy environment is and what developing countries' policy environments are. But in encouraging this recognition, the question arises, Why don't countries learn from each other?

One thing that is absent from this conference is a positive theory of liberalization. You really need a discussion on this issue. I think it would be a great complementary conference to have, given that we have already got these papers together.

Let me try to elaborate.

There are lots of different national experiences throughout the world and lots of different cases of liberalization. To my mind, they seem to be generated by very different causes. For example, in China the idea of financial liberalization seems to arise because they need a better allocation of credit for a more efficient economy.

In Chile, my impression is that there may have been some need for a better allocation of credit, but there was also clearly an idea that the government itself has not been able to back the deposits that it has guaranteed and that there was an embarrassment on the part of the government. If it gets too darn embarrassing for the political system to keep hands on, it makes a case for let's get hands off and get out of the fire.

In the U.S. that kind of argument seemed to be operative in the 1970s. With high interest rates as a result of inflation, other market mechanisms, such as money market funds, came about to give consumers a high interest rate at a time when the banking sector had ceilings. Banks then lost interest in having themselves regulated, because they couldn't compete with the other opportunities that consumers had to have. So the U.S. regulatory system shrank because there was incomplete coverage in the first place. Then, when macro policy made interest rates rise, the government was forced to shrink back regulations under consumer pressure and pressure from the banking industry.

The lesson from the S&L crisis, it seems to me, is not that deposit insurance cannot work; it is that political management of deposit insurance can create tremendous inefficiencies. In this case, it was that the House of Representatives could not get its act together. They could not pass legislation on a closure policy for S&Ls when they knew, economically speaking, they ought to be closed one by one as they become insolvent.

Interestingly enough, if the government has a guarantee in place and a particular bank becomes insolvent, that generates a government liability whether or not the bank is closed.

If you were doing correct economic accounting, the instant any kind of guaranteed institution became insolvent, the liability would be added to the government budget whether it was funded currently or not. It was, in part, because the public didn't understand the extent of the hidden liabilities being generated this way that the House was not pressured sooner to appropriate funds for a comprehensive closure policy.

In addition, as is becoming widely understood, pressure from individual S&L owners who were benefiting from delayed closure made it very difficult for congressmen to vote for closure. In a nutshell, I think the main Achilles' heel of the S&L deposit insurance program was the closure policy.

But there is a solution. You don't want the government to have the sole power to trigger closure. You want to set up the financial institution so that another group of claimants may be holding subordinated debt.

That can be achieved by making financial institutions issue uninsured subordinated debt to claimants who would have the right to trigger closure in the event of a default.

I think if you did that you could very greatly reduce the cost of having deposit insurance in a way that you wouldn't have to throw out the baby with the bath water.

GARY GORTON: We already have this system. We have uninsured banks with subordinated debt. I have looked at exactly whether or not these crises are sensitive at all to bank risk measures. They are not. That would suggest to me that there is an implicit insurance. If you can have that, that would be great.

PHILIP BROCK: I think what you are saying anticipates some of this afternoon's first session where we will be looking at the Chilean banking law. There are aspects of that law that we will have a chance to look at in a concrete way and say, Well, do we think this law is actually going to work or not, and why? So I am glad you brought this up now.

There are obviously other people in this group who have talked about subordinated debt. Paul Horvitz in his book on safe and sound banking has devoted attention to that issue. So it is an important issue.

I think that what Gary is saying is that as far as he can tell the data indicate that people with subordinated debt think that they are insured also. That interpretation is an open topic that we should return to when this seminar's second Chilean paper is addressed.

PATRICK HONOHAN: I just want to make one quick point. Of the many very interesting pages in the paper, one which jumped out at me was Table 2.13 showing the debt/GDP rate by sector and how it grew so rapidly between 1977 and 1980 to figures like 65 percent in the agricultural and building sector.

It struck me that probably one of the most important things behind the subsequent banking crisis was really excessive leverage in the economy, the banks giving a par value guarantee to depositors backed by a claim equivalent to 65 percent of agriculture's GDP. Probably encouraged by the implicit or explicit deposit insurance guarantees, banks were able to build up that amount of leverage.

What seems to have been missing were instruments that could channel risk funds for investment—funds that didn't carry a par value guarantee. If the investment had been financed in this way, the risk of bank failure would have been reduced. If the banks had been smaller in the economy and if the equity holdings had been larger, then this very risky situation might not have emerged, and you might not have had all these present-value gambles being taken by under-capitalized banks.

This leads me to suggest that the policies to ensure that there is an adequate development of the stock market and of equity contracts may be equally important for attaining financial stability as is policy for regulation of the banking system and proper behavior by bank management.

I wonder whether the authors might have some comment on the failure of the stock market to develop adequately.

SALVADOR VALDÉS: I think we should not confuse two things. The aggregate savings-investment balance is one thing. The other one is what type of claims are financing the investment. A smaller share of the investment that existed was financed through equity, and more was financed through debt, specifically debt through the banking sector.

It is natural to think that that should be so when you start with a very repressed banking system. The total bank loans-to-GDP ratio at the start of the liberalization process was very, very small, on the order of 15 percent. When it rose to 50 percent, I would say up to then you have the natural consequence of any financial liberalization. You get a higher degree of intermediation through these institutions.

It continued rising, to 70 percent by the end of 1982. That is quite ahead of what is common for developing countries of Chile's income level. You begin to think something is wrong. In our paper we expand on how many things went wrong. There was huge overexpansion of the banking sector.

The rise from 15 percent to, say, 40 or 50 percent shouldn't be surprising. It took four or five years. I would say it is the expected result of any liberalization.

PATRICK HONOHAN: What I am really suggesting is, yes, I understand why the banks grew, but why was the stock market not also strong in this period?

SALVADOR VALDÉS: It did grow. The market value of the stock market multiplied by fifteen times between 1976 and 1980. So it grew at even a faster rate than the banking sector in market value terms.

SERGIO DE LA CUADRA: Ten years ago equity as a percentage of gross national product in Chile was about 10 percent. Today it is about 30 percent. So there has been a fantastic growth there. One must recognize that part of this growth corresponds to privatization accomplished in the last five years. But even before this privatization there was important growth of the equity-to-GNP ratio in Chile.

PHILIP BROCK: I think one issue that Patrick was raising was the amount of leverage in the economy during this period. Banks in Chile at the start of the Great Depression were operating with debt-equity ratios of 4:1. That ratio was 20:1 in the 1970s.

In Charlie's paper, banks in the 1920s were operating somewhere around 10:1. If you are thinking of operating in an economy that has macro fluctuations because of copper or oil or whatever, what is the size of the equity cushion you want in banks and in firms?

What I would read into what you are saying is that both banks and firms in Chile in the 1970s had smaller equity positions than they do now. What is the optimal equity position for banks, and is there a role for regulation in making banks take on more equity than this 5 percent of assets that is more or less typical in Chile?

SALVADOR VALDÉS: In the first place, when talking about aggregate debt/equity ratios, one should distinguish what the country as a whole has as a debt/equity ratio. In the aggregate, the debt must be only the foreign debt. That is very important for the terms-of-trade shocks that you were talking about. A country that has a lot of foreign debt and also has a lot of fluctuation in terms of trade is incurring a high risk. Of course, its creditors are also incurring a high risk.

I think you are actually referring to the internal debt situation. Keep the foreign debt constant. Then what difference should higher intermediation within the economy make?

PHILIP BROCK: It is the debt/equity ratio that they are operating with. What difference does that make?

SALVADOR VALDÉS: We have talked many times with Sergio that in Chile the debt/equity ratio should be lower than, say, in the U.S. as a whole or in Western Europe because of precisely this phenomenon. It is a reasonable reaction to that.

You shouldn't talk about the 1970s in Chile as a static situation. It was very different in 1976 than in 1980. There was a huge difference because of the financial liberalization.

SERGIO DE LA CUADRA: Not only financial liberalization. We had across-the-board liberalization in all the markets.

The trade liberalization, I am sure, imposed an important demand on credit for reallocating resources in response to the new tariff policies, and it was also a period of development of new exports. This also caused a higher demand for credit. There was also an important fiscal reform that finished with the fiscal deficit. Previously, many of the savings were going to the government to finance the fiscal deficit.

There were many things done at the same time. It is very difficult to just compare two points in time without consideration of all these other changes.

SALVADOR VALDÉS: I have a question for Charlie Calomiris. Say we have free banking whereby, as defined by Sergio, there is no government intervention, and banks, coordinating among themselves, establish a clearinghouse that turns into a cartel or a self-regulating cartel, or whatever. The question is, What is the real resource cost of that market structure?

Say you have a cartel that regulates its members to keep liquidity in crisis. That problem is solved. That's true. But what about the spread between lending and borrowing rates over time? Worse than that, what about the political power of that kind of cartel?

CHARLES CALOMIRIS: You are getting a little bit ahead of the story. This is the punch line of my discussion later. That's the antitrust issue, which in principle is fairly straightforward to deal with by regulating entry of membership in these groups and by arranging the groups in ways so that groups compete.

In the U.S. today futures and options markets compete with each other for business. They are competing coalitions in which the clearing members coinsure and regulate each other to facilitate trading even in the face of large price movements. I don't believe the Mercantile Exchange or the Board of Trade is a monopoly. Nevertheless, they perform this function.

I would argue we have very good examples of ways to solve payment system problems and yet maintain the kind of competitiveness that you are worried about. That is a very important consideration.

SERGIO DE LA CUADRA: I want to make an additional comment on the question of the growth in the debt-to-GDP ratio. I think a good argument for what has biased the financing of the corporation in favor of debt is the tax system we had in Chile in the 1970s. We don't have an effective tax on interest income. On the other hand, interest paid by the debtor of the corporation is not taxable. So it is much better to take your money to the bank, to make a deposit, and then receive a loan from the bank with your own money. You are going to save taxes in this way.

The problem is not only in our law. The control of taxable interest income is quite difficult.

JOHN BOYD: I don't mean to particularly pick on Charlie Calomiris today. However, to keep our facts straight, the options and commodities exchanges, as Gary pointed out, aren't cartels as we normally think of the term.

Secondly, it is not clear (whatever sort of coalitions they are) that they have solved their liquidity problems. In 1987, when they truly needed liquidity, they turned to the banking system and indirectly to the discount window.

CHARLES CALOMIRIS: This takes us very far afield, but as part of my research project I have been talking to people at the Mercantile Exchange and the Board of Trade. I would be prepared to argue that they operate as coalitions, and a great deal of what they are focusing on is coinsurance. They do depend somewhat on the banking system, but they also employ collateral requirements and margin calls to ensure market stability for the group. Individual clearing members have relations with banks, but the clearinghouse association is a cartel, and it depends on very strict regulations, not just a credit line with some banks.

JOHN BOYD: It is simply a matter of fact that the La Salle Street clearing institutions turned to the banking system for hundreds of millions of dollars in October. It is going to be difficult to argue, therefore, that this coalition has solved their liquidity problems.

MARVIN GOODFRIEND: That example is really inappropriate, though. Here you had a massive drop in the equity value that proved long-lasting. So it was not a liquidity crisis. No organization in which the members cooperate to help each other out in such situations and therefore coinsure each other could be expected by themselves to withstand that sort of shock.

JOHN BOYD: Well, Charlie said this topic is very far afield.

DON MATHIESON: Just a couple of comments. It seems to me, that even if there are cartels, they are subject to pressure from abroad.

GARY GORTON: Let me just say something about these clearinghouses. These aren't cartels.

The important point about these clearinghouses is that there are strong forces which cause banks in unregulated systems when they are not well diversified to form certain kinds of organizations which don't fit into any microeconomics textbooks. The motivation for joining is these very externalities which the government through deposit insurance is trying to prevent the effects of. That means that price-setting behavior by the cartel is not motivated for the same reasons that we find in the usual microeconomics textbooks.

It is the presence of these externalities associated with banking panics which causes bank regulation. That is the history of bank regulation.

The question is whether it has anything to do with anything going on today. I think Charlie and I disagree on this. It seems to me that the examples where this worked very well are situations in which we didn't face problems of credible commitments by governments to bail out these systems.

When you didn't have that, then I think there is plenty of evidence for looking at the social cost. In particular we could look at losses on deposits during nineteenth-century American banking panics and the number of failures versus what has happened later. If you make that comparison, I am afraid it looks like we should not have government regulation. It seems that that is not really important since there is no going back in terms of this issue of precommitment.

DON MATHIESON: There are a couple of things that struck me in this discussion. I guess I fall into the camp that says that in all major financial systems there is essentially an official safety net even when there isn't explicit deposit insurance. The public seems to have the perception that the authorities will step in during a financial crisis and that the largest financial institutions will not be allowed to fail. This reflects an implicit assumption on the part of both the public and the authorities that the costs of maintaining the safety net are viewed as smaller than the cost of a financial disturbance. One of the problems we have in dealing with this is that we don't know what the cost of a financial panic would be. We are making decisions on maintaining or expanding the safety net in the absence of complete information.

When one does look at the cost of a panic, especially in major financial systems, it would not be adequate to look at what the historical costs of earlier panics were in a single country. We have a system now where shocks are rapidly transmitted across countries. I don't know what would happen in the system if we had a real liquidity crunch in the United States.

GARY GORTON: I don't think this question of cost is as hard as you make it out. Part of the problem is that we sort of lose sight of what it is that these regulations were designed to prevent to start with.

It seems now that there is this presumption that we are trying to prevent all bank failures, and we are trying to prevent shocks from percolating through the system, and we are trying to prevent problems in shifts, and everything is an externality.

It seems clear to me that the initial motivation for banking regulation has sort of been lost and it has become something else. For example, it is not clear that when the Bank of New York couldn't make its big payment, there would have been an unmitigated disaster for the clearing system if there had been no intervention.

Part of the problem in making these statements is that in an environment where there is already this huge Big Brother standing around ready to do something, everybody assumes that it will act. If we didn't have that, it is not clear that private arrangements couldn't work very well.

It is hard to sort all of that out. That may be a problem, but it may be a problem that has been induced by how we have come to think about regulation. It is straightforward to compare the costs in unregulated systems to costs in regulated systems. You can look at the historical data. I think it comes out the wrong way. It is just that people don't want to concede that some kinds of panics and collapses are desirable and have social benefits.

PATRICK HONOHAN: One of the issues that arises in the context of a panic is this question of contagion from bad banks to good banks. It is all right if people are only running from bad banks. That's good discipline. But they may run away from good banks because they are not sure what is going on and they think the whole banking system is affected.

Was this a problem in the various Chilean episodes of failures of different institutions? Were fundamentally sound banks also affected by depositor runs? If so, one could discriminate between support given by the authorities to essentially failed banks or insolvent banks and support given for purely short-term liquidity needs which were able to be reversed later on. In some other countries I think what we find is that depositors run from the bad banks to the good banks and that there is a not a significant loss of deposits to the system as a whole.

SERGIO DE LA CUADRA: In Chile people move from good banks to bad banks. The interest rate differential is so huge that they move to bad banks.

(Laughter.)

PHILIP BROCK: When I was in Chile in 1981, I looked for the place that paid the highest interest. I think it was Financiera Ciga. That was one of the ones that was liquidated by the government after I left.

In concluding this session, I would like to comment on one thing that I am seeing. I don't want to start off Paul's session with this. There has been a lot of discussion on financial regulation in general, which mirrors a lot of what is in the literature. And there has been some discussion on the aspect of small open economies that are facing shocks.

During the next session you are encouraged to think beyond the problems and policy responses attending financial regulation in the case of Texas; you are encouraged to consider Texas as a small open economy and to compare its external links to the rest of the United States with the links between Chile and the rest of the world.

3   *Paul M. Horvitz*

The Causes of Texas Bank and Thrift Failures

During the 1950s, 1960s, and 1970s, bank failures were relatively rare events in the United States. The greatest number in any of these years was sixteen in 1976, and the average number of failures per year was five. What bank failures did occur tended to be concentrated in states with many small banks.

Virtually no large banks failed during the 1950s and 1960s, and only a few failed during the 1970s. Each of the large bank failures was viewed as an aberration, although I suggested in 1975 that we were likely to face such failures on a regular basis in the future (Horvitz, 1975).

A similar story could be told about failures of thrift institutions, although the thrift industry did suffer significantly from the first interest rate crunch in 1966 and in subsequent periods of high interest rates, such as 1974 and 1979. To protect the thrift institutions from commercial bank competition during such periods, the government set ceilings on deposit interest rates and made them binding on commercial banks and thrift institutions in 1966.

For both commercial banks and thrifts, however, the 1980s have been an entirely different story. Bank and thrift failures have become much more common and have included the largest institutions in the industry. American Savings, at one time the largest savings and loan in the country, failed in 1988, and Continental Illinois National Bank, the ninth largest commercial bank in the country, failed in 1984.[1] Other money center banks, such as Bank of America and Manufacturers Hanover, underwent severe pressure during the 1980s but did not fail.

A number of mostly macroeconomic explanations have been given for the recent increase in financial failures. The cause has been variously identified as the increased volatility and record high levels of interest rates following the change in Federal Reserve operating procedures in 1979, the inflation that followed the first oil crunch in 1973 and the ultimate deflation in the early 1980s, the decline in bank capital ratios, a decline in the value of the bank charter as a result of increased competition. Some writers trace the problem to changes in regulation—elimination of deposit rate ceilings, broader powers for thrifts, increased deposit insurance coverage. A sizable literature has developed that analyzes the thrift problem, including useful books by Carron (1982), Brumbaugh (1988), and Kane (1989). Book-length treatments of the failure of Penn Square National Bank by Singer (1985) and Zweig (1985) and the problems of Bank of America by Hector (1988) have made useful contributions to our understanding of the national problem.

My aim in this chapter is different. I focus on the collapse of the banking industry and the savings and loan industry in Texas. *Collapse* is the correct term since virtually all the large savings and loans failed during the 1980s, along with seven of the ten largest commercial-banking organizations (two others were acquired by out-of-state bank holding companies at a fraction of their precrisis price). During 1988 Texas bank failures totaled 113, a number that was exceeded in 1989. Of course, the national or macroeconomic factors that led to increased failures in the United States during this period affected Texas as well, but those factors and normal variability do not seem sufficient to explain the Texas situation. Problems at the national level cannot be expected to affect all fifty states equally (as the pre-1980 bank failure data suggests), but the Texas situation seems well beyond what might be expected from national considerations and normal state-to-state variability.

The Economic Background

The Texas economy enjoyed great prosperity during the 1970s and into the 1980s. The increased price of oil following the first Organization of Petroleum Exporting Countries (OPEC) action in 1973 meant an immediate increase in exploration and production in the state. Houston enjoyed a boom as a world center of oil service operations. As the center of new development, Midland/Odessa became the metropolitan area with the highest ratio of millionaires to population.

Following the 1973 OPEC price increase, oil prices remained under $15 through the second half of the 1970s, until the second oil price shock in 1979 brought the price to almost $40 per barrel for a brief time in 1980 (see Figure 3.1). Even after a decline to $35 in 1981, many energy economists were predicting "$85 in '85," a forecast that, despite its symmetry, turned out to be far off the mark. It must be emphasized, however, that this forecast was shared by responsible observers of the industry and not just the dream of perennially optimistic wildcatters.

The price gradually slipped to $26.50 in 1985 and then collapsed to under $10 in July 1986. While the recovery in prices has been substantial, the impact of the 1986 crash has persisted. The possibility of future price declines discourages investment in exploration or development that would be profitable if current prices were certain to be maintained. Drilling in the United States virtually stopped in 1986, as the number of active rigs fell from about 4,500 in 1981 to under 1,000 (see Figure 3.2). Many "conservative" oil loans

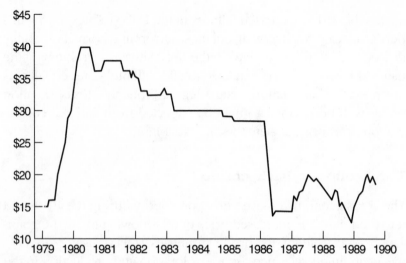

Figure 3.1 Posted Price of West Texas Intermediate Crude, 1979–1990 (per barrel) **Source**: Amoco Production Company.

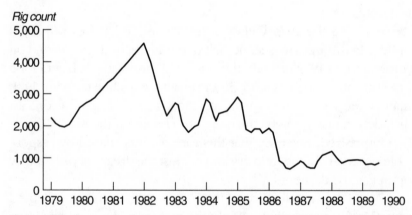

Figure 3.2 Rotary Rig Count in the United States, 1979–1990 (working rigs, by month) **Source**: Baker Hughes, Inc.

collateralized by oil reserves were protected with oil at $20 but became at risk at the 1986 price levels. Further, the finances of the state of Texas are tied to the price of oil to an inordinate extent. *Ad valorem* oil and gas severance taxes make up a large part of state tax revenue, representing 13.6 percent in 1970 (before the first price increase) and 21.0 percent in 1985.

The effect of the price changes on employment is interesting because the employment data suggest less of an economic disaster than is generally believed. The first price decline was associated with a net loss of over 200,000 nonagricultural jobs in the state from the 1982 peak to the 1983 trough, but this decline was made up by 1983. Much of the 1982–1983 decline was concentrated in Houston (see Figure 3.3). Dallas experienced a flattening of employment growth, but employment continued to increase until 1986.[2] Total nonagricultural jobs in the state peaked at 6.7 million in early 1986, dropped to 6.4 million in the next year, and expanded gradually to exceed 6.8 million in 1989.

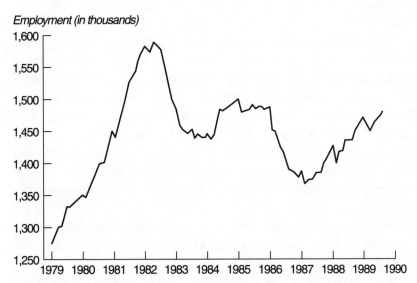

Figure 3.3 Nonagricultural Wage and Salary Employment in the Houston Primary Metropolitan Statistical Area, 1979–1990 **Source**: Bureau of Labor Statistics.

The job loss was significant, representing a 44 percent peak-to-trough decline in the mining (oil) sector and a 24.9 percent decline in the total industrial employment base. The mining sector represented over 15 percent of the state's real gross product in 1980. Recovery in the oil-related sector of the economy has been meager, although activity in the chemical industry has benefited from lower prices of oil used as a raw material. It is important to recognize, however, that employment and other measures of the real Texas economy now exceed the previous peak. Retail sales, for example, totaled $125 billion in 1988, finally exceeding the 1985 peak of $124 billion.

The decline in employment is comparable to that experienced during other downturns in the primary industry of other states—the auto industry in Michigan, the steel industry in Pennsylvania, the coal industry in West Virginia, or the textile industry in New England. Those industry declines had serious economic effects, but they did not lead to bank failures (or even loan losses) to an extent at all comparable with the Texas experience. The decline in Texas was perhaps more rapid, and that may have exacerbated the effect on banks.

One explanation for this difference is that many oil-related loans were tied to the price of oil rather than to the level of production. That is, banks did not take losses on loans to General Motors or U.S. Steel or Exxon. Banks in Michigan made loans to suppliers to the auto industry, and banks in Texas made loans to independent oil producers and oilfield service firms. The auto-related firms were able to handle their obligations as the industry cut production, but the oil-based loans depended on oil as collateral. Perhaps the past experience of Michigan banks led them to be more conservative in underwriting loans to the auto industry or to be more careful about maintaining a diversified loan portfolio. Many lenders in Texas had the view that the price of oil could only go up, and "worst case" scenarios looked at current prices.[3]

These data focus on the nonagricultural sectors of the Texas economy, but Texas has a large agricultural economy (third largest in the United States, following California and Iowa). One might hope for some benefits from that diversification, but it turned out that problems in the agricultural sector coincided with the decline in the manufacturing-mining sectors (a coincidence that occurred nationally during the Depression of the 1930s). All the major Texas agricultural commodities—cotton, corn, wheat, and cattle—hit new low prices for the decade in 1986 (these prices recovered sharply in 1987). A large number of Texas bank failures were due to agricultural problems (prices and drought), but the Texas experience here is akin to that in Kansas, Iowa, and other farm states during the mid-1980s. The number of such failures declined in 1988 and 1989 as the farm problems eased.

Most analyses of the Texas economy focus on oil and gas, but there have been some attempts to put this into a broader context. Weinstein and Gross argued that

> what is playing out in the 1980's is the reversal of forces that benefited the state during the 1970's. . . . Texas was a regional beneficiary of the high inflation rates that characterized the 1970's. As is always the case during inflationary periods, commodity prices rose faster than those of fabricated products; so Texas received more for the energy and agricultural products it sold relative to the prices it paid for finished goods produced in other regions. The result was a substantial transfer of real income from other sections of the U.S. to Texas. (Weinstein and Gross, 1986)

In a later paper they argue that along with the change in terms of trade, there was also a change in the international value of the dollar that first benefited, and then harmed, Texas exports. This development was accompanied by an increase in foreign protectionism that particularly affected Texas products—beef, citrus, semiconductors, construction, and engineering services. In fact, Weinstein and Gross conclude, "the strong dollar and foreign protectionism probably had a greater negative impact on Texas than the drop in oil prices during the 1981–1985 period" (Weinstein and Gross, 1988).

It is important for an analysis of the Texas economy to distinguish between the "real" production economy and the real estate market.

As noted, the real economy has recovered and is now operating at levels above previous peaks, but the real estate market is still in a very depressed state. Opinions differ on whether or not real estate prices have begun to move up. There is some scattered evidence indicating that they have risen, particularly residential prices in Houston, but it is clear at least that prices are not declining (see Figure 3.4). Of course, declines in house prices of this magnitude are virtually unprecedented in our post-1930s experience. It is difficult to be precise about price trends on apartments and commercial property because sales are infrequent (aside from sales of properties that banks have acquired through foreclosure). It is not unusual for the real estate market to lag behind the real economy in an upturn, particularly when there is a large backlog of unoccupied rental space. In any case, it is clear that the performance of the financial sector was more closely tied to the real estate market than

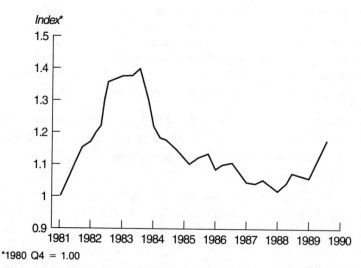

*1980 Q4 = 1.00

Figure 3.4 Houston Quarterly Home Price Index, 1981–1990 **Source**: University of Houston Center for Public Policy.

to the real economy. We will return to the reasons for this problem later in this chapter.

Why Is Texas Different?

The Texas banking structure is different from that of the rest of the United States. Texas has a long-established populist, antibank tradition (including, for a time, a constitutional prohibition of banking). This tradition is embodied in the prohibition of branch banking that was in effect until 1987. This prohibition, in a very large state with a prosperous economy, yielded a predominance of unit banks. In 1980, before the wave of failures, Texas had over 1,500 banks. As of 1987 Texas had 10.5 banks per 100,000 population, compared to 3.5 in Florida (which also had severe restrictions on branching until recently) and 1.1 per 100,000 in New York. Texas allowed multibank holding companies, however, which led to the creation of a number of very large holding companies.

This structure, consisting of a great many small banks, has implications for bank failures, since it is virtually impossible for a small bank to be well diversified. Large banks may fail to diversify or choose not to diversify, but small banks are at the mercy of their local economy. This is a significant factor in explaining the number of bank failures in Texas during the mid-1980s (when farm banks in the rest of the Midwest were also failing in record numbers), but it does not explain the failures of the large banks in Texas.

Texas has long had a large savings and loan industry. Growth in Texas led to a large demand for housing and, traditionally, commercial banks were not active in residential mortgage lending.

Nationally, the majority of savings institutions are organized as mutuals, but in Texas, stock institutions still predominate.[4] Until recently, stock institutions could not obtain a federal charter. Thus, the majority of Texas thrifts are state-chartered, stockholder-owned institutions.[5] Although this structural difference was not significant during the 1960s and 1970s, it became important in the 1980s, because Texas savings and loan law was extremely liberal as to the powers of state-chartered institutions.[6] In addition, savings and loans were allowed to branch, even though commercial banks were not. S&L branches thus proliferated because they provided the consumer with convenience facilities that commercial banks could not provide.

Some other aspects of the Texas economy and culture must be kept in mind. First, the Texas economy is not well diversified now and was even less diversified until recently. The dependence on oil and oil-related business is substantial, as described earlier. The loan portfolios of the major banks were even more dependent on the energy sector than was the economy as a whole. Given this situation, the decline in the price of oil during the 1980s would have had a significant effect on Texas banks.

The Texas economy, and particularly Texas real estate, had enjoyed a long period of prosperity. Although Texas had historically experienced dramatic cycles in oil prices, similar cycles had not taken place in real estate in the major cities. This long history of price increases in real estate may have led lenders to be unduly optimistic in their approach to such lending. Several of the large Texas banks also had traditionally been active in construction lending and other nonresidential real estate lending. After all, the booming growth in Texas during the 1960s and 1970s meant that a tremendous amount of construction was going on, and financing that activity was logical for the local banks.[7] As compared with past real estate lending problems for banks, the Texas banks concentrated their real estate lending in local markets that they thought they understood. It is easy to criticize bank managements that took losses in lending to real estate investment trusts (REITs) in the 1970s to finance developments in Florida or Atlanta or Tennessee, but out-of-area lending was not the source of the Texas real estate lending losses. In fact, lending in Texas has been a major source of such losses for non-Texas banks. The last downtown skyscraper built in Houston was completed in 1987 and financed (to the extent of over $200 million) by Bank of America. That building remained empty years later.

Federal tax policy deserves some of the blame. The Economic Recovery Tax Act of 1981 (ERTA) allowed investors to write off roughly 40 percent of their investment in real estate projects during the first five years of the project (pre-ERTA depreciation rules allowed a five-year write-off of 22.6 percent). James Christian, chief economist of the U.S. League of Savings Institutions, recently wrote, "Early on, it was generally known that tax syndicators were having a field day with ERTA and that projects were being built just to milk the tax benefits."[8] The Tax Reform Act of 1986 represented a drastic change in the tax incentives for investment in real estate. The five-year depreciation write-off was reduced to 18 percent. Passive loss treatment was restricted, limiting the ability of investors to deduct from other income the tax losses resulting from depreciation of income-producing property. Further, preferential capital gains treatment was repealed. This meant that in 1986 and 1987 few investors were interested in buying the projects developed in response to the incentives of ERTA. And because of the growth in Texas until 1983, a disproportionate amount of the development inspired by ERTA was located in Texas (and financed by Texas banks and thrifts). Christian's point is well taken—in the absence of tax benefits many of these projects were uneconomical from their conception.

A final consideration is more speculative and less susceptible to quantitative measurement. There appears to be a prevalent Texas attitude that the appropriate action when things are going badly is to double the bet rather than cut one's losses. As we shall see, Texas banks had opportunities to accept the fact that the decline in the oil business meant significant losses and a halt to their growth. Most could not accept that economic reality, and instead attempted to continue growth by shifting into the other major Texas industry— real estate.[9] For example, Republic management decided to take over Interfirst rather than concentrate on seeking to work out of their own problems, and MCorp attempted to remain independent. The decision of Texas Commerce to cut its losses and sell (at what appears to have been an attractive price under the circumstances) is the exception. The general willingness of Texas managements to

take additional risk as their situation worsened was intensified by
certain incentive aspects of the federal deposit insurance system and
the policies of the supervisory agencies.

The Sources of the Losses

Obviously, the decline in the oil industry led to losses for the large
Texas banks, but these losses would not have been sufficient to cause
failure in most cases. Energy-related lending accounts for much of
the loan loss suffered up to 1983 or 1984. After the 1981 oil price
decline the widely followed strategy was a massive switch into real
estate lending. The reasons for this can only be found in the success
with real estate lending in the past and the absence of significant real
estate downturns in the past. The pattern can be seen by reviewing
changes in the First City Bancorp portfolio over this period.[10]

First City was one of the most aggressive energy-lending institutions in Texas, and its failure is widely believed to have resulted from
the oil collapse. At the end of 1982 First City's energy portfolio
amounted to $2.4 billion, about 15 percent of its total assets. This
figure stayed roughly constant over the next several years. But First
City was also an active real estate lender, with a portfolio of about
$1.8 billion at the same time. About 70 percent of these loans were
for construction or land development.

During 1983 and 1984 First City dramatically expanded its real
estate lending, so that such loans totaled $3.4 billion (nearly 20
percent of assets) by the end of 1984. First City continued to grow
during this period. Charge-offs of real estate loans were much
smaller than energy-loan losses, but by 1986 nonperforming real
estate assets ($404 million) exceeded nonperforming energy loans
($337 million).

Commercial banks lagged in responding to the decline in real
estate, which was dragging them down. (First City's 1986 real estate
charge-offs amounted to only $34 million.) Some of this delay was
no doubt a deliberate attempt to postpone recognizing problems
until recovery in the real estate market should make such recognition

unnecessary. But some was due to error. At least with respect to the commercial banks, it seems that the major error was a failure to recognize the loss potential in *performing* loans. That is, real estate loans on which the borrower was making payments were not viewed as potential problems, *even though the value of the property fell below the amount of the loan.* A borrower will carry such debt only so long, particularly if there is no personal liability. In many cases the amount of debt swamps the personal resources of the borrower, so that personal bankruptcy is the likely outcome. If the real estate downturn had been short-lived (even if sharp), these loans might have come through without loss. The length of the real estate depression ensured that all such projects would result in loss.

The decline in the energy and real estate sectors would have led to losses by banks no matter how prudently they were managed. The economic decline would not have led to widespread failures, however, if the banks had been more diversified. U.S. restrictions on interstate banking make diversification more difficult or more expensive. We have noted that diversification may be impossible for small banks. It appears, however, that Texas banks were not concerned about their concentration on energy loans—they did not view them as risky assets that called for diversification. Even those banks emphasizing the risky sector of the market—oilfield-servicing—seemed to believe that their risk could be diversified by holding a portfolio of such loans. It is somewhat harder to explain the concentration in real estate, other than to point to the previously mentioned long upswing in Texas real estate.

In recent years several states, including Texas, have changed their laws regarding interstate banking. The changes in the Southeast were not related to concern about bank failures, but the changes in law in the energy belt states (Texas, Oklahoma, and Alaska) were clearly intended to facilitate rescue of failing institutions. It is interesting to speculate as to whether Interfirst or Republic would have failed if either had been owned by NCNB Texas National Bank throughout the 1980s. The answer to that question may depend in part on the rules for interaffiliate transactions of bank holding companies, such as the Federal Reserve's "source of strength" concept, or the recently enacted requirement for subsidiary cross guarantees.

Savings and loans did not lend directly to the oil industry and had few losses as a result of the first oil price shock. Their problem, of course, was real estate lending, which also ultimately did in the banks. It is obvious in retrospect, but was apparently not so clear to the participants, that the real estate projects being financed in the early 1980s in Texas were based, directly or indirectly, on the energy business. It should have been obvious that a loan for a housing development in Midland could be recoverable only if there were employment increases in the oil business. Similarly, a strip shopping center in Houston depended, in the final analysis, on the viability of the Houston economy, and this, in turn, depended on the fortunes of the oil patch.

The real estate collapse, when it came, was so severe that virtually all savings and loans were severely affected. It has become difficult to distinguish between the reckless operators and the sound managements on the basis of financial results alone. That is, as recently as 1986 or 1987 it was reasonable to view the most insolvent institutions as badly managed (or worse). But by 1988 and 1989 even those institutions with highly regarded managements were massively insolvent. In several cases highly regarded managements were recruited to serve as managers of insolvent thrifts in the Management Consignment Program (MCP) of the Federal Savings and Loan Insurance Corporation (FSLIC) and then were themselves taken over by FSLIC. University Savings of Houston managed three MCP institutions before being put into receivership. Merabank acquired one of those MCP institutions (State Savings of Lubbock) as FSLIC acted to put the institution under sound ownership and management, and then Merabank itself ran into severe problems. When the FSLIC's Southwest plan for case resolutions was announced in early 1988, such institutions as Commonwealth Savings, San Antonio Savings, and Olney Savings were viewed as well-run potential acquirers of insolvent institutions under the program. By the end of 1988 all were insolvent themselves (and Olney was actually acquired under the Southwest plan).

Finally, it must be stressed that lending institutions as a whole were not simply innocent victims of an unprecedented real estate depression. Overbuilding took place, and all of it was financed by lenders. If it had not been for the availability of financing, much of the development would never have taken place. It is an old (but true) saw that developers will build anything for which they can get financing. What we found in Texas was that at least some lenders will finance anything on which they are promised 50 percent of the profits. Had the lenders been more skeptical during this period, or had the supervisors stepped in earlier, the overbuilding (and the subsequent depression) would have been much less extensive.

Many discussions of the savings and loan problem emphasize fraud. Fraud was indeed present in many failed savings and loans and small failed commercial banks (no one alleges that fraud was responsible for any of the large bank failures). A General Accounting Office (GAO) study found fraud present in 25 percent of a sample of failed savings and loans. But the presence of fraud does not mean that fraud caused the failure or that fraud was responsible for most of the losses suffered in those institutions. A recent review of FSLIC's 1988 experience in handling 205 failures concluded that no more than 10 percent of FSLIC's cost in these cases could be attributed to fraud.[11]

Some fraud took place after the fact, in an economic sense. That is, when it was clear to owners and managers that the institution was doomed to fail, some fraudulent transactions were undertaken to funnel assets out of the bank or thrift. Also, some of what is frequently thought of as fraud is really an insider abuse that does not necessarily have fraudulent intent. A developer who owns a bank or thrift may be inclined, improperly or illegally, to use the bank's funds to finance his development projects. He may believe that the project is sound and that it represents a good opportunity for the bank. It is not, of course, my intent to defend fraud or self-dealing but rather to argue that many discussions exaggerate the importance of fraud in explaining FSLIC losses.

The Economics of Financial Institutions

Conceptually, the economics of depository institutions is rather simple: Banks raise funds from the public and lend those funds to individuals or institutions that need them. Profitable earnings spreads arise from the ability to charge a higher rate on loans than must be paid for funds, although profitability is achieved only if these spreads are sufficient to cover the operating costs of the institution.

The markets in which most institutions raise and invest funds are rather competitive, so spreads are relatively narrow.[12] It is clear that noninterest operating costs play a key role. But perhaps more important than interest rate spreads or noninterest expense is the relationship between the volume of interest-earning assets and interest-costing liabilities.

Obviously, in an accounting sense, total assets must equal total liabilities plus capital. But not all assets yield income, and not all sources of funds require an interest payment. Banks do not earn interest on fixed assets and cash. They always have some loans that are not performing and perhaps some real estate that has been obtained through foreclosure of nonperforming loans. On the liability side, equity capital does not require an explicit interest payment (although, of course, the owners expect a return on their investment). Commercial banks historically have obtained a large fraction of their funds from demand deposits on which interest payments are prohibited by law. Since the introduction of NOW accounts, only corporate checking accounts are interest-free sources of deposit funds.[13] Despite their decline in relative importance on commercial bank balance sheets, however, these deposits significantly affect the ratio of earning assets to costing liabilities.

This ratio is important in understanding the differing performance of banks and thrift institutions in Texas and the differences between Texas institutions and those in the rest of the country. Traditionally, commercial banks have had higher ratios of capital to assets. The minimum regulatory requirements in place during the early 1980s were a 6 percent ratio for banks and a 3 percent ratio for thrifts. Further, thrift institutions do not have interest-free demand deposits. Given the low capital ratio and the need for some amount of cash and fixed assets, it is very difficult for a thrift to maintain an earning asset/costing liability ratio of 100 percent. Most commercial banks routinely have a ratio in excess of 100 percent.[14]

The major impact on these ratios has come from nonperforming assets.[15] At the end of 1985 commercial banks in Texas had nonperforming assets equal to 2.7 percent of total assets, compared to 1.9 percent for other banks (as of 1982 the Texas figure had been only 1.6 percent). By the end of 1987 the ratio in Texas had climbed to 6.9 percent while the figure for non-Texas banks had increased to only 2.3 percent. There was a great deal of variation in these figures. For example, First Republic's nonperforming loans exceeded 15 percent of total assets in 1987. With an excess of costing liabilities over earning assets, it is very difficult, in competitive markets, to earn positive profits.

The picture is much more dramatic when we look at Texas thrifts. At the end of 1985, 1.8 percent of assets in Texas were owned by lenders who had acquired them by foreclosure. By the end of 1988, such ownership by foreclosure constituted 12.4 percent of Texas's assets. In comparison, the corresponding percentages for the United States at those respective dates were 1.5 and 1.8. Total nonperforming assets represented 5.9 percent of assets of Texas thrifts at the end of 1985, 16.5 percent in 1986, and 23.4 percent at the end of 1987. If troubled assets equal 15 percent of assets, there is no way for a savings and loan to earn enough on the remaining 85 percent of assets to cover its interest costs on virtually 100 percent of liabilities. Such a situation tends to worsen as operating losses reduce capital and hence further reduce the earning asset/costing liability ratio.

The Impact of High Interest Rates: 1979–1982

The distinctly Texan failure addressed in this chapter took place in the mid- and late-1980s. It was affected, however, by the national experience of record high interest rates following the change in Federal Reserve operating procedures in October 1979. This was particularly true of the savings and loans.

A rise in interest rates is potentially devastating to financial institutions that, like traditional thrifts, use short-term deposits to fund long-term, fixed-rate loans. In 1980 adjustable-rate mortgages (ARMs) were virtually nonexistent. In 1981 and 1982, as deposit costs rose with market rates and interest income on the mortgage portfolio increased only slowly, thrifts found themselves with negative interest spreads.

This situation can be expressed in terms of the income statement or the balance sheet. It meant substantial operating losses for those thrifts that paid going market rates. Any institution that attempted to limit interest payments to what it could afford faced heavy deposit outflows that eventually forced it to pay market rates.

The increase in interest rates also meant a decline in the market value of fixed-rate mortgages. If the assets and liabilities of banks and thrifts were reported on a market value basis (as are those of securities firms, for example) or on the basis of cost or market, whichever is lower (as are those of many firms), they would have shown a substantial negative net worth. It is only a peculiar accounting convention that allows these institutions to carry their loans and investments at their historical cost rather than fair market value that presented the illusion that most were solvent.

The accounting conventions have real effects on behavior (which is why the industry has so vigorously opposed suggestions for market value accounting). The supervisory agencies have generally been reluctant to take over or close an institution that is solvent on a book (historical cost) basis.[16] If Texas banks and thrifts had been closed in recent years when the market value of their assets was less than their liabilities, the cost to the insurance agencies would have been much less. Also, removal of these institutions from the market would have precluded construction of some projects that contributed to the overbuilding in Texas and would have reduced the demand for funds by insolvent institutions that bid up rates in Texas and contributed to the "Texas premium."

Savings and loan managements were not deceived by the illusion of solvency created by their accountants. They knew that in an economic sense they were under water. Only limited strategic choices were available to them. The simplest option was simply to continue as they were doing and pray for lower interest rates. While this strategy may have been unimaginative, it turned out that such prayers were answered. Rates declined in late 1982 and 1983 and, following a mild increase in 1984, declined again from 1984 to 1987. Those who followed that strategy—the majority of the industry—are healthy today.

Another strategy was to attempt to grow out of the problem. A thrift with $50 million of deposits and a negative (real) net worth of $5 million is in serious condition. If it could increase its deposits by $500 million and earn a 1 percent return on the marginal funds, it could erase its deficit. In the 1970s such a strategy would not have been available, since a $50-million institution could not generate $500 million of new deposits. But the end of interest rate ceilings resulting from the Depository Institutions Deregulation and Monetary Control Act of 1980 made that feasible. That legislation also increased the coverage of federal deposit insurance to $100,000, so that by offering somewhat more than going market rates, a bank or thrift could attract virtually unlimited funds. The fall in computer and communication costs made it possible for money brokers to raise large amounts of funds to be divided into insured deposits.[17] During 1983 and 1984 savings and loan deposits increased by 18.7 percent and 20.3 percent, an extremely rapid rate of growth, particularly when commercial bank time deposits declined during this period. Texas savings and loans grew even faster than the national average—32.4 percent in 1983 and 37.7 percent in 1984. The problem with this strategy was not in raising the funds but in finding a way to invest huge volumes of high-cost funds at a profit. Few who adopted this approach were successful.

A third strategy, often combined with the second, was intentionally to invest in high-risk assets. The Garn–St. Germain Act of 1982 broadened considerably the powers of federal savings and loans, particularly in commercial lending. Several states already granted broad powers to state-chartered thrifts, and others, particularly California, amended their restrictions in accordance with the federal changes. The California law was most liberal, allowing state-charted institutions to invest virtually all their assets in anything they wanted. Texas has long allowed state-chartered institutions to invest substantial portions of their assets in real estate development. Some institutions used these new powers wisely, diversifying their portfolios by expanding into commercial and consumer lending and thereby reducing their exposure to interest rate risk. Many were unsuccessful, particularly when the move to riskier assets was accompanied by rapid growth.[18]

An example of this phenomenon can be seen in the investments in development and land loans—a risky activity—during this period. Such assets represented less than 5 percent of assets for savings and loans in the United States (and in Texas) in 1980. By 1985, following the liberalization of powers by the deregulation act, the U. S. average rose to about 5 percent. The forty Texas thrifts that were in the worst shape in 1985 (this includes Vernon Savings, Sunbelt, and others of their ilk) held nearly 30 percent of their assets in this form, and the remaining Texas thrifts held in excess of 20 percent.

An important element of the high-risk strategy involved seeking assets that promised the potential of very high returns—that is, those assets with an equity participation. Some savings and loans would make loans only on projects in which they were promised a share of the profits. The philosophy of some managements and owners was simply that they were so far under water that an extra percentage point or two in returns would not be sufficient to get them back in the black—they literally needed to take a flier with a chance for a big hit in order to be resurrected.

This situation led many to take a final option—sell out. But this leads to an obvious question: Why would anyone buy a business that was insolvent and losing money? Some buyers were probably fooled—after all, we have already noted that thrift accounting was misleading. But most knew what they were doing. Some might have seen an opportunity to adopt the second or third strategies profitably. Some, however, were focusing not on the negative net worth they were acquiring but on the large assets they were controlling for a small investment. They saw opportunities to divert some of those assets to their own pockets. It has become common to attribute much of the savings and loan mess to fraud and insider abuse. As noted earlier, the importance of fraud has been exaggerated, but some did take place. Many of those whose intent was fraudulent, however, came into the business because the economic circumstances led those concerned with profitability to sell out to those more interested in the volume of assets they could control for a small investment.

The effect of the high interest rates of the early 1980s on commercial banks was not comparable to their effect on the savings and loans. Commercial banks are generally not as exposed to interest rate risk as thrift institutions, and the Texas banks were better balanced than the typical commercial bank. At this time Texas banks tended to have higher-than-average loan/asset ratios, and most of the loans were short-term or floating rate loans. Thus their interest income increased as their interest costs increased. In retrospect it is clear that the riskiness of bank portfolios increased during the 1980s, but this was not in response to losses imposed by the interest rates of 1981–1982.

The Role of Deposit Insurance

Deposit insurance played an important part in the failure of Texas financial institutions, even though it fulfilled its designated role of maintaining stability in the system in the face of stress. In the absence of deposit insurance a fractional-reserve banking system is vulnerable to runs in response to adverse information. Depositors have little to lose in withdrawing their funds in response to bad news, even if they believe the information is false. In that case, prompt withdrawal of funds may protect them against a failure caused by a run by other depositors.

With deposit insurance, no one has an incentive to participate in a run. It is rather remarkable that despite the wave of failures in Texas during this period and the reams of adverse publicity (including discussions of the insolvency of the FSLIC), serious runs did not occur. Some institutions suffered brief runs, as well as significant long-term outflows of funds, but no bank or thrift failure was caused by a run. In fact, no insolvent institution was forced to close its doors because of a run.

If stabilization were the only effect of deposit insurance, we would chalk it up as a great success. Unfortunately, deposit insurance also has a rather insidious side effect that exacerbated the problem. With deposit insurance, depositors have no incentive to choose their banks on the basis of financial soundness. Weak banks have virtually the same access to funds as healthy banks.[19] This essentially equal access allowed insolvent banks to stay in operation long after market forces, in the absence of deposit insurance, would have closed them. What is worse, these institutions had every incentive to take greater risks, for which they were able to obtain virtually unlimited funds. Deposit insurance did not cause more banks to become insolvent; hence it is incorrect to blame the failures on deposit insurance. It did, however, make the public cost of failure much greater than it would otherwise have been.[20]

If insolvent banks are identified and closed as soon as their net worth is depleted, the cost to the deposit insurance system is small. That is, if banks are closed when the value of assets is approximately equal to the value of the liabilities, only stockholders suffer a loss. If, on the other hand, insolvent institutions operate for a long time, the losses will probably be much larger when they are finally closed. An empirical study of FSLIC losses found that the length of time between insolvency and FSLIC action was an important explanatory variable.[21]

There is a difference between the banks and thrifts that might be noted, although it is hard to document. It is clear that in the early 1980s many thrift operators recognized that their situation was hopeless and that desperate measures might be appropriate. In response, many consciously adopted high-risk strategies. That does not seem to be true of the large banks, most of which seemed to believe that if they could just hang on, real estate recovery would eventually bail them out. Many banks seemed to fail to recognize just how precarious their position was. To take the extreme example, Republic's acquisition of a clearly troubled Interfirst without Federal Deposit Insurance Corporation (FDIC) assistance does not seem to have been intended as a doubling of the bets; rather, it was an unwarranted, perhaps arrogant, belief that Republic had sufficient management capability and resources to pull it off successfully. On the other hand, many thrift acquisitions of other weak or insolvent thrifts were clear attempts to increase the stakes. Of course, whether it is employed consciously or not, the ability to operate in a risky manner once insolvent is a result of deposit insurance, because without deposit insurance the bank could not obtain the funds with which to take the risks.

The Supervisory System

This discussion raises the question of the efficiency of the supervisory process in detecting impending failures and acting in response to them. The Federal Home Loan Bank Board (FHLBB) has received a great deal of criticism and a great deal of the blame for the Texas S&L catastrophe,[22] but there has been relatively little criticism of the banking agencies for the bank failures. This disparity exists because of the public cost of the S&L failures rather than differences in the failure rate.

The United States has a complicated system of regulation of

financial institutions. Both banks and thrifts can be chartered by either the federal government or the states. At the federal level, banks and thrifts are supervised by different agencies, and federal deposit insurance is available through different insurance agencies to both types of institution, whether state or federally chartered. The principal supervisor of each institution is its chartering agency—the state for state-chartered institutions, the Office of the Comptroller of the Currency (OCC) for national banks, and the Federal Home Loan Bank Board for federal S&Ls. The deposit insurance agencies (the FDIC and the FSLIC) have somewhat limited supervisory authority over the institutions they insure, though the Financial Institutions Reform, Recovery, and Enforcement Act of 1989 (FIRREA) does strengthen the FDIC's powers.

Several inherent conflicts in this situation have been glossed over for many years. An extreme view of the relationship between federal and state regulators is that both seek to expand their power by gaining new "constituents" and that the result is a "competition in laxity."[23] There seems to be little support for that view, but there is basis for concern that the chartering authorities will have less interest in risk, bank failure, and its cost since the insurance agency, not the chartering agency, bears that cost. The problem is greatest with respect to the powers of state-chartered institutions.

Until recently most states have been rather cautious in approving broader powers for state-chartered institutions. There have long been some discrepancies between the powers of state and federally chartered institutions, but these were not believed to impose an intolerable risk on the federal insurance system (partly because no institutions appeared to abuse those powers). For example, Texas-chartered S&Ls have long had the power to invest in real estate development through service corporation subsidiaries, but this was usually done in modest amounts and was generally profitable during the 1970s. In the interest of comity between federal and state regulators, the general posture of both the FDIC and the FSLIC was simply to tolerate those differences.

During the 1980s these differences became more important, as several states broadened the powers of state-chartered institutions. Several different motives were at work here. Some states sought to attract out-of-state institutions after observing the benefits South Dakota gained by attracting Citicorp's credit card operation. As noted earlier, some states broadened the powers of their institutions in response to the broader powers granted to federal S&Ls by the Depository Institutions Deregulation and Monetary Control Act (DIDMCA) and the Garn–St. Germain Act of 1982. From the point of view of the states, such actions were costless as long as they required federal deposit insurance. The FSLIC was forced to respond to this initiative by requiring California institutions to file business plans promising to limit their use of these broadened powers.

The broadening of powers was not a significant factor in Texas. There were no significant changes that affected either state-chartered banks or S&Ls. Federally chartered thrifts did gain broadened powers by DIDMCA and Garn–St. Germain, but most of the larger S&Ls in Texas were state chartered and already had broad real estate investment powers. Most losses in Texas thrifts were accounted for by greater *use* of powers that they had had for many years and used only modestly—investments in real estate development and loans for acquisition, development, and construction (ADC loans) of real estate projects (many of which were made with "equity kickers"). The commercial bank losses were accounted for by traditional commercial bank activity—farm loans by smaller, rural banks and energy and real estate lending by the major banks.

"Deregulation," then, in the sense of a broadening of powers, was not a factor in the Texas failures (although it may have played a role in the California S&L failures). As noted, though, deregulation of interest rate ceilings did allow institutions that wanted to take greater risks to obtain all the funds that they needed. This did not increase the probability of failure, since most of these institutions were already insolvent or close to it because of their interest rate risk problems. What it did was to make the *amount* of the losses greater. The distinction between Texas bank and thrift failures lies in the ultimate cost to the insurance funds (and the taxpayer), and not in differences in the number of failures or the size of the failed institutions. After all, no Texas S&L failure involved such a volume of assets as the failures of First Republic, First City, or MCorp.

The explanation for this lies in bank supervision and administration of the deposit insurance system. The role of supervision is not necessarily to prevent failures but to monitor the condition of weak institutions so that they can be closed (or other appropriate action taken) when they become insolvent or close to it.[24] Regardless of the risk posture of a bank, if it is closed when its net worth is depleted, the cost of the failure is borne entirely by stockholders or subordinated creditors who are paid to take that risk. To the extent that the regulators are successful in detecting insolvency, the cost of failure to the insurance system is small.

The FDIC has been much more successful at this than the FSLIC. Most of the large bank failures have been resolved at a cost to the FDIC of only a few cents per dollar of deposits.[25] There is some reason for concern about a deterioration in the FDIC record in Texas in view of the long delay in dealing with the insolvencies of many of the subsidiary banks of MCorp, National Bancshares, and Texas American Bancshares. Nevertheless, the record is vastly different from that of the FSLIC, which is incurring losses of 50 cents or more per dollar of liabilities.

Part of the reason for that is simply that resolving cases takes money, and the FSLIC for some time has not had the resources needed to dispose of insolvent S&Ls efficiently. Many insolvent institutions have been allowed to continue operating and losing money, so that the ultimate resolution cost is increased. But it must also be recognized that the FSLIC supervisory mechanism has not been strong. To a considerable extent, the magnitude of the S&L losses in Texas can be viewed as a failure of supervision.

The supervisory failure in Texas was caused in part by inadequate personnel—in both numbers and quality—and also by a poor organizational structure. The supervisory problem needed attention by 1983, when many institutions, weakened by the high interest rates of the previous years, were moving into higher-risk activities. The savings and loan examiners were trained and experienced for the relatively simple tasks they had had—evaluating portfolios consisting mostly of single-family mortgage loans. In 1983 they were confronting portfolios of complicated commercial real estate development projects. Even if they had been able to analyze these deals, such analysis take a great deal of time. There were simply too few examiners to do the job, so that many weak institutions went much longer between examinations than was appropriate.[26] The problem was recognized (some would say, "recognized too late") by the chairman of the Federal Home Loan Bank Board (FHLBB), Ed Gray, who attempted to convince the Reagan administration to increase his budget so that the number of examiners could be increased. He was turned down by administration officials, who were committed to a policy of deregulation and failed to see the difference between regulation and supervision.[27] Had they been familiar with the experience of Chile, the outcome might have been different.

At this time the supervisory efforts of the Federal Home Loan Bank system were organized in a peculiar fashion. The examiners were employees of the FHLBB. They did their on-site investigations as fact gatherers and submitted their findings to the FHLBB. The examination reports were then sent to the supervisory staff of the individual Federal Home Loan Banks. All supervisory efforts were handled by the district banks, whose president served as principal supervisory agent (PSA) for the district. There are some historical reasons for this distinction between examiners and supervisors, but they are not good ones. The system was an awkward one, with virtually no direct contact between examiners and supervisors, and it was easy for problems to slip between the cracks.[28] In numerous cases, problems spotted by examiners have not been acted on promptly. As congressional hearings have made clear, the case of Empire Savings of Mesquite was a most egregious example. It is true that fraud played a large role and the books were showing substantial profits up to Empire's closing in 1984, but the examiners had pointed out problems much earlier.

Even if the structure worked effectively, there were too few supervisors to handle the task. In 1983 the Federal Home Loan Bank was in the process of moving from Little Rock to Dallas. The forty-eight-person supervisory staff at Little Rock would no doubt have proved inadequate for the task, but in fact only eleven members of that group (mostly clerical and junior supervisors) made the move to Dallas. Efforts were immediately made to recruit and train new employees, but certainly the numbers and experience level were too low at least through 1984. During the twelve months before relocation of the Federal Home Loan Bank (October 1982 to September 1983), 116 examinations of Texas savings and loans were conducted. During the following twelve months, the number dropped to 100 and dropped even further, to 91, from October 1984 through September 1985, just when the need for increased examinations was becoming obvious.[29]

How different would the result have been if the supervisory effort had been handled effectively? I believe that earlier recognition of the problems could have had a profound effect on the ultimate failures and losses of commercial banks as well as savings and loans. This is so even though the FSLIC would clearly not have had the resources to deal with all these cases in 1983–1987.

Many S&Ls were operating out of control. They were making vast numbers of imprudent loans, in many cases based on little more than a desire for the up-front fee income generated. The worst offenders were already insolvent, so action taken against them would not have prevented failure. The losses of these institutions would have been smaller, even if they could not have been closed but only put into the FSLIC's Management Consignment Program—a sort of holding action that removed untrustworthy management. More important, an earlier removal of those institutions would have considerably reduced the competitive pressures to pay higher interest rates on deposits thus adversely affecting the healthy S&Ls (and banks) in Texas. Perhaps even more important in the long run, a great many ill-conceived real estate projects in Texas would never have been built. In the absence of some of these projects, some better-run thrifts might have survived, and some bank failures would have been avoided.

Conclusion

It is difficult to summarize a complex story briefly. Lack of diversification clearly played a key role in causing the failure of Texas banks. The oil price collapse would not by itself have led to massive failures if the bank response had been cautious and conservative. The attempt to continue growing in the face of the energy-lending problems, and particularly to expand in real estate lending, represented a risk exposure of a different order of magnitude. This was exacerbated by the reckless lending of many thrifts.

If the United States had had a system of national banking in place before 1980, many of the failures might have been avoided. Failures of supervision, particularly in the savings and loan industry, bear a heavy responsibility for the magnitude of the losses. Deposit insurance itself, which allowed the losses to accumulate without touching off financial panic, contributed to the size of the loss.

There is now rather general agreement within the academic community concerning the sort of financial restructuring or deposit insurance reform that is necessary to prevent a recurrence of the disaster. Congress clearly agreed that major change was necessary and refused to appropriate funds to cover the losses without some significant reform. It is clear, however, that the legislated changes embodied in FIRREA do not represent the sort of reform that is needed.

There is agreement that a high capital requirement is essential to sound banking in order to provide a cushion against losses but also (and more important) to make sure that the incentives of the owners are compatible with the public interest in bank safety. There must be a good monitoring system to enable the supervisors to ascertain that the capital is real. Such a system requires both on-site examination and market value reporting of asset and liability values. Also, the supervisory authorities need the power to act before net worth is depleted, either by forcing owners to inject new capital or by taking over the institution. Interstate banking is clearly desirable to allow greater diversification.

There are two principal alternatives to this type of regulatory structure: first, the "narrow bank" approach, a more radical reform that would limit bank investments to riskless (or, in some versions, marketable) assets so that failure could not occur; second, a return to pre-1980 type regulation, restricting the powers of thrifts and perhaps reinstituting deposit interest rate ceilings. While the first does not seem to be politically realistic, there is support for the second (and the stiffened qualified thrift lender test in FIRREA is a step in that direction). In my view that is the wrong message to draw from the Texas experience.

Peter Diamond

Comment

I greatly enjoyed reading this paper, particularly the rich description of the sequential events. I found the presentation clear and compelling. There is really nothing in the presentation with which I would disagree. Instead, I want to talk about some of the areas that are not covered in the presentation.

The first thing that amazed me as someone whose knowledge of the Texas bank and thrift crisis came solely from reading the sports pages of the Boston *Globe* was that Jim Wright was not mentioned—not only Jim Wright the individual, but all the other political factors that Jim Wright can stand for in this discussion.

Particularly in the context of Chapters 1 and 2, this seems to me to miss one of the big messages around here, namely, political economy. The interaction between politicians and regulators may be the most important aspect of what is going on.

In Chapter 1, Philip Brock reported on numerous restrictions on what governments are allowed to do in Latin American countries. It is unclear whether those will in fact prove to be binding restrictions.

I think a focus on that sort of question is essential, and I will get back to that at the end of my remarks.

The second area not covered in the paper—and which I was expecting—was a contrast between the FDIC and the FSLIC. My belief, which may or may not be soundly based, is that they differ quite a bit in regulatory powers as well as in relation to the industry and the politicians. It would be interesting to see if there are any lessons to be drawn by relating differences in outcome to differences in regulatory powers. There may be nothing very interesting there, however; what really matters is the speed with which a bank can be closed when necessary and the difference in speed between the two insurance corporations. One doesn't need very subtle analysis to reach that conclusion.

One element in the paper that again relates to the Chile paper is the inherent danger from new activities and inexperienced regulators in a changing system. I think that story comes out in both papers.

This paper does not contain much discussion of the extent of change in activity that the regulators faced. That was obviously not a big story, but if we think of a paper focused on how we learn lessons rather than how we explain the big story, that might be something to consider. The general area of paying experienced bank examiners enough also seems relevant. That gets back to the political economy.

One element struck me as being in sharp contrast to the paper in Chapter 5, by Charles Calomiris. If I have the picture right, the outcome described here is the reverse of what was expected from branching. If I have the facts, banks can't branch in Texas and S&Ls can, but S&Ls turned out worse than banks—presumably because the other factors overwhelmed the ability of branching to avoid problems. I think this is something that needs to be sorted out between the two papers.

I also want to consider the contrast between Texas and Chile, with regard to the role of interstate branching to protect Texas. I think the two places may be on a close footing. Both of them can invite Citibank and Bank of America to open branches. Given that kind of diversity, I don't know that there is necessarily an enormous difference in the opportunities available in Texas and Chile. It is unfortunate that we don't know a great deal more than we do about two issues raised in Chapters 2 and 3: the political economy of banking and the problems of efficiency analysis. We don't have much understanding of the basic workings and implications of believable political economy models, and lessons may not generalize well across countries because the outcomes may depend on different underlying political practices. Gary Gorton very forcefully addressed the subject of efficiency in his comment on Chapter 2. We are concerned not only with bank failures or bank panics but with the efficiency of the resource allocation system. Bank panics and bank failures are a piece of the description of what is going on.

The problem is that we don't have really good models of the role of intermediaries in the efficiency of resource allocation. We don't have them because there aren't intermediaries unless there are frictions, and we don't have good models with frictions. What we all have down pat is the frictionless system. That is just not going to help with this problem.

The same issue arises with the time dimension. Obviously the role of intermediaries has to do in large measure with the lags that occur with any human action. The lag structures associated with all sorts of economic activities are critical for what the financial system is all about.

We don't have good models for situations in which the decision process and the resource allocation process are significantly spread out in real time. One of the things we learned from the stock market crash of 1987 is that even the markets we think of as having the least friction can have frictions that are important in the time dimension of attempted trades. Obviously I am not faulting the paper for failing to develop fundamental theoretical models that we are all missing.

Some of the remarks that have been made in this seminar contain some implicit model of the efficiency issue. First, there is a basic contrast between people who think that the money supply, the medium of payment, is what efficiency is really all about and people who see an important role for a richer intermediary structure. Even if we are thinking of microeconomics rather than macroeconomics, that contrast has to be faced and sorted out. The other side of the same coin is to sort out externalities. Which externalities are important may tie into which of these views you think captures what is really important.

Part of the problem of evaluating a panic or crash is how to think of it in these terms. Very little has been done about that. Let me just mention a couple of interesting things that I have looked at in that regard. In New York in 1907 withdrawals from the banking system were suspended, but transactions within the banking system were allowed. There was a lag, but a market opened up where you could sell deposits. There was about a 2 percent premium for cash over deposits. A question is whether the premium that occurred adequately measures the costs of suspension of convertibility. If so, this 2 percent number can be considered either very big or as very small. It is not clear what is a big number and what is a small number in intermediation.

One of the points Gary Gorton has made in his earlier work is that bank failures don't come out of the blue: They aren't sunspot events; they come with problems in the economy. I think that makes it particularly difficult to evaluate the importance of failures. Both the economy and the banking system are having problems, and you know the causation runs both ways. It is very hard to tease out believable, extrapolatable evaluations of the importance of the different pieces. Ben Bernanke is the most notable person to attempt to measure this.

I have been intrigued by the Irish bank strikes, of which I believe there have been two. (I have found some discussion of this but not in the detail I would like.) The banking system was closed for a while. Before the strike, the economy was not in serious trouble. The money supply collapsed enormously as the strike took place, but the economy went on: It didn't collapse. I am sure there were some problems. Checks with lots and lots of signatures on the backs started passing from hand to hand as currency, representing growth in the money supply. Like the creation of a market for nonconvertible bank deposits, it was a substitute for what might otherwise have been a much larger problem.

The Irish strikes could be viewed as a destruction of the Friedmanite view on the role of money. If you want to measure money by what is still available, it's just currency.

Let me mention one other element that came up earlier—the issue of contagion. One recent example of contagion occurred in Ohio, where worry about the Ohio deposit insurance fund set off a run on sound banks. The run did not occur because people had information that the banks were in trouble—deposit insurance for sound banks wouldn't seem terribly important—but there was an instant run on the whole system. I believe, therefore, that contagion remains a very serious concern.

Let me turn to the externality issue. Obviously, when you think about efficiency you must also think hard about externalities.

When we look at the huge bills that have been run up and we want to measure the social cost associated with that, two things naturally come to mind. One is fraud, which is a redistribution of wealth but still not liked by some social welfare functions. Second is bad investments. I thought Paul Horvitz did a nice job of bringing out the endogeneity of the quality of investment with respect to the behavior of the banking system, the pecuniary externality that becomes a real externality when mistakes are made. I think that is a very good point.

But consider a purely bad investment. A bank lends to someone who is going to invest in a project with a large variance and a low mean because that is what the bank wants. That is the classic moral hazard of systems that are in trouble. Clearly a lot of the bad investment externality is associated with not closing banks quickly.

There is another externality that, depending on whether you take the money or intermediary point of view, comes from disrupted transactions. One probably shouldn't think of such transactions as being lost but rather in terms of the cost of restructuring transactions: the cost of finding alternative ways of carrying them out, plus the cost of lost efficiency in investment when borrowers are unable to borrow because the banking system is temporarily not functioning well. How big the costs are, how we would try to measure them, how they relate to different systems of regulation—I think these are all basic and rather important questions.

Let me turn to political economy. I think there are two themes here. One that I think I agree with is the fact that governments hand out money after large losses, whether they result from the most recent earthquake or significant bank failures, whether one big bank or a whole system of small banks fails. That can probably be taken as an axiom of political economy.

It is a little unclear how important that is. It relates, for example, to the system we have for closing banks. The fact that the losses fall on the taxpayers rather than the depositors may be of limited significance as a redistribution issue. If regulators operate successfully, the allocation elements may not be big. If this is the underlying political economy, then the issue of regulation becomes the issue of how you regulate to hold down the costs that come with this underlying political economy.

We see that in earthquake and flood insurance; the government tries, first, to get the financial costs off its books by subsidizing people to buy such insurance and second, by some degree of direct regulation, to hold down the assets that are at risk from floods and earthquakes.

I think we could perhaps usefully think about the regulation of banks in the same way, but it requires having a political economy in which we have some confidence. The trouble is that we don't have very much in the way of either systematic cross-country and -time histories focused on the political economy. We just have lots of horrifying anecdotes, so we are all aware that really terrible things can happen. It is generally the case that if you want really big disasters, the government is capable of generating bigger ones than the private market.

Let me offer a small example. What if the government would allow small banks to fail but would not let big banks fail? And what if the important costs associated with the system come from not letting banks fail? Then maybe, contrary to Gary Gorton's remarks, what we want is a system with lots of small banks and no big banks. We would have lots of failures, but that may be much cheaper than having big banks get in trouble but not fail.

We generally look at countries like England, which have a small number of big banks, as systems that are not subject to the kinds of problems we have in the United States. But if all we had in the United States were the big ten banks and if we had nothing underpinning them, I wonder whether they all would have gone belly up during the less-developed-country debt crisis, and if not, whether they would have failed if there had been widespread coordinated repudiation of debt by LDCs.

I think we need some rich models so we can track back and forth between the political economy and the implications for regulation. I like the paper by de la Cuadra and Valdés because of its recognition of this chain of reasoning.

Response and Discussion

PAUL HORVITZ: I think Peter Diamond's comments are well taken. Jim Wright should have been discussed. I think that is a significant omission—not because I think that Jim Wright himself was that important in this picture, but because of the whole issue of the interaction of the political considerations and forbearance. There were pressures for forbearance on the supervisors from many directions, other congressional directions besides Jim Wright. As a matter of fact, the House did not seem particularly upset about the ethics charges against Jim Wright with his intervening on behalf of his constituents.

The other interesting aspect is that the supervisory agencies have frequently been subject to such pressure and it has traditionally been a lot easier for the Federal Reserve, the Comptroller of the Currency, and the FDIC to resist those pressures than the Home Loan Bank Board. There is a difference in culture there. That may play a large part in the decision to dismantle the Home Loan Bank Board.

The pressures for forbearance go also to the decision makers themselves. That is, from the supervisor's point of view there is a tendency—I guess this is the time-inconsistency problem again—to delay taking action and to hope that things are going to get better.

I think a more egregious problem than Jim Wright, in terms of delay, was the delay all during 1987 and 1988 when the bank board was clearly aware that the problem was vastly greater than the resources that the FSLIC had at its disposal.

In the tendency of Chairman M. Danny Wall to assure Congress, at least until after the 1988 election, that there were sufficient resources to handle the problem without the need for taxpayer funds to resolve the problem, we lost a lot of time and a lot of money. The point is well taken that these political issues deserve more attention.

The contrast between the FDIC and the FSLIC is discussed in the paper. I would argue that the difference is not a difference in powers. The powers are very similar. Ken Scott may be able to be more specific about that.

The main things that kept the FSLIC from taking more definitive action earlier were (1) a lack of money—a key difference between the FDIC and the FSLIC—and (2) a difference in the capability of the supervisors to recognize the magnitude and extent of the problems.

The new powers that Peter mentioned are relevant, though new powers did not add directly to the losses in Texas. They may have in some other places. But there was a supervisory problem: The supervisors were not prepared to deal with the new powers.

Savings and loan examiners were accustomed to examining a portfolio of single-family mortgage loans, which are pretty easy to evaluate. You check whether there is appropriate collateral and whether the loan is current, and that is about it. In looking at complicated loans to finance commercial real estate, there are literally file drawers of information and backup material that has to be analyzed in order to determine the quality of a loan. The savings and loan examiner who had been trained in the 1960s and 1970s simply was not prepared for that.

The issue of branching is an interesting one. I do not think savings and loan branching helped very much in terms of diversification. The branches were largely means of generating deposits. The lending was undiversified despite the branching, and hence I do not believe that the branching capability of savings and loans in Texas greatly improved the diversification of the asset portfolio. Maybe it should have, but as it turned out, all of the major markets in Texas had substantial real estate declines: Austin, Houston, Dallas, and San Antonio. It really did not matter whether one had a branch structure throughout the state or whether it was concentrated in Houston. At least in this case, diversification within the state did not help, and broader branching would have been necessary.

KENNETH SCOTT: Let me follow up on the point Paul was just making about what you can learn from the presence in Texas of banks and S&Ls and FDIC and FSLIC. And let me assume that he is correct about the historical proposition that the FSLIC and the Federal Home Loan Bank Board have had a different tradition with respect to vulnerability to political pressure.

One should always ask why. One very superficial answer is to say that there are a few words in the law that are different. If you go back to the Homeowners' Loan Act of 1933, you can find some language in there about the mission of the bank board to establish and create and organize a federal savings and loan system, and therefore you can argue that it was more a promoter than a regulator. I do not think those few words in the law explain a great deal fifty years later.

If you think about an administrative agency's susceptibility to political pressure from the industry and from constituents—how that is brought to bear—essentially it comes through two different channels. One is the executive branch, the White House, the national committee of the party in power. The other is through the Congress.

There is not a great deal of distinction so far as White House pressure is concerned between FDIC or FSLIC. In fact, my perception was that White House pressure was not particularly an issue. The pressure came from the Hill.

The distinction between FSLIC and FDIC on the Hill is very clear-cut, I think. FDIC, like the Fed and like the Comptroller, does not go to the Hill either for appropriations or for authorization with respect to its budget. The bank board did not go to the Hill for appropriations, but they did have to go to the Hill for authorization with respect to their budget. So they were directly able to feel the pressure from not only the oversight committees, the banking committees, which is also true for FDIC, but they were also susceptible to pressure from the appropriations subcommittees in the House and in the Senate, which is a fact that did not escape the industry's attention. If you want to squeeze, that is a key point at which to squeeze.

The other point Paul raised was this matter of differences in powers. There I would argue that, if anything, the difference in powers cuts in the other direction. You have been talking about closure policy as being a key issue with respect to outcomes in a system of bank failures or deposit insurance. The FDIC as insurer has no closure power.

The closure power with respect to banks is possessed by the primary supervisor or the chartering authority: the comptroller of the currency or the state bank superintendent. They are the ones who can make the determination factually and physically that the institution will cease operations or will be taken over and the management displaced by a government appointee. FDIC has no such power. In contrast, FSLIC effectively had that power with respect to all federal S&Ls by virtue of the fact that the Federal Home Loan Bank Board was the primary supervisor: It was the chartering authority for the federal savings and loan system as well as being the operating head of the Federal Savings and Loan Insurance Corporation.

So if you talk about differential powers, that part of it should have cut the other way in Texas and elsewhere. So I think it was not a question of powers; I think it was very much a question of resources, as Paul was suggesting.

PAUL HORVITZ: The powers in dealing with closing are interesting in terms of the structure. When a bank is in trouble, deciding how to handle that insolvency or threatened insolvency is a rather complex, interagency negotiation. The regulator is either the state or the Comptroller of the Currency. It is the FDIC that has the money to resolve the insurance problem, and it is the Federal Reserve that is the source of liquidity to keep things going until the solution is worked out.

In the savings and loan industry we had a unified system that, it seems to me, was organizationally a much more efficient way of dealing with difficulties in the industry. We had a Home Loan Bank Board that controlled the supervision, controlled the FSLIC, was the insurer, and controlled the Federal Home Loan Banks, which were a source of liquidity. That structure has been broken. Now there is a separate Office of Thrift Supervision, the insurer being the FDIC, and the Home Loan Banks being an entirely separate agency. So it seems we have clearly moved to a less efficient organizational structure for dealing with problems.

I want to give some indication of where I think my paper fits in with the discussion we have had already this morning.

Whenever I talk about problems in Texas, whether it is before an audience of economists or at a cocktail party, people are always searching for the cause or the answer to the question of what was responsible for the problems in Texas. And I think some readers may be disappointed in the paper that I don't have any single answer. There is no single cause.

People in Texas would like to view it as being a single answer, to view the problem as being caused by the collapse of the price of oil and hence as resulting from an external factor beyond anyone's control. People outside of Texas like to search for the cause as being fraud and self-dealing. While both of those factors played a part, there are many factors involved.

Part of the reason there are many factors involved is that there are really three different questions that are being asked. The three different questions are, What caused the number of bank failures that we experienced? What caused the number of savings and loan failures? And third, what accounted for the huge cost of the savings and loan failures?

Those are really three separate questions. The factors involved in those, while they are interrelated, are somewhat different. With respect to the one that has gotten the most attention, the cost of the savings and loan failures, I think it is of interest to put that in the context of the point that Gary mentioned earlier, that if we have bank regulation, that seems to lead to failure; if we do not have bank regulation, that leads to failures.

But one thing we can be clear on. If we had a free-banking system in the absence of deposit insurance, while I cannot predict what the number of bank failures or savings and loan failures would have been in Texas, it is completely clear that the cost would have been much less.

Some of that goes to what in the paper this morning was discussed as "moral hazard." We are often a little sloppy, I think, about defining moral hazard in these contexts. In the insurance literature moral hazard really refers to people acting differently because they are insured.

In the banking case the moral hazard is not simply that people's attitude toward risk changes because of the existence of deposit insurance but that the existence of deposit insurance allowed risk-prone entrepreneurs to take risks where they could not have gotten the funds in the same magnitude if it were not for deposit insurance. So it is not just that it modified their attitudes. They simply would not have had the amount of funds available if it were not for deposit insurance.

As I say, there were a number of factors involved. For a disaster to be this great it took several elements to be involved, including several elements of bad luck in that some of these things happened at the same time. There was a significant element of bad luck in the Texas situation.

I think it is unlikely that that experience would be repeated to that extent even if we did nothing about reforming the system. That leads me to conclude that what is needed are relatively modest revisions of the system rather than a wholesale, total change in the system.

There are modest changes that involve applying the lessons we have seen from Chile or from Texas. What is rather discouraging from the point of view of public policy is that I do not think frankly we learn a great deal from my paper, or from the paper on Chile, which I found interesting. I do not think we learn much from Charlie's paper on bank failures during the 1920s. We knew those things.

It is somewhat discouraging that we do not do anything about the things we learn we already know—that is, the issue of moral hazard or the question of deregulation and free banking.

It should have been clear that as we move in the direction of deregulation of the financial system, whether we are talking about Chile or Texas, if that is to be done in the context of either explicit deposit insurance guarantees or implicit government guarantees, then there must be some amount of prudential supervision.

In the U.S. banking industry, it seems to me, there was recognition of that. In the savings and loan industry, particularly in Texas, there was lack of recognition and a lack of preparation. That is evident in the Reagan administration's refusal to allow the Home Loan Bank Board to increase its staff of examiners and supervisory people at the time the need for increased supervision should have been apparent to everyone.

One of the key issues that seems to run through both the Chilean and the Texas situations is the very difficult problem of deciding when the supervisors should intervene.

One of the controversies in Texas, for example, had to do with whether the examiners should classify or criticize loans that were current; that is, loans on which interest was being paid but on which the value of the collateral for the loan had declined to less than the amount of the loan.

This was a matter of considerable controversy between bankers in Texas and the regulators, and there was some congressional intervention to prevent the regulators from classifying loans which were current but in which the collateral had become inadequate.

This is where the vast majority of the unrecognized losses, or the delay in recognizing losses, occurred. What I have in mind is a situation where a lender makes a loan of $8 million secured by an office building worth $10 million. Payments on the loan were made on a current basis for some period of time. As the real estate market declined, that building became worth, say, $6 million. As long as the loan was being paid, the bankers argued that the examiners should not classify that loan. But a borrower is going to pay for only a limited period of time on an $8 million loan on a property that is worth $6 million. A default and a loss are almost inevitable.

The question of when you intervene also involves the very difficult issue of whether to go by book value or market value. Despite Gary Gorton's comments this morning, I do not think the question of market value or book value is a red herring. It may be impossible to come up with proxy market values for some amount of the assets. But that is the difficulty in deciding when to intervene to protect the deposit insurer.

There is one other point that I want to stress in making a distinction between a Texas and Chile situation. Chile is a small open economy. No matter what Chile does, it may be impossible to protect the financial sector from disruptions or shocks that come from outside the financial sector.

Texas is not in that same situation, in that it is a matter of choice that led Texas to have a banking system that was undiversified. Texas could have chosen to have a branch banking system or diversification that could have prevented the declining price of oil from affecting the whole banking system.

That choice is not inevitable in the structure of the U.S. financial system. Congress decided to allow states to determine their own banking structure and to preclude interstate branching. That was not an inevitable choice, and there is no need necessarily to have a state banking system that is subject to the lack of diversification that exists in Texas.

So while it may be impossible to protect the banking system in Chile against the decline in the price of copper, it should be possible to shield the banking system of the U.S. from having significant losses as a result of a decline in the price of oil.

ROBERT BARTELL: By way of background, I have been an S&L supervisor and I have been a bank supervisor and I ran a big savings and loan in Texas, so I have an unusual perspective on this subject. If I sound like an academic, it is because I have also done that a bit.

Let me explain the difference between bank and savings and loan failure rates in a way that is different from what Paul Horvitz and others, Ken Scott in particular, have suggested.

There are basically three factors that can be used to explain differences in failure rates. By this, I am referring to the frequency as well as the severity of failures, because it is the amount of the loss per incidence of failure that truly differentiates S&L and bank failures.

The first one is fraud or bad management, and along with that, inadequate monitoring by the regulatory agency. Fraud has been a problem in both savings and loan failures and bank failures for a long time. It has been studied quite extensively. I believe that in most cases the regulatory agencies have been reasonably even in terms of their inability to detect fraud and to take action to prevent it from causing failure.

The two factors that it seems to me distinguish bank and S&L failure rates and have relevance in terms of trying to understand deposit insurance are, one, technological change accompanied by regulatory inflexibility, and, two, economic crisis and a destruction of asset values.

It is very clear that technological change in the financial services industry, combined with regulatory inflexibility, had a far more serious adverse impact on savings and loan associations than it did on commercial banks because of the fact that the technological change took place in the liability and asset areas that were the S&L specialty, and it was regulatory inflexibility that prevented savings and loans from getting out of the short-term deposit and long-term loan mismatch quickly.

The interesting thing is that technological change and regulatory inflexibility generated a closure policy, or lack of closure policy, that was considered politically acceptable. If you remember, in 1981–1983 there was a large number of savings and loan associations that very clearly failed, but they were not closed. Some were merged, of course, but they were merged with the encouragement and assistance of the bank board, and in many cases the management of the failed institution was absorbed into the management of the surviving institution or else they were able to take their pensions and go off without feeling any great pain.

What happened in this era was an unwillingness to mark to market and to close institutions when the value of their liabilities was considerably greater than the value of their assets. These failures, of course, were caused by technological change in financial markets and regulatory restrictions on the ability to pay market rates on deposits and to offer variable rate loans.

It was perceived that the failures did not come about as a result of managers who were bad people—that is, fraudulent activity and bad management did not create the problem—so it was thought that the institutions did not need to be closed and that they should be given forbearance. In Garn–St. Germain both the FDIC and the FSLIC were given the authority to provide "capital" to these institutions to carry them through this period when the regulatory inflexibility would be done away with and the technological change could be accommodated.

What happened in Texas, and other energy and farm states, is an example of the third factor that causes failure, and that is an economic crisis which destroys asset values.

The initial closure policy in Texas was not one that said economic destruction of values should be blamed on the people who ran the institutions. In other words, the breakup of the OPEC oil cartel was not the fault of savings and loan management. It was something that came from outside the system. So initially the regulators did not close institutions in Texas when they became insolvent; they did not mark their assets to market, as Paul Horvitz pointed out. There was a lot of pressure not to mark the assets to market and to keep the institutions technically solvent.

Of course, what happened was that the institutions were able to continue to attract funds because of deposit insurance. Some of them tried to grow out of their problems with regulatory encouragement, but they ended up paying a very high cost for their deposits because of a very prevalent perception that Texas deposits were risky and FSLIC insurance was not as good as FDIC insurance. The cost structure of the S&Ls became uneconomic in itself because they had to pay a much higher rate than FDIC-insured institutions.

It has been estimated that the cost of FSLIC deposits as compared to FDIC deposits during this period of time, 1985–1987, was something on the order of 100 basis points. That was in large part because FSLIC insurance was perceived as being not as good as FDIC insurance, and it was the Texas S&L institutions, in particular, that had to pay that higher cost. In addition, the value of real estate assets, which collateralized virtually all S&L loans, dropped as much as 50 percent. You would have to be a magician to keep an institution alive under these circumstances.

What is a realistic closure policy? We should identify fraud quickly and make sure that the institutions where there is fraud and bad management be closed quickly. But that is not what causes failures of insurance systems. Fraud and mismanagement are relatively isolated factors.

The closure policy that exempts institutions that are run by decent people who are overcome by technological change and regulatory inflexibility or who are overcome by an economic crisis that destroys asset values is one that is going to run into serious political problems.

As long as the people who manage these institutions can go to their representatives and senators and to the regulators and say, look, we did not cause this, somebody else caused it; we are suffering, so please provide forbearance, provide capital, and so forth, I think the normal response of government is to say, okay, these people did not cause the problem, it was caused by an external force, and therefore we should help them. This is a reasonable description of the bailout of the farm credit system.

What has happened recently is a reversal of that. In other words, what has happened in Congress is that the stories of fraud and mismanagement have taken control, and Congress now is saying closure policy is going to have to be tightened up; we are going to have to penalize these people if their institutions fail. The reason I think Congress is willing to do that now is because they are convinced that it was fraud that caused all these problems in Texas and elsewhere and not technological change and regulatory inflexibility, for which Congress is partially responsible, and not because there was an economic crisis that destroyed asset values. So now the legislative and regulatory approach is the "ayatollah" approach. That is, if your institution fails, you must be a crook so off with your head. How long this attitude will prevail is not clear, but while it does prevail, it is very dangerous to be a manager or stockholder of a Texas banking institution.

GARY GORTON: I would like to agree with this point about technological change and add something. I was a bit surprised at Paul's somewhat mild reaction to what happened in Texas, as to its being a rare event. It is exactly these kinds of events that we are supposed to prevent.

The situation, it seems to me, is quite different now in the U.S. markets. The particular pattern of markets that are open now is different than it was a few short years ago. The pattern of markets which are open or closed is extremely important.

In the case of the U.S. it is clear that important markets are open and particular markets for bank assets are either opened or opening. By that I do not mean just mortgage-backed securities or even other asset-backed securities, but the market for home loan sales.

That has two immediate implications. One is that it is possible for banks to diversify in ways they could not have done three or four years ago. Today, loans originating in Texas can be sold throughout the banking system of the U.S., with the proceeds purchasing a diversified portfolio. That was not possible three or four years ago.

That is a $280-billion market now, which receives no attention whatsoever in any of these discussions, perhaps because others share my conviction that the regulators are going to close it in the next few years.

It also has immediate implications for bank regulation. Bank regulation is predicated upon the illiquidity of bank assets and on information asymmetries that may derive from that. If bank assets are liquid, then we are in a completely different ball game.

What I found interesting about the paper was that, as Paul points out, there was an increasing number of commercial bank failures, which he predicted. Those were occurring, it seems to me, because of technological change, whereas the conclusion I draw from the S&L crisis was that it resulted from poor regulation that did not anticipate consistently high interest rates.

We cannot anticipate every possible future contingency, so we are always going to be Monday morning quarterbacking about what we should have done to cut the losses.

The S&L industry has just been laid bare. It is an industry which no longer serves a useful purpose, and we should develop some policies to somehow get rid of this industry. I do not know what those should be.

In the case of commercial banks, it seems that the regulatory proposals are just completely bankrupt. It seems to me that that should not be the way we think about the S&L issue either. I was quite surprised by the conclusions at the end of your paper.

PAUL HORVITZ: Surprised by what, that they did not flow from what came before?

GARY GORTON: No, not that they were logically inconsistent, but that they did not seem to address the problem of technological change, as Bob Bartell suggested.

PAUL HORVITZ: My argument on the bank side is that we have identified the sources of the problems or we knew them earlier anyway. The steps that are under way are the right steps to deal with the problem in the context of the assumption that we want the stability that comes with deposit insurance. I think, for better or worse, we have rejected the idea of free banking or accepting the disruption that goes with the possibility of loss on deposits.

We are going to have deposit insurance. The question then is not one of whether occasional panics are a better approach to it. I think we have adopted the view that we are going to protect depositors. Then the question is, What kind of regulatory framework is optimal for minimizing the adverse costs of that? We recognize there are costs to providing full or close to full protection.

I think what is needed is relatively simple and well identified, and that is capital and monitoring and closure policy.

You talk about bank assets becoming marketable. One could move a little farther than that. The approach that Jack Guttentag and Dick Herring have argued for is to limit banks to investment in marketable assets; banks can invest in anything as long as it is marketable and marked to market, as the securities industry, in effect, is. Then you can prevent loss.

But banks do create value by dealing in unmarketable assets, or what up to now, at least, have been unmarketable assets. I prefer a regulatory system that is designed to keep those contributions of banks while trying to minimize the losses or the costs that are associated with trying to protect depositors.

GARY GORTON: I agree with your perspective about deposit insurance if you are talking about Chile, where a different pattern of markets is open.

It seems to me that when the structure of markets just changes in certain ways, in a sense there is not really a policy choice. The only policy choice, it seems to me, with respect to commercial banking is not what you or I think but whether we are going to close this market. If we are not going to close it, then the whole ball game, including how we think about these problems, is completely different.

It is not clear to how this can all happen, that banks can sell loans and so on, but it strikes me that there has been this change that has enormous ramifications for bank regulation. One of the motivations for selling loans is that you do not have to hold equity against them.

If you say to a banking system, Well, we want you to raise your debt/equity ratio, it seems to me that that would work as perhaps a binding constraint in a world where you could not sell bank loans. But if bank loans can be sold, this is simply not going to be a good policy unless you simultaneously say, Well, there is a lot of risk associated with these loans, so we are going to close these loans down. That is an attempt to re-create this previous technological environment. That would be something which seems to me to be extremely costly socially. We ought to welcome the opening of this market.

PAUL HORVITZ: I welcome it. But it does not avoid the need for equity against it. If those loans are to be sold, someone has to provide some credit enhancement. If the bank guarantees those loans itself, obviously the regulators treat them, I think appropriately, as staying on the balance sheet. If there is to be some other credit enhancement, if someone else is going to guarantee them, then whoever that is needs some equity.

CHARLES CALOMIRIS: If you think as do I that the banking securitization question that Gary raised is controversial, let's leave that aside. I think banks still make some loans that are not going to be easily securitized.

In savings and loans it seems like that really is not an issue any more. To say it differently, the necessity for savings and loans to initiate and hold portfolios of mortgages seems to be a thing of the past.

Normally we think of having very high capital requirements, for example, on intermediaries as being costly, because they may keep the size of the intermediary's balance sheet small. That is an argument for why we do not have 100 percent capital requirements on banks and why we have to worry about deposit insurance instead. That argument does not exist for savings and loans, because they do not as a group do anything that requires that they have these large balance sheets.

I would like to propose that there really is a different regulatory question about deposit insurance for savings and loans and banks. There may still be a lot of issues to be resolved in bank deposit insurance. I think it would be hard for anyone to explain to me why we cannot immediately pass 100 percent capital requirements on savings and loans. So what if their balance sheets fall by 50 percent or more? Who cares?

SERGIO DE LA CUADRA: Like a mutual fund?

CHARLES CALOMIRIS: Yes.

JOHN BOYD: That is perfectly feasible, Charlie, because as a matter of fact there probably will not be any of them in a couple of years anyway. At least not as we now know S&Ls.

(Laughter.)

I was really fascinated with Peter Diamond's comments, and I found several of them to be a veritable breath of fresh air. But I am surprised that some of the people in this room were not incensed by what he said.

It has been very trendy in the last couple of years to argue that if banks could just diversify enough, you would not have many of these problems. In fact, several people in this room have written papers along this line, and so have several people from my shop, advocating national branch banking.

But as Peter Diamond observed, in Texas, S&Ls can branch and banks cannot, at least not as much. Yet there it is clear the S&Ls got the worst of it, and branching did not help them much.

Peter also raised the issue of whether big banks are necessarily safer than small banks. He asked, What if we had forced all the large money-center banks in the United States to mark their assets to market at the peak of the LDC crisis, and did not provide government support. How many of them would have been closed? That is a good question!

The point is, it is not clear that enhanced diversification or national branch banking is a panacea to the problems under discussion. How is greater concentration in banking going to solve them? Besides, the largest banking firms operate all over the United States already. Beyond that, they can and do lend anywhere in the world they want.

PAUL HORVITZ: The evidence suggests that banks have not diversified to the extent that is possible within the framework that exists. Banks have resisted diversification. The banks in Texas were not constrained to be as heavily loaned to the oil business as they were and certainly not constrained to be as heavily loaned to real estate as they subsequently became. The evidence suggests that bankers are comfortable with certain kinds of assets, certain kinds of borrowers.

While I would favor broadening the ability to diversify, I think a greater problem is the question of whether or not banks will seek to diversify. As a matter of fact, one might argue that banks should appropriately specialize where they have the greatest expertise and in an efficient market leave it to the investor to hold a diversified portfolio of specialized banks.

PATRICK HONOHAN: Even if the Texas banks were not sufficiently diversified, they were in some way integrated into the much larger U.S. economy generally. The manifestation of that was ultimately the bailout of the depositors by the deposit insurance system.

In Chile as well you had a moderately small economy facing a shock, in some way parallel, maybe, to the real estate shock in Texas. That banking system was also integrated into the world economy in a certain way—not in the way of, say, setting the loan portfolio in a properly diversified manner, but by the banking system itself having borrowed from international banks, as I read Sergio's and Salvador's paper this morning.

The resolution of that situation was entirely the opposite, the inverse of the resolution in the case of the United States. Instead of the losses being transmitted through this integration with the world economy to the more widely held international banks, it was quite the opposite. The losses were all funneled right back into the small Chilean economy to be borne there by the state in undertaking the guarantees.

I think this raises important issues of international integration of banking for small economies. There are a lot of economies that are a lot smaller than Chile and facing comparable or greater shocks. I think there is a public policy issue that is linked into the resolution of the international debt crisis here.

PHILIP BROCK: Let me ask Sergio if he would say something about what happened in Uruguay in 1982 or so.

SERGIO DE LA CUADRA: In the early 1980s there were more than thirty banks operating in Uruguay. Of these thirty banks, one was a state-owned bank, one was a private Uruguayan bank, and all the rest were branches of foreign banks operating in Uruguay. The crisis that they suffered in Uruguay made the portfolios of these banks very bad. They had big losses in their loans. They said, If you do not buy all of our bad loans at face value, we are not going to renew any loans we have in Uruguay. So the Central Bank of Uruguay had to buy all these bad loans made by the foreign branches operating in Uruguay at their face value with no repurchase agreement.

PHILIP BROCK: This was something around 15 percent of GDP, I think. A large number.

SALVADOR VALDÉS: Let me say something about it. I think there is a very large difference between diversifying assets or investments and diversifying liabilities. The second one places demands on the deposit insurance of local authorities. That is a clear indication that you want the first type of diversification, not the second one.

PAUL HORVITZ: One aspect of diversification and the point Peter made about how we might prefer a system of lots of small banks. If we had allowed interstate banking in the U.S. ten years ago, it is possible that if First Republic of Texas and NCNB Texas National Bank had been operated jointly or had been merged in 1980, as occurred following the failure of First Republic, then we would have seen a failure of the combined entity and not just a failure of First Republic. So that diversification would have had a perverse effect.

ROBERT BARTELL: But would their losses have been greater?

PAUL HORVITZ: The losses would have probably been the same.

SALVADOR VALDÉS: I would like to raise one question on the political economy side, and that is, How much do you want regulation to be in only one hand? It is an old problem: Who regulates the regulators?

In particular, if you have regulatory delay in the sense that maybe a problem is detected in a bank but still it may be the case that regulators do not want to acknowledge the fact, then that delay might be due to inappropriate provisioning policies or something related to the quality of their own supervision.

I don't know how important that problem is, but if it is important, that would speak in favor of dividing the regulatory authority into two parts, one that supervises and one that takes over and bears the losses. The latter has the highest incentive to supervise the supervisors.

I will leave that question open.

MARVIN GOODFRIEND: I wanted to make a couple of comments, one on the sale of loans and another on diversification evidence.

This is addressed to Gary in part because Gary has written a lot on this. The fact that there is a market in loan sales that is growing doesn't indicate to me that there is a fundamental shift in any kind of regulatory need for banking. Banking provides an essential service, which is basically to make loans to firms that are too small to access the credit markets directly through commercial paper.

That is a fundamental fact which is not going to change over time. In the U.S. roughly half of GNP is produced by relatively small companies, those with under 500 employees. So you are always going to have a considerable volume of loans originated based on information-intensive lending.

Banks in the past have originated a variety of loans, some less information-intensive than others. As we move further into the computer age, it is reasonable that some portion of bank loan portfolios is going to be salable, but it is by no means clear how big that portion will become.

Also, it seems to me that it is very important who buys these loans. If they are bought by other information-intensive lenders and not tended thereafter, then the loan sales are merely an efficient means for better diversification of risk of information-intensive loans among banks. If the U.S. moves toward branching in the next ten years, that might slow somewhat the spread of loan sales.

Also, if these loan sales are basically traded among information-intensive lenders, then loan sales will not change much the liquidity of the banking system as a whole because when you consolidate the banking system balance sheet, you are still going to have roughly the same proportion of information-intensive "illiquid" loans that regulators have to worry about today.

It is far from clear to me that the spread of loan sales means the end of banks as we know them or the end of a need for bank regulations as we know them.

The other point, looking at current evidence on nationwide banking for evidence of the extent to which they wish to diversify, is really fraught with problems. The extent to which large banks want to diversify is greatly influenced by the "too big to fail" current regulatory environment. It may be that large banks do not now diversify as much as one might expect because they obtain sufficient guarantees from the deposit insurance program. So you really have a chicken-and-egg problem getting evidence on this issue, I think.

PHILIP BROCK: Thank you. That is Peter's point also on having lots of small banks that you can allow to fail.

JOHN BOYD: That's exactly right. If you don't solve the too-big-to-fail problem, diversification potential doesn't buy you anything.

KENNETH SCOTT: It seems to me the short way to put that is that diversification has a cost. Why should an institution incur it unless it is going to save something? In this fully insured world you are not saving anything, and therefore why incur that particular cost?

I want to switch back to another point that Paul made: The deregulation events of the early 1980s in a deposit insurance environment necessitated an enhancement of supervision.

I would like to advance the counterargument that this reflects a confusion of cause and effect. The real issue is that of incentives. If management has excessive risk-taking incentives, then all the deregulation is doing is affording them some new channels through which they can adopt that preferred policy.

In rebuttal, you have to make the argument that deregulation greatly increases the supply of risky investment and makes it much cheaper for management to go into risky investment than would otherwise have been the case. That is an empirical issue. I suppose it must in principle be true to a degree. The question is, Is the degree large or trivial? My own perception is that it isn't hard to create risk if you wish to choose a risky investment policy. Whether you are in a wide-spectrum investment environment or a relatively confined one, you can find ways to do it.

When the bank board, for example, took over control of Financial Corporation of America, they said to American Savings: Don't go into all of these new and fancy things. So they didn't. They just continued to make a heavy bet on interest rate futures by making longer fixed rate mortgages.

So you can always go for a high-risk strategy. It's a cinch. I don't think deregulation is therefore a very critical factor. At most, it facilitated (by reducing some of the cost) following that kind of a policy, but the critical factor to look for is incentives, not the deregulation.

PAUL HORVITZ: I disagree. There is a spectrum out there of management with different attitudes toward risk. In the world of Regulation Q ceilings, they are limited in the amount of funds they have. With deregulation those who are risk-prone can get access to unlimited amounts of funds.

KENNETH SCOTT: I thought you were talking about asset deregulation. You are talking instead about taking the cap off of Regulation Q?

PAUL HORVITZ: Both. Your point is well taken with respect to the first.

DON MATHIESON: I think one issue that relates to how much you need diversification of portfolios is how well you can estimate the covariances between the yields on different loans. I remember in late 1982 when we were discussing the debt crisis with one of the bankers in New York, the question came up as to how his bank's portfolio could ever get so concentrated in loans to problem countries. I had the impression that he had viewed his loans to Chile, the Philippines, and East European countries as a diversified portfolio. They looked at the expected returns and the variance on their loans, but they forgot about the covariances of the yields across countries when a systemic shock occurs.

The point here is that diversification will not do much for systemwide shocks. For example, in a country like Chile a major change in the terms of trade or the price of copper would affect all sectors of the economy. Another problem is that as financial markets integrate, the covariances of the yields on assets tend to increase. This is especially evident in the major industrial countries where financial markets have been integrating much more rapidly than goods markets. This means that even if a bank starts with what looks like a diversified portfolio, it may become over time less diversified. This raises the general question of how one constructs financial positions or contracts when the underlying variance-covariance structure is shifting over time.

MARVIN GOODFRIEND: I want to follow up on this point, which I think is very interesting. If you have a small country like Chile, one of the things you would want to do to get around the fact that you can't diversify very well internally is to invite international business to the country. Yet my understanding from countries I have visited, like Switzerland, is that there is some reluctance to do that, because the banking industry in the country itself wants to keep business in-house.

It seems like there is a political decision to keep foreign banks out because of the competition. Yet that is what you would want to do, to diversify your banking system against the idiosyncratic risks associated with the terms-of-trade shock.

Is that true? If it is, can you see any way to get around that political impediment?

SERGIO DE LA CUADRA: In the case of Chile we have a very long experience with competition of foreign banks in the country. A couple of years following the turn of the century, foreign banks started coming to the country. By the 1920s my recollection is that more than 50 percent of the assets in Chilean banking belonged to foreign banks.

The financial repression in the country started in the 1930s. These foreign banks left the country, with some exceptions. Citibank remained there until the regime of Mr. Allende, when all foreign banks were closed down. Since we reopened our market in 1974, a lot of foreign banks came back to the country.

I was trying to think what this has meant for a more stable banking system in the country. It is not so clear to me. It has benefits. It has made our domestic banks much more competitive, more productive, and they offer us as good a service as you can get from the foreign banks. There is very fair competition and very strong competition.

In the domestic market you don't observe any advantage of a foreign bank competing with a domestic bank, but what have they added to the stability of the system? The only thing I would say is they are backed by their headquarters.

I have in mind the case of a branch of an American bank there—I am not going to give the name—which was doing operations that were not allowed by Mr. Ramírez and other superintendents in Chile. They were recently fined the highest fine ever placed on a bank operating in Chile. As a result of this they brought more capital to the country to have a more sound operation there.

Maybe they can help with international corporations that want to operate in Chile who trust the American banks more. In that sense they have been helpful.

SALVADOR VALDÉS: When a country has a repressed financial market, then banks may have access, depending on the type of regulation, to huge profits—say, when deposit interest rates are fixed below the inflation rate or that kind of thing. In that case it is very understandable that a country doesn't want foreign banks to get a piece of the cake.

In a liberalized financial market, except for the common desire for protection of the domestic banking industry, I don't see any reason for the country to close up its market to foreign banks.

SERGIO DE LA CUADRA: Do you think they can add stability to the system?

SALVADOR VALDÉS: I think that the stability issue is complicated by the local deposit insurance problem. If the foreign banks get local deposit insurance and they are not supervised correctly, they may add to the instability rather than the other way around.

PHILIP BROCK: Do you want to follow up?

MARVIN GOODFRIEND: I would like to pursue this later. I am sure we will get a chance.

It seems to me that there is an analogy between interstate branching prohibitions in the U.S and the extent to which a small country's banking system is connected to international banks.

SERGIO DE LA CUADRA: Completely open for many, many years.

MARVIN GOODFRIEND: It would strike me that you have an alternative to deposit insurance that you might want to rely on. Depositors might want to leave their deposits at Citibank.

SERGIO DE LA CUADRA: There are many, many Latin Americans that are benefiting from deposits to the U.S. banks. The amount of money deposited by Latin Americans in the U.S. is huge.

MARVIN GOODFRIEND: Let's just pursue this move conceptually a bit more. It strikes me that large international banks might be better diversified, and it is only because the local banks are getting deposit insurance that individuals are willing to hold funds there at all.

PHILIP BROCK: The amount of equity that is at stake is the local amount, right? For example, Citibank in Chile. The amount of equity they can lose is just what they have in Chile.

SALVADOR VALDÉS: The foreign bank may behave just to keep its reputation abroad, but I think that in the case of Chile a misbehavior of the Chilean branch might not affect the worldwide reputation of Citibank.

PHILIP BROCK: There is this Uruguayan example, too, where it didn't matter that they were foreign branches. They just told the government, You had better buy these loans from us or else.

SERGIO DE LA CUADRA: In Chile our pension funds are forced to invest only in assets that have been rated by approved rating companies. So if they want to make a deposit in a bank, that bank must be rated. I think one or two years ago the rating given to the Bank of America branch in Chile was not very good.

CHARLES CALOMIRIS: Phil, you were the one that suggested this to me, so I will hang it on you. This is really a jurisdictional question.

It is one thing to open up a bank in another state within the United States, knowing that if there were a bad realization in that place and you wanted to move funds from that branch to another, you would be freely allowed to. But there may be jurisdictional problems that would make U.S. banks or other foreign banks reluctant to move into another country, and there may be political economies of staying within a particular jurisdiction too that are related to political influence.

The difference of political jurisdiction across countries seems to create fundamental differences in the economics of branching from what you would expect from branching behavior within a country.

4

Guillermo Ramírez
and Francisco Rosende

Responding to Collapse: Chilean Banking Legislation after 1983

The financial crisis that struck the Chilean economy during the early 1980s threatened the stability of the market reforms that had been implemented in the economy during the mid-1970s. The serious difficulties encountered by the financial system not only necessitated in-depth strengthening and rehabilitation of the sector but also pointed to the pressing, unavoidable need to draw up a new and more efficient banking law that would be consistent with a stable market economy.

The paper in this volume by de la Cuadra and Valdés has provided the historical and conceptual framework for the origins of the 1981–1983 financial crisis in Chile. This paper focuses on the evolution of the financial sector after 1983. The two sections that follow this introduction contain a summary of the major steps taken by the economic authorities to revive the financial sector beginning in 1983 and a discussion of the conceptual framework for the 1986 amendments to the banking law.

A third section examines the more substantive points of Chilean banking legislation with special emphasis on the mechanisms for bank capital adjustment, and a fourth section discusses difficulties that might be encountered when implementing the new mechanisms for banking suspension and adjustment. The concluding section then describes the evolution of the Chilean financial market after the reforms became effective. We wish to stress that the principal purpose of this chapter is to describe the origin and scope of amendments made to Chilean financial legislation rather than to analyze the causes of the crisis or the theoretical foundation of the law.

The Banking Rehabilitation Program

The weak net worth position of major Chilean banks, which called for intervention in January 1983, led the government to grant priority attention to rehabilitating the financial system. Private sector debts to the financial system were first rescheduled in 1983, in conjunction with a reduction in the real interest rate charged on rescheduled loans. The operation was addressed primarily to small-scale debtors and involved a substantial volume of nonmonetary debt issue by the central bank. Debts were rescheduled again in 1984 by amending interest rates and repayment terms for outstanding obligations with the banking system. The associated restructuring costs were again borne by the central bank. In all, during 1983–1984 about one-third of the loans granted by the banking system were included in long-term reprogramming at substantially lower real interest rates (5–7 percent per annum in real terms) than the initial real rates that were contracted privately.[1]

A vigorous bank capitalization program was carried out in 1985 and 1986, based on the sale—to new owners—of stock in the banks under intervention. In the case of Banco de Chile and Banco de Santiago, the process became known as *capitalismo popular*, or popular capitalism, since the process was based on the purchase of stock in these banks by small-scale stockholders using special credits granted by the state through the Chilean development agency, Corporación de Fomento de la Producción (CORFO). The loan was secured by the shares purchased. Simultaneously, a bank capitalization process was promoted by the Superintendency of Banks as a form of access to a state guarantee on deposits. The capital base of banking institutions was thus expanded in a manner consistent with the levels of debt incurred, degree of concentration, and portfolio quality of each bank.

Between 1984 and 1987 the banking system collected new capital on the order of U.S. $900 million, or a gross increase of about 60 percent for the system as a whole. Two-thirds of this figure was accounted for by popular capitalism, while the balance was a direct contribution by domestic and foreign investors, largely undertaken as the consequence of the incentives under the foreign debt conversion process. As a result, seven banks, which in 1986 accounted for 60 percent of the loans granted by the private financial system, returned to the private sector.

Another central element in the Chilean financial rehabilitation program conducted between 1982 and 1986 involved transferring at book value all debts with low probability of redemption in the banking system to the central bank. This operation was known as "purchase of past-due portfolio." As counterpart to transferring the banks' bad debts to the central bank, the program required the banks involved to enter a commitment whereby all profits—net of dividends to popular capitalists, who were preferred creditors— would be devoted to repurchasing the portfolio. At the end of 1986, the total loans transferred to the central bank in this way amounted to about U.S. $3 billion, or 28 percent of the loans in the entire financial system.

No less complex and significant than the task of confronting the net worth problems suffered by the Chilean financial system after the crisis is the task of delineating the future institutional framework for the financial sector. Indeed, the crisis made it clear that the prevailing institutions were incapable of detecting financial sector problems in a timely manner and of providing well-functioning adjustment mechanisms for problem banks.

Two alternative paths suggested themselves. One was for the government to regulate the financial sector more heavily. This path would have sought closer control of banking risk so as to limit the extent of the commitment that the economic authorities—particularly the central bank—assumed by granting depositor insurance. The other path was to proceed to effective privatization of the financial system by providing explicit private adjustment mechanisms in the case of banking net worth difficulties and simultaneously introducing a risk variable into deposits.

The latter option was perceived to be more consistent with the spirit of an economic system based on the development of private initiative. The 1986 amendments to the Chilean financial legislation, which are described later, were based on the notion that stability in the financial sector requires proper incentives. Although private forms of financial market control and adjustment were considered more consistent with a market economy than public forms, the difficulties faced by the banking sector after the crisis, along with the external debt problems affecting the nation as a whole, recommended a conservative introduction of reforms to avoid speculation against domestic financial assets. The amendments are therefore an attempt to combine a greater ability to forecast financial problems with a more important role for the private sector in the supervision and adjustment process. Nonetheless, since the legislation retains some degree of deposit insurance, the Superintendency of Banks still has a major supervisory role to play.

The Bases of Current Banking Legislation

Of the many factors involved in the Chilean financial crisis that subsequently gave rise to the amendments to the prevailing financial legislation, some deserve special mention. First, the supervisory apparatus of the Superintendency of Banks was clearly inefficient in the early 1980s and allowed the difficulties suffered by financial institutions to be identified at a very late stage. Legislation in force in the early 1980s failed to provide sufficient preventive measures for the Superintendency of Banks—or ideally the management of the banks themselves—to correct an unfavorable situation before it turned into a major problem.[2] Furthermore, the recent history of the Chilean financial market, as reflected in the behavior of bank loans and interest rates paid on deposits when the financial crisis was in full force, seems to reflect the banks' preference for betting on the emergence of some form of exogenous rescue rather than for taking steps to adjust their net worth.[3] Although massive loan renewals plus higher deposit interest rates helped banks to overcome immediate liquidity problems, these actions were obviously explosive in terms of the performance of the financial system as a whole.[4]

Another major issue facing legislative reformers was how to introduce incentives for depositors to discriminate among institutions according to portfolio risk. Similarly, stimuli had to be provided for banks to want to exhibit solvency to depositors. This was a crucial issue among intended amendments to the banking law, for achievement of a stable financial market required the creation of a system in which insurance on bank indebtedness had a price that would encourage greater transparency in the brokerage process.

The precise way in which risk was to be introduced into bank deposits was not easy to determine. The Chilean economy, with a currency "dominated" by stronger currencies and burdened with the aftermath of financial crisis and substantial external payments problems, found it difficult to do without official insurance on bank debts, both internal and external.

Furthermore, aside from state-owned and foreign banks, if the financial market was to make a positive contribution to the development of production, it appeared unwise to establish conditions likely to jeopardize the performance of normal payments in the economy, which would happen, for instance, if convertibility of demand deposits were not fully guaranteed.

The explicit introduction of a risk variable into depositors' decision-making processes had to be designed to give the rule being set the most credibility possible. In other words, given Chilean economic history, it seemed difficult to think that in the event of poor performance of one or more banks, a loss could be imposed on depositors that would be sufficient for banks to recapitalize fully. It was therefore advisable for the new law to allow depositor losses, but only for nondemand deposits. This stipulation was intended to prevent completely paralyzing the payments system in the face of actual or apparent difficulties in the banking system and to limit risk to a certain percentage of time deposits.

Another significant issue in the banking law reform was the search for alternative channels of official intervention in case of net worth or liquidity problems affecting financial institutions. That idea was of course reflected in the introduction of some degree of risk into deposits, which in practice became an automatic mechanism for bank capitalization. It was nonetheless necessary to seek other alternatives, such as the establishment of explicit conditions under which a bank could be capitalized by other financial institutions. This strategy was viewed as a way of providing other options of bank capitalization also based on agreement among private agents, although these options obviously had to be consistent with overall banking legislation, in terms of controlling risk levels and loan concentration.

Finally, it seemed unrealistic to disregard the possibility of official intervention in a bank in difficulty, although this option was deemed less desirable than recapitalization mechanisms in terms of the stability of a market economy. The fact was, however, that this option had been employed in the past and would most likely continue to be a major path to bank adjustment. Once the validity of the official intervention mechanism had been recognized, it was reasonable to include the rules to govern the intervention process in the banking law.

The issues just discussed basically involve incentives for bank operations and net worth adjustments. Nevertheless, having recognized that demand deposits were fully secured by law and that time deposits would be secured for only a percentage of their value, the

Superintendency of Banks still had a significant role in supervising bank operations. This task emerged as a supplement to the adjustment mechanism and involved overseeing compliance with provisions for implementing asset adjustment of banks in an initial stage of distress as well as making sure that institutions maintained the proper level of capital for the level of risk they were running with their loans. Such official supervision of the risk factor of banks' portfolios was seen as particularly significant in the process of financial rehabilitation following the crisis.

The New Institutional Framework for Banking in Chile

The new Chilean banking legislation enacted in late 1986 (Law No. 18,756) and supplemented in 1988 (Law No. 18,707) and 1989 (Law No. 18,818) reflects to a considerable extent the economy's experience with financial liberalization from the mid-1970s until the crisis of the early 1980s. The amendments made to the banking law in 1986 were the outcome of a process that the Superintendency of Banks had begun, partly by administrative means, in the early 1980s. In view of the emerging crisis, the superintendency took the first steps in that direction in 1980, setting guidelines for rating loan portfolios, measuring the volume of related credits, and making provisions following the same procedure.[5] In 1984–85, following the financial crisis, efforts were made to increase the degree of the public's information regarding the actual position of banks. This was accomplished by initiating a policy of disclosing "significant facts" and modifying bank accounting procedures so that assets and revenues of financial institutions would clearly and accurately reflect bank conditions. Accounting concepts were thus brought closer to the equivalent economic concepts.

The main mechanisms provided for in the banking law are described in the next three subsections.

Preventive control and transparency of the banking business. The banking law, including the 1986 amendments, provides (under Articles 13 *bis* and 14 of the Organic Law of the Superintendency of

Banks and Financial Institutions and under Articles 116, 119, and 126 of the General Banking Law) for an active role of the Superintendency of Banks in rating the quality of banking investments, along the lines of the mechanisms in effect since the early 1980s.[6] Although the regulations that have historically been applied to a bank's net worth condition, such as a minimum debt/equity ratio or minimum capital requirements, are still in force, they have given way in importance to automatic recognition of expected losses chargeable to surpluses or capital. As a result, accounting net worth comes closer to economic net worth. The emergence of solvency problems in a bank is now said to occur when "the value of its assets less provisions, after deducting losses not covered by provisions, and subtracting its legally contracted liabilities, is equal to or less than 40 percent of the bank's paid-in capital and reserves as of January 1 of the year in question, after adjusting for inflation during the intervening period" (Article 119).

A primary element for proper operation of the law is a set of indicators that accurately describe a bank's soundness. Such indicators should give timely notice of impending asset or liquidity problems, given the strong emphasis that the law lays on anticipating banking distress. The Chilean law seems to be unique in the amount of information delivered to economic agents regarding the financial condition of each banking institution. The Superintendency of Banks is explicitly forbidden by law to permit any accounting delay in recognizing a bank's losses (Article 14). At the same time the Superintendency is required to publish in a newspaper of national circulation, at least three times a year, a detailed report on each bank's compliance with capital requirements and the results of a procedure by which assets are rated according to an estimate of expected losses (Article 13 *bis*). This practice is apparently unique in Latin America and has been in force since 1987. Through the end of 1989 seven such publications had been made.

In addition the banking law (Article 20) and the security market law (Law No. 18,660) set significant limits to "bank secrecy," which have been reduced exclusively to protecting a depositor's privacy.

Removal of this legal barrier is a major step in the new legislation, for exaggerated bank secrecy in the past—and also in other countries—was one cause of bank problems that eventually required government intervention.

Based on the new legislation, private risk-rating firms were organized to evaluate the condition of banks in order to provide information to depositors. Under the law each banking institution must be subject to two private ratings each year.[7] The task of rating the level of portfolio risk is of course highly complex. Moreover, the liberal view cannot comfortably accommodate the fact that the Superintendency of Banks should directly or indirectly conduct the process. Although problems are undeniably linked to this method, some degree of government guarantee on bank debts unavoidably gives the Superintendency of Banks a degree of responsibility for bank supervision.

From the standpoint of financial stability and suppression of discretionary practices, it would of course be highly beneficial if some form of impersonal procedure could be found to rate banking portfolio risk, on the basis of a set of rules governing the size of provisions to be made by the bank, consistent with the level of portfolio risk. The present legislation is an effort to advance in that direction by giving the private sector a role in risk rating; it seems unlikely, however, that the action of the Superintendency of Banks could be regulated to the point of suppressing its discretionary authority. As mentioned before, the action of the superintendency in rating a bank's portfolio risk is the logical outcome of the need to keep up some degree of government guarantee on deposits and is intended to strengthen the stability of financial activity.

The new banking law also contemplates additional liquidity requirements designed to improve the ability of banks to face possible changes in the volume of demand deposits. The presence of liquidity problems that could possibly affect a bank's ability to meet its demand deposit obligations is revealed when the bank fails to comply with the provision requiring a technical reserve to be maintained for any demand deposits exceeding two and one-half times its capital. A bank must report the failure to comply with this provision to the Superintendency of Banks on the next business day following the event, along with the steps it plans to take to comply with the regulation. Should such failure continue for more than fifteen days, the bank's board of directors must submit a recapitalization proposal to creditors, except those with priority status, as in the case of demand deposits. In any event the superintendent of banks has the power to designate a provisional administrator or to order the bank to liquidate.

Another case of liquidity problems covered in the law is the repeated violation of the financial management requirements imposed by the central bank on a specific commercial bank that has been granted emergency loans for more than fifteen days or has renewed those already existing. In such cases the law presumes that there is an ongoing liquidity problem.

A major issue in the new banking law, which stems from the financial crisis in Chile and elsewhere in Latin America, is the establishment of stringent restrictions on the power of banks to do business with related parties. The various loans granted to firms owned by the same group of shareholders are viewed as a single individual loan subject to relevant loan limitations—5 percent or 25 percent of the bank's capital and reserves, depending on whether valid guarantees are involved (Article 84, No. 2). In addition, the agreed-upon terms for such debt must be market terms. The superintendency is also legally empowered to object to various kinds of contracts executed by the bank and related parties (Article 19 *bis*).

Adjustment mechanisms. As mentioned before, one of the fundamental elements in the framework of the new Chilean financial legislation is the explicit recognition that part of a bank's liabilities may not necessarily be fully convertible so that, as a result, the risks of bank operations are shared by stockholders, depositors, and the state.

The basic elements of the adjustment process, discussed in the following subsection, are outlined here:

1. The law provides for full convertibility of liquid debts in the banking system, where liquid debts are defined as close substitutes of central bank money; that is, demand deposits and time deposits with a residual maturity of ten days or less. To avoid disturbing the means of payment in the economy in the event of a banking crisis, debt service is ensured by support from the central bank. To minimize the effect on monetary policy of distress in the financial sector, whether in isolated cases or overall, the banking law requires each commercial bank to set up a technical reserve for liquid debts exceeding two and one-half times the bank's capital and reserves (Article 80 *bis*). This requirement is designed to prevent runs on banks that might jeopardize normal operations of the economy's payments system. Simultaneously, this provision induces banks to structure liabilities in a more conservative fashion, for illiquidity risks are thereby penalized.

2. In the event of moderate solvency problems the new law peremptorily requires stockholders to put back an amount of capital sufficient to ensure a debt/equity ratio of 20:1 (Article 116).

3. In the event of severe ongoing insolvency or illiquidity problems, which have not been possible to overcome through the usual banking-market channels—such as capital replenishment, sale of a portion of the loan portfolios, or merger—the law provides that creditors or depositors holding bank debt, except holders of liquid liabilities, may enter into an agreement with the distressed bank whereby the debt is converted into capital in the bank. Such an agreement by creditors safeguards the bank's continuity as a firm in operation and provides an alternative to liquidation by the bank's creditors (Articles 118–125).

   The attractiveness of this mechanism has recently been reinforced by a new amendment to the law. The amendment's intent is to minimize conflicts among the parties by granting a number of benefits to creditors who are required to turn their deposits into shares. To this end the law provides for a basic debt/equity swap agreement in an amount sufficient to return the bank to a debt-equity ratio of 14:1. The law also provides for repurchase of such shares with bank surpluses belonging to the original share-holders (Articles 121 and 124).

The operative mechanism of these agreements is a key part of the new law and incorporates the principle of shared risks. As before, in an environment of conservative banking regulation and abundant market information, this procedure breaks away from full convertibility of bank debt and gives way to a floating scheme that depends on the price of the bank's assets. In establishing this mechanism, much weight was attached to Chile's experience during the period of full, explicit, or de facto state guarantee on deposits. The establishment of this mechanism also suggests a pessimistic view of the prospect of setting up a deposit guarantee fund, aside from central bank contributions, that is financed by differentiated premiums duly calculated according to the risks assumed.

4. As a result of the crisis suffered in 1981–1983, the government was forced to grant full guarantee on deposits until 1986, when the banking rehabilitation program was completed. Subsequently, as a transitional measure in 1987 and 1988, guarantee was granted upon payment of a uniform premium by the financial system, to which financial institutions adhered on a voluntary basis; the guarantee involved gradual reduction of insurance coverage from 90 percent in early 1987 to 60 percent at the end of 1988 (Transitional Article 1, Law No. 18,576).

   Now that this transitional period has ended, a form of government guarantee remains, free of charge, which involves 90 percent of deposits held by small-scale investors (about U.S. $2,000 each). In practice this provision effectively puts an end to the government guarantee on bank liabilities (time de-posits) and becomes the keystone of the new financial regulatory system (Articles 141–150).

5. Finally, in an effort to privatize the costs of a banking crisis and promote self-regulation in the market, the law allows private

banking institutions to share in rescuing a bank in distress by granting a subordinate loan accountable as capital (Article 137). Clearly, to the extent that "sound" banks perceive a greater risk in the externality arising from a run on the bank than in investment, they will be prepared to make use of this mechanism. In addition it is reasonable to assume that the banks participating in such a capitalization will impose clauses on the loan in order to improve the probability of its repayment.

The adjustment process. As mentioned, one of the major innovations included in the current Chilean banking legislation is the establishment of private adjustment channels to resolve difficulties in a bank's financial situation. The purpose of these channels is to prevent government intervention from being the only option available to overcome difficulties affecting the financial sector. The Chilean banking law retains the legal category of intervention by the Superintendency of Banks in financial institutions as a way to respond to nonperforming managements or repeated violations of the law. Nevertheless, the possibility of avoiding government intervention is critically dependent on the ability to diagnose and undertake the solution to a crisis in a financial institution at an early stage. It is thus reasonable to think that the private sector will take a positive role in capitalizing a bank if it can be ascertained that the bank's difficulties are minor and do not compromise its medium-term performance. Conversely, if a recapitalization proposal (discussed later) is submitted to a bank's creditors in a context of serious bank distress, then, even if creditors must share in the financial restructuring, it is highly likely that a flight of deposits to other banks will ensue, compounding the distress and finally calling for official intervention. Both from the standpoint of watching over economic stability and in order to enhance the privatization of the bank adjustment process, therefore, the necessary tools should be designed to detect financial difficulties at an early stage.

In order to contribute to a swift solution of liquidity and/or solvency problems affecting the normal operation of a financial institution, the law contemplates specific situations that would trigger an adjustment process. There is the case of noncompliance with the technical reserve requirement, which requires a creditor recapitalization proposal if the problem is not promptly resolved. The same applies if the bank's debt/equity ratio is higher than 20:1 as of January 1 of any given year. Bank recapitalization is also in order when the value of assets adjusted by nonprovisioned losses is less than 40 percent of capital or when the bank finds it difficult to meet its obligations. Ongoing illiquidity is also assumed when the rules for the central bank's lender-of-last-resort loans have been repeatedly violated (Article 119).

It is worth noting that these provisions, especially regarding solvency, are quite stringent, in the sense that fairly moderate variations in the value of bank assets require speedy adoption of capital adjustment policies. In principle these rules, which might be viewed as a source of financial instability, in fact help to make the shared-risk scheme possible, for they encourage bankers to adopt more conservative policies.

The main aspects of adjustment mechanisms for a bank's assets in the event of financial distress are described in the following section, with special reference to alternatives to government intervention.

The recapitalization proposal. The recapitalization proposal, which in essence is an adjustment in bank net worth by variation of the "exchange rate" of its obligations, may take the form of

1. Total or partial capitalization of bank liabilities

2. Extension of nonpreferential debt maturities

3. Remission of part of the debt

4. Any other legal method with respect to debt payment between a bank and its creditors

As in the external debt agreements, this agreement contains a *pari passu* clause to the effect that all recapitalization proposals must be similar for all applicable creditors. This provision is complemented by the central bank's agreement to make available to the bank any amounts required for the necessary convertibility of demand deposits.

After the board of directors of a bank has identified a situation in which the institution is undergoing solvency or liquidity difficulties, the board must make a recapitalization proposal to its creditors, except preferential ones. Detection by bank management of problems in the bank's financial statements thus opens an adjustment channel through which creditors help to raise bank capital and thereby alter the structure of liabilities to restore a more solid asset position.

As we have already pointed out, the effectiveness of bank capitalization through a creditors' recapitalization proposal depends primarily on the magnitude of the difficulties to be resolved. The prompt response of management to problems threatening to affect the bank's asset position makes a creditors' agreement more likely to succeed as an adjustment tool. In particular the magnitude of the problems faced by the institution not only determines the feasibility of counting on the agreement as the sole adjustment variable but also affects the reaction of creditors and depositors at large regarding the funds they keep in the bank once the agreement has been concluded.

In this context, bank management is faced with conflicting motivations. On the one hand, adverse operational results in the bank make prompt action necessary to minimize the cost of adjustment. On the other, there is a strong tendency to defer adjustment as long as possible to try to reverse the unfavorable results and preserve the status of the bank president or director. The decision whether or not to defer is made by the bank management in the space allowed by regulations of the Superintendency of Banks, which sets the adjustment process in motion by force of law.

In the original version of the amendments to the bank law introduced in 1986 the board had to submit a recapitalization proposal to creditors once the existence of problems affecting the bank's solvency was confirmed. The creditors had to evaluate this proposal and vote approval or disapproval within fifteen days of the date of the proposal's publication in the *Official Gazette*. The proposal in question was deemed accepted when approved by creditors representing the majority of the total voting liabilities. Should the recapitalization proposal be rejected by the creditors, however, mandatory liquidation of the bank would ensue, upon a favorable resolution of the Superintendency of Banks and the central bank.

In the original version of the banking law these amendments gave creditors few options and practically forced them to approve the recapitalization proposal as submitted by the bank's board; otherwise, they would have faced mandatory liquidation of the bank.[8] Moreover, under the law the liquidator had three years to complete his task, which entailed an additional cost to creditors, aside from the uncertainty as to the amount of the capital increase required by the bank. In spite of the obvious benefits to the normal operation of a market economy and to macroeconomic stability arising from the existence of private channels to adjust bank asset problems, it therefore appeared that the creditors' recapitalization formula, as originally set forth in the 1986 amendments to the banking law, could have been used by a bank's board of directors to exploit the bank's creditors, in as much as rejection of their proposal would lead to mandatory liquidation of the bank.

The difficulties surrounding the creditors' recapitalization formula in its original form produced a bias in favor of applying the traditional intervention scheme to confront banking problems. For this reason amendments were made in 1989 to strengthen the ability of the creditors' recapitalization proposal to resolve a bank's problems by means of an analysis by the Superintendency of Banks of the proposal's capacity to obtain actual improvement of the bank's financial statements. In addition, the amendment contemplated a "standard" recapitalization proposal for cases in which the formula originally submitted by the board was rejected:

> The recapitalization proposal made by the board shall be judged by the Superintendency of Banks with regard to its effect on the actual improvement of the financial institution, in particular, whether the

partial remission of debts proposed is indispensable. The Superintendency will issue a ruling within five business days; should it fail to do so, the creditors' recapitalization proposal may be submitted. If the Superintendency raises objections the board shall accept them within two business days. If the board's proposal is rejected or the objections of the Superintendency are disregarded, a recapitalization proposal shall be submitted as provided under article 121.[9]

The following "standard" recapitalization proposal is submitted to creditors for consideration once the original proposal of the board has been rejected:

> If the recapitalization proposal made by the board of directors is rejected, the board within the next three days shall submit to the same creditors another proposal based on reducing the bank's deposits and obligations to third parties to fourteen times its paid-in capital and reserves, by capitalizing the relevant credits. In the case of a "financiera," the reduction will be to ten times.[10]

If, however, this further proposal is also rejected by creditors, mandatory liquidation applies.

Clearly the recent amendments to the bank law governing the use of a recapitalization proposal are designed to offer an intermediate option between the board's initial proposal and mandatory liquidation, so as to place a "floor" on the volume of nonpreferential deposits in the bank open to capitalization.

Mandatory liquidation. If it proves impossible to resolve the bank's net worth problems by a creditors' recapitalization proposal, or if the superintendent finds that the bank lacks the necessary solvency to continue in operation, the bank's charter will be revoked and the bank will be declared under mandatory liquidation, following a resolution to that effect by the Executive Committee of the Central Bank of Chile. As mentioned, the liquidator designated by the Superintendency of Banks will have a renewable period of three years to carry out this task.

Consistent with the spirit of the law, the available cash funds invested in central bank notes will be used to ensure convertibility of demand deposits. If such funds are insufficient, the central bank will put up the necessary resources and give preference to those creditors over others who do not hold demand deposits.

Mandatory liquidation implies a number of priorities, and thus the liquidator must first reserve resources as necessary to meet the costs of liquidation and pay off preferential creditors, then distribute the balance among ordinary creditors in proportion to the amount of their respective credits. Finally, the Superintendency of Banks may give shareholders any resources available after paying off the credits of depositors and other creditors and covering liquidation costs.

Interbank capitalization. Another alternative for confronting solvency problems in a financial institution is an interbank loan to strengthen the capital position of the distressed bank. The terms and conditions of such a loan must be agreed upon in the stockholders' meetings of both financial institutions and must also be approved by the Superintendency of Banks. Under prevailing legislation no bank may grant loans of this nature in an amount equivalent to more than 25 percent of its paid-in capital and reserves.

This loan will be treated as capital of the borrowing bank, for purposes of the margins provided in the banking law, and may be repaid only if the debtor bank is duly capitalized, irrespective of the loan.

Under the law, if the loan is not repaid within the agreed-upon term, it may (1) be capitalized if the two banking institutions merge; (2) be used for making a capital increase as resolved by the lending institution, provided the shares issued are underwritten by a third party; and (3) be used to underwrite and pay for a capital contribution. In this event the shares acquired shall be disposed of in a formal secondary market within 180 days from the date of capitalization.

This mechanism offers a private adjustment channel for the bank's net worth position as an alternative to submission of a creditors' recapitalization proposal. If problems are discovered that affect the solvency of a particular bank, it is reasonable to think that other banks will be interested in helping to rehabilitate it if they believe that the difficulties requiring replenishment of the bank's capital can be resolved within a reasonable period. To avoid the cost of calling a creditors' recapitalization proposal and of intervention, the management of the bank in distress may want to negotiate such a loan with other banks in a stronger financial position. Granting this loan may not only be good business for the lending bank but it is also backed by whatever share of the market the distressed bank may have. If the loan's agreed-upon terms and conditions are not met, the lending bank is likely to capitalize the loan and take over management of the debtor bank, thus benefiting from possible scale economies in the financial intermediation operations of both banks.

This interbank support mechanism basically encourages private negotiation among the parties. It differs in this respect from deposit guarantee funds operating in certain countries, such as the United States and Spain. The Spanish deposit guarantee fund provides limited guarantee to depositors in the event that a bank suspends payments or becomes bankrupt. The fund can also take over control of the distressed bank should the latter prove unable to overcome its difficulties on its own. Thus, in the words of one analyst,

> The Fund is an institution that acquires banks in distress as one of its essential aims, in order to restore such banks to a sound footing in a fairly brief period. To this end, the Fund takes over direct control by underwriting the increase in equity capital of banks in financial distress owing to explicit or implicit losses jeopardizing the bank's normal operation and necessary solvency.[11]

Unlike the Chilean case, this fund is formally part of the Spanish financial organization and operates with the support of the banks and Banco de España. Private banks join the fund or withdraw from it voluntarily, and the fund operates in the purview of the Ministry of Economic Affairs.

Under Chilean banking legislation the prospect of interbank support loans is limited by banks' available capital and does not depend on an institutionally organized "mutual aid association."

Should such an association arise, however—for example, through banking syndicates that would guarantee the convertibility of members' debts—the degree of supervision exercised by the association on the quality of the members' portfolio would very likely be at least as stringent as that of the Superintendency of Banks in order to safeguard the reputation of the syndicated banks.[12]

Potential Weaknesses of the Devices of the Banking Law

The broad measures of banking-market liberalization enacted after 1975 did not initially pay enough attention to strengthening the institutional mechanisms for regulation and supervision. The post-1986 amendments to the banking law represent significant steps toward preventing a repetition of the problems of the early 1980s. These amendments appear to preserve the solvency and stability of the banking system in a competitive environment.

Nonetheless, an effort should be made to pinpoint possible weaknesses in the Chilean system. To begin with, it should be recognized that the experience is unique and that the system is still new. The qualities of the system will become apparent only in the course of time.

Similarly, despite the rigorous delineation of the mechanisms involved and the law's shared-risk philosophy, it is very difficult to give an unambiguous opinion concerning the stability that it offers to the financial system, primarily because in the past four years the Chilean economy has enjoyed a sound economic position with appreciable GDP growth and successful macroeconomic management. In the face of sectoral or external shocks, for instance, the indicators of financial market conditions will show a decline in the net worth position of banks. Obviously, no banking law can hold back the damage caused by a major shock; however, a regulatory scheme that systematically moderates the risks assumed and that promptly triggers asset adjustment mechanisms will tend to reduce the vulnerability of the system in the face of such disturbances, provided that it contains incentives for proper assessment of the risk involved in intermediation.[13]

In all countries, but perhaps especially in small countries exposed from time to time to economic and political fluctuations, the first steps taken to overcome an economic crisis often depend substantially on the individuals with authority to face the crisis. The use of private adjustment mechanisms for banking problems may be virtually nullified if the authorities prefer historical support measures based on bank intervention.

In countries with a tradition of governmental guarantee on deposits the establishment of adjustment devices such as those provided by the Chilean banking law will always clash with the general public's ignorance on the subject or with popular expectations arising from such a guarantee. Although the promotion of transparency schemes partly helps to resolve the problem, there will nevertheless always be a disparity between the information costs of institutional investors and those of other depositors that might warrant government intervention for the sake of small-scale depositors.[14]

Finally, the strict application of such adjustment devices in Chile may be limited in the near future, given that a substantial portion of banking rehabilitation following the crisis of 1981–1983 was conducted with the help of government financing through popular capitalism and the sale of the banking system's past-due loan portfolio to the central bank.

The 1986 Law and the Evolution of the Financial System

The Chilean economy today exhibits a reasonable degree of monetization and financial deepening. A brief examination of the financial market shows that the Chilean banking community handles financial assets on the order of U.S. $21.2 billion (about 95 percent of GDP), which break down into U.S. $13.5 billion in loans and U.S. $7.7 billion in holdings of financial investments. Total deposits and domestic financial obligations amount to about U.S. $11.7 billion, and the assets held by all banking institutions add up to some U.S. $1.9 billion, in the hands of forty-one banks and *financieras*. By loan volume, domestic banking institutions constitute 70 percent of the market, Banco del Estado de Chile constitutes 17 percent, and branches and affiliates of foreign banks, about twenty in all, more or less cover the remaining 13 percent.

According to information available for January 1987 to April 1989, the dynamics of the financial system following the 1986 amendments to the banking law show substantial growth in intermediation levels. Loans increased at an average annual rate of 7.4 percent, while domestic demand and time deposits averaged 10.6 percent annual growth. Both figures grew somewhat faster than GDP.

From another angle, the different treatment that the law grants to demand as opposed to time deposits does not seem to have affected either type of deposit to date. The behavior of demand deposits has in fact been rather erratic, apparently influenced by variations in money demand during the period.[15] Time deposits, supposedly more seriously affected by the lack of deposit guarantee, have grown at highly positive uniform real rates, averaging about 15 percent, far beyond GDP growth rates.

It is interesting to explore whether the mechanisms of the banking law have realigned the market toward institutions perceived as safer or endowed with more than average support—specifically, whether investors have tended to prefer Banco del Estado de Chile or foreign banks to domestic financial institutions. Contrary to what one might have expected, the participation of domestic banks in total domestic banking obligations has tended to increase. The most relevant case is participation in total time deposits, where the share of deposits held by domestic institutions rose from 56 percent in 1986 to 63 percent in April 1989.

A substantial increase in local borrowings from the public by domestic banks stems from an effort to replace foreign obligations by peso liabilities as part of the intense process of foreign debt repayment and conversion into domestic assets that began in

1985. Isolating this factor, the next question is whether private banking institutions have declined, with respect to Banco del Estado and foreign banks, in their volume of operations, especially loans. The figures for 1987–1989 show that domestic banking institutions have gained ground considerably, relative to the greater dynamism shown by foreign banks before 1985. While the share of domestic banks has risen in real terms at annual rates on the order of 8 percent, somewhat lower than the 10-percent rate of foreign banks, the former have retained their share in the market at about 70 percent.

At the same time the relative share of bank obligations to total financial assets has declined from 55 percent in 1985 to 44 percent in 1989. To say that this is the result of amendments to banking legislation would be unreasonable. Rather, the explanation seems to lie in the severe shock of the crisis in the capital market and the subsequent recovery, along with the increased rate of economic activity and favorable business expectations. In addition, the Chilean authorities have modernized the legislation governing the nonbanking capital market. Finally, it is not surprising that as the degree of financial modernization grows in a country, there is an inevitable tendency toward the development of more sophisticated forms of financial intermediation.[16]

It is worth wondering whether the conservative nature of the shared-risk scheme and the supervision system that links bank provisions and net worth to the outcome of loan portfolio ratings have distorted the structure or competitiveness of the banking market. Although we have not conducted an exhaustive study, it appears that few symptoms have justified such concern. For example, in late 1986 the Herfindahl concentration index was 0.1027, against 0.0825 in late 1988. Similarly, in the same period the share of the five main institutions in total loans fell from 61 percent to 55 percent and intermediation costs, though slightly higher according to partial information available, have been within reasonable bounds. Indeed, the real average rate of gross annual return on financial assets has stabilized at between 3.0 percent and 3.3 percent, while the average spread between deposit and lending rates ranges between 3 percent and 3.8 percent.[17]

These figures indicate that the new institutional scheme enforced in Chile since late 1986 has not engendered enough uncertainty to block the development of the banking industry. On the contrary, it appears to have stabilized that development as the process of risk internalization progresses.

We wish to emphasize, however, that the system has been operating for only a few years and that both Chilean banking and the Chilean economy are going through an extremely favorable period of growth. From 1986 through 1989 GDP has shown sustained growth at an annual rate of more than 6 percent, while bank surpluses from 1987 through 1989 accounted for an average return of 19 percent on the industry's capital, up from 12 percent from 1985 through 1986. Obviously, the healthy asset position prevailing today in the financial system contributes to the system's strong performance.[18] Consequently, time is still required to demonstrate the full benefits of Chile's new banking legislation.

Kenneth E. Scott

Comment

The paper by Messrs. Ramírez and Rosende starts by saying that it is descriptive, not analytical. I think that is being a bit modest, because there is clearly an underlying analytical perception in the chapter and in the legislation.

I want to begin by taking as given that banks are going to experience external shocks from time to time that are of a sufficient magnitude to produce losses throughout the banking system. Their origins may be domestic, such as unstable fiscal or monetary policy, or foreign, such as an international recession or the formation of an oil cartel.

Note that I think the kind of shock we are talking about gives the lie to the fraud explanation of what happened in Texas or the Southwest. Here is the current issue of *Common Cause* magazine: "It's a Wonderful Life, the Sequel." "The harrowing epic of a small town S&L gone bad, starring Jimmy 'the Greek' Stewart as 'Bailout' Bailey," and so on. "Warning: This movie contains explicit scenes of unbridled greed."

Well, it may contain scenes of unbridled greed, but that is not exactly the same thing as fraud. Fraud, I think, is not much of a problem for the stability of the banking system. It creates losses, but it is essentially idiosyncratic. It does not create a wave of failures that tends to swamp the whole system. Why would there be an epidemic of fraud in Texas? Are the bank examiners like Typhoid Mary, carrying the disease from one bank to the next?

If you assume that there are going to be periodic waves of losses, then it seems to me that in any country the existence of diversification just means that you are going to encounter them maybe a little less often. But how can Chilean banks be diversified? Chile is too small a country. It's like saying Oklahoma should be diversified.

So given periodic waves of losses, I think there are two related questions: Who is going to bear them? and How are you going to minimize them? It seems to me that the second is the more important. In his comment on Paul Horvitz's paper, Peter Diamond suggested that whether taxpayers or depositors bear the brunt of banking losses may not make a huge difference as to the consequence of those losses. The obvious response, I suppose, is that if the private owners and management of a bank bear the losses, they have the incentives to monitor and minimize risk exposure and loss, whereas if the government bears the loss, the owners and managers lack those incentives, and worse still, they have incentives to create greater risk exposure and loss. This is the moral hazard issue.

If that is true, then the initial question would have to be, Why don't you leave the matter of loss minimization fully private? I think the paper and the literature tend to offer three kinds of response to that, and two of them the legislation addresses to some extent.

One reason for not leaving this matter solely private is the run contagion argument—that you are going to have a large number of unnecessary secondary failures of solvent but illiquid institutions. The argument is that the public is unable to distinguish the solvent from the insolvent institution, and therefore many solvent banks are unnecessarily terminated.

Whether that is factually correct as a matter of history is disputable, I believe. The legislation, in any event, addresses that issue. If there is a run contagion problem, it is an information externality and the legislators tried to do something about increasing the amount of information available to the market with respect to the condition of banks. Does that eliminate the problem? No. What they hope is that they have alleviated the problem significantly. It will be interesting to see how that works.

The second argument for not leaving loss minimization to private handling is that bank failures may disrupt the payment system, which can create losses for other participants. It has never been clear to me that this is necessarily a matter of externality, because the other participants are all linked in contractual chains of arrangements and can adjust pricing and monitoring and other behavior with one another to try to reduce this kind of risk.

How do the Chilean legislators address such a risk? Essentially they provide free deposit insurance to sight deposits and to a certain fraction of term deposits. Guillermo Ramírez estimated that it represents insurance of about 40 percent of the liabilities in the banking system.

The fraction remains at 40 percent, however, only if the political pressure toward full bailouts of depositors—the third explanation for deposit insurance—is effectively resisted. Even if it were, there would still be perverse incentives created by the government's free risk bearing of 40 percent of the liabilities of the system.

It is the perverse incentive problem, it seems to me, that hurt the United States in the S&L disaster on two levels: Preinsolvency and postinsolvency. On the preinsolvency level, free deposit insurance obviously constitutes a subsidy to risk taking. So there will be more risk taking; the bank is not going to have to pay the full added cost of the additional risk to the holders of insured liabilities. The postinsolvency problem is the explosion of gambling behavior that we witnessed throughout the savings and loan industry. If you leave the old management and stockholders in operating control, if you do not have closure, you will get a lot of "bet the bank" activity.

In addition to these two private incentive problems, there is also a governmental incentive problem involving management of the banking system and of the insurance scheme. First, take the preinsolvency subsidy to private risk taking. What is the Chilean response to that as indicated by the legislation? In large part it seems to me they are relying on supervision to monitor and control that added exposure. It is what was at one time favorably touted in this country as preventive supervision. You try to keep the institution from getting into a position of added or, in the supervisor's language, "excessive" risk.

I think that approach is unrealistic because it fails to recognize the limits of effective supervision. Supervisors have much poorer information than the management of the institution. They get that information with a time lag, they add to the time lag as they process the information through their organization, and they can never undo positions already taken.

As I indicated in an earlier remark, it seems to me that if management of the institution wants a certain risk profile, supervision and regulation simply cannot effectively keep them from attaining that goal. I therefore doubt that the 1980s experience demonstrates a genuine failure of supervision at this preinsolvency level, either in Chile or in the United States. I think the objective was simply beyond supervisory capacity.

Another way to try to deal with the issue of risk subsidy is to make the insured obligations essentially risk-free. You can address that through capital requirements. There is, for example, a provision (Article 80) in the Chilean law for a so-called "technical" reserve, which in a sense is a 100-percent collateralization of sight obligations beyond a certain level.

If you make those requirements high enough, I suppose it is a workable strategy. It certainly is the strategy that all the major banking authorities around the world are trying to promote under the Basle accord of July 1988.

The problem is that the capital numbers that would be required to make the debt truly risk-free are quite high, and the numbers in the legislation and the Basle accord are not that high.

In the Chilean law (Article 81) the minimum level of debt to equity is presently 20 to 1, or about a 5 percent capital requirement. Operationally, as I understand it, they intend to try to achieve about a 6-percent capital level or slightly above that.

At those capital levels, however, the debt is still quite risky. Consumer credit or commercial credit companies, for example, normally operate at equity ratios twice as high or more, and they are still paying a substantial risk premium on their debt. So even under the kind of capital and collateralization arrangements in the law, it seems to me that the perverse incentive remains and the banks can be expected to exploit the free deposit guarantee by taking greater risk positions than they otherwise would.

The important point about the postinsolvency incentive problem is obviously that it is vital not to let banks operate with trivial or negative net worth. If we didn't learn anything else from Texas, we should have learned that.

Under the Chilean banking law, the closure rule is rather interesting. The statutory scheme (Article 116) is that below a debt/equity ratio of 20 to 1 or below an equity level of around 5 percent (which is supposed to be a risk-adjusted 5 percent, as I understand it), management has to raise more equity or it has to present a recapitalization proposal to the term creditors of the bank, which in essence will involve a swap of debt for equity on a pro-rata basis to restore the capitalization ratio to 20 to 1, or in the new draft legislation to perhaps 14 to 1. If this proposal is accepted by majority vote of the creditors, it binds all these nonguaranteed creditors.

This imposes added risk on the bank debt holders. If the proposal is not accepted by the creditors, the statutory scheme presumably calls for the bank to go into liquidation. Again, this assumes that the politicians do not succumb to bailout pressures.

That means in theory that either the bank is going to get more equity or it is going to be liquidated if it goes below the 5 percent capitalization level. At that point, it would be below 5 percent but supposedly not insolvent, so the only losses on liquidation should go to the stockholders.

I think there are some foreseeable problems here. One is that these capitalization numbers, these debt/equity ratios, and these asset values and so on are presumably all book values. In other words, they are accounting numbers; they are historical costs; they are not current market values.

Interestingly, the banking law (Article 14) contains authority for the supervisor to prescribe accounting rules to show the "real situation" of the bank. Apparently, the supervisor has the power to try to move the Chilean system further in the direction of reflecting market values than, for example, we have yet moved our banking system. I hope he succeeds in such an endeavor.

Absent that, and maybe even with it, it is probable that banks may for some period of time be, first, economically insolvent, and second, under the control of private stockholders. This sets up the gambling explosion phenomenon.

When this process unfolds, banks become insolvent and gamble, and then, after a lag, the supervisors catch up and shut them down. If such insolvency is a result of random bad luck striking individual institutions, the state can probably absorb the losses without a lot of public complaint. The losses will be larger than they need be, but they may not be dramatic; that was the way we operated for the first fifty years of FDIC and FSLIC experience.

The real problem comes, as Paul Horvitz suggested earlier, when a series of shocks occur so that, first, many banks become insolvent, and second, their gambles mostly come up losers. Then you get an S&L-scale disaster.

If such a series of shock occurs, what can the supervisors do? I don't think they can prevent institutions from choosing to accept a higher risk policy than they would if they were paying the full risk premium to all their sources of financing, but with somewhat better information the supervisors can, at least in theory, respond to insolvency or near insolvency by takeover.

But now the problem of political incentives raises its head, as the authors clearly recognize throughout their chapter. I would like to direct my final comments to the issue that has come up a number of times already—the nature of incentives in the political dimension of this problem. Can you forestall a political bailout of all creditors? Or even worse, of stockholders as well? That is a more difficult issue, it seems to me.

The question is how you can alter political incentives. We can think of ways to alter the incentives of the management of the institution, but how can we alter the incentives of elected politicians?

I have no answer, but a few suggestions. Some of them are based upon the proposition that you may have different political dynamics *ex ante* and *ex post*.

Ex ante, before all this takes place, we may be able to reach a consensus that it is undesirable for the government to follow a bailout policy. The problem, of course, comes *ex post*, when the particular failures occur and there emerges a concentrated and effective lobbying group who may win financial concessions from a much more diffuse group of losers.

Bailout bills often pass in such situations—and not just for banks, but for Lockheed or for Chrysler or for other large enterprises that can muster this kind of concentrated political pressure. Then the question becomes, Can you devise some form of *ex ante* agreement that will make this *ex post* tendency to renege on a "no bailout" position harder to maintain? Can you adopt, for example, some kind of special metarule or constitutional rule to make it harder to alter a previous position? Suppose you put into the organic law an explicit repudiation of bailout. What you have in the Chilean banking law at the moment is not that in the least. What you have is tacit recognition of the prospect of bailout by the Central Bank of Chile and authority to proceed in that direction (see, for instance, Article 127). Suppose you want to try to forestall that course. How would you go about it?

You do find efforts to do that kind of thing, obviously, in written constitutions. That is the function of a constitution, to establish some kind of a metarule: for example, the Bill of Rights. You back it up with super-majority requirements for amendment and then you enforce it against the legislative and executive branches through the courts.

Can you do anything along these lines on less than the constitutional level? There are some efforts that I think are quite interesting on the legislative level.

Let me cite two examples from the last Congress. First, take the base-closing bill, which established a special procedure. The Defense Department has tried to close certain unneeded military bases for decades. Every time it tried to close them and get the necessary authorization from Congress, all the affected districts banded together and effectively log-rolled a veto against the base closure. But *ex ante* there was general agreement that there were a lot of unnecessary bases and it would make sense to close them.

How was that general principle upheld? The bill established a commission outside Congress to identify bases to be closed. This was not necessarily done on the basis of pure merit, but in any event the commission came up with a list.

Then you turn the burden around. Both houses have to override that list by legislation subject to presidential veto, or it goes into effect under the terms of the previous law. So in essence you have turned the veto position around.

Another example is the Gramm-Rudman deficit reduction legislation. If you want to get a waiver of what counts as a deficit under Gramm-Rudman—this is an issue that came up in the S&L bailout bill—what does it require? The waiver requires not a majority vote in the U.S. Senate; it requires a super-majority vote, a 60 percent vote.

These aren't foolproof devices, obviously. There are ways to get around any of these things if there is a determined and large legislative majority that wishes to do so. All you are doing is changing the odds. But by doing that you are making your "no bailout" pledge more credible and therefore making it more likely that management will act accordingly and without the perverse incentives that you are concerned about on the level of bank management.

A final thought on the subject: One can try to alter the structure of political pressures on the legislature. For example, suppose that in advance you identify the loser in the event of a bailout as not the taxpayers at large but a narrow, specified group.

For example, build into the insurance fund law some form of

ex-post levy on other financial institutions. That doesn't mean it stays there, but that is the way the law reads. All it takes to keep it there is a veto power.

If you have done that, what is the sequence? You have created a counterlobby to the institutions that are seeking the bailout, that are seeking to get the management of the banking agencies and the insurance funds to operate in their interest, because you have now created a smaller, more politically effective, concentrated group that has an incentive to avoid the *ex-post* assessment.

Are any of these measures guaranteed to work? No. Might they change the odds? I think so. At any rate, I think the subject is worth trying to think hard about, rather than just bemoaning the fact that we don't have a good clear answer to the political economy problems, which are a very real part of the problem.

At this point, though, on the basis of admittedly no more than a superficial acquaintance with Chilean banking legislation, my instinct is to wish Chile luck, because I fear that both we and they may still be in the same soup.

Response and Discussion

GUILLERMO RAMÍREZ: I appreciate Mr. Scott's comments on the paper, and would like to respond to two or three of his observations. I also invite Mr. Valdés and Mr. de la Cuadra to contribute to my response. Their knowledge of Chile's banking law is extensive. Indeed, my colleague Mr. de la Cuadra was an adviser in designing the law.

The law reflects an intensive effort to clearly circumscribe and define the role of the superintendent of banks and of the state more generally relative to the participation of the private sector. The role of the regulators in this case is twofold.

First, the role of the supervisor is to try to assess bank risk for the purpose of putting this information in the hands of the public. The idea is not just to try to produce prudential regulation to avoid 100 percent of the cost of a bank failure; the main idea is to put this information in the hands of the public.

For instance, every quarter we produce a loan classification according to risk. I am required to sign a resolution of each of these quarterly loan classifications, and their outcomes are published in the official magazine of the country. I believe this is a very strong way of disclosing information to the market.

The second role of the supervisor in this scheme is to attempt to approximate the accounting value of the assets to the market value. The intent of this inspection is to force banks to retain enough earnings to cover any risk that we found in the assets.

We even require evaluation by private experts of the value of the fixed assets of the banks. Then this must be adjusted to market value on the books of the bank.

This is more or less the role of the supervisor. They must not become involved in trying to produce the idea in the public that banks cannot fail because they are well regulated or well examined.

The second is the amount of the relation of equity to assets, which in this case is 5 percent. I believe that it could be important to have a better coefficient of equity to assets. I believe in practice that this 5 percent is not so bad for the following reasons. First, we put a lot of emphasis on trying to compute in this ratio all of the balance sheet liabilities. This is not assets to equity; it is liability to equity. The second is that we try to adjust asset and capital or equity to market value.

In many fields of life not all things depend on the law. Many things depend on individuals. Of course, political authority may change and despite the law may adopt some other decision. But I believe there are some facts in the Chilean banking law that probably help.

The main agent that takes the losses in Latin America is the central bank. We have approved another recent law by which the central bank is an autonomous institution backed by constitutional regulations. Of course, if the central bank has to be careful with its net worth, probably the central bank will be conscious of that and will not help banks with problems at once as in the past.

The other is not, of course, a final solution, but at least helps. In the same banking act is the obligation of the superintendents to make a decision as to the asset quality on site. If the law says depositors should take some part of the losses, it is more difficult just to pay, based on political decisions. Of course, a more generic banking act that says nothing about this could be a worse situation. Thank you.

PHILIP BROCK: I think at this point comments that give more information about the law will be helpful to everybody here.

SALVADOR VALDÉS: I will try to give more details about the current Chilean banking law in order for the audience to appreciate all the details. I think that Ken Scott provided a very clear outline for doing this.

First, the contagion among banks. I think that Guillermo Ramírez is right in saying that the law contains the obligation for the superintendency to publish a lot of the information it has gleaned from bank examinations. Risk classification of banks is regularly published.

I understand that Chile is now the only country in the world where the bank examiners publish such information. We have observed that the big pension funds keep special personnel looking at the risk rating of banks all the time. That allows us, in my view, to reduce contagion to a large extent because there is more information.

About protecting the means of payment and these externalities, the new Chilean law insures only the liquid liabilities of banks plus a small amount from small depositors. The main thing is liquid liabilities, and those are sight deposits and deposits payable on demand, and also those deposits that have a maturity less than thirty days.

In addition, any longer-term deposit is insured in the last ten days before its maturity. A 180-day deposit is insured during the last ten days before its maturity. That is a lot of the banking system liabilities, but it clearly protects explicitly the means of payment.

If you only do that, perverse incentives remain. I agree on that.

How does the law manage the remaining risk for the government treasury?

First, it does rely on supervision. Ken says it is unrealistic to rely too much on supervision. I think we can rely somewhat on that. Something can be gained from that.

Second, there are provisions for subordinated debt that were recently introduced. Subordinated debt holders would in the future be able to introduce some clauses that will allow them to intervene in the administration of a bank that gets into trouble. However, that is only a possibility for the future because no such thing has been issued up to now. The law that authorized that was approved, I think, a couple of months ago.

Finally, there is this issue about the risk-adjusted capital requirement. There is a lot of risk adjustment. The asset values that the bank can register are adjusted by the superintendent's assessment of risk. That is not a market value, of course, because there is no market, but at least it has a lot of information within. Only after subtracting those provisions is the 5 or 6 percent capital requirement assessed. So it is above those provisions.

Ken Scott points out that the required level of capital for a bank, say 5 percent, is still too small given the fact that almost 40 percent of bank liabilities are insured because almost 40 percent are liquid.

There is one element that is missing from that. The law provides for central bank loans to a bank in order to cover this liability to liquid deposit holders. But these central bank loans have priority in any capitalization swap procedure later. In effect, the government, although it is issuing this guarantee for 40 percent of the deposits and it requires only 5 percent capital, it also makes sure that the central bank loans required to cover the losses of demand deposit holders have priority over other creditors. So the effective risk for the government in insuring this is rather small. All that risk is shifted to the uninsured depositors.

What is actually very new from the Chilean banking law is this feature of forced capitalization in the sense that when a bank is declared insolvent, the superintendent can call for a swap where depositors get shares of the bank and part of their deposits are transformed into equity. That has to be voted on.

The only alternative of the depositors is liquidation. Our assessment is that liquidation is usually a very bad alternative, because you lose the operating value of the bank.

So that creates a potential source of funds to govern the losses. Uninsured depositors can be called upon to make up for the losses.

The problem is that the law, even though it creates this swap system, still keeps the alternative path, a takeover by the government. That paths means full insurance of all depositors. So the law is in this sense ambivalent.

PHILIP BROCK: The general way I view the Chilean banking legislation is in line with what Ken was saying about constitutions sometimes mattering. The question is whether regulations such as the ones adopted for Chile have any meaning at all in terms of the problems we are discussing or whether in the end they probably don't mean much.

GARY GORTON: One of the things I find intriguing about this law is its disclosure requirements.

Every theory of banking panics supposes in some form or another that the need for regulation emanates from information asymmetries. In a sense, then, it seems quite natural and quite logical to surmise that if such missing information can be supplied, then the problem of information externality would be to some extent, if not completely, mitigated.

I find this idea that the information should be published and that banks should have these independent ratings extremely interesting. It corresponds, I think, to the debate in the U.S. about whether the list of problem banks should be published or whether CAMEL (capital, assets, management, earnings, liquidity) ratings should be published, and so on.

I want to say a few things about this now. We can consider various scenarios here. Suppose that we have banks that rate 1, 2, or 3 (if they are the best, lowest risk, they are rated 1, and so on). In the absence of published information about these ratings, we would conclude that if the spreads between the rates of interest they pay on deposits and the appropriate risk-free rate were zero for all three categories, then everybody believed the implicit guarantee. If they were positive for all three categories, we would conclude that there is no implicit guarantee of insurance.

Now suppose we condition our judgment with knowledge gained by looking at the published information. We would expect the third category to have the highest spreads and the first category to have the lowest. To the extent that these spreads differ by rating, we might be led to conclude that the information on the riskiness of banks is in fact being represented in market prices and the information asymmetry is being eliminated.

It is not clear to me that any new information is necessarily provided. If there was no implicit guarantee, either people would have an incentive to produce this information themselves or if it really is extremely costly to produce, then we might be led to conclude that there is no implicit guarantee and it's in the market prices.

There is one slight problem with this. I think there is a natural tendency for government information producers or bank examiners to treat "type one" and "type two" errors differently than the market.

In the United States there is a lot of evidence that the error in bank examinations is the mistake of calling a good bank a bad bank. Of course you trade this off against the other error, and you end up calling many bad banks good banks.

For example, Penn Square's CAMEL rating six months before it collapsed was something like a 3, which would not be very good, but it wouldn't be what you expected for Penn Square six months before it failed. That suggests it would be hard to figure out why these spreads conditioned on the ratings are different.

I think it might be hard to unravel whether the information that is being announced and produced by these ratings agencies is really serving the right purpose. I think it's a great idea. Somebody should definitely study all this. I would be really interested to know the answers to these questions.

JOHN BOYD: I want to make one small observation on attempting to solve this incentive bailout problem via a constitutional amendment or something like that.

The very problem that you are trying to solve militates against ever passing the amendment. There is no strong public mandate behind a constitutional amendment in this country or, I suspect, in Chile at the present time. True, the public is to some extent upset because of the FSLIC bailout. However, the powers that be have done an extremely good job of clouding the bailout cost, spreading it over many years, etc. Thus, the expected public hue and cry has simply not occurred. Support for an amendment would be diffuse at best. At the same time, there are well-defined interest groups and effective lobbying organizations which would fight such an amendment tooth and nail.

I see the chances of actual passage as slim or none at all.

GARY GORTON: I disagree with that. I think that misunderstands one of the points that Ken made, which was that there is a difference between the *ex ante* situation and the *ex post* situation.

In the case of this counterlobby, which I thought was an excellent idea and was how nineteenth-century clearinghouses behaved, *ex ante* every bank might agree that if there is to be bailout *ex post*, we all agree *ex ante* that we are going to tax ourselves, thinking that this will prevent this state from occurring, and then *ex post*, if it occurs, the information is different.

So if you could get the *ex ante* agreement, it would change the incentives *ex post*.

JOHN BOYD: Wait a minute, Gary. I was not talking about the idea of setting up this incentive mechanism in advance. I was simply talking about the probability of passing a constitutional amendment along these lines. Although I don't make large wagers, I would be glad to make you a small wager that it won't happen in the next five years.

GARY GORTON: Since it's a small wager, I will extract the information for that.

SALVADOR VALDÉS: Concerning Gary's proposition about studying the spreads, actually I made an econometric study in Chile after this law was passed, trying to see if the spread would depend on the bank ratings, and it didn't at all. Maybe the data has been changing. I used data only up to a year and a half ago. That was when the law was first introduced. Maybe there is a learning process.

GUILLERMO RAMÍREZ: It is absolutely correct that it is difficult to convince the public. I agree that it is difficult. I am not 100 percent sure that the public will take into account this piece of information.

We tried to make every effort in that regard. For instance, in the case of Chile TV advertising of banks, the banks have to put in a very straightforward sentence that the state is not going to pay if that bank fails and therefore people should be informed about it.

During the last ten months two banks ran into difficulty. We observed these two banks were paying a higher interest rate on deposits. This was the case of Banco Nacional and Banco del Pacífico. This mechanism of the law, despite the fact that it is extremely young, in these two cases functioned rather well. Two banks in Chile is not meaningless, because we have just forty-five financial institutions. Medium-size banks and small banks account as groups for 6 to 7 percent of the total market.

It works. New owners bought these banks, and the state didn't put any money up. That was because of the scheme in the law requiring them to inform us as soon as possible of the problem at its outset.

The decision of the government in this case was that if no private investors were interested in these banks because they were not profitable, then a swap agreement would be called for.

But I believe it is very difficult to change the mind of the public. We have lived with fifty or sixty years in which the state always had to pay the bill. Therefore it is very deep in the mind of the people.

SALVADOR VALDÉS: I just wanted to add some institutional information about what Guillermo said. We have been talking as if the only two insolvency resolution procedures were either takeover and fully insure everybody or the swap agreement.

What Guillermo has pointed out is that the new law enacted in 1986 introduced several other mechanisms that are different. Basically they give powers to the superintendent to force the administration of a bank to engage in searching for partners and getting the original owners to put up more capital while it still has positive net worth but it is below 5 percent or 6 percent of assets.

He points out that in the last year there have been two banks that have gotten into trouble, but both of those cases could be managed through these intermediate procedures. Both of them found investors who put up new capital. So there was no need to make the hard choice between a full takeover and full guarantee and the swap procedure.

GARY GORTON: What happened to the spreads in the case of these two versus the other banks?

SALVADOR VALDÉS: My sample was up to before these problems came. That's the next research project.

PHILIP BROCK: In Chile the superintendent of banks collects information from all the banks who have to evaluate the loan quality of the loans to every single one of the borrowers from the bank. The superintendent gets to see how each bank rates each lender. For example, if four banks are rating low as to one firm, they are rating it as a C, and one bank is rating it as an A, the superintendent has information on that.

The superintendent also compiles all this information so each bank knows the total outstanding loans to a firm from the whole banking system although it doesn't know what the ratings are that have been given to it by other banks.

There is a tremendous amount of information that is being collected by the superintendency now and then being given back out to the banks. I think that is something else interesting about the way the system works.

CHARLES CALOMIRIS: My point relates to this question of whether the spreads should reflect anything about ratings. I may be misunderstanding the way this law works, but from what I understood from the discussion, when you get a rating of being a riskier firm, that also means that you will be required to maintain a higher amount of capital, or at least there is a good chance that you are going to have to come up with a higher amount of capital.

These capital requirements are risk-related; is that right? If that is right, then there are two alternative conclusions you could draw from the fact that the spreads don't reflect changes in the portfolio ratings.

You might conclude that there is implicit insurance for all these guys; nobody believes that the government is going to give anybody a haircut.

Alternatively, you might conclude that this law works very well because there is an automatic adjustment in capital to stabilize debt risk.

So I am not sure what to conclude from the spreads.

GARY GORTON: How about if we look at changes in the spreads?

I think you could unravel this by looking at when the ratings change, the response to when the ratings change. There should still be a difference. Suppose a bank is rated a 1, and then it goes to a 2. Your argument, I take it, is that this means that the bank is going to be forced to put up more capital. So conditional on that, they just do what, be a 1 again?

CHARLES CALOMIRIS: Even if they don't become a 1, they have to come up with more capital, and this is predictable. The combination of more capital and a higher risk portfolio may be roughly the same as less capital and a lower risk portfolio in their effects on the value of the subordinated debt.

5   *Charles W. Calomiris*

Do "Vulnerable" Economies Need Deposit Insurance? Lessons from U.S. Agriculture in the 1920s

To justify the substantial protection that governments offer banks, regulators frequently refer to banks' unique position as the channel through which payments clear and through which essential short-term commercial and working-capital credit is provided to parties whose access to other sources of funds is limited. Banks are "special" because all other industries rely on them to maintain their operations and execute their transactions in a timely, convenient way. In particular, whether one defines the payments system narrowly to include only check clearing or more broadly to include lines of short-term credit to bank borrowers, it would be hard to conceive of a payments system without banks.[1]

Thus, shocks that threaten the viability of banks, encourage financial disintermediation, and cause disruptive bank failures or suspensions of deposit convertibility can be very costly to society; and these costs may be far greater than the reduced profits, or bankruptcy costs, incurred by banks. In recent research the peculiar severity of the Great Depression and the vulnerability of agricultural producers to banking disturbances in the 1980s have received particular emphasis as examples of socially costly financial disruption (see Bernanke, 1983; Calomiris, Hubbard, and Stock, 1986). The externalities generated by banks' special roles as check-clearing agents and commercial credit suppliers, therefore, may provide a rationale for regulation of banks.

Notwithstanding this presumed vulnerability of the payments system and the essential role of banks, critics of current government interventions into banking have argued that the government has gone too far in guaranteeing bank liabilities and consequently has promoted an unacceptable degree of socially undesirable risk taking by banks. For example, from a theoretical perspective, Calomiris and Kahn (1991) argue that demandable-debt banking and the first-come, first-served rule of bank repayment to depositors were part of an incentive-compatible equilibrium in which informed depositors (often other banks) were rewarded for investing resources in monitoring banks. Insurance removes the reward, and hence the incentive, that encourages such monitoring. Insured banks' incentives to undertake excessively risky projects are magnified by shocks that reduce bank capital. Such shocks increase the bank's potential gain from pursuing long shots by increasing the implicit value of the put option inherent in deposit insurance (see also Merton, 1977). Empirical evidence of excessive risk taking by insured financial intermediaries, especially in response to adverse shocks that reduce bank capital, has been provided by Kane (1988) and Brewer (1991), among others.

Furthermore, critics argue that regulators underestimate to what extent the financial "safety net" can be provided with little or no government insurance of banks. For example, private clearinghouses historically provided coinsurance among member banks that reduced the incentive for depositors to remove funds from banks during periods of financial uncertainty. Mutual regulation and monitoring ensured that members would not get a free ride on the group protection (see Cannon, 1910; Gorton, 1985). Coordination among banks, sometimes even across state lines, was enhanced in and among states that permitted branch banking—in particular, in the antebellum American South (see Calomiris, 1989).[2] With fewer and better-diversified banks it was easier for banks to respond to crises as a group, again effectively coinsuring by continuing to "make markets" in other banks' deposits and notes.

Similarly, in three unit-banking states of the antebellum North, statewide bank liability insurance plans (which predated clearinghouse private coinsurance) managed to protect the payments system and limit (or eliminate) bank failures and suspensions of convertibility without encouraging excessive risk taking by members. These plans gave member banks authority to enact and enforce regulations and provided the incentive for effective self-regulation and monitoring by making member banks fully and mutually liable for the liabilities of any failing banks. These systems managed to maintain smooth functioning of the payments system within and across states and saw few, if any, bank failures relative to states that lacked an effective means of bank coordination. A review of the experiences of these antebellum bank insurance success stories, and the very different experiences of other state bank insurance schemes, is provided in Calomiris (1989).

The apparent lesson of historical bank clearinghouses, early Southern branch banking, and mutual-guarantee self-regulating insurance plans under government sponsorship is that banking coalitions can act to coinsure effectively against many threats to the payments system. The successful operation of private clearinghouses in today's financial markets—the Clearinghouse for Item Processing Services (CHIPS) network, for example, or the futures and options clearinghouses—indicates that these lessons can be applied successfully in the modern context as well.

Private coinsurance schemes, however, cannot offer unlimited protection against financial collapse in all circumstances. Private insurance is not effective in preventing disintermediation by depositors who question the ability of the coalition to guarantee the losses of its members. Once a shock becomes large enough to threaten the capital of the group of banks as a whole—rather than simply a small subset of its members—coinsurance ceases to be credible.

Furthermore, the geographic distribution of privately coinsuring groups—and consequently the potential for coinsurance—may be restricted by laws that limit branch banking and thus impair the ability of bankers in different locations to communicate, monitor one another, and coordinate their behavior. Most financial crises in U.S. history began as small disturbances, relative to aggregate bank capital, which were insurable in principle by mutual protection among banks. Reasonable fears of insolvency of a subset of banks, confusion as to which banks had suffered most from the shock, and the absence of a mechanism for mutual protection at the state or national level, however, provided incentives to depositors, who were unable to determine the precise incidence of the disturbance, to withdraw their funds (see Gorton, 1989; Calomiris and Gorton, 1991). Lacking effective means to coinsure against such disturbances, the thousands of independent and geographically distant unit banks were sometimes forced to suspend convertibility as a defensive reaction during such economywide bank runs. Suspensions of convertibility limited depositors' and noteholders' liquidity and reduced the desirability of placing funds in banks, thereby reducing the supply of loans and forcing banks to adopt more conservative lending practices than under normal circumstances. In a few cases, large numbers of banks were liquidated when the banking system failed to coordinate timely suspension (see Calomiris and Schweikart, 1991).

The relative success of statewide systems of branching banks, or mutual-liability banks, in meeting crises such as the Panic of 1857 suggests that, for an economy as diverse nationally as the United States, a combination of full nationwide branch banking and government-sponsored, privately managed mutual-liability insurance may be sufficient to prevent large sector- or region-specific shocks to bank capital from becoming a threat to aggregate bank capital and, therefore, the payments system.[3]

One could argue, however, that this approach might not be sufficient for economies with intrinsic vulnerability to large sector-specific shocks. In the United States, full interstate branching could virtually eliminate the risk to banks from regionally concentrated shocks to the terms of trade, which have proved particularly important for the agricultural and oil-producing sectors (see Alston, 1983; Stock, 1984; Calomiris, Hubbard, and Stock, 1986). In smaller countries with less-diversified economies, however, the risk from terms-of-trade shocks is large (see Brock, 1988), but the potential for reducing payments-system risk through diversification is more limited because national sovereignty limits the development of full international branch banking. These limitations can be viewed as an example of the "time inconsistency" problem. Banks chartered in country X may decide to leave their local branches in country Y stranded rather than pay for their losses during bad times, and there may be no way for country Y to force them to do so. Furthermore, governments may find it advantageous to limit the repatriation of bank profits to support bank branches in other countries.

The central question I will address in this paper is this: Should the governments of such intrinsically risky economies stand ready to rescue banks in the event of a large shock to the economic base? The question may be divided into two parts: How great are the advantages of a government's insuring the payments system (whether narrowly or broadly defined) from the strains of such shocks rather than relying on a privately administered, mutual-guarantee system? Are the social costs of excessive risk taking by banks, which the existence of bank deposit insurance engenders, greater or less than the supposed benefits of insurance?[4]

The specific historical cases I will discuss are the experiences of agricultural areas of the United States in the 1920s—a period that witnessed a rapid, sharp terms-of-trade reduction for agricultural producers and an unprecedented rate of farm, business, and bank failures in the most affected regions. The 1920s provide a particularly useful context to investigate the role of different regulatory regimes in reducing or magnifying the effects of the shock on financial intermediaries. Interstate branch banking was not permitted, although some states allowed full, or limited, intrastate branching. Furthermore, some states had enacted deposit insurance before the crisis. Finally, the existence in each state of nationally chartered banks (under a common regulatory regime across states) provides a point of comparison for the magnitude of the shock to banks in each state, the relative performance of the various state-chartered banking regimes, and the significance of deposit insurance or branch banking in magnifying or lessening the impact on banks.

In Calomiris (1989) I presented evidence from the 1920s of higher initial growth, and higher subsequent failure rates, for four state-chartered, insured banking systems relative to national banks operating in the same state, which were prohibited by the U.S. comptroller of the currency from joining state deposit insurance funds. While this comparison was a useful first step, it is important to establish that the differences between insured state-chartered and uninsured national-chartered bank failure rates are not merely an artifact of different exposure to agricultural risk, due to different locational patterns (rural or urban) for state- and national-chartered banks or more restrictive regulations on national-chartered banks— in particular, stricter limitations on real estate loans.[5] Here I look at all eight of the insured systems. I compare the performance of national- and state-chartered banks within and across states, taking account of differences in economic and regulatory environment (for example, the existence of branching and deposit insurance) and using additional indicators of bank performance.

No single historical example can provide a conclusive answer to the broad question of whether government deposit insurance is socially desirable in price-sensitive economies. Only through the accumulation of evidence—from examples of the costs of such crises and the consequences of the decisions to provide insurance or allow branching—will policy makers be able to make informed choices in the difficult matter of bank regulatory policy.

The following section provides cross-sectional evidence of price, income, and wealth movements and of indicators of financial distress experienced by various states in the 1920s. The next section measures changes in the size, number, and portfolio structure of national- and state-chartered banks before and during the crisis. The third section evaluates differences in the performance of the state-chartered banking systems in response to the crisis—specifically, differences in the rates of bank suspension and bank failure, the costs to depositors of failures, and the ability of the banking systems to recover from the crises under different state regulatory regimes. The fourth section returns to the central question of whether deposit insurance is desirable for economies with intrinsic vulnerability to large income disturbances.

The Post–World War I Agricultural Crisis

Typically, wars have been prosperous times for farmers. World War I, like the Napoleonic Wars and the Crimean War, witnessed a rapid expansion of agricultural income. As with previous wartime booms, however, the end of war brought a severe decline in the agricultural terms of trade. Declines in price and income translated into declines in farm land values. Farmers who had used debt financing to expand operations during the boom found their incomes slipping as their leverage ratios rose, often to levels that were unsustainable.

The crisis was quite sector- and region-specific. Indeed, for most sectors in the United States the 1920s were a "new age" of unprecedented stability and growth. In many states with a heavy reliance on agricultural earnings, however, the period was one of declining income and financial collapse.[6] Differences from state to state in the degree of agricultural stress reflected different movements in earnings and wealth, as well as differences in farmers' financial vulnerability to those declines.

Table 5.1 provides indices of real gross farm income and its components for 1910–1930. These figures show that the post–World War I decline in agricultural income affected virtually all producers, although the timing and severity of decline varied across activities, with staple foodstuffs and textile raw materials suffering the worst percentage declines from 1919 to 1921.

The uneven sectoral decline within agriculture produced different responses in income and wealth across states. Furthermore, Alston (1983) finds that similar reductions in farm wealth and earnings produced far greater rates of farm foreclosure in some states than in others. Holding declines in wealth and income constant, one finds that states that had expanded both farm acreage and farm leverage during the wartime boom suffered much higher rates of farm foreclosure.

Foreclosure rates for farms throughout the country during the 1920s and 1930s reached historic highs that have never been exceeded. For 1921–1940 foreclosure rates averaged more than five times the highest average levels for any other decade from 1913 to 1980. While the national average was high during the interwar period, the uneven incidence of foreclosure across states made matters far worse in some states. In Montana, from 1921 to 1923, 28 percent of farmers lost farms or property.[7] From 1926 to 1930, foreclosures in Montana relative to owner-operated farms in the state averaged 52.2 per thousand per year.[8] Other northern and western states with extremely high foreclosure rates (per thousand owner-operated farms per year) for 1926–1930 include South Dakota (70.4), North Dakota (58.0), Oklahoma (50.0), Iowa (48.3), Arizona (42.7), and Colorado (42.4). South Carolina (68.0), Georgia (56.5), Mississippi (47.7), and Louisiana (40.1) had substantially higher rates of foreclosure than the other southern states. Arkansas (39.7), Nebraska (38.4), Idaho (37.6), and Missouri (34.1) also experienced farm foreclosure rates considerably above the national average of 27.1 per thousand per year.

Tables 5.2 and 5.3 provide a variety of measures of economic conditions for each of the forty-eight contiguous states during the period 1919–1930. Table 5.2 contains data on the following: gross farm income change from 1919 to 1921; changes in total net income from all sources received by farm and by nonfarm populations from 1919 to 1921; the percentage difference in the value of crops sold from 1922 to 1925 and from 1925 to 1928; and the percentage change in the state-specific crop price index from 1919 to 1924.

Table 5.3 reports the change in the value of farm real estate per acre over the periods 1913–1920, 1920–1925, and 1925–1930; the ratio of mortgage debt to farm real estate value in 1920; the farm-to-total population ratio for 1920; and the farm foreclosure rate for 1926 to 1930.

The choices of dates for each series in Tables 5.2 and 5.3 reflect data availability as well as the peaks and troughs of the agricultural cycle. Whereas the income, wealth, and price variables in Tables 5.2 and 5.3 are all expressed in nominal terms rather than adjusted for aggregate price level movements, the GNP deflator was roughly constant for the years 1919–1929, except for 1920, according to recent estimates by both Romer (1989) and Balke and Gordon (1989). These estimates are reproduced in Table 5.4. Moreover, from the standpoint of the sustainability of farms and farmers' ability to repay debt to banks, it is nominal income and wealth that matter, since debt and debt service are set in nominal terms.

Tables 5.2 and 5.3 indicate that the first years of the agricultural crisis (1920–1930) can be divided into three stages: the initial shock of 1920–1921, a period of partial recovery from 1922 to 1924, and a subsequent period of decline. Because of differences in crop mix, supply-side variation, and financial vulnerability, the experiences of the various states differed considerably during these three stages, as the tables show.

No single indicator provides an adequate measure of the experience of a particular state during one of these stages. First, income and price indicators are extremely sensitive to the specific dates over which they are calculated. As an example, 1924 was a relatively good year for Montana and North Dakota; it differs markedly from either 1923 or 1925 in this respect. Second, some income or price movements are perceived as transitory, while others are viewed as more permanent. Aside from the immediate cash-flow effects of such

TABLE 5.1

Indices of Gross Farm Income, by Products and Total Production, 1910–1937 (1909–1913 = 100)

Year	Twelve important crops[a]	Staple foodstuffs[b]	Fruits[c]	Dairy and poultry products	Textile raw materials[d]	Meat animals[e]	Meat animals, adjusted[f]	Total farm production	Total farm production, adjusted[g]
1910	99.8	93.2	101.6	100.3	105.3	99.7	96.1	101.4	101.5
1911	97.6	97.7	106.8	88.7	96.0	89.9	83.0	95.3	94.2
1912	102.4	101.0	108.5	101.5	99.5	95.2	92.7	102.1	102.4
1913	101.3	99.6	102.4	103.9	110.0	107.7	110.9	105.6	107.7
1914	102.4	131.3	109.0	105.5	77.0	107.5	117.3	106.5	110.6
1915	112.1	146.5	117.7	104.5	85.9	104.4	112.2	110.1	113.6
1916	143.3	154.6	126.0	117.1	134.3	129.0	133.1	134.2	136.9
1917	220.3	222.2	147.3	158.6	201.6	180.8	189.5	194.6	199.2
1918	239.5	284.2	189.2	191.7	231.9	242.7	232.8	231.5	231.3
1919	269.4	326.2	260.7	223.1	255.4	239.0	219.5	253.5	250.5
1920	177.5	252.7	269.4	241.6	136.5	186.6	173.6	204.0	202.3
1921	109.6	150.7	183.5	173.8	84.7	116.4	112.5	132.6	132.8
1922	132.9	140.5	222.3	167.0	135.6	129.1	126.5	146.3	147.0
1923	150.2	127.3	203.1	189.4	179.2	132.0	122.5	160.0	158.7
1924	167.9	162.0	222.8	191.3	195.4	135.8	118.6	169.6	166.1

246

1925	167.9	176.4	223.6	211.9	198.8	163.2	147.4	182.8	180.0
1926	142.4	176.8	231.5	223.8	145.6	172.8	163.5	178.0	177.3
1927	156.6	177.3	220.1	223.6	167.6	158.9	155.2	179.5	180.2
1928	147.0	144.9	221.0	234.9	170.6	163.6	164.1	180.4	182.4
1929	143.7	159.7	233.6	245.0	161.7	171.4	172.6	184.1	186.4
1930	87.5	106.8	184.4	205.7	90.3	146.5	147.6	141.0	143.0
1931	56.7	65.5	150.0	157.1	62.3	102.6	105.8	100.9	103.0
1932	50.5	51.9	102.9	119.8	53.1	68.2	73.4	76.7	79.0
1933	74.1	83.0	137.3	112.3	80.9	73.8	76.7	89.0	90.7
1934	71.2	73.4	145.6	126.0	87.0	86.0	64.8	95.0	89.7
1935	82.4	88.0	160.8	155.5	83.0	114.1	110.8	115.8	116.1
1936	110.3	116.3	166.5	160.8	107.1	139.2	130.3	133.1	132.0
1937	105.4	121.2	195.7	169.7	111.0	141.8	136.2	139.6	139.5

aWheat, corn, oats, barley, rye, buckwheat, flaxseed, hay, potatoes, sweet potatoes, cotton and cottonseed, tobacco.

bWheat, rye, potatoes, sweet potatoes, dry beans, rice.

cOrchard fruits, citrus fruits, grapes.

dCotton and cottonseed, flaxseed, wool.

eCattle, calves, hogs, sheep, and lambs slaughtered, and live cattle exported.

fAdjusted for changes in inventory values.

gAdjusted for changes in inventory values of meat animals.

SOURCES: See Data Appendix.

TABLE 5.2

Price and Income Changes, by State, 1919–1928

| | Percentage change | | | | | |
| | 1919–1921 | | | | | |
	Gross farm income	Total net farm income	1919–1921 Total net nonfarm income	1919–1924 Crop price index	1922–1925 Value of crops sold	1925–1928 Value of crops sold
Alabama	-44	-38	25	-29	2	-16
Arizona	-37	-26	14	-35	18	44
Arkansas	-44	-49	27	-33	1	-10
California	-24	58	82	-45	20	0
Colorado	-41	-19	56	-43	41	-24
Connecticut	-7	162	44	-36	-7	-19
Delaware	-39	-39	39	-34	13	-15
Florida	-35	8	51	-37	8	31
Georgia	-57	-78	20	-54	11	0
Idaho	-39	-58	20	-54	61	-22
Illinois	-50	-89	45	-45	11	-4
Indiana	-48	-101	23	-55	10	-14
Iowa	-50	-113	3	-50	5	3
Kansas	-45	-66	39	-32	9	19
Kentucky	-46	-32	51	-48	-10	-2
Louisiana	-47	-64	35	-43	-23	-43
Maine	-26	24	48	-65	-60	-65
Maryland	-42	-10	45	-45	-20	-45
Massachusetts	-14	111	53	-41	-35	-41
Michigan	-34	-6	27	-55	-23	-55
Minnesota	-48	-75	38	-34	-23	-34

Mississippi	-51	-54	17	-37	-25	-37
Missouri	-48	-116	42	-51	-14	-51
Montana	-30	NA	34	-47	2	47
Nebraska	-51	-92	16	-37	23	2
Nevada	-38	NA	53	-38	0	-3
New Hampshire	-12	222	40	-49	10	-39
New Jersey	-29	17	44	-51	8	-11
New Mexico	-37	40	47	-18	51	-6
New York	-25	35	61	-50	19	-36
North Carolina	-41	-40	29	-47	4	-9
North Dakota	-46	-39	69	-1	21	-16
Ohio	-44	-49	25	-56	11	-21
Oklahoma	-50	-76	14	-32	21	0
Oregon	-30	-32	29	-48	17	-13
Pennsylvania	-32	11	42	-46	23	-34
Rhode Island	-22	64	61	-48	18	-42
South Carolina	-56	-88	-6	-62	6	-14
South Dakota	-53	-101	-19	-36	3	-14
Tennessee	-39	-28	42	-39	-10	-6
Texas	-44	-63	37	-16	-15	27
Utah	-43	14	37	-50	43	-16
Vermont	-15	77	43	-44	1	-30
Virginia	-41	-36	32	-46	-5	-7
Washington	-21	-21	37	-55	41	-25
West Virginia	-33	1	43	-48	14	-22
Wisconsin	-30	1	40	-54	26	-26
Wyoming	-43	106	77	-34	28	1

SOURCES: See Data Appendix.

249

TABLE 5.3

Farm Land, Population, and Foreclosures, by State, 1913–1930

	1913–1920 % change in value farm real estate per acre	1920–1925 % change in value farm real estate per acre	1925–1930 % change in value farm real estate per acre	1920 Ratio of farm mortgage debt to farm value	1920 Ratio of farm population to total population	1926–1930 Average annual farm foreclosure (per 1,000 farms)
Alabama	77	-11	-7	.12	.57	29.5
Arizona	65	-56	2	.20	.27	42.7
Arkansas	122	-20	-12	.11	.65	39.7
California	67	10	-2	.13	.15	16.3
Colorado	41	-31	-10	.17	.28	42.4
Connecticut	37	10	2	.13	.07	5.3
Delaware	39	-3	-1	.15	.23	13.7
Florida	78	75	0	.08	.29	11.1
Georgia	117	-40	-14	.08	.58	56.5
Idaho	72	-34	-6	.21	.46	37.6
Illinois	60	-27	-21	.09	.17	29.0
Indiana	61	-32	-22	.08	.31	23.8
Iowa	113	-34	-17	.16	.41	48.3
Kansas	51	-19	-2	.12	.42	27.2
Kentucky	100	-30	-9	.09	.54	20.2
Louisiana	98	-22	-6	.10	.44	40.1
Maine	42	2	0	.10	.26	10.5
Maryland	66	-5	-6	.13	.19	16.8
Massachusetts	40	8	-1	.13	.03	6.5
Michigan	54	-6	-9	.15	.23	21.6
Minnesota	113	-27	-16	.15	.37	36.2

Mississippi	118	−34	−10	.11	.71	47.7
Missouri	67	−30	−18	.14	.36	34.1
Montana	26	−37	−4	.22	.41	52.2
Nebraska	79	−32	−8	.13	.45	38.4
Nevada	35	−41	−3	.20	.21	21.0
New Hampshire	29	11	−2	.10	.17	7.3
New Jersey	30	24	1	.16	.05	7.2
New Mexico	44	−31	2	.13	.44	26.3
New York	33	3	−7	.16	.08	13.8
North Carolina	123	−7	−16	.06	.58	23.4
North Dakota	45	−28	−13	.19	.61	58.0
Ohio	59	−23	−18	.08	.20	16.4
Oklahoma	66	−20	−3	.16	.50	50.1
Oregon	30	−13	−3	.14	.27	17.4
Pennsylvania	40	−4	−6	.10	.11	6.9
Rhode Island	30	14	5	.08	.02	6.0
South Carolina	130	−34	−25	.07	.63	68.0
South Dakota	81	−37	−19	.13	.57	70.4
Tennessee	100	−19	−10	.09	.54	20.5
Texas	74	−14	−5	.12	.48	23.7
Utah	67	−20	−3	.16	.31	13.5
Vermont	50	−7	−2	.18	.36	10.6
Virginia	89	−7	−13	.07	.46	15.6
Washington	40	−17	−3	.13	.21	20.0
West Virginia	54	−8	−13	.04	.32	9.0
Wisconsin	71	−12	−10	.21	.35	22.6
Wyoming	76	−54	−2	.15	.34	26.3

SOURCES: See Data Appendix.

TABLE 5.4
GNP Deflator Estimates, 1917–1929

	Balke and Gordon (1989)	Romer (1989)
1917	11.36	13.06
1918	13.35	15.20
1919	15.23	15.58
1920	17.58	17.75
1921	15.30	15.12
1922	14.22	14.30
1923	14.63	14.69
1924	14.64	14.51
1925	14.90	14.77
1926	14.98	14.84
1927	14.72	14.48
1928	14.60	14.59
1929	14.64	14.60

SOURCES: See Data Appendix.

changes, the economic impact of income shocks on farmers' wealth and financial survival depended on market perceptions of how permanent these disturbances were. Third, the impact of a wealth or income shock depends on the vulnerability (leverage) of farms— that is, how severe the shock is relative to previous expectations of future income. Some of the highest foreclosure rates occurred in states with a relatively high ratio of farm mortgage debt to farm real estate value (Table 5.3). While changes in prices and income provide measures of the magnitude of disturbances, these considerations suggest that changes in the value of farms and the farm foreclosure rate are more indicative of likely (anticipated) long-term changes in farm income associated with those shocks.[9]

Finally, in evaluating the impact of agricultural shocks on state-wide bank performance, the proportion of state income derived from farming and the proportion of the labor force employed in farming are obviously important. The geographical isolation of farming communities is also relevant, for it affects the abilities of merchants or bankers in these areas to diversify.

The links (explored in a later section) between economic conditions, for which indicators are reported in Tables 5.2 and 5.3, and the threat to banks in a given state are therefore subtle. Ideally, in analyzing these links, one would want to take account of the perceived permanence of different income shocks, the degree of financial leverage, the rapidity and cumulation of shocks, and the relationship between the degree of concentration of income in agriculture and the impact on banks from agricultural shocks.

This study investigates the role of regulatory regimes in limiting the incidence and costs of financial disruption in the face of a major challenge to the financial system. To evaluate the influences of the different state regulatory decisions in propagating adverse shocks, I compare the performance of banks in thirty-two states that were substantially affected by the agricultural depression.

The sample of states whose financial systems are later analyzed in greatest detail include any state that (1) experienced a farm real estate value reduction (per acre) exceeding 20 percent from 1920 to 1930, or (2) had an average annual farm foreclosure rate exceeding 20 per 1,000 from 1926 to 1930. This sample includes states that suffered extreme depression, as well as those with more moderate commercial failure rates and bank failure experiences (discussed in a later section). The states in the sample are listed in Table 5.5 according to their deposit insurance and branch banking laws.

Bank Membership and Balance Sheet Patterns across States

The influence of regulation on membership, location, and risk. In 1920 the same regulations governed national banks in each state. The experience of these national banks provides a state-specific benchmark against which to compare the behavior of state-chartered banks across states. Bank entry and asset growth, as well as financing and portfolio decisions of state-chartered banks, can be compared with one another in absolute terms as well as relative to the behavior of national banks in the respective states.

Of course, national banks were not identical across states, and they faced different exposure to agricultural risk. In every state, national banks were larger on average and located more often in

TABLE 5.5

Regulatory Regimes (in thirty-two "agricultural crisis" states)

	No deposit insurance	Compulsory insurance	Voluntary insurance
Full intrastate branching allowed	Arizona North Carolina South Carolina Virginia		
Limited new branching	Kentucky Louisiana Michigan Ohio Tennessee		
No new branching, old branches remain	Alabama Arkansas Georgia[a] Indiana Minnesota Wisconsin	Nebraska (1911–1930) Mississippi (1914–1930)	Washington (1917–1921)
No branching allowed	Colorado Idaho Illinois Iowa Missouri Montana Nevada New Mexico Wyoming[b]	North Dakota (1917–1929) Oklahoma (1908–1923) South Dakota (1916–1927)	Kansas (1909–1929) Texas (1910–1927)

[a]New branching prohibited in 1927.
[b]Branching authorized by legal implication; none allowed in practice.
SOURCES: See Data Appendix.

cities than their state-chartered counterparts. These differences from state to state were important. Also, urban national banks that served as regional reserve centers for agricultural areas were more likely to suffer asset depletion due to the impact of agricultural disturbances on correspondents. In what follows, I try as much as possible to control for these differences across states.

Before 1920 several states established deposit insurance systems. Incentive problems due to insurance are often said to have made insured banking systems grow at a "reckless" rate, limit the growth of capital, and overextend themselves in the farm loan market (Thies and Gerlowski, 1989; Calomiris, 1989; White, 1983; FDIC, 1956; American Bankers Association, 1933; Robb, 1921); however, no systematic quantitative comparisons of the behavior of the different state-chartered systems have been made before, to my knowledge.

It is difficult to distinguish between incorrect expectations of continuing prosperity and excess risk taking induced by deposit insurance without a standard against which to measure the behavior of insured banks. When one controls for differences in economic environment by using uninsured state banking systems in other states and national banks in the same state, one has provided such standards of comparison.

The dates for which the different state deposit-insurance systems came into and out of operation are given in Table 5.5. For three states (Kansas, Texas, and Washington), participation in state-run deposit insurance was voluntary. Numbers and deposits of participating and nonparticipating state banks in these states are given in Table 5.10. All state-run insured banking systems were in operation during the boom of 1918–1920; except for Washington, the state-operated insurance systems were the dominant component of the state-chartered systems by 1920. In Texas, state banks not belonging to the state-run system were privately insured, as required by regulation, while in Washington and Kansas state-chartered banks could avoid insurance altogether.

In describing the peculiar incentives of insured banks, one should distinguish between voluntary and involuntary state systems. Under voluntary insurance legislation, banks could retain state charters without joining the insured system. Since national charters were a costly means for many banks to avoid the insurance fund, state banking without insurance was an important option.

The laws governing withdrawal from a state's insurance plan were extremely important as well. In two of the three voluntary systems (Washington and Kansas), banks opting out of state-run insurance could avoid any form of insurance. These two systems also limited the effectiveness of insurance—and thereby reduced risk subsidization among banks—by allowing member banks to leave the insurance system at any time. Washington's system went further, and provided essentially no protection for large losses, because it allowed banks to withdraw at any time without even retaining liability for past losses. In Washington, low initial insurance premiums and the ability to leave the voluntary systems seem to have encouraged many banks that were not egregious risk takers to join, only to withdraw once troubles began. In Texas, voluntary withdrawal was not permitted until the insurance law was amended in 1925. Of course, banks could also opt out of any of the compulsory or voluntary state systems by securing a national charter. To do so, however, would have been costly for banks that relied on activities prohibited by national law or for those with insufficient capital.

Although all state-chartered Texas banks were required to have some form of insurance, the privately insured banks were unlikely to have had the same opportunities as those insured by the state to take advantage of insurance through excessive risk taking. While there is much evidence that supervision and regulation were lax in the state-run plans, historical examples of privately run insurance (see Calomiris, 1989) indicate that excessive risk taking was not a problem because of strong incentives by insurers to provide effective regulation and supervision. Thus Texas state-chartered banks that chose private rather than state-run insurance are likely to have assumed risks comparable to those of uninsured banks in other states.

Both compulsory and voluntary insurance during this period differed from current U.S. federal deposit insurance in several important respects. Typically, interest rates on insured deposits were restricted by law (except in Nebraska), and capital requirements were much higher than today (typically, 10 percent of deposits for insured banks). While interest rate ceilings were sometimes hard to enforce because of outright fraud, or the use of discounts as an alternative to interest (see Cooke, 1910), they limited the availability of funds somewhat, unlike FDIC regulations that allow risk-taking members to attract funds by offering insured certificates of deposit at unusually high interest rates. Furthermore, as in virtually all state systems and throughout the national banking system, stockholders in privately insured banks had extended liability equal to the amount of capital in the bank. Such liability was not equivalent to a doubling of the capital stock, because collections from assessments on the stockholders of failed banks averaged less than 50 percent of assessments for all state banking systems from 1921 to 1930.[10] Finally, the state systems were not insured by the state treasuries, but rather by member banks as a group, through an insurance fund to which banks contributed annual assessments. These assessments had upper bounds annually, meaning that the liability of solvent banks was limited. Furthermore, solvent banks that belonged to the insured systems in the 1920s were able to avoid much of the liability to depositors of failed banks by leaving the system or forcing repeal of the insurance statute by threatening to do so (more on this later). All these considerations suggest that the effective protection of depositors and the potential for excessive risk taking would have been less under past insured systems than under current federal deposit insurance. Evidence on incentive problems in these plans provides an *a fortiori* case for potential excessive risk taking under government-guaranteed insurance of the kind currently available in the United States.

Evidence of the effects of deposit insurance. Tables 5.6 through 5.10 present measures of state banking system averages and aggregates, broken down by type of bank charter and by state, for the thirty-two "agricultural crisis" states for various dates. The indicators include the following: the number of banks (Table 5.6), the proportion located in towns or cities of 2,500 or more and the average total assets per bank (Table 5.7), aggregate total asset growth (Table 5.8), the ratio of capital to assets (Table 5.9), and the participation of banks in voluntary insurance systems (Table 5.10).

As the data for the various state- and national-chartered systems show, not all types of banks were equally likely to join one or another system. Larger minimum capital requirements and more

TABLE 5.6

Number of State and National Banks, 1914–1929 (in thirty-two "agricultural crisis" states)

	National banks					
	1914	1918	1920	1923	1927	1929
Alabama	90	91	101	106	105	106
Arizona	13	18	20	20	15	14
Arkansas	57	72	83	88	79	73
Colorado	124	122	141	143	124	121
Georgia	115	97	93	97	83	80
Idaho	55	68	81	73	52	43
Illinois	463	469	480	505	490	487
Indiana	255	258	254	251	233	224
Iowa	341	352	358	349	287	265
Kansas	212	234	249	266	257	247
Kentucky	143	132	134	139	142	138
Louisiana	31	31	38	34	32	33
Michigan	99	105	112	119	134	133
Minnesota	273	294	331	344	277	272
Mississippi	37	33	30	31	36	35
Missouri	130	131	136	132	135	134
Montana	61	126	145	121	74	69
Nebraska	228	191	188	182	153	158
Nevada	10	10	10	11	10	10
New Mexico	37	43	47	42	29	28
North Carolina	73	81	87	83	77	73
North Dakota	146	165	181	184	141	125
Ohio	379	369	370	368	340	323
Oklahoma	343	340	348	459	350	307
South Carolina	51	81	82	84	65	53
South Dakota	105	125	136	131	98	93
Tennessee	113	106	98	105	104	99
Texas	518	543	556	561	649	623
Virginia	133	149	165	181	167	164
Washington	77	80	87	115	109	106
Wisconsin	131	147	151	155	156	157
Wyoming	32	38	47	45	30	25

(*continued on facing page*)

TABLE 5.6 (*continued*)

	State banks					
	1914	1918	1920	1923	1927	1929
Alabama	267	238	251	254	251	244
Arizona	47	60	67	55	32	34
Arkansas	425	389	404	403	376	347
Colorado	206	236	262	224	175	159
Georgia	675	659	686	586	412	362
Idaho	134	136	141	109	92	94
Illinois	1,439	1,434	1,489	1,416	1,358	1,319
Indiana	664	773	798	854	827	757
Iowa	1,410	1,561	1,564	1,506	1,222	1,129
Kansas	932	1,037	1,100	1,068	923	830
Kentucky	467	444	450	474	444	432
Louisiana	217	218	229	232	200	193
Michigan	702	740	739	765	739	718
Minnesota	863	1,141	1,177	1,151	912	794
Mississippi	282	266	302	303	290	277
Missouri	1,337	1,407	1,516	1,495	1,304	1,191
Montana	226	277	286	242	136	129
Nebraska	749	946	1,037	968	896	714
Nevada	21	23	23	24	25	25
New Mexico	47	74	76	59	30	30
North Carolina	384	434	491	477	432	399
North Dakota	619	693	718	648	390	309
Ohio	746	778	772	745	724	703
Oklahoma	574	580	612	446	348	344
South Carolina	329	336	379	345	216	170
South Dakota	526	517	543	556	319	303
Tennessee	378	415	450	466	418	393
Texas	1,038	1,037	1,125	1,071	852	791
Virginia	274	300	331	343	334	321
Washington	296	281	306	274	224	233
Wisconsin	652	778	819	838	810	801
Wyoming	72	98	113	89	58	62

SOURCES: See Data Appendix.

TABLE 5.7
Total Assets per Bank, and Bank Location, 1914–1929 (in thirty-two "agricultural crisis" states)

	Average total assets per bank (thousands of dollars)					
	National banks					
	1914	1918	1920	1923	1927	1929
Alabama	806	1,224	1,516	1,449	1,944	2,311
Arizona	1,215	1,299	1,766	1,389	1,863	2,608
Arkansas	607	818	1,020	1,004	1,285	1,352
Colorado	1,069	1,614	1,801	1,695	2,116	2,244
Georgia	884	1,676	2,145	1,704	3,299	3,377
Idaho	546	811	1,088	827	1,079	1,094
Illinois	1,912	2,764	3,562	3,068	3,737	3,295
Indiana	960	1,319	1,667	1,635	1,890	2,097
Iowa	692	1,010	1,301	1,144	1,264	1,381
Kansas	531	839	977	870	1,016	1,104
Kentucky	900	1,474	1,824	1,957	2,118	2,162
Louisiana	2,075	3,677	4,119	3,416	3,846	4,099
Michigan	2,054	2,826	3,784	3,634	4,324	4,991
Minnesota	1,220	1,682	1,979	1,785	2,325	2,468
Mississippi	756	1,281	1,843	1,956	2,589	2,702
Missouri	2,820	4,276	5,507	4,162	4,887	4,509
Montana	895	746	761	766	1,191	1,489
Nebraska	694	1,342	1,566	1,424	1,496	1,615
Nevada	972	1,545	1,823	1,529	1,990	2,299
New Mexico	612	879	963	968	1,047	1,331
North Carolina	921	1,379	2,064	2,086	2,544	2,634
North Dakota	338	499	563	528	644	702
Ohio	1,545	2,484	2,912	2,470	2,638	2,785
Oklahoma	343	766	1,096	848	1,219	1,448
South Carolina	908	1,244	1,818	1,520	2,048	2,371
South Dakota	446	718	862	731	733	871
Tennessee	1,026	1,583	2,352	2,070	2,459	3,033
Texas	705	1,081	1,588	1,356	1,567	1,771
Virginia	1,265	2,045	2,461	2,110	2,381	2,347
Washington	1,610	2,570	3,039	2,482	2,958	3,306
Wisconsin	1,592	2,065	2,720	2,476	2,979	3,413
Wyoming	630	1,102	1,365	1,369	1,442	1,711

(*continued on facing page*)

TABLE 5.7 (*continued*)

	Average total assets per bank (thousands of dollars)						Proportion of banks in towns of more than 2,500 people, 1920[a]	
	State banks						National banks	State banks
	1914	1918	1920	1923	1927	1929		
Alabama	283	368	543	522	578	545	.55	.26
Arizona	555	807	974	974	1,745	2,107	.70	.54
Arkansas	164	304	456	404	445	492	.66	.31
Colorado	263	397	460	514	437	477	.42	.23
Georgia	224	355	534	519	489	538	.75	.31
Idaho	162	335	487	334	436	568	.58	.25
Illinois	739	996	1,322	1,610	2,085	2,584	.52	.31
Indiana	352	451	609	628	769	806	.57	.37
Iowa	314	423	563	542	562	596	.36	.15
Kansas	146	269	326	285	304	320	.43	.18
Kentucky	245	389	497	537	651	826	.63	.24
Louisiana	581	950	1,592	1,472	2,029	2,184	.79	.31
Michigan	635	988	1,470	1,505	2,272	2,555	.71	.25
Minnesota	235	287	425	403	443	466	.34	.18
Mississippi	238	450	664	552	632	660	.80	.28
Missouri	350	493	572	631	722	741	.63	.22
Montana	269	391	436	393	605	680	.28	.16
Nebraska	155	298	335	319	365	383	.40	.12
Nevada	593	817	1,030	947	1,063	1,228	.60	.39
New Mexico	197	277	347	364	365	466	.47	.37
North Carolina	232	345	578	565	744	809	.77	.28
North Dakota	106	165	248	211	262	289	.16	.06
Ohio	806	1,162	1,645	2,167	3,095	3,271	.59	.41
Oklahoma	95	228	346	211	279	292	.51	.21
South Carolina	241	342	536	424	471	588	.72	.43
South Dakota	136	271	395	344	272	318	.27	.07
Tennessee	240	396	562	558	626	714	.65	.23
Texas	159	242	375	304	379	429	.49	.24
Virginia	329	478	613	656	819	878	.50	.29
Washington	449	637	752	520	606	703	.56	.29
Wisconsin	365	440	626	634	776	752	.62	.24
Wyoming	148	242	300	307	431	514	.47	.13

[a]Branches excluded.
SOURCES: See Data Appendix.

TABLE 5.8

Asset Growth, 1914–1930 (percentage change in thirty-two "agricultural crisis" states)

	National banks					
	1914–1918	1918–1920	1920–1923	1923–1927	1927–1929	1929–1930
Alabama	53	37	0	33	20	60
Arizona	48	51	−21	1	31	3
Arkansas	70	44	4	15	−3	17
Colorado	48	29	−5	8	0	7
Georgia	60	23	−17	65	−1	35
Idaho	84	60	−32	−7	−16	−47
Illinois	46	32	−9	18	−12	−6
Indiana	39	24	−3	7	7	11
Iowa	51	31	−14	−9	1	−21
Kansas	74	24	−5	13	4	12
Kentucky	51	26	11	11	−1	22
Louisiana	77	37	−26	6	10	−14
Michigan	46	43	2	34	15	57
Minnesota	48	32	−6	5	4	2
Mississippi	51	31	10	54	1	71
Missouri	53	34	−27	20	−8	−19
Montana	72	17	−16	−5	17	−7
Nebraska	62	15	−12	−12	12	−13
Nevada	59	18	−8	18	16	26
New Mexico	67	20	−10	−25	23	−18
North Carolina	66	61	−4	13	−2	7
North Dakota	67	24	−5	−7	−3	−14
Ohio	57	18	−16	−1	0	−17
Oklahoma	121	46	2	10	4	17
South Carolina	118	48	−14	4	−6	−16
South Dakota	91	31	−18	−25	13	−31
Tennessee	45	37	−6	18	17	30
Texas	61	50	−14	34	9	25
Virginia	81	33	−6	4	−3	0
Washington	66	29	8	13	9	33
Wisconsin	46	35	−7	21	15	30
Wyoming	108	53	−4	−30	−1	−33

(*continued on facing page*)

TABLE 5.8 (*continued*)

	State banks					
	1914–1918	1918–1920	1920–1923	1923–1927	1927–1929	1929–1930
Alabama	16	56	−3	9	−8	−2
Arizona	86	35	−18	4	28	10
Arkansas	70	56	−12	3	2	−7
Colorado	73	29	−4	−33	−1	−37
Georgia	55	57	−17	−33	−3	−47
Idaho	94	51	−47	10	33	−22
Illinois	34	38	16	24	20	73
Indiana	49	39	10	19	−4	26
Iowa	56	33	−7	−16	−2	−24
Kansas	105	28	−15	−8	−5	−26
Kentucky	51	30	14	14	23	60
Louisiana	64	76	−6	19	4	16
Michigan	64	48	6	46	9	69
Minnesota	61	53	−7	−13	−8	−26
Mississippi	78	68	−17	10	0	−9
Missouri	48	25	9	0	−6	2
Montana	78	15	−24	−13	7	−30
Nebraska	142	23	−11	6	−16	−21
Nevada	51	26	−4	17	16	30
New Mexico	121	28	−19	−49	28	−47
North Carolina	68	89	−5	19	0	14
North Dakota	75	56	−23	−23	−13	−50
Ohio	50	40	27	39	3	81
Oklahoma	142	60	−56	3	3	−53
South Carolina	45	77	−28	−30	−2	−51
South Dakota	96	46	−6	−55	11	−47
Tennessee	81	54	3	1	7	11
Texas	52	68	−23	−1	5	−19
Virginia	59	41	11	22	3	39
Washington	35	29	−38	4	11	−29
Wisconsin	44	50	4	18	−4	17
Wyoming	122	43	−19	−9	27	−6

SOURCES: See Data Appendix.

TABLE 5.9

Capital as a Percentage of Total Assets, 1914–1929 (in thirty-two "agricultural crisis" states)

	National banks					
	1914	1918	1920	1923	1927	1929
Alabama	14	10	8	9	7	7
Arizona	7	7	5	6	5	5
Arkansas	15	10	8	9	7	7
Colorado	8	5	5	5	5	5
Georgia	15	8	7	8	7	7
Idaho	12	7	6	8	6	6
Illinois	9	6	5	6	5	6
Indiana	11	8	7	8	7	7
Iowa	10	7	6	7	7	6
Kansas	11	7	7	8	7	7
Kentucky	14	9	7	7	7	6
Louisiana	11	7	6	7	7	7
Michigan	8	6	5	6	5	5
Minnesota	8	7	5	7	6	6
Mississippi	13	9	7	8	6	6
Missouri	10	7	6	8	7	6
Montana	10	8	8	8	6	5
Nebraska	10	6	6	7	6	6
Nevada	15	9	8	9	7	7
New Mexico	9	7	7	8	7	6
North Carolina	13	8	7	8	8	8
North Dakota	11	8	7	8	6	6
Ohio	11	7	6	7	6	7
Oklahoma	13	6	6	8	6	6
South Carolina	17	9	8	10	7	8
South Dakota	9	6	5	6	6	5
Tennessee	11	8	6	8	7	7
Texas	14	9	7	9	8	8
Virginia	11	7	6	8	8	8
Washington	9	6	5	6	6	7
Wisconsin	9	6	6	7	6	6
Wyoming	9	5	5	6	6	5

(*continued on facing page*)

TABLE 5.9 (*continued*)

	State banks					
	1914	1918	1920	1923	1927	1929
Alabama	17	12	9	9	10	9
Arizona	7	6	6	9	7	6
Arkansas	20	12	8	10	9	9
Colorado	12	8	8	8	8	7
Georgia	20	12	10	11	12	12
Idaho	17	9	8	10	7	6
Illinois	10	8	7	7	7	7
Indiana	13	10	8	9	8	7
Iowa	10	8	7	7	7	7
Kansas	14	8	8	9	9	9
Kentucky	17	11	9	9	8	9
Louisiana	12	8	6	7	6	6
Michigan	8	6	5	6	5	5
Minnesota	10	9	7	8	6	6
Mississippi	16	8	7	7	6	6
Missouri	12	9	7	8	8	8
Montana	14	10	9	10	7	7
Nebraska	14	8	8	9	8	8
Nevada	14	9	7	8	7	6
New Mexico	19	13	12	12	11	8
North Carolina	13	9	7	9	8	8
North Dakota	14	10	8	10	9	9
Ohio	8	6	5	6	5	6
Oklahoma	16	8	7	10	8	8
South Carolina	16	11	8	11	10	9
South Dakota	12	7	6	7	9	8
Tennessee	16	9	8	9	9	9
Texas	21	14	11	13	11	10
Virginia	15	10	11	12	10	10
Washington	12	9	7	9	9	8
Wisconsin	9	8	6	7	6	6
Wyoming	16	10	9	10	7	6

SOURCES: See Data Appendix.

TABLE 5.10

Banks in States with Voluntary Insurance Systems

	Kansas				Texas[a]				Washington[b]			
	Participating		Not participating		Participating		Not participating		Participating		Not participating	
	Number	Deposits[c]	Number	Deposits[c]	Number	Deposits[c]	Number	Deposits[c]	Number	Deposits[c]	Number	Deposits[c]
1917	577	152	430	73	828	204	46	12	46	40	239	109
1919	649	205	427	88	907	321	41	15	104	80	191	123
1920	683	191	409	81	990	266	41	14	116	75	190	107
1922	698	180	369	62	936	252	34	11				
1924	651	195	371	75	896	302	37	21				
1926	399	79	547	154	34	3	748	226				
1928	39	3	794	219								

[a]Texas had no state-insured banks after 1927.
[b]Washington had no state-insured banks after 1920.
[c]In millions of dollars.
SOURCES: See Data Appendix.

restrictive portfolio regulations for national banks meant that small banks, particularly those that wished to specialize in agricultural credit backed by real estate, would be attracted to the state-chartered systems. As Table 5.7 shows, although there was considerable variation among states, national banks were always larger on average and always had a higher proportion of banks located in cities.

Because the potential benefits of deposit insurance are greater for small rural banks, historical accounts and economic theory lead one to expect that deposit insurance for state-chartered banks will reinforce this propensity for small rural banks to belong to the state system, and for large urban banks to join the national system. White (1983: 198–200) found that support for deposit insurance regulation was greatest among small bankers operating in unit banking states with low minimum capital requirements. For large urban state banks (which generally opposed deposit insurance legislation), deposit insurance was seen as a burden, a legislated subsidy from large to small banks.[11] Interest rates on insured deposits typically had ceilings that kept insured banks from being as competitive in the market for large, sophisticated depositors as in the market for deposits in rural areas.[12] Capital requirements in the insured systems (typically 10 percent of deposits) were more of an impediment to risk taking for large banks than for smaller banks operating in the geographic periphery. A group of oil prospectors, ranchers, or farmers could organize a small bank to finance their expansion, while placing limited funds of their own at risk.[13] Many large city banks found advantages to operating in a more disciplined environment, with stockholders and subordinated debtholders keeping watch over conflicts of interest between bank and banker. For urban banks, the expanding opportunities in trust activities and alternatives to standard demand-deposit banking as a means of finance were the wave of the future; for small rural banks, deposit-financed agricultural lending was the way to expand.[14] There were exceptions. Some particularly unscrupulous large city banks chose to enter the insured systems, intending to use them as a means to create and exploit conflicts of interest and to finance speculative expansion on a scale that would not have been possible for a rural unit bank.[15]

Bank membership and balance sheet patterns indicate that deposit insurance was an important force in determining who joined or left the various systems and in influencing bank expansion and risk taking during the boom and bust. No single indicator in Tables 5.6 through 5.10 provides a litmus test of the importance of deposit insurance for adverse selection in bank membership and excessive risk taking; but a combination of factors apparent in the tables indicates that state systems featuring deposit insurance constituted a distinct group, during the eras of both expansion and contraction.

During the boom period of 1914–1920, the insured banks grew more rapidly than others. The fastest-growing state banking systems from 1914 to 1920 are shown in Table 5.11. Of these sixteen systems, seven were insured (one of the voluntary systems, Washington, is excluded from this list). The compulsory systems ranked first, fourth, fifth, sixth, and eighth in asset growth over this period. Two of the voluntary participation state systems (Kansas and Texas) ranked tenth and eleventh. High growth by itself does not imply excessive risk taking. As Table 5.11 shows, high growth was not confined to insured systems, as the experiences of Wyoming and Idaho demonstrate.

Three factors, however, made the high growth rates of the insured state banking systems unique: They accomplished high growth mainly through increases in the numbers of banks (see Table 5.6), rather than in assets per bank (Table 5.11); growth seems to have been concentrated in relatively sparsely populated regions; and insured banks operated with low capital-to-asset ratios, typically observed only in systems of larger-than-average size. Of the eight state banking systems that averaged less than $400,000 in total assets per bank in 1920, six were insured banking systems, with the frontier states, Wyoming and New Mexico, accounting for the remaining two.

The West as a region was experiencing an era of extraordinary banking growth, comparable to the growth of New England banking in the early national period (1790–1830) or the South from 1820 to

TABLE 5.11

High-growth States: Insured and Uninsured

	Assets in 1920/ Assets in 1914		Assets per bank in 1920[a]		Capital/total assets in 1920	
	National banks	State banks	National banks	State banks	National banks	State banks
Uninsured						
Arkansas	2.45	2.64	1,020	456	.084	.085
Colorado	1.92	2.22	1,801	460	.048	.083
Idaho	2.93	3.16	1,088	487	.059	.077
Iowa	1.97	1.99	1,301	563	.057	.067
Minnesota	1.96	2.46	1,979	425	.054	.069
Missouri	2.04	1.85	5,507	572	.063	.072
Montana	2.02	2.04	761	436	.077	.091
New Mexico	2.00	2.84	963	347	.073	.119
Wyoming	3.18	3.17	1,365	300	.048	.090
Average	2.27	2.49	1,755	448	.063	.084
Insured						
Kansas	2.16	2.63[b]	977	326[b]	.066	.079[b]
Mississippi	1.98	2.99	1,843	664	.069	.066
Nebraska	1.86	2.99	1,566	335	.057	.082
North Dakota	2.06	2.72	563	248	.068	.081
Oklahoma	3.24	3.86	1,096	346	.060	.070
South Dakota	2.50	2.85	862	395	.053	.062
Texas	2.42	2.56[b]	1,588	375[b]	.071	.112[b]
Average	2.32	2.94	1,231	391	.064	.078

[a]In thousands of dollars.
[b]The data for Kansas and Texas state banks includes insured and uninsured banks.
SOURCES: See Data Appendix.

1860.[16] But the insured banks differed in certain respects from those in other high-growth western states. In New Mexico, state-chartered banks operated in more populous areas, on average (see Table 5.7); and the fragility inherent in such rapid growth and small size were partly offset by the unusually high capital-to-asset ratio of banks (12 percent) in 1920, as shown in Table 5.9. Wyoming's capital-to-asset ratio of 9 percent was higher than any of the other insured banks of comparable size, as well. Thus if one uses the combined standard of high growth, small bank size, and low capital-to-asset ratios, then the insured banking systems appear especially vulnerable at the peak in 1920. Texas operated with a relatively high capital ratio because its law required capital as a percentage of deposits of between 10 and 20 percent (depending on deposit size), while other insurance systems required 10 percent.

It is important to verify that the high growth and unique vulnerability of the insured state systems relative to other state systems are attributable to different banking responses, rather than to different fundamental economic conditions. To this end, additional comparisons of insured systems with other banking systems within and across states are instructive. Specifically, I consider three standards of comparison: the relative growth of insured and uninsured state banks in states where insurance was optional; the growth of state-chartered banks across states, relative to the growth of national banks in the same state; and the growth of insured banking relative to uninsured state-chartered banking in adjoining states with similar "economic fundamentals."

For two of the three states with voluntary systems (Kansas and Texas), the growth differences between national- and state-chartered banking before 1920 (Table 5.8) were clearly due to the disproportionate growth of state-run insured banking, as Table 5.10 reveals. These two voluntary systems grew rapidly during the pre-1920 boom period relative to other state banking systems, in both number of banks (Table 5.6) and total deposits. The Texas system—which did not allow voluntary withdrawal by member banks and therefore provided more anticipated insurance protection than the Washington or Kansas system—was the fastest growing of the three voluntary insurance systems, relative to national or uninsured banks in the state. In Texas, the deposits in banks of all types in the state grew by 271 percent from the end of 1914 to the end of 1919, while those in insured banks grew by 402 percent.[17] The total number of banks in the state increased by 11 percent, while the number of insured banks increased 25 percent, from 1914 to 1920. In Kansas, total deposit growth was 131 percent for 1914–1919, while insured-banking deposit growth was 173 percent.

In the third voluntary-insurance state, Washington, the state-chartered system as a whole grew slowly compared with the national system; and the insured system never accounted for more than 41 percent of state-chartered deposits (FDIC, 1956: 50). Several features of the Washington experience made it a special case. First, Washington's free-exit provision provided virtually no protection and hence no encouragement for excessive expansion. Second, its insurance system was the last to be established (in 1917), and there was less time for banks to join before 1920. Third, Washington's banking growth during this period was concentrated more in the large urban banks. Its national banking system was fifth among the sample of thirty-two states in average asset size of banks in 1920 and experienced above average growth in assets from 1914 to 1920. The lack of a rural/agricultural boom in Washington—farm land prices grew a modest 40 percent from 1913 to 1920 (see Table 5.3)—further limited any perceived advantages to small rural banks of membership in the insured system.

A second standard for comparing growth during the boom—one that controls for state-specific economic conditions—is the relative growth of state and national systems between states with and without insurance. Typically, state banking systems grew faster than national systems. In some states this difference is especially pronounced; in others it is actually reversed.

A rough comparison is provided in Table 5.12, a four-by-four matrix that arranges states according to the quartile growth rates of their national- and state-chartered banking systems for 1914–1920. Only two state-chartered systems ranked two or more quartiles higher in growth of assets than the quartile rank of their state's national banks: Mississippi and Nebraska. These were two of the five compulsory insurance states.

A more formal approach to comparing state-chartered banking growth to national bank growth across states is presented in Table 5.13. Using cross-sectional data for the sample of thirty-two states, I performed a regression of state-chartered bank asset growth for 1914–1920 on the following: national-chartered asset growth, the

TABLE 5.12

Bank Growth Quartile Comparison, 1914–1920 (in thirty-two "agricultural crisis" states)

	State-chartered banking systems			
National-chartered banking systems	First quartile	Second quartile	Third quartile	Fourth quartile
First quartile	Nevada, Illinois, Kentucky	Colorado, Georgia, Indiana, Ohio		*Nebraska*
Second quartile	Iowa, Missouri, Montana	Minnesota, Wisconsin	New Mexico, Tennessee	*Mississippi*
Third quartile	Alabama, *Washington*	Michigan, Virginia	Arizona, *Kansas, North Dakota, Texas*	
Fourth quartile			Arkansas, South Carolina	Idaho, Louisiana, North Carolina, *Oklahoma, South Dakota,* Wyoming

NOTE: First quartile states had the lowest growth rates; fourth quartile states had the highest. Italicized states had state-insured banking systems.

SOURCES: See Data Appendix.

272

TABLE 5.13

Regression Results: Early Asset Growth of State-chartered Banks (in thirty-two "agricultural crisis" states)

Dependent variable: Growth in total assets of state-chartered banks, 1914–1920

Independent variables	Coefficient	Standard error	Prob > 1T1
Intercept	0.156	0.468	0.741
National bank growth	0.682	0.147	0.000
(Reserve center) × (national bank growth)	−0.115	0.063	0.080
Growth in land values, 1914–1920	0.526	0.334	0.127
Ratio of farm to nonfarm population	−0.328	0.655	0.621
Presence of voluntary insurance	0.327	0.251	0.205
Presence of compulsory insurance	0.609	0.189	0.004

$R^2 = 0.683$
$\bar{R}^2 = 0.607$

Dependent variable: Growth in total assets of state-chartered banks, 1914–1920

Independent variables	Coefficient	Standard error	Prob > 1T1
Intercept	0.101	0.465	0.829
National bank growth	0.681	0.147	0.000
(Reserve center) × (national bank growth)	−0.132	0.060	0.038
Growth in land values, 1914–1920	0.555	0.333	0.107
Ratio of farm to nonfarm population	−0.283	0.654	0.669
Presence of voluntary or compulsory insurance	0.518	0.165	0.004

$R^2 = 0.670$
$\bar{R}^2 = 0.607$

percentage rise in farm land value per acre, the ratio of farm population to total population, and dummy variables for the presence of insurance. In the first version I separate the voluntary insurance states—Kansas and Texas—from the compulsory insurance systems. Washington is excluded from the set of insured states altogether. I also add a dummy variable (which interacts with the growth of national banking) for states that contained especially important "reserve centers." National asset growth is included as a measure of state-specific opportunities for expansion, holding regulation constant. The growth in the value of farm real estate is included to control for different expectations of long-run profitability from agricultural loans (which should have a disproportionate effect on state banks). The reserve center dummy is included to control for peculiarities in the growth of national-chartered banks due to interstate influences through correspondent relations.

The regression results confirm that insurance was associated with very high relative rates of growth of state-chartered banks and that national banks in reserve-center states grew more than national banks elsewhere. As predicted, the effect of compulsory insurance is stronger than that of voluntary insurance because voluntary plans provide less cross-subsidization and because (in Kansas) withdrawal was allowed by law. Even in Kansas and Texas, however, the effects of insurance dummies were important (accounting for an additional 33 percent of asset growth from 1914 to 1920), although the few degrees of freedom and the consequent high coefficient standard errors limit the power of hypothesis tests.

Finally, comparisons among state banking systems in the same regions also support the conclusions that insured banking growth was unusually high and that insured states were more vulnerable during the boom. First, consider the states in the western region adjoining the western insured states: Arkansas, Colorado, Idaho, Iowa, Missouri, Minnesota, Montana, New Mexico, and Wyoming. How do these states compare, in growth, bank size, and capitalization, to the insured states of Kansas, Nebraska, North Dakota, Oklahoma, South Dakota, and Texas? Data on the ratio of state-chartered bank assets in 1914 relative to 1920, average state-chartered bank size, and capitalization are reported in Table 5.14. Then consider a similar comparison between Mississippi statistics and those of the uninsured states in the deep South: Alabama, Georgia, and South Carolina. (Louisiana is excluded because of the special role of New Orleans as a financial center.)

These data reveal that the nine uninsured state-chartered systems of adjoining western states had larger banks on average, grew less, and had somewhat higher capital than their counterparts in the insured systems. On average, uninsured western asset growth from 1914 to 1920 was 138 percent, compared to 186 percent for the insured

TABLE 5.14

Regional Comparison of Insured and Uninsured State-chartered Banks

	Assets 1920/ Assets 1914	Assets per bank in 1920 (thousands of dollars)	Capital/total assets in 1920
West			
Uninsured			
Arkansas	2.64	456	.085
Colorado	2.22	460	.083
Idaho	3.16	487	.077
Iowa	1.99	563	.067
Minnesota	2.46	425	.069
Missouri	1.85	572	.072
Montana	2.04	436	.091
New Mexico	2.84	347	.119
Wyoming	3.17	300	.090
Average	2.49	450	.084
Insured			
Kansas[a]	2.63	326	.079
Nebraska	2.99	335	.082
North Dakota	2.72	248	.081
Oklahoma	3.86	346	.070
South Dakota	2.85	395	.062
Texas[a]	2.56	375	.112
Average	2.94	338	.081
South			
Uninsured			
Alabama	1.81	543	.087
Georgia	2.43	534	.097
South Carolina	2.56	536	.085
Average	2.27	538	.090
Insured			
Mississippi	2.99	664	.066

[a]Data for Kansas and Texas include uninsured banks.
SOURCES: See Data Appendix.

group. The average total assets of banks in the uninsured group was $450,000, while for the insured banks the average was $338,000. The historic vulnerability of small banks explains why, other things being equal, their depositors required them to maintain higher than average ratios of capital to deposits.[18] But in this sample, capital averaged 8.4 percent of assets for the uninsured group and 8.1

percent for the insured. When Texas—the insured state with a high legally mandated capital-to-deposit ratio that exceeded "market-determined" bank leverage in other states—is excluded the difference becomes even greater (8.4 percent, compared to 7.5 percent).

The relation between Mississippi and its neighbors is similar. Asset growth averaged 122 percent in the uninsured states, as compared to 194 percent in Mississippi. The ratio of capital to assets for the uninsured states was 9.0 percent, as compared to 6.6 percent in Mississippi. Average bank size in Mississippi was greater than that of the other states in the deep South ($664,000 as compared to $538,000), but this size difference is partly attributable to the much higher growth in assets in Mississippi. From 1914 to 1920 their assets tripled, compared with those of the other states whose assets on average roughly doubled over the same period. Also, Mississippi's state-chartered banks included older, relatively large branching banks (ten banks with twenty-four branches in 1920) that were allowed to continue operating even though new branching was not allowed. Finally, as discussed in the following section, many of Mississippi's rural banks had failed during the boll weevil crisis of 1912–1913, and the state banking regulators were notoriously restrictive in granting entry by new banks.

Insured banking: from boom to crisis. Having established, by several standards of comparison, that deposit insurance was associated with high growth and greater bank vulnerability (small size and low capital) during the boom, I now evaluate the effects of insurance on the membership and balance sheet responses of state banking systems to the crisis. As several authors (American Bankers Association, 1933; FDIC, 1956; White, 1983; and Calomiris, 1989) have documented, the insurance plans did not provide effective protection to the states' payments systems or to bank depositors. Reimbursements to depositors were neither timely nor complete, and exit from the insured systems relieved solvent banks of the responsibility to cover insolvent banks' liabilities. Here I quantify the role of deposit insurance, and the vulnerability it entailed, in preventing state-chartered banking systems in states with insurance from responding to the crisis as well as other state systems.

As one would expect, failures and assessments rose during the collapse, and there was widespread defection of relatively healthy insured banks to alternative systems, as shown in Table 5.15. In all cases, there was a net transfer of banks from the insured state systems to the national system.

Table 5.15 reports data on changes of charter across the two systems within each state from 1921 through 1930. During this period the forty-eight contiguous states as a group experienced a total of 361 net conversions from state- to national-chartered banking. All eight states with deposit insurance had positive net conversions over this period, and as a group they accounted for 278 of the 361 net conversions. At the same time, the group of Montana, Iowa, Colorado, Idaho, Wyoming, Oregon, Arizona, Arkansas, Minnesota, and New Mexico had only five net conversions in all. Furthermore, only eight states other than those with insurance plans had net conversions of greater than five: Alabama, California, Illinois, Minnesota, Missouri, Oregon, Virginia, and Wisconsin. This group of states—unlike the insured states—did not suffer a collapse of state banking during this period. Alabama's state system showed essentially flat total assets over the period; California's, Wisconsin's, and Virginia's state systems experienced growth; in Illinois only a small percentage of banks converted, and total state banking assets grew substantially relative to that of national banks; in Minnesota, the percentage that converted was also small; and Oregon was not an "agricultural crisis" state. Thus the insured state-chartered systems were virtually the only cases for which national banking gained at the expense of state banking in response to the agricultural crisis.

In the states with voluntary state-run insurance participation (Table 5.5), there was widespread movement to the other state systems as well (Table 5.10). In Kansas and Texas, banks switched en masse from 1924 to 1926. The demise of the Texas system reflects the fact that withdrawal was illegal until 1925. In Kansas, the failure in 1923 of the largest bank in the insured system, and a court ruling in

TABLE 5.15

Bank Charter Switches, 1921–1930

	From state to national charter	From national to state charter	Net increase in banks under national system
Alabama	10	0	10
Arizona	1	1	0
Arkansas	7	4	3
California	16	0	16
Colorado	6	1	5
Connecticut	0	1	−1
Delaware	0	2	−2
Florida	4	6	−2
Georgia	7	0	7
Idaho	0	13	−13
Illinois	13	3	10
Indiana	3	7	−4
Iowa	2	2	0
Kansas	14	2	12
Kentucky	7	3	4
Louisiana	0	2	−2
Maine	0	1	−1
Maryland	1	1	0
Massachusetts	4	1	3
Michigan	4	0	4
Minnesota	19	5	14
Mississippi	10	0	10
Missouri	10	4	6
Montana	1	0	1
Nebraska	31	0	31
Nevada	0	0	0
New Hampshire	0	1	−1
New Jersey	2	11	−9
New Mexico	1	1	0
New York	7	8	−1
North Carolina	6	5	1
North Dakota	12	0	12
Ohio	2	1	1
Oklahoma	113	50	63
Oregon	7	0	7
Pennsylvania	11	8	3
Rhode Island	0	1	−1
South Carolina	4	1	3
South Dakota	4	1	3
Tennessee	8	3	5
Texas	130	8	122

(*continued on facing page*)

TABLE 5.15 (*continued*)

	From state to national charter	From national to state charter	Net increase in banks under national system
Utah	0	0	0
Vermont	0	1	−1
Virginia	16	3	13
Washington	27	2	25
West Virginia	2	0	2
Wisconsin	9	1	8
Wyoming	1	6	−5

SOURCES: See Data Appendix.

1926 absolving banks that chose to withdraw from liabilities for prior bank failures (above the amount of securities already deposited in the state fund), explain the timing of withdrawal. In Washington, the failure of one bank—again, the largest in the state, which accounted for one-fifth of insured deposits—prompted all other insured banks to leave the system.[19]

Thus, while deposit insurance produced abnormally high growth during the boom, it caused abnormally low state-chartered growth during the crisis. Table 5.16 reports regression results analogous to those of Table 5.13 but for the periods 1920–1926 and 1920–1930. The average annual rate of business failure from 1921 to either 1925 or 1929 divided by the average rate for the four years prior to 1921 is included in the regressions to capture better the financial distress banks faced in each state. The regressions are run for two subperiods because, before 1930, Nebraska's insurance fund chose not to close many insolvent banks that had suspended convertibility; this action contaminated the measure of solvent bank deposits. For this reason I exclude Nebraska from the dummy for insured states in the 1920–1926 regression. Results for the 1920–1930 regression are reported with and without including Nebraska in the dummy banking variable.

The regressions show that the presence of insurance was associated

TABLE 5.16

Regression Results: Late Asset Growth of State-chartered Banks

Dependent variable: Growth in total assets of state-chartered banks, 1920–1926

Independent variable	Coefficient	Standard error	Prob > 1T1
Intercept	0.400	0.458	0.391
National bank growth	0.598	0.239	0.019
(Reserve center) × (national bank growth)	0.213	0.098	0.039
Ratio of farm to nonfarm population	−0.251	0.347	0.477
Growth in land values, 1920–1925	0.269	0.540	0.622
Business failure rate, 1921–1925 / Business failure rate, 1917–1920	−0.048	0.039	0.233
Presence of deposit insurance (excluding Nebraska)	−0.271	0.123	0.036

$R^2 = 0.537$
$\bar{R}^2 = 0.426$

Dependent variable: Growth in total assets of state-chartered banks, 1920–1930

Independent variable	Coefficient	Standard error	Prob > 1T1
Intercept	1.482	0.554	0.013
National bank growth	0.063	0.225	0.782
(Reserve center) × (national bank growth)	0.141	0.135	0.308
Ratio of farm to nonfarm population	−0.648	0.475	0.185
Growth in land values, 1920–1930	−0.091	0.659	0.891
Business failure rate, 1921–1929 / Business failure rate, 1917–1920	−0.095	0.053	0.088
Presence of deposit insurance (excluding Nebraska)	−0.194	0.171	0.267

$R^2 = 0.405$
$\bar{R}^2 = 0.262$

Dependent variable: Growth in total assets of state-chartered banks, 1920–1930

Independent variable	Coefficient	Standard error	Prob > 1T1
Intercept	1.467	0.529	0.010
National bank growth	0.055	0.220	0.803
(Reserve center) × (national bank growth)	0.130	0.133	0.337
Ratio of farm to nonfarm population	−0.593	0.465	0.214
Growth in land values, 1920–1930	−0.065	0.641	0.920
Business failure rate, 1921–1929 / Business failure rate, 1917–1920	−0.094	0.052	0.079
Presence of deposit insurance (including Nebraska)	−0.240	0.155	0.134

$R^2 = 0.429$
$\bar{R}^2 = 0.292$

with lower growth during the decline. Growth for the insured systems from 1920 to 1926 was 27 percent lower (as a fraction of the 1920 level) than in uninsured state systems. Not surprisingly, the difference in growth is lessened if one chooses a longer period (1920–1930) to gauge recovery from the crisis. When the postponed collapse of Nebraska is included for the 1920–1930 sample, there is a change from a 19 percent to a 24 percent slowdown in growth during the decade. Other variables generally have the expected signs—higher business failure rates and farm population concentration are associated with lower growth; and controlling for omitted variables by including national bank growth is important for the 1920–1926 period. Land value changes add little to the reliability of the regression equation once these other control variables are taken into account.

Insured banks were not the only ones that saw a decline in growth during the crisis. Many states experienced a considerable decline as agricultural earnings fell and bankruptcies rose. There was, however, substantial variation in the rate of recovery from the crisis across states, and across banks within states. As Table 5.8 shows, in the period 1927–1929 the uninsured state systems of Arizona, Idaho, and Wyoming saw high growth rates that essentially reversed the negative growth of the previous seven years. In all three cases, state-chartered banking growth for the period 1920–1929 exceeded the growth of national-chartered banks in those states.[20]

Furthermore, within states the growth of state-chartered banks was not identical across banks. With the exception of the insured systems, the average size of state-chartered banks was somewhat stationary or even increased from 1920 to 1929 (Table 5.7). In some extreme cases assets per bank approximately doubled (Arizona, Illinois, Michigan, Ohio, and Wyoming).

Growth of bank asset levels and increases in average bank size are positively related during this period, as exemplified by the experiences of Arizona and Wyoming, in particular. This correspondence suggests that, as small rural banks failed, they were not likely to be replaced by similar institutions, but rather by larger banks. White (1985) found that the surge in bank mergers from 1919 to 1933 was partly the result of the desire to move away from a system of small, fragile unit banks. While several factors could account for variations across states in the extent of consolidation (for example, a reduction in the perceived desirability of rural farm loans and a change in emphasis toward industry located in cities and towns where larger unit banks operate), this variation may also reflect different regulations across states—in particular, laws governing branch banking.[21]

In states that allowed branch banking, the acquisition of small rural banks that failed or their replacement with new branches should have been easy because the cost (including risk) of establishing branches was lower than that of opening a bank.[22] Chapman (1934: Chapter 11) provides evidence of relatively high growth of branching banks for the nation as a whole during the 1920s. A thorough analysis of the relative growth of branching banks and unit banks during the 1920s in states that permitted branching would require a study at the level of individual banks, which is beyond the scope of this paper. Instead, using available data, I examine the growth in the number of branching banks and their branches at the state level and link it to total banking growth, in number and total assets.

Branch banking and banking system recovery. Table 5.17 summarizes data on the growth in the number of total banks, branching banks, and branches of national and state banks for 1924 (the earliest available data) and 1928 (the last disaggregated data available for the 1920s), categorized according to state banking laws on branching in the thirty-two agricultural crisis states. The state-bank regulatory regimes are divided into four groups: full free entry for branching banks statewide, full free entry with locational limitations on branches, limited (or zero) entry of new branching banks but continuation of existing branching, and total legal prohibition of branching.[23]

National banks were often permitted to maintain any branches that existed at the time of their conversion to national charters; thus

TABLE 5.17

Growth in Branch Banking (in thirty-two "agricultural crisis" states)

	National Banks					
	1924			1928		
	Total facilities	Branching banks	Branches	Total facilities	Branching banks	Branches
Statewide branching allowed						
Arizona	19	0	0	15	0	0
North Carolina	86	2	3	83	4	6
South Carolina	84	2	3	66	3	8
Virginia	352	7	11	182	9	16
Limited branching allowed						
Kentucky	145	3	7	155	4	15
Louisiana	41	1	8	41	1	8
Michigan	144	10	23	181	9	48
Ohio	363	4	4	338	7	7
Tennessee	110	2	2	122	7	19
Preexisting branching allowed						
Alabama	105	0	0	107	0	0
Arkansas	88	0	0	79	0	0
Georgia	101	2	7	97	4	16
Indiana	248	0	0	229	1	2
Minnesota	345	3	11	285	2	6
Mississippi	36	1	1	37	1	1
Nebraska	177	2	2	160	2	2
Washington	114	1	2	111	1	2
Wisconsin	157	1	2	159	1	2
No branching						
Colorado	141	0	0	123	0	0
Idaho	70	0	0	46	0	0
Illinois	502	0	0	484	0	0
Iowa	347	0	0	270	0	0
Kansas	260	0	0	250	0	0
Missouri	134	0	0	134	0	0
Montana	93	0	0	70	0	0
Nevada	11	0	0	10	0	0
New Mexico	33	0	0	29	0	0
North Dakota	165	0	0	136	0	0
Oklahoma	421	0	0	333	0	0
South Dakota	116	0	0	97	0	0
Texas	573	0	0	638	0	0
Wyoming	37	0	0	26	0	0

(*continued on next page*)

TABLE 5.17 (*continued*)

	State Banks					
	1924			1928		
	Total facilities	Branching banks	Branches	Total facilities	Branching banks	Branches
Statewide branching allowed						
Arizona	64	6	20	53	8	23
North Carolina	535	39	64	437	39	73
South Carolina	347	7	17	247	12	28
Virginia	216	24	34	376	30	47
Limited branching allowed						
Kentucky	483	1	5	480	29	34
Louisiana	303	33	85	299	42	103
Michigan	906	53	309	989	55	374
Ohio	947	47	199	960	52	243
Tennessee	512	19	51	446	20	42
Preexisting branching allowed						
Alabama	276	5	19	269	5	19
Arkansas	400	2	3	361	2	3
Georgia	608	19	46	394	15	21
Indiana	863	4	8	808	3	7
Minnesota	1,081	0	0	855	0	0
Mississippi	346	10	24	313	10	24
Nebraska	925	0	0	746	0	0
Washington	272	4	5	247	3	4
Wisconsin	839	6	7	817	6	7
No branching						
Colorado	201	0	0	164	0	0
Idaho	107	0	0	94	0	0
Illinois	1,408	0	0	1,337	0	0
Iowa	1,438	0	0	1,169	0	0
Kansas	1,033	0	0	864	0	0
Missouri	1,478	0	0	1,231	0	0
Montana	155	0	0	132	0	0
Nevada	23	0	0	25	0	0
New Mexico	43	0	0	29	0	0
North Dakota	523	0	0	354	0	0
Oklahoma	388	0	0	337	0	0
South Dakota	437	0	0	315	0	0
Texas	1,046	0	0	816	0	0
Wyoming	79	0	0	60	0	0

(*continued on facing page*)

TABLE 5.17 (*continued*)

	All Banks			
	1924		1928	
	Total	Branching banks and branches	Total	Branching banks and branches
Statewide branching allowed				
Arizona	83	26	68	31
North Carolina	621	108	520	122
South Carolina	431	29	313	66
Virginia	568	76	558	102
Limited branching allowed				
Kentucky	628	16	635	82
Louisiana	344	127	340	154
Michigan	1,050	395	1,170	486
Ohio	1,310	254	1,298	309
Tennessee	622	74	568	88
Preexisting branching allowed				
Alabama	381	24	376	24
Arkansas	488	5	440	5
Georgia	709	74	491	56
Indiana	1,111	12	1,037	13
Minnesota	1,426	14	1,140	8
Mississippi	382	36	350	36
Nebraska	1,102	4	906	4
Washington	386	12	358	10
Wisconsin	996	16	976	16
No branching				
Colorado	342	0	287	0
Idaho	177	0	140	0
Illinois	1,910	0	1,821	0
Iowa	1,785	0	1,439	0
Kansas	1,293	0	1,114	0
Missouri	1,612	0	1,365	0
Montana	248	0	202	0
Nevada	34	0	35	0
New Mexico	76	0	58	0
North Dakota	688	0	490	0
Oklahoma	809	0	670	0
South Dakota	553	0	412	0
Texas	1,619	0	1,454	0
Wyoming	116	0	86	0

SOURCES: See Data Appendix.

national banks operated branches in some states. In no states before 1927, however, did national banks maintain significant branching systems. Upon passage of the McFadden Act (February 1927), limited national bank branching was allowed in states that permitted branch banking. Even under the McFadden Act national banks were still restricted to establishing branches within the "city, town or village" of their main office. Thus there was little variation across states in national bank branching during the 1920s.

Several patterns are visible in Table 5.17. Because of switching between national and state charters, let us focus on branching within the states for national and state banks in aggregate. Of the eighteen states that allowed branches to exist, only three saw a reduction in the number of total branch-banking facilities from 1924 to 1928. All these reductions occurred in states that prohibited the establishment of new branches but allowed existing branches to be maintained (Georgia, Minnesota, and Washington). In all three cases, the departure (failure or closing) of a single bank accounts for the reduction.[24] In the other six states that allowed branching to continue but prohibited the establishment of new branches, the number of branching facilities remained the same. In the nine states that allowed new branching, branching facilities uniformly increased at a rapid rate, often as the total number of banking facilities declined; and branching thus came to comprise a much larger fraction of total banking facilities.

Moreover, the recovery of total bank asset levels was higher for systems that permitted growth in branch banking. Arizona, Kentucky, Louisiana, Michigan, North Carolina, Ohio, Tennessee, and Virginia all saw relatively high rates of asset recovery (Table 5.8) in the late 1920s relative to other states. These were also the states that experienced the largest increases in the average size of banks (Table 5.7). South Carolina was the only exception to the rule, with negative asset growth in both banking systems during this period. Clearly, this exception "proves the rule," as South Carolina witnessed a more than doubling of its branch banking facilities from 1924 to 1929, even though the combined growth of unit and branching banks was negative.

More formally, in Table 5.18 I report regressions of bank asset growth from 1920 to 1926 and 1926 to 1930 on the same variables used in Table 5.16, with the addition of branching dummies for city-restricted and out-of-city branching. Out-of-city branching includes statewide branching systems and Ohio, which allowed limited out-of-city branching. I also report regressions using the change in

TABLE 5.18

Regression Results: Late Asset Growth and Bank Size of State-chartered Banks

Dependent variable: Growth in total assets of state-chartered banks, 1920–1926

Independent variable	Coefficient	Standard error	Prob > 1T1
Intercept	0.544	0.450	0.239
National bank growth	0.602	0.235	0.018
(Reserve center) × (national bank growth)	0.178	0.098	0.084
Ratio of farm to nonfarm population	−0.404	0.346	0.254
Growth in land values, 1920–1925	0.037	0.541	0.946
Business failure rate, 1921–1925 / Business failure rate, 1917–1920	−0.040	0.038	0.308
Presence of deposit insurance (excluding Nebraska)	−0.190	0.126	0.146
Out-of-city branch banking	0.179	0.124	0.163
Within-city branch banking	0.204	0.132	0.136

$R^2 = 0.601$
$\bar{R}^2 = 0.462$

Dependent variable: Growth in total assets of state-chartered banks, 1920–1930

Independent variable	Coefficient	Standard error	Prob > 1T1
Intercept	1.539	0.449	0.002
National bank growth	0.124	0.200	0.539
(Reserve center) × (national bank growth)	0.078	0.115	0.502
Ratio of farm to nonfarm population	−0.936	0.405	0.030
Growth in land values, 1920–1930	−0.386	0.551	0.490
Business failure rate, 1921–1929 / Business failure rate, 1917–1920	−0.072	0.044	0.118
Presence of deposit insurance (excluding Nebraska)	−0.065	0.140	0.647
Out-of-city branch banking	0.398	0.150	0.014
Within-city branch banking	0.428	0.161	0.014

$R^2 = 0.625$
$\bar{R}^2 = 0.495$

(*continued on next page*)

TABLE 5.18 (*continued*)

Dependent variable: Assets per bank for state-chartered banks, 1926

Independent variable	Coefficient	Standard error	Prob > 1T1
Intercept	1341.96	739.24	0.082
National bank growth	0.101	0.115	0.385
(Reserve center) × (national bank growth)	0.084	0.072	0.256
Ratio of farm to nonfarm population	−1782.05	580.74	0.005
Growth in land values, 1920–1925	−160.61	884.00	0.857
Business failure rate, 1921–1925 / Business failure rate, 1917–1920	−40.55	60.60	0.510
Out-of-city branch banking	593.49	198.93	0.007
Within-city branch banking	540.64	257.51	0.047

$R^2 = 0.688$
$\bar{R}^2 = 0.597$

Dependent variable: Assets per bank for state-chartered banks, 1930

Independent variable	Coefficient	Standard error	Prob > 1T1
Intercept	1868.64	847.17	0.037
National bank growth	0.072	0.128	0.577
(Reserve center) × (national bank growth)	0.100	0.079	0.219
Ratio of farm to nonfarm population	−2642.12	725.33	0.001
Growth in land values, 1920–1930	−375.72	952.96	0.697
Business failure rate, 1921–1929 / Business failure rate, 1917–1920	−24.39	75.20	0.749
Out-of-city branch banking	876.91	244.74	0.002
Within-city branch banking	736.32	330.63	0.036

$R^2 = 0.700$
$\bar{R}^2 = 0.612$

average bank size as the dependent variable. While the availability of the few degrees of freedom in the regressions prompts a cautious interpretation of the results, both branching indicator variables were relatively large and statistically significant. Indeed, branching indicators have a larger, more significant, and more persistent effect on total asset growth than deposit insurance indicators in the regression. These results indicate that, from the standpoint of *long-run* banking recovery, the distinction between unit and branch banking was more important than the distinction between insured and uninsured banking. Deposit insurance mainly caused a retreat from the state-chartered systems until the time that the insurance fund was dissolved; then the state systems as well as other unit banking systems gradually recovered. In contrast, the effect of branching on banking growth and average bank size increases with time.

These comparisons understate the difference in growth between branching banks and independent unit banks, because many unit banks operated as members of bank "chains." The Federal Reserve, which collected data on "chain" banks, distinguished true chains from other banking conglomerates. Chains were defined as groups of corporately independent banks "under centralized control."[25] As was recognized at the time, chains sometimes served as a "second best" substitute for branches in states where branching was prohibited. While banks in chains were separate corporate entities, they imitated to a lesser degree some of the advantageous features of branch banks. First, chains of banks could reduce individual bank risk by coordinating their response to crises and coinsuring as a group. Second, chains pooled resources and staffs to reduce overhead expenses and improve account management procedures (see Chapman, 1934: 322–63). The potential for chains to allow member banks to diversify bank portfolios seems to have been more limited, as the high failure rates of chains relative to branching banks indicate.[26]

As Table 5.19 indicates, the freedom to branch was inversely related to the prevalence of chain banking. Table 5.19 reports the number and proportion of chain banks in the state- and national-chartered systems for our sample of thirty-two agricultural crisis states. States with branching restrictions saw much higher incidence of chain banking, and that incidence increased with the extent of the branching prohibition.

Summary of findings. The evidence on overall growth, average size, and membership patterns of banks during the 1920s indicates that the states can be grouped into three categories according to the

TABLE 5.19

Chain Systems and Participating Banks by State (as of June 30, 1929)

		Banks in chain systems	
	Number of chain systems	National	State
Statewide branch banking permitted			
Arizona	1	1	5
California	4	20	10
Delaware			
District of Columbia			
Maryland			
North Carolina			
Rhode Island	1	1	2
South Carolina			
Virginia	—	—	—
Total	6	22	17
Branches restricted as to location			
Kentucky	1	4	
Louisiana	2	6	4
Maine	1	2	3
Massachusetts	4	19	14
Michigan	11	3	68
Mississippi			
New Jersey	12	22	27
New York	17	58	53
Ohio	1	3	3
Pennsylvania	9	12	26
Tennessee	3	6	4
Total	61	135	202

(*continued on facing page*)

banking systems in use at the time: states where deposit insurance made the system more fragile, magnified the expansion in response to the agricultural boom, and worsened the contraction during the bust; other unit banking states with less extensive swings in aggregate growth; and states with branch banking systems (restricted or statewide) that managed to respond most successfully to the challenges brought by the declining terms of trade in agriculture.

How can one reconcile the fact that deposit insurance created

TABLE 5.19 (*continued*)

	Number of chain systems	Banks in chain systems National	State
	Branches prohibited by law		
Alabama	3	11	11
Arkansas	4	13	50
Colorado	2	8	5
Connecticut			
Florida	4	13	19
Georgia	6	8	15
Idaho	3	7	16
Illinois	11	20	61
Indiana	1	2	1
Iowa	12	33	59
Kansas	10	15	40
Minnesota	34	130	149
Missouri	4	7	19
Montana	2	4	11
Nebraska	9	15	48
Nevada	2	2	12
New Mexico	1	4	2
Oregon	6	14	18
Texas	6	7	30
Utah	5	12	38
Washington	11	26	36
West Virginia			
Wisconsin	5	14	21
Total	141	365	661
	Branches prohibited in practice		
New Hampshire			
North Dakota	7	20	40
Oklahoma	8	41	18
South Dakota	5	10	20
Vermont			
Wyoming	2	3	7
Total	22	74	85
Grand Total	230	596	965

SOURCES: See Data Appendix.

moral hazard during the boom but did not protect depositors ultimately? I would argue that the precipitous collapse of agricultural prices was a small-probability event with major consequences. Insurance would have protected (at least the first few) individual banks from individual failures absent cataclysmic declines, and thus depositors may have been less mindful of bank risk taking before the bust. The large withdrawals of assets from insured banks after insurance was removed are certainly consistent with the notion of depositor discipline through withdrawals from troubled banks.

Bank Failure Costs and the Role of Regulation

Combined data on numbers of banks and their assets over time do not distinguish voluntary exits by banks from bank failures. In particular, one might conceive that the decline in insured banking was primarily the result of voluntary exit in response to rising assessments once a few banks had failed, in conjunction with laws that permitted banks to switch charters. If this were the case, skeptics regarding the failings of the insured systems might argue that the prohibition of voluntary exit would have been sufficient to make the systems viable.

Evidence on bank failures and their costs therefore provides a complement to the results reported in the previous section. A study of the characteristics of bank failures permits one to distinguish exits from failures and supplies further direct evidence on the extent of risk taking during the boom under different regulatory regimes.

The American Bankers Association (1933), Calomiris (1989), and Thies and Gerlowski (1989) provide evidence that insured banks were more likely to fail than (a) national banks in the same state, (b) uninsured state banks in the same state, and (c) uninsured state banks in other states. While the within-state comparisons made by these authors of the failure propensities of insured and uninsured state banks in Kansas (summarized later) are compelling, the other evidence is less so. One must control for differences in states' product specialization, and differences across states in the relative agricultural risk exposure of national and state banks (because of other regulatory differences between national and state banks) if one wants to isolate the role of deposit insurance regulation in promoting risk taking.[27]

Furthermore, the definitions of bank failure may differ across these studies in ways that are not always clear. In analyzing bank failures, I restrict attention to involuntary liquidations. Some banks suspended operations and reopened; other banks were acquired by other institutions; some banks chose to close while still solvent. Suspensions, consolidations, and voluntary closings have social costs—consolidations and closings may reduce the supply of banking services in some areas, and suspensions disrupt the payments system. I focus on liquidations because they offer a clearer index of the costs of the crisis—forced permanent departure of banks and depositor losses—and provide a clearer measure of the risk taking of banks, since closings, acquisitions, and suspensions often have explanations other than bank insolvency.[28] I also focus on average failure rates for several years rather than year-by-year comparisons across states. Differences in state closure rules (in particular, the long delay in closing insolvent banks by the Nebraska Guaranty Fund) argue for this approach.[29]

I examine three dimensions of the failure "performance" of banking systems: the rate of bank failure; the severity of bank failure, measured as the ratio of claims on failed banks to their remaining resources (excluding payments by insurance funds); and the efficiency of the bank liquidation process, with emphasis on the roles of deposit insurance and branching regulations.

Bank failure rates. Table 5.20 presents data on average annual bank failure rates, by state and type of banking system, for various subperiods from 1918 to 1929 for the sample of thirty-two agricultural crisis states.[30] These data echo the wide variation in economic fundamentals and banking system responses across states and types of banks evidenced in earlier tables. Clearly, the Cotton Belt and the grain-producing states suffered disproportionately during the 1920s. Table 5.20 illustrates the pitfalls of using the difference

TABLE 5.20

Average Annual Percentage Bank Failure Rate, 1918–1929 (in thirty-two "agricultural crisis" states)

	1918–1920		1921–1924		1925–1929		1921–1929	
	National banks	State banks	National banks	State banks	National banks	State banks	National banks	State banks
Alabama	.00	.14	0.25	0.70	0.57	1.17	0.44	0.97
Arizona	.00	.00	3.75	7.09	0.00	3.11	1.67	4.31
Arkansas	.50	.34	0.30	1.05	1.36	2.92	0.94	2.06
Colorado	.00	.29	0.71	2.96	1.56	2.49	1.18	2.37
Georgia	.00	.31	0.27	3.10	1.91	5.80	1.19	4.02
Idaho	.00	.00	4.32	5.67	2.86	2.80	3.29	3.70
Illinois	.00	.16	0.05	0.39	0.44	0.48	0.28	0.43
Indiana	.00	.18	0.10	0.53	0.56	1.22	0.35	0.96
Iowa	.00	.04	0.28	1.06	4.32	2.78	2.45	1.89
Kansas	.00	.17	0.40	1.43	0.54	2.19	0.49	1.78
Kentucky	.00	.07	0.00	0.67	0.00	1.14	0.00	0.96
Louisiana	.00	.16	0.66	1.64	0.00	1.47	0.29	1.50
Michigan	.00	.05	0.00	0.17	0.17	0.10	0.10	0.14
Minnesota	.12	.46	0.53	1.95	3.11	3.96	1.98	2.89
Mississippi	.00	.00	0.83	1.41	0.57	1.47	0.74	1.43
Missouri	.00	.22	0.00	1.02	0.75	2.33	0.41	1.72
Montana	.00	.00	6.72	10.14	3.23	1.94	4.14	5.09
Nebraska	.00	.07	1.73	1.81	1.60	4.27	1.60	2.98
Nevada	.00	.00	0.00	1.09	0.00	0.00	0.00	0.48
New Mexico	.00	.00	7.98	8.89	1.82	5.12	4.26	5.56
N. Carolina	.00	.00	0.86	1.88	1.93	2.40	1.40	2.20
N. Dakota	.00	.10	3.59	7.10	3.64	6.69	3.44	5.87
Ohio	.09	.04	0.14	0.13	0.17	0.59	0.15	0.37
Oklahoma	.10	.18	1.72	4.82	1.47	2.89	1.76	3.16
S. Carolina	.00	.00	0.00	2.31	3.70	7.94	2.03	4.87
S. Dakota	.00	.07	4.04	5.99	4.83	5.86	4.09	5.28
Tennessee	.00	.00	0.00	0.39	0.37	2.12	0.23	1.38
Texas	.00	.20	0.58	1.69	0.63	1.40	0.62	1.47
Virginia	.00	.34	0.15	0.98	0.11	0.92	0.13	0.97
Washington	.00	.23	0.57	1.96	1.07	1.13	1.02	1.42
Wisconsin	.00	.00	0.33	0.36	0.52	0.96	0.44	0.69
Wyoming	.00	.00	4.26	6.20	1.62	5.06	2.60	4.72
Average	.03	.12	1.41	2.71	1.42	2.65	1.37	2.43

SOURCES: See Data Appendix.

between state and national bank failure rates for a given state (as in Calomiris, 1989) to measure the role of deposit insurance. While the differences between state and national bank annual failure rates for 1921–1929 are greater for insured states than for uninsured states on average (1.4 percent for compulsory-insurance states, as compared to 1.0 percent for states without deposit insurance), in all but one state (Iowa) the failure rate for national banks was less than for state banks, presumably because of the smaller average bank size and more liberal real estate lending regulations of the latter.

Similarly, comparisons between states across state-chartered systems reveal several cases where uninsured systems fared worse than insured. The difference in annual failure rates between the uninsured (2.26 percent) and insured (2.92 percent) state-chartered banking systems for 1921–1929 on average is 0.68 percent, but by varying the definition of region—a control used in Thies and Gerlowski (1989)—one could easily conclude from such simple comparisons that insured state-chartered banks had less experience of failure than uninsured state-chartered banks. For example, one could define Texas and Oklahoma as being in the same region as Arizona and New Mexico, or define Mississippi as being in the same region as Alabama, Georgia, Louisiana, and South Carolina.

Regional distinctions, of course, are intended as rough classifications of economic environments under which banking systems operate. Thus, rather than experiment with different definitions of economic regions, I included measures of economic environment directly in weighted-least-squares regressions to capture the marginal effects of deposit insurance on bank failure propensities.[31] I do not report these results because I found that, depending on the precise mix of control variables one uses, the calculated impact of deposit insurance (and of the control variables) varied greatly and was typically positive and insignificant.[32] In other words, given the few degrees of freedom available, regression results seem unable to deliver much information on the contribution of deposit insurance to bank failure propensities. The only robust findings from this analysis were the strong positive association between commercial failure rates and bank failure rates and the strong negative relation between average bank size and bank failure rates.

Perhaps the best evidence of excess failure rates for insured banks remains the simple comparison of the failure tendencies of insured and uninsured state-chartered banks operating in Kansas. Kansas provides a unique "controlled experiment" because it was the only state with a large number of both insured and uninsured state-chartered banks. The annual failure rate for insured banks in Kansas from 1921 to 1924 (before the mass conversions of banks to uninsured charters) is 1.90, compared to an annual failure rate of 0.67 percent for uninsured banks.[33]

The severity of bank failure for insured and uninsured systems. It would be a mistake to place too much emphasis on rates of bank failure as indicators of the costliness of financial crises. Bank failures are discrete events; particularly severe financial crises force many banks to cross the threshold of failure. For this reason, bank system performance may be better gauged by the overall losses of depositors, rather than the tendency to fail, which may show relatively little variation.

Data exist with which to perform cross-state and cross-system comparisons of asset shortfalls of insolvent banks in the 1920s as a means to measure the average severity of bank failures across states. Complete data for insured banking systems are provided in FDIC (1956), but data for the rest of the U.S. banking systems are available only for banks whose liquidations were completed by 1930 (see Data Appendix). As Table 5.21 shows, for some state-chartered systems only a small percentage of liquidations that had occurred during the 1920s were processed by 1930. The ratio of repayments to total unsecured deposit claims from the limited sample in each state is likely to be a biased indicator of the total sample; for example, banks with higher losses might take longer to liquidate.

Despite this problem, there is little doubt that insolvent insured banks suffered worse asset depreciation in the 1920s than state-chartered banks in other states. The rates of shortfall for insured state banks were among the highest in the country (Table 5.21). Regional comparisons are particularly telling. Consider the low ratios of repayments from assets to total claims of North and South Dakota (17 and 24 percent, respectively) and their neighbors' ratios: Montana (52), Idaho (49), Wyoming (54), Colorado (68), and Minnesota (48). A comparison of insured banking in Nebraska (35) with that in Iowa (54), Missouri (53), Colorado, and Wyoming is similarly revealing.

Kansas, Oklahoma, Texas, and Mississippi showed ratios more similar to the average experience of their neighbors. Note that two of these were voluntary insurance states, and the exceptionally high required capital ratio of Texas may have played a role here as well.

Oklahoma's compulsory insurance system lasted only until 1923 and thus should have had relatively little influence on failure propensity for the 1920s as a whole. As current critics of deposit insurance emphasize, many of the losses that occur in an insured system reflect bank responses to adverse shocks that reduce bank capital and magnify the incentives for risk taking (see Kane, 1988; and Horvitz, this volume). By closing its system early in the 1920s, Oklahoma may have avoided this magnification of risk taking.

Mississippi had the lowest rate of asset shortfall of the five compulsory insurance states, as well as the lowest rate by far of bank failure for that group for the period 1921–1929. Mississippi's special experience may reflect, in part, the circumstances for the creation of its compulsory-insurance system. The Mississippi deposit insurance law was passed in response to the state banking crisis of 1912–1913, induced by the destruction of cotton crops in those years by the boll weevil. The relatively low failure rate (Table 5.20) and degree of asset shortfall (Table 5.21) in Mississippi during the 1920s may indicate simply that many of the most vulnerable banks in that state had collapsed before the period of deposit insurance coverage. The surviving banks on average were larger and more urban and thus were less likely to use deposit insurance protection to promote high-risk agricultural expansion. Entry by new banks seeking to take advantage of deposit insurance was notoriously difficult in Mississippi as

TABLE 5.21

Bank Liquidations, 1921–1930 (as of 1930)

	National banks			State banks		
	Number completely liquidated	Number in process of liquidation	Repayment ratio[a]	Number completely liquidated	Number in process of liquidation	Repayment ratio[a]
Alabama	2	11	1.00	9	39	.59
Arizona	2	0	.50	4	20	.91
Arkansas	3	15	.87	37	96	.36
Colorado	8	9	.60	62	9	.68
Georgia	5	11	.51	120	130	.44
Idaho	17	4	.47	28	11	.49
Illinois	2	31	.76	9	131	.63
Indiana	1	12	.77	6	109	.88
Iowa	14	69	.69	182	130	.54
Kansas	4	10	.79	119[b]	0[b]	.53[b]
Kentucky	0	3	NA	18	41	NA
Louisiana	1	0	.69	16	19	.41
Michigan	0	4	NA	2	8	.72
Minnesota	13	43	.58	50	245	.48

Mississippi	2	.88	64[b]	0[b]	.52[b]
Missouri	2	.66	109	200	.53
Montana	38	.34	27	28	.52
Nebraska	13	.44	317[b]	0[b]	.35[b]
Nevada	0	NA	0	0	NA
New Mexico	12	.51	18	19	.70
North Carolina	4	.71	2	87	1.00
North Dakota	21	.45	340[b]	0[b]	.17[b]
Ohio	3	.66	0	42	NA
Oklahoma	25	.43	139[b]	0[b]	.56[b]
South Carolina	8	.51	16	189	.66
South Dakota	16	.51	242[b]	0[b]	.24[b]
Tennessee	1	.93	12	61	.83
Texas	21	.58	138[b]	0[b]	.54[b]
Virginia	1	.90	4	41	.57
Washington	4	.84	1[b]	0[b]	.75[b]
Wisconsin	2	.30	20	40	.66
Wyoming	8	.70	15	13	.54

[a]The repayment ratio is defined as the ratio of deposits repaid from asset liquidation for banks that were completely liquidated.
[b]Insured banks only. Includes liquidations completed after 1930.
SOURCES: See Data Appendix.

well, because of the strict chartering standards set by the state's regulators.[34] Thus Mississippi seems to have avoided the higher failure rates of the other compulsory systems mainly because its insurance system was enacted after a major agricultural depression and because its regulators prevented the entry of small rural unit banks that were so common in the other insured states. This view is consistent with the comparatively large average size of banks in 1918 and 1920 in Mississippi relative to its neighbors or relative to other insured banking systems (see Table 5.7).

Inefficient bank liquidation procedures in insured states. A final interesting difference between insured and uninsured banking was the efficiency of bank liquidation procedures. Delays in winding up the operations of banks impose costs on depositors of illiquidity and forgone interest, apart from the ultimate larger losses due to asset shortfalls. Delays in closing banks, or in final liquidation of closed banks, may also afford insolvent bankers greater opportunities for risk taking or fraudulent behavior.

On average, for the United States as a whole during the 1920s, it took three years eleven months for state bank liquidations to be completed, and for national banks it took four years two months. For the agricultural crisis states for which data are available, state bank liquidations averaged four years four months, and national bank liquidations averaged three years eleven months (Table 5.22). In the five compulsory insurance states delays for insured state banks were much longer than for state banks in other states and much longer than for national banks in those states (see Table 5.22). In Nebraska, state-chartered banks that were liquidated before 1930 took an average of six years four months to be liquidated, compared to four years nine months for national banks. In North and South Dakota, state-bank liquidation delays averaged six years three months and five years seven months, respectively, compared to four years and four years eight months for national banks in the respective states. In Oklahoma, delays averaged five years, compared to three years eight months for national banks. Voluntary insurance state systems had

TABLE 5.22
Average Time between Closing and Completed Liquidation of Banks, 1921–1930 (in thirty-two "agricultural crisis" states)

	National banks		State banks	
	Years	Number of banks	Years	Number of banks
Alabama	3.17	2	3.25	8
Arizona	4.83	2	3.67	3
Arkansas	2.42	3	2.83	37
Colorado	4.42	8	2.92	60
Georgia	3.75	5	3.67	113
Idaho	4.17	17	4.50	28
Illinois	3.25	2	3.83	8
Indiana	7.50	1	4.33	5
Iowa	3.67	14	3.58	179
Kansas	3.25	4	3.33	117
Kentucky	n.a.	n.a.	3.33	17
Louisiana	7.17	1	4.25	14
Michigan	n.a.	n.a.	6.25	2
Minnesota	4.00	13	5.58	48
Mississippi	1.08	2	6.00	2
Missouri	3.50	2	3.17	109
Montana	4.50	38	4.33	23
Nebraska	4.75	13	6.33	15
Nevada	n.a.	n.a.	n.a.	n.a.
New Mexico	4.42	12	5.00	17
North Carolina	2.92	4	7.08	1
North Dakota	4.00	21	6.25	35
Ohio	3.42	3	n.a.	n.a.
Oklahoma	3.67	25	5.00	64
South Carolina	3.83	8	3.92	8
South Dakota	4.67	16	5.58	22
Tennessee	0.92	1	3.92	6
Texas	4.00	21	3.75	19
Virginia	4.67	1	3.92	4
Washington	4.17	4	4.08	32
Wisconsin	3.67	2	3.17	20
Wyoming	4.83	8	3.33	10

n.a. = not available.
SOURCES: See Data Appendix.

average delays roughly comparable to those of national banks operating within the same states, as did virtually all other agricultural crisis states.[35]

What can explain this phenomenon? That deposit insurance systems redeemed the losses of depositors slowly and partially, owing in part to the limited resources of the funds, is well established (see American Bankers Association, 1933; FDIC, 1956). The present analysis reveals that even the liquidation of failed banks was more protracted in the insured systems than otherwise. One explanation for the inordinate delays is political. Perhaps solvent banks and bank regulators sought to delay the liquidation of insolvent bank assets to limit the rate of increase of the obligations of the guarantee funds. The evidence of delayed closure of banks, especially in Nebraska, is consistent with this interpretation of delayed liquidation. That lag is akin to the FSLIC's recent policy of delaying the closure of insolvent savings and loans, purportedly at the behest of members of Congress or savings and loan owners.[36] State politicians of the 1920s may have acted similarly; and solvent banks had a motive for encouraging delays, to give themselves an opportunity to switch charters in anticipation of increasing obligations and assessments. Whether political motives or other factors explain delays in closures and liquidations must await further historical research into the process of bank liquidation in these states.

The unusual survivability of branching banks. In the previous section I established that branch banking flourished in response to the crisis of the 1920s. Although it is likely that the physical costs of entry of branches was lower than that of unit banks in many cases, another dimension of the advantage to branching—one that was noted even in the 1920s—was that branching banks suffered lower risk of failure.

References to this phenomenon were quite common (for example, Cartinhour, 1931). The congressional hearings of 1930 on "branch, chain, and group" banking provided data that allow some quantification of the lower risks of branch banking in the United

States during the 1920s. From 1921 to 1929, only thirty-seven branching banks, operating seventy-five branches, were liquidated. More
than two-thirds of these banks operated a single branch, and no
more than six of them operated three or more branches.[37] In 1924
714 banks were operating 2,293 branches. Thus only 112 of the 3,007
branch banking facilities in existence in the middle of the decade, or
roughly 4 percent of branching facilities, failed over the entire
decade.

Of course, national comparisons can be misleading. California
and other states that were relatively prosperous during this period
account for a large percentage of branching facilities. In 1924, the
thirty-two agricultural crisis states contained 1,312 of the 3,007
branch banking facilities. Breakdowns of failures by type of bank and
by state are not readily available; but even if all branching failures
had been concentrated in these states during the 1920s, the annual
rate of failure for branch banking facilities would have been only
0.85 percent. This is a very low rate of failure compared with those of
state systems on the whole (see Table 5.20). Only four state-chartered
systems had failure rates lower than 0.85 percent—Illinois, Michigan, Ohio, and Nevada—and none of these states was among those
most affected by the crisis; for example, they all had below-median
farm foreclosure rates for the sample of thirty-two agricultural crisis
states (see Table 5.3).

In some cases, specific within-state comparisons are possible. In
the states that prohibited new branching from 1924 to 1928 but
allowed branching banks to continue to operate branches (Alabama,
Arkansas, Indiana, Minnesota, Nebraska, Washington, and Wisconsin), branch bank failures can be derived from the difference
between the number of branches in operation in 1928 and the
number in operation in 1924.[38] In this sample of seven states, twenty-
eight branching banks operated fifty-eight branches in 1924; and
twenty-six branching banks operated fifty-three branches in 1928, for
a remarkably low annual failure rate (for all facilities) of 0.02
percent.

Finally, for other states, branch-bank failure experiences can be gleaned from data on bank "disappearances," using *The Bankers Encyclopedia* to trace the presence or absence of banks from 1920 to 1929. In all cases, a careful review of entries revealed whether disappearances were due to acquisitions or to closings. I traced the entries for the branching banks of three states over this period: Mississippi, Arizona, and South Carolina. I chose these states because they experienced high rates of bank failure, they had a small number of branching banks (making data collection easier), and branching banks in these states operated branches mainly outside their home city. In Mississippi, all twenty-four branches in operation in 1920 were located outside their banks' home cities. The same was true of Arizona's twenty branches in operation in 1920. In South Carolina, thirteen out of fifteen branches operated outside the home city. These banks, therefore, provide a useful measure of the potential advantages of statewide branching during a crisis.

Arizona permitted statewide branching throughout the period. In 1920, eight Arizona banks operated twenty branches. By 1929, two of these (each operating one branch) had been acquired by larger branching banks. One of the branching banks (operating one branch) failed. In the interim, three new branching banks had entered, thus explaining the stability in the total number of these banks (see Table 5.17). The average annual failure rate for total branching facilities was therefore 1.6 percent for 1921–1929, compared to 4.3 percent for the state-chartered banks as a whole.

Mississippi had allowed branching outside home cities but later prohibited branching except for the establishment of limited agency facilities within home cities. Nevertheless, the existing statewide branches were permitted to continue operating. During the 1920s none of the ten branching banks operating twenty-four branches failed, whereas the average annual failure rate for state-chartered banks as a whole was 1.4 percent.

In South Carolina from 1920 to 1929, four out of eight branching banks in operation in 1920 closed, but all of these were banks that operated a single branch, and two of the four operated branches within their home city. Thus, of the twenty-three towns or cities in which branch banking facilities were located, nineteen retained them. This fact is important since the lack of available banking facilities in thinly populated areas (where virtually all branches were located in Arizona, Mississippi, and South Carolina) increases transaction costs in those locations and can inhibit the flow of capital to worthy enterprises located there. The overall failure rate of existing branching facilities in South Carolina was 2.9 percent, compared to a rate of 4.9 percent for all state-chartered banks.

Entry into branch banking was especially strong in South Carolina, and entrants apparently learned the importance of establishing multiple branches. Two new entrants—The People's Bank of South Carolina and the South Carolina Savings Bank—entered during the 1920s and established eighteen and nine branches, respectively, operating outside their home cities.

The lessons of the high survival rates of branching banks during the crisis apparently were not lost on bankers. As Table 5.17 shows, and these examples confirm, in states where it was allowed, branching flourished and increasingly took the form of multibranch banks, where that was allowed. Four of the eight states that had enacted deposit insurance legislation before the 1920s passed laws in the aftermath of the crises of the 1920s and 1930s allowing branching. By 1939 North Dakota had provided for limited branching, and Mississippi had reversed its previous prohibition on new branches to allow limited branching as well. South Dakota and Washington permitted full statewide branching. For the United States as a whole by 1939, nineteen states allowed full branch banking, and seventeen allowed limited branching, compared to twelve statewide and six limited branching systems in operation in 1924.[39]

Unfortunately, policy makers in many agricultural unit banking states did not change their regulations with respect to branch banking after the debacle of the 1920s and 1930s. Thus, the same patterns of high failure rates of unit banks repeated in states hit by the agricultural crisis of 1980–1985. As in the earlier period, branching banks weathered the storm far better than unit banks. In California, where branching dominated, despite relatively high farm loan delinquency rates and loan charge-offs, only one bank (a unit bank) failed during the crisis (see Calomiris, Hubbard, and Stock, 1986: 469).

Lessons for Policy in Price-sensitive Less-Developed Countries

It has been widely known that deposit insurance systems enacted in the 1920s failed *ex post facto* to offer sufficient and timely protection to depositors or to the payments system more generally. In this chapter I have shown that deposit insurance created costs as well. It provided incentives for excess risk taking by banks and hampered the recovery of the banking system from the agricultural crisis because of the costs to solvent banks of remaining in the insured banking system. The excessive growth during the halcyon days of 1914–1920 was matched by the excessive failures of banks and decline in banking operations in insured states as a response to the crisis.

Voluntary insurance systems provided less coverage than compulsorily insured systems. In the extreme case of Washington's free-exit policy, there was virtually no insurance protection. The positive aspect of the failed voluntary plans, however, was that the limits on depositor protection also limited the cross-subsidization of risk among banks. This fact explains the differences between the observed growth and loss rates under voluntary and compulsory insurance.

During the boom, voluntary insurance systems grew less than compulsory insurance systems but more than unit banking state systems without insurance plans. Voluntary insurance states also showed intermediate failure rates and liquidation delays. Branching banks suffered much lower risks of failures and enjoyed disproportionately high rates of growth and entry during the 1920s relative to unit banks. From the standpoint of desirability of outcomes during the 1920s, the various regulatory regimes could be ranked (in descending order) as follows: full statewide branching, limited branching, uninsured unit banking, voluntary-insurance unit banking, and compulsory-insurance unit banking (recall that branching was not permitted in insured states).[40]

The contrast between the effects of branch-banking regulations and deposit insurance regulations is ironic, since the two regulatory choices were viewed as alternative solutions to the problem of providing stability in the banking system, without sacrificing banking services in remote areas, during the years of active bank regulatory reform after the Panic of 1907 (White, 1982 and 1983).[41] The history of the 1920s reveals that branching and deposit guarantee in fact had opposite effects with respect to generating banking stability. From this perspective, deposit insurance represented an added cost because it was incorrectly perceived as an alternative to branch banking and thereby helped to perpetuate unit banking.

Proponents of deposit insurance, however, might argue that it was the manner in which deposit insurance was implemented, not insurance per se, that caused systemic collapse in the 1920s. They might argue that higher capital requirements, better supervision, risk-based insurance premiums, and government financing of the insurance fund might have produced a better result. Clearly, with high enough capital requirements and sufficiently strict entry barriers (as in Mississippi), the moral hazard and adverse selection problems of deposit insurance will be reduced and may disappear, but at the expense of higher financing costs to banks and less entry of banking into peripheral areas. Elsewhere (Calomiris, 1989) I have argued that a more successful, efficient, and historically proven organizational scheme for deposit insurance would be a mutual guarantee system of self-regulating branching banks in which the government's main role would be to provide an antitrust policy to define membership for mutually insuring groups of banks. Mutual-guarantee systems were extraordinarily successful in dealing with financial panics during the pre–Civil War years in the United States, while providing access to affordable loans in geographically peripheral areas. Unlike almost all governmental deposit insurance regulators, banks regulated and monitored one another effectively, discovered and corrected unsound banking practices quickly, and kept the payments system operating smoothly in the face of financial crises.[42] Evidence of similarly successful self-regulating systems in other countries is provided in Bordo and Schwartz (1989).

A possible objection to this approach is that limited aggregate banking capital can make it difficult for banks as a group to insure themselves against very large disturbances. In such circumstances, a systemic collapse could occur. Furthermore, given this possibility, it might be impossible for the government to commit credibly to allowing the banking system to fail. Knowledge of this implicit guarantee may provide incentives for risk taking.

I have two responses to this objection. First, if an economy is prone to shocks of this magnitude, deposit insurance may be inadvisable altogether. Why should not banking capital in aggregate be allowed to fall drastically at a time when the investment opportunities of an economy have been devastated? In the presence of free entry and branch banking, one would expect new banks or branches to arise to take the place of failed ones, as in Arizona and South Carolina in the 1920s. Furthermore, it seems inadvisable for an economy devastated by a terms-of-trade shock to attempt a rescue of the banking system, particularly in a developing economy that relies on indirect (often financial) taxation to finance such bailouts. It might be more advisable to act in advance to subsidize new industries in an attempt to diversify the economy, rather than focus on the solvency of the banking system as a panacea. The fundamental problem of such an economy, after all, is not its financial system but its economic base.

My second response to the supposed need for government-financed and government-regulated deposit insurance is an empirical one. In most cases during the 1920s, total banking capital within each state would have been sufficient to repay losses to depositors of failing institutions—and thus mutual guarantee, self-regulating systems operating even at the state level would have been feasible.

Table 5.23 reports total deposits of suspended banks (deposits of failed banks are not available) by state from 1921 to 1930 for national and state banks in the thirteen states with the largest total bank failure rates and provides estimates of the total shortfall of assets in failed banks of each type. A rough indication of the rate of asset shortfall for national and state-chartered banks that failed in these states can be derived from Table 5.21, although these data are imperfect indicators. To obtain an estimate of total asset shortfalls, I multiply the total deposits of suspended banks by the shortfall rate from Table 5.21 (one minus the repayment rate) and multiply this product by the ratio of failed banks to suspended banks. As Table 5.23 shows, in many states the number of bank suspensions far exceeded the number of bank failures because banks were sometimes reopened or acquired rather than placed in receivership. A comparison of the average size of failed banks (estimated from data on completed liquidations) and the average size of suspended banks revealed that larger banks were more likely to avoid liquidation after suspension. I thus adjusted for the average difference in size between suspended and liquidated banks in estimating the total asset shortfalls. To summarize, the estimated shortfall of assets (the difference between depositor claims and receipts from asset liquidation) is given by the product of four terms: total deposits of suspended banks, the ratio of liquidations to suspensions, the shortfall ratio (estimated from data on completed liquidations), and the ratio of the average size of liquidated banks to the average size of suspending banks (again, estimated from data on completed liquidations).

These estimates appear in Table 5.23 for national and state-chartered banks. The level of bank capital plus surplus (bank book equity) of solvent banks in 1930 is provided for comparison. Only three of the thirteen states show a ratio of shortfall to bank equity approaching or above unity: Nebraska, North Dakota, and South Dakota. For all other states, banks as a whole would have had sufficient capital to support failing banks. The national banking failures in all the states could have been absorbed by surviving national banks, and state-chartered systems could have covered losses of failed banks in every state except Nebraska, North Dakota, and South Dakota. These three state systems, however, suffered bank losses several times the size of remaining state banks' equity.

TABLE 5.23

Estimated Asset Shortfalls of Failed Banks (relative to equity of remaining banks in "severe failure" states)

| | Deposits of suspended banks 1921–1930[a] | Ratio of liquidations to suspensions | National banks | | Estimated shortfall[a] | Total bank equity June 1930[a] |
			Average size ratio of liquidated banks to suspended banks	Rate of asset shortfall[b]		
Arizona	1,256	.67	.83	.50	349	3,815
Colorado	11,003	.94	.45	.40	1,862	13,776
Georgia	16,538	.84	.09	.49	613	39,064
Idaho	10,601	.81	.65	.53	2,958	4,612
Iowa	55,984	.79	.50	.31	6,855	35,750
Minnesota	28,338	.97	.59	.42	6,812	69,387
Montana	16,287	.87	.44	.66	4,115	9,999
Nebraska	13,695	.80	.94	.56	5,767	26,083
North Dakota	17,438	.84	.80	.55	6,445	9,210
Oklahoma	27,364	.72	.70	.57	7,861	41,251
South Carolina	12,153	.92	.57	.49	3,123	11,665
South Dakota	21,109	.93	.60	.49	5,772	8,477
Wyoming	9,154	.91	.45	.30	1,125	4,819

State-chartered banks

All banks

	Deposits of suspended banks 1921–1930[a]	Ratio of liquidations to suspensions	Average size ratio of liquidated banks to suspended banks	Rate of asset shortfall[b]	Estimated shortfall[a]	Total bank equity June 1930[a]	Ratio of shortfall to equity
Arizona	15,056	.80	.06	.09	65	8,496	.03
Colorado	12,187	.95	.95	.32	3,520	10,273	.22
Georgia	46,318	.75	.70	.56	13,618	39,805	.18
Idaho	9,185	.85	.63	.51	2,509	4,983	.57
Iowa	138,995	.75	.66	.46	31,649	74,935	.35
Minnesota	80,634	.77	.47	.52	15,174	38,417	.20
Montana	31,361	.89	.47	.48	6,297	9,947	.52
Nebraska	78,093	.85	1.04	.65	44,872	27,760	.94
North Dakota	45,199	.92	1.05	.83	36,240	9,695	2.26
Oklahoma	38,986	.79	.28	.44	3,794	11,493	.22
South Carolina	50,970	.91	.58	.34	9,147	17,069	.43
South Dakota	91,619	.77	1.00	.76	53,615	10,848	3.07
Wyoming	7,536	.80	.48	.46	1,331	3,844	.28

[a]In thousands of dollars.
[b]The rate of asset shortfall is a product of (1) the total deposits of suspended banks; (2) the ratio of liquidations to suspensions; (3) the shortfall ratio; (4) the ratio of the average size of liquidated banks to the average size of suspended banks.
SOURCES: See Data Appendix.

Significantly, these were the *only* states that had compulsory insurance for most of the 1920s (this criterion excludes Oklahoma) and that also allowed substantial entry by new banks (this criterion excludes Mississippi). These states had foreclosure rates and land depreciation experiences comparable to several other states (see Table 5.3)—notably Montana, Georgia, and South Carolina—but none of the state-chartered systems in these other states approached the banking losses relative to remaining equity of the three long-lived, compulsory insurance systems.

This conclusion is supported by the evidence from balance sheet data and the evidence on failure rates and failure severity that has been reported here. Moreover, it agrees with the hypothesis that, absent compulsory deposit insurance (and free entry), the fundamental disturbances experienced in these states would have had different consequences for their banking systems. If statewide branch banking had been permitted within these states, bank failures would have been even lower, and the entry of banking capital during the 1920s would have been higher. Moreover, in a mutual-liability, self-regulating system of banks (like that of three states in the pre–Civil War era) risk taking by banks would have been substantially circumscribed by self-imposed regulations and vigorous supervision of other banks.

Of course, no degree of regulatory wisdom could, or should, have made the 1920s a profitable time for banks in agricultural regions affected by drastic declines in prices and land values. In the face of these shocks, some failures were inevitable. What regulation could have done, but did not do, was make the system as a whole less susceptible to shocks and more resilient in its response to failures.

Data Appendix

Income and Price Data. Data on indices of gross income by type of farm product reported in Table 5.1 are taken from Strauss and Bean (1940: 31). Data on income—farm and nonfarm, gross and net—and farm and nonfarm population are taken from Leven (1925: 192–209, 259). The state-specific crop price index is defined as the relative price in 1924 of the bundle of crops sold in 1919. These data are reported in U.S. Department of Commerce (1927). Data on the value of crops sold, by state, were compiled by the Bureau of Agricultural Economics, Department of Agriculture, and reported in U.S. Department of Commerce, *Statistical Abstract of the United States*, various years.

Farm land values, mortgages, and foreclosures. Data on farm real estate values per acre, total real estate value, and amount of farm mortgage debt are provided in Clifton and Crowley (1973). Farm foreclosure data are from Stauber (1931).

GNP deflator estimates. Alternative annual estimates of the GNP deflator, reported in Table 5.4, are from Balke and Gordon (1989) and Romer (1989).

Branch and chain banking. Data on state branching regulations, numbers of branch banks and their branches, and banking chains are taken from Board of Governors (1924, 1926, 1927, Feb. 1929, Dec. 1929).

Bank balance sheet data. Bank balance sheet data, and total numbers of banks, disaggregated by state and by type of charter, are taken from Board of Governors (1959) and—for insured banking systems—from FDIC (1956: 66–67).

Locations and survival of individual banks. Data for individual banks, and bank locations, are taken from Bankers Encyclopedia Co., various years.

Numbers of bank liquidations. Liquidations of national banks are reported in the *Annual Report* of the Comptroller of the Currency. State bank liquidations for each state were published in the comptroller's *Annual Report* as well. The definition of banks employed in Board of Governors (1959) is used to construct state-level series for failed "state" banks. This definition includes trusts and unincorporated banks, as well as narrowly defined state-chartered banking corporations. It is not possible to derive consistent series of narrowly defined state-chartered bank balance sheet or failure data using these sources.

Bank charter switching. Data on bank charter switching are taken from Board of Governors (1937: 1087–1122).

Business failures. Business failures and number of solvent enterprises for each state are reported in U.S. Department of Commerce, *Statistical Abstract of the United States*.

Number and deposits of suspending banks. The number and deposits of state and national bank suspensions are reported in Board of Governors (1943: 286–91). These are used to derive the average size of suspended banks in Table 5.23.

Data on liquidated banks. Data used in Tables 5.21–5.23 on the number, deposits, losses, and time taken to liquidate banks for which liquidations had been completed by 1930 are reported in Goldenweiser and colleagues (1932: vol. 5, 191–207).

Richard Webb

Comment

My immediate reaction when I first heard of the topic for this seminar and of the specific papers that were being planned was a complaint. Why had Phil Brock and Jerry Jenkins not done all this eight years ago, *before* I was ordered home from a quiet job in the World Bank and put in charge of the central bank in Peru and suddenly presented with banks failing to the left of me and to the right of me?

Of course, even eight years ago would have been too late. Whatever useful lessons for financial regulation are drawn from this seminar would have had to be applied some fifteen or twenty years ago to reduce the odds of bank failures in the early 1980s or to reduce the size of the resulting losses. The cards had been dealt long before I arrived at the central bank in 1980. And indeed, whatever new cards are dealt in LDCs over the next few years, the result of this seminar might make the life of the central bank governors some ten years from now somewhat easier.

I thought it an interesting idea to look at the experience of U.S.

regional economies that were highly dependent on agricultural exports as a way of finding clues to improve financial regulation in LDCs. My impression is that very little has been written on this topic in LDCs. And the fact that they had considerable dependence on commodity exports means that banks in U.S. regional economies must have been subject to the same macroeconomic instability now faced by most LDCs.

I think all readers will agree that this chapter is an attractive piece of scholarship. For me it was a pleasure to read. The argument is clearly put and well documented. What helps a great deal in selling the argument is the fairness with which alternative interpretations are discussed along the way. I find it hard to comment directly on the argument or evidence of the paper, partly because I find it so convincing but also because it is a subject about which I know little. I will limit myself then to some comments on the lessons that might be drawn for LDCs.

One point that affects possible lessons is that the set of cases chosen by Calomiris may be one of *more* export commodity-centered instability than is now the rule in LDCs. According to the World Bank (1988), only 8 to 9 percent of gross domestic product in all developing economies originated in commodity exports in 1986. Calomiris does not provide similar figures for the states examined in his paper, but my guess is that their dependence on commodity exports was higher. In eleven of the thirty-two states listed in Table 5.5, for instance, half or more of the total population lived on farms. In any case, the experience of these regional economies is directly comparable to those LDCs that *are* highly dependent on commodity exports.

The seminar's issue, however, is how to deal with macro-economic instability, whatever its source; and since LDCs are subject to considerable instability from sources in addition to commodity exports, such as changes in government spending, the Calomiris study should be looked at as a case of high aggregate instability irrespective of the exact source. Nevertheless, we should keep in mind that the source of that instability may make a difference in the way in which it affects banks.

My main question with regard to lessons for LDCs has to do with institutional, rather than economic, structure comparability. And here I am also limited by insufficient familiarity with LDC banking structures. My impression, nevertheless, is that banking structures in LDCs now look quite different from those of the United States in the 1920s. The biggest difference is the large growth in practice of the government as both an owner and a regulator of interest rate and credit policies. A related aspect is that LDC central banks are a much bigger part of the banking scene, as regulators and as sources of money (unfortunately), than was the case in the United States. Another difference is the substantial presence of foreign branch banks. Finally, national branch bank systems are the rule rather than unit banks. What all this adds up to, I think, is this:

1. Less vulnerability to exogenous macroeconomic disturbances

2. More vulnerability to changes in government finance and government policies

3. A weaker moral case for not bailing out

On the bailout question, I am not quite sure whether Calomiris is saying no to bailing out the owners and depositors or just to the owners. I agree on not bailing out owners, partly for the practical reasons that he argues, and partly for moral reasons. But I cannot swallow the idea of not bailing out depositors. The Peruvian constitution has an article (154) that says that "the State promotes and guarantees private savings." My reading of that article was that depositor bailouts were mandatory in Peru. But, in addition, I thought it right. The government goes to a lot of trouble to approve who can bank and to look over that individual's shoulder. Even then, with all the resources at its command, the government continually fails to see a coming bank collapse. Depositors cannot simply be told to look out for themselves, all the more since the source of the major macroeconomic disturbances is often the government itself.

Calomiris's most interesting recommendation, as I interpreted his conclusions, was in favor of mutual-guarantee, self-regulating systems of insurance and supervision. The case for this idea, however, is not fully developed in this chapter, and I suggest that more could be said on that alternative in future works, since it seems especially innovative and interesting.

Charles W. Calomiris

Response

I believe Richard Webb is right in arguing that government policy shocks may be more important in many countries today than terms-of-trade shocks. I was interested in investigating the response of banking systems to a historically large shock that tested their capabilities. My findings that branching banks did remarkably well and that coinsurance would have been feasible at the state level make an *a fortiori* case for the capabilities of such systems under less extreme exogenous aggregate risk. Of course, governments can and do institute regulatory and macroeconomic policies that threaten the solvency of the banking system. My argument is that better mechanisms are feasible. I have not thought about how to devise a banking system that is "government-proof." It's an interesting question.

I disagree about the desirability of an unconditional commitment by the government to insure depositors. Under current policy, there is no threat of loss to those that place their funds in banks, and there will be little hope of constraining bank risk taking. As Charles Kahn and I have argued in a recent paper, part of the beauty of bank contracts historically was that they allowed uninformed depositors to benefit from the discipline imposed on banks by informed depositors (often other bankers). One should not remove this discipline, at least not without establishing an alternative mechanism that reduces the incentive for excessive risk taking.

There are mechanisms one could design in which government deposit insurance would not be so disastrous. Suppose, for example, we relied on banks to discipline one another by some form of mutual-liability plan, in which the risks taken by one bank create potential costs for others. In this case the government might provide an ultimate guarantee for deposits at little cost, but only if a substantial "deductible" is charged to banks in the self-regulating group to make up losses of failed banks.

Alternatively, if there were demand for absolute protection of small depositors, then this could be accomplished by creating a separate class of insured bank accounts, backed by Treasury bills.

It is quite appropriate that we have at least some discussion of U.S. financial history, because I would argue, as Bordo and Schwartz have in a recent paper (1989), that deposit insurance really is an example of intergovernment contagion. That is, deposit insurance came from the peculiar historical experience of the United States and was adopted later in other countries that decided to imitate some U.S. government policies. So I think it is important to explore the peculiarities of the United States and whether deposit insurance in some sense was necessary in that context.

In my comments I want to summarize some of the main points in the paper and then also try to point out where I think the points that I am making relate in specific ways to questions that have come up in the other papers. I hope that that will stimulate some discussion.

One of the main messages of the paper is that moral hazard, adverse selection, and incompetence are not just theoretical constructs. They are very important empirically.

I want to echo and emphasize what Paul Horvitz said, that risk taking is not just a matter of conscious intent (that is, people intending to take on more risk than they otherwise would) or adverse selection (that is, firms or individuals tending to have access to riskier projects being selected by deposit insurance). Deposit insurance creates a higher level of tolerance for individuals who may be misguided or ignorant. I think there is room for all three of these kinds of stories: adverse selection, moral hazard, and higher tolerance for incompetence.

In the period I discuss there is even greater reason to believe in this third element. Just about every war that I can think of witnesses a rapid increase in basic commodity prices, particularly in grains and livestock. I could tell this story about the Napoleonic Wars, the Crimean War, the Civil War in the United States; and it is no surprise that this happened during World War I.

What is a little surprising is that this boom was associated with a lot of long-run expansion in clearing of land and in new cultivation, especially in some states. You might ask the question, Well, shouldn't people have known better? In a way, that is my point. It is quite likely that under a different regime we wouldn't have seen such expansion. That is why I think that there is not just an element of moral hazard or adverse selection, but also a tolerance for ignorance. I could make the same point about U.S. agriculture in the late 1970s as well.

I think another theme that we have seen today is that these problems seem to be magnified by booms and only make themselves apparent during busts. That is, excessive risk taking during good times doesn't show up as bank failures. Expectations of people who are misguidedly sanguine are reinforced when there are positive realizations on commodity prices. You are going to see a deposit insurance collapse when there is a big boom, which ignorant or risk-taking people magnify, followed by a big drop in the terms of trade. So it is not surprising that this magnification through perverse incentives shows up only during times of rapid booms followed by busts. The design flaws, of course, are always there, but they are not always apparent.

Another point that I make in the paper, referring mainly to an earlier paper, is that the externalities of the payments system—that is, the potential for systemic disruption of the payments system—can be handled in other ways more successfully. Informal or formal self-regulating groups of banks were extraordinarily successful. I want to mention just a few of those examples.

Southern banks in the pre–Civil War period in the United States were allowed to branch, unlike their cousins in the North, and during the panics of both 1837 and 1857 were extremely successful. When suspensions of convertibility occurred, the banks were able to get together and coordinate, to maintain markets in each others' notes and deposits, to keep the clearing system functioning effectively—and they did this through effective and credible self-regulation.

Of course, Gary Gorton and others have talked about clearinghouses and the way that they established formal rules and formal coalitions that did the same thing. But interestingly, U.S. bank clearinghouses imitated an earlier government innovation, which was an early form of bank liability insurance.

There were three successful experiments with insurance out of six in the pre–Civil War period. All three operated at the state level; all three were unlimited mutual-liability insurance systems among member banks. There were roughly thirty banks in each of these systems.

Unlimited mutual liability was combined with the authority of the banks to establish boards to pass regulations and to monitor each other. This is, of course, exactly what clearinghouses later would do. The first experiment of this kind was 1834 in Indiana.

These systems of mutual liability were extraordinarily successful, more successful than city clearinghouses or perhaps branch banking coalitions. During the Panic of 1857 the states with unlimited mutual liability insurance didn't even suspend convertibility. They had virtually no bank failures. In Indiana there was never a bank failure of an insured member.

The boards detected unsafe or fraudulent practices early, and they had virtually no incidence of them. They would suspend the offending treasurer, or they might threaten the bank that it couldn't pay out dividends until it had corrected its violations. Interestingly, unlike all the other insured systems, these mutual-liability systems found problems early and corrected them. The others only found problems after banks had failed.

The third point that I want to make is that the peculiar feature of the U.S. unit banking system prevented self-regulation from being an answer to the nationwide problem of banking panics. Banking panics resulted from confusion about the incidence of a particular shock across a large number of banks, often a shock that was small relative to aggregate bank capital.

Unit banking increased the possibility for such confusion. Consider the shock to the railroad securities market in 1857. In an economy with only ten banks there would have been no risk that any bank would fail. In an economy with 2,000 banks there was quite a substantial risk that one of the New York City banks would fail, and this was sufficient to induce a nationwide banking panic. So the first problem with unit banking was that it increased the uncertainty about the distribution of the effects of these shocks.

The second problem was that physically separating banks made it much harder for banks to coordinate and self-regulate. Clearinghouses were typically confined to cities where banks could police each other and establish the kinds of credible self-regulating mechanisms that were necessary. If you restrict the system to unit banking, though, simple geographical and communication limits make it difficult to extend that sort of network beyond the confines of a small area.

Another potential limit to the self-insurance of banking is the size of the shocks against which the banking system has to insure. Coinsurance works very well for shocks that are small relative to aggregate banking capital but might not work so well for shocks that are large relative to aggregate banking capital.

The United States, in the 1920s, experienced shocks comparable to those we are worried about in an economy like that of Chile or other similar LDCs today. Do such shocks threaten the aggregate capital of the banking system and thereby make self-regulation impossible?

Before I address that question, I want to talk a little bit about why the 1920s in the United States provides such a good case study. In the United States many of the states were fairly specialized, either in agriculture or in some cases in oil. They shared many of the properties of a small open economy with a high degree of specialization.

The other thing that is interesting about the specialized states is that because of the peculiar structure of dual banking regulation in the United States, states experimented with a wide variety of different regulatory regimes. In some states we have simply unit banking; that is, bank branching is restricted, and there is no insurance. In other states we have branch banking, sometimes limited to cities, sometimes allowed throughout the state, and in some unit banking states we have deposit insurance systems created.

Note that these were not government-financed deposit insurance funds; they were government-created and government-supervised deposit insurance, but they were funded solely by premiums charged to the individual member banks. Accumulated funds from these premiums were the only backing for insured deposits. That fact turns out to be quite important. That system is very different from the unlimited mutual-liability arrangement of a small self-regulating group of banks.

Each of these states had national banks existing side by side with the state banks. Thus, we can do comparisons within states to see how the behavior of the national banks differed from that of the state-chartered banks. We can also do comparisons across states, seeing for a given behavior of the national banks across states, conditioned on the different regulatory regimes of the state-chartered banks, how they performed.

This is really an ideal sort of experiment in the sense that we have some meaningful controls. We know things about income and wealth changes in these states. We know about the behavior of national banks under a common regulatory regime. And we have a lot of poorly diversified small open economies that are linked by being part of the United States but not linked in their regulatory systems.

I look at both sides of the boom and the bust. First I examine how the different systems responded to the incentives created by deposit insurance before the collapse. Than I measure their behavior during the bust.

First, I find that deposit insurance in the 1920s was associated with higher growth, *ceteris paribus*; and this finding was due to high growth by smaller banks that were thinly capitalized. Of the thirty-two agricultural crisis states in my sample, the combination of high growth, thin capital, and small-sized banks distinguishes the insured states.

When the bust came, the insured systems all fell apart. They were all illiquid and insolvent. They could not make payments out of their immediate funds, and they had no prospect of ever being able to accumulate enough from their funds.

But more importantly, the loan losses of the banks that were members of these deposit insurance funds were much higher. Their rates of failure were higher too, but that was not the biggest difference between their performance and the performance of other unit banking systems. The real difference was that the asset shortfalls of insolvent insured banks were much greater.

Interestingly, branching was the political alternative in many of the debates that led up to the development of deposit insurance after the Panic of 1907. People understood very well at the time that branching stabilized the banking system. They had had a lot of experience from other countries and from U.S. history before the Civil War; and that experience confirmed the stability that branching afforded.

But there was a coalition between the interests of the unit bankers and, for some reason, the populist movement that worked to preserve unit banking by developing deposit insurance. That coalition was the important political impetus for deposit insurance. It was the way to create, they thought, stability and at the same time to preserve unit banking.

Those were the origins in the twentieth century of deposit insurance. What is interesting, though, is that branching banks, which were thought of as more or less an equal alternative by a lot of the legislatures, turned out to be much better. That is, unit banks performed worse than branching banks, and insured banks performed even worse.

Branching banks had much lower rates of failure. Not only that, but in states that allowed branching the recovery from the crisis, in terms of the total asset growth of the banking systems, also was much greater. In terms of both the vulnerability of banks and the resiliency of the banking system, branching was far superior to its alternatives.

I said one of the questions I wanted to address was whether coinsurance could work in small open economies subject to large shocks. This boom and bust cycle in the agricultural states of the 1920s is an example of a large shock. Table 5.23 provides a means of getting at this question.

For the thirteen states that had the highest rates of bank failure, I separated banks into national and state-chartered banking systems, estimated the total asset shortfalls of the banking systems, and compared this estimate with the total equity of surviving banks. That estimate is my basis for answering the question, Could the banking system as a whole have coinsured against these risks?

I find, first of all, that none of the national banking systems saw asset shortfalls approaching the total equity of surviving banks. In the state systems that fact is also true, with three interesting exceptions.

Those three exceptions were the only three states in the United States that had compulsory deposit insurance with free entry, allowing virtually any bank to join, and that kept compulsory deposit insurance in place throughout the 1920s. These systems maximized the cross-subsidization of risk taking among banks.

If you answer the question, What is the set of states that had compulsory long-lived free-entry deposit insurance? you have also answered the question, What are the three states that would have found it impossible for their state-chartered banking systems to have supported themselves through coinsurance?

What these data tell me is that insurance had a very substantial effect on the amount of aggregate bank capital relative to bank capital placed at risk. I conclude from this evidence that absent compulsory free-entry long-lived deposit insurance, bank capital would have been quite adequate to support coinsurance at the state level. And I would add that if these banking systems had employed intrastate branching, which was all that was allowed during this period, they would have performed even better.

Let me just make a few other quick points.

On this question of time consistency, John Boyd earlier said that it is a long-standing historical rule that governments just can't help themselves. They will always intervene. This is a fairly recent phenomenon. In fact, out of all the failed insurance systems that I looked at, eight postbellum and three antebellum, in only one case did the state government intervene to come to the assistance of a failed state deposit insurance fund.

What is consistently true about the political economy of deposit insurance is that in virtually every case where politicians were granted regulatory influence or authority—that is, the three antebellum failures and all eight of the postbellum systems—there was political abuse or regulatory neglect. Nebraska's insured system kept failed banks going for about eight years in the 1920s.

Let me mention just a couple of other points to make connections to the other papers. Earlier someone asked, How much is enough capital? Is 5 percent enough, for example?

In the systems I looked at, the ratio of total equity to deposits was in excess of 10 percent. There was double liability too. *Ex post facto* this liability can be hard to collect, and some collections were not forthcoming on extended liability. But regardless of how you count capital relative to deposits, these systems had very high rates of capital relative to the ones in the Chilean legislation or the United States today.

Not only that, but typically the insurance funds of the 1920s also had interest rate ceilings on deposits. Furthermore, this system was not government-financed insurance. Therefore, the protection wasn't so great as today; the interest ceilings were in place, thus the potential for getting funds wasn't so great; and capital was much higher. This provides an argument *a fortiori* for similar potential problems today. If you see large losses in the 1920s under those circumstances, then it is no surprise that you can get hundreds of billions in losses in the S&Ls today.

I want to close by saying that I recognize there are many ways to solve the incentive perversities of deposit insurance. I believe that self-regulation, especially in an environment of branch banking, is feasible.

It is also likely to be the lowest-cost method. If you let banks, which presumably are the best informed about the relevant economic tradeoffs (for example, the tradeoff between regulating more and monitoring more), decide what regulations to pass, and if you let banks monitor each other, given that they will probably be the most efficient processors of information about each other, self-regulation must be a less costly method than government supervision and regulation.

The first question is feasibility. If you believe that such systems are feasible, then there is every reason to believe that they are also optimal.

Discussion

PAUL HORVITZ: I am a little distressed at this rehabilitation of the role of bank cartels and clearinghouses. When I grew up, we viewed those as monopolistic, anticompetitive operations. There were, in fact, antitrust suits against clearinghouses for setting service charges and limits on hours.

If you give a group of bankers in a state the power to set regulation, clearly they will make the business less risky. They will cut hours. They will prohibit or limit interest on deposits. They will be safer. There is no question about it. In some sense the costs will be low, but the costs will be borne by the consumers of banking services.

I think it is reasonable to look at those costs and consider that alternative, but I am somewhat surprised at your—Gary has indicated some of this also—sort of admiration for the benefits of these competition-restricting operations.

CHARLES CALOMIRIS: I responded to that a little bit before, but I think I can make it more explicit now. I am not suggesting that the government get out of the business of antitrust regulation. I am simply saying if we have a good mechanism for banking stability, let's combine that mechanism with a good mechanism for competitiveness.

Let me give you a specific example. I am not sure this is the best way to do it, but this certainly will do it.

Suppose you defined four regions in the United States in such a way that every region had overlapping banking groups. The government will make sure that entry into each banking group is free and the government will make sure that the definition of the regional range of any group is such that it is always competing with other groups. As I argued before, the clearinghouses and futures and options markets compete with each other. There are ways of designing this system so that you make the groups compete with each other as well.

If you are worried about antitrust violations, such concerns arise in any industry. We are not going to redesign our telephone lines because we are worried about antitrust in the telephone industry.

PAUL HORVITZ: No, but you are proposing to make anticompetitive arrangements easy by setting up a framework by which the supposed competitors get together. It is not like antitrust in other industries. Maybe it is worthwhile, but the tradeoffs really have to be faced up to.

During periods of stability, during the 1960s, this issue was confronted. Certainly the consensus among economists was that we would be better off if we had a more competitive system with more failures and more competition. Now we have moved in that direction. Perhaps we have gotten more failures than we would like and maybe the optimal is in some sense to go back, but I fear you are going back too far.

CHARLES CALOMIRIS: I just don't think there is any reason why we can't have it both ways.

(Laughter.)

ROBERT BARTELL: An ineffective cartel?

CHARLES CALOMIRIS: No. Competing coalitions.

SALVADOR VALDÉS: I want to raise further questions on cartels. Assume that this cooperative group shares information on risk. They have to supervise each other. Say you are a firm in a city where all banks share information among themselves. Wouldn't they be able to charge a very high premium?

CHARLES CALOMIRIS: You are defining the group to be geographically specific. I want to make sure that that is not the case. The relevant market in which a bank monopolizes is a particular place. Unit banking under the current regime is a great example of monopoly banking. What I would like to do is see branch banking where not only are a lot of banks competing within the same range, but also independent groups of banks are competing within the same range.

Also, you have to keep the size of this group small. If the size of a group of banks that are coinsuring each other gets too large, there is no incentive for one to monitor another, because the gains from monitoring another bank are shared with all group members and the costs are private.

What made these antebellum systems successful, once again, is that they had twenty or thirty banks that were members throughout a state. So they had enough geographical proximity, and they had a small enough group to make mutual regulation incentive compatible. If you had a branch banking system, you could extend that geographic range quite a bit.

PETER DIAMOND: There are two things I want to pursue. First of all, I find the basic story on the various effects of insurance on the system very plausible. On admittedly casual reading of the paper, not going through it in detail, I have some concern about the degree of support that comes from the data because of the self-selection problem.

Let me spell that out. It would be good to divide the bad outcomes among the different causes you have identified—moral hazard, adverse selection, inducement of particular kinds of individuals into banking.

What troubles me is the endogenicity of the kind of charter a bank has. You have a table of banks changing. So the natural thing to wonder is, first of all, whether it isn't the banks that want to grow fast that become the state banks or become the insured banks when you have that split.

The natural way to try to control for that in a test would be to take subsets of banks that existed before the insurance systems were set up and classify them by where they were then. This might give you a four-way classification, depending on where they were earlier and what kind of system they were under, and try to repeat some the tabular analyses that you have done to sort that out.

CHARLES CALOMIRIS: I thought about that. Part of what I am interested in measuring is selection bias. The argument I believe for why banks grew so fast in the insured systems is that they were taking advantage of cross-subsidization. So I believe that story. What I want to measure is what is unusual about these insured states, which is partly reflected in these conversions from the national system to the state system and then back after the crisis.

I agree with you, but I don't want to control for that. I want that to be in there.

PETER DIAMOND: You might want to separate out the effect this has on existing banks.

Let's go to the failure rate. I think this is where the clearest story is. Let's assume, which I don't believe, that there is absolutely no effect of insurance on absolutely anything, except a bank that sees it is in deep trouble and about to fail and gets itself insured. Then you will see enormous failure rates in the insured system, and as a corollary, higher failure rates in the state system; and you haven't measured any of the things you are interested in.

CHARLES CALOMIRIS: That I did control for. In Table 5.23 I reported separately the asset shortfalls relative to bank equity for the state system, for the national system, and for all banks in that state. What I am able to show is that it isn't just that the insured states had higher failure rates for this sort of reason. In those states there was a threat to all banking capital in aggregate. In other words, switching won't explain this phenomenon. So I did try to control for that in that one table.

PETER DIAMOND: I think breaking out the pieces more generally might be quite instructive.

In some of the regressions, I wasn't quite sure from going quickly through the descriptions whether you were adjusting various growth measures for these changes in category, which would obviously matter a lot for the regression results.

You are calculating a regression of state bank asset growth on national bank asset growth. That coefficient will mean one thing if the national bank growth is measuring the underlying economy, because you have netted out the transfers. If you get banks switching from state to national, that would introduce a negative coefficient if that were the only thing going on.

CHARLES CALOMIRIS: Given the high minimum capital requirements and strict limitations on mortgage lending for national banks, and the concentration on agricultural lending by state-insured systems during the boom, I think there was likely little differential "crowding out" of national bank chartering by the chartering booms of state banks in the insured states.

As you know from looking at the table, virtually the only states where switching was important during the bust were Texas and Oklahoma.

PETER DIAMOND: I wonder how you end up interpreting the coefficients where you have several things going on simultaneously and you don't break them out separately.

The other issue that I wondered about is the extent to which variables were proxies for other variables. If, for example, large banks fail less than small banks and large banks are associated with branching, it may be that size is what matters rather than the diversity that comes with branching.

CHARLES CALOMIRIS: I am not able to say.

PETER DIAMOND: There is a set of issues there that I think at least needs flagging.

I want to turn to the interesting suggestions you are making on alternative ways of regulation. It seems to me that one could be more imaginative in pursuing them.

The underlying premise, which seems to me to be a very sound one, is that banks would be better examiners than government examiners. So I asked myself whether we could get the banks into the examining business without necessarily getting them into the full range of potential cartel interactions.

If you think of the incentives for individual banks with a group of twenty banks, you don't have to mutually insure. You could, for example, have the government pick up 90 percent of the loss and have 10 percent borne by individual banks.

Then you might have a rule, for example, that requires a bank that wants deposit insurance to be the examiner of another bank of approximately the same size, with contingent liability if the examined bank fails. The two banks could be in different states, taking advantage of the fact that we haven't had interstate branching.

No doubt there are many variations on this theme that could be thought up. The idea here is that we are privatizing the regulation system, not the insurance system.

CHARLES CALOMIRIS: I think I may even have phrased it that way in the earlier paper. When I say coinsurance, I mean things as general as group-contingent insurance premiums. You don't have to have real coinsurance, but just something that links banks' costs to other banks' behavior.

PETER DIAMOND: But you were pursuing this also in order to select bank regulations. That is part of what the mutual group does. But if you want to state small, you could just do this for examination. Bank A in Massachusetts must examine Bank B in Ohio; if you are not in the examining business, you can't have deposit insurance. If examination is the nub, that's a way of addressing it.

ROBERT BARTELL: But, Peter, what does Bank A do when it finds out that Bank B is taking excess risk and therefore is going to cost Bank A some money? What does Bank A do?

PETER DIAMOND: If your scenario is that the main problem is not cutting banks off promptly enough, presumably Bank A goes to the regulators and says that Bank B is in trouble and needs to be closed quickly. When you say close a bank, you would have to have penalties associated with both types of errors.

Some of the problems we have had have been problems with the examination system. Obviously the problems that come from the process dragging out, of not closing a bank that the regulators would like to close, are not improved by this system. You would have to go further.

ROBERT BARTELL: So Bank A loses its coinsurance obligation as soon as it blows the whistle on Bank B.

PETER DIAMOND: You could imagine coming in and doing an evaluation at that point. But if you blow too soon, there would be a penalty going the other way. You would have to have penalties going both ways to create a balance of incentives over the two kinds of errors.

CHARLES CALOMIRIS: There is an interesting point here. Even in these failed systems of the early twentieth century the designers of these systems believed that banks were the best monitors of other banks. So they tried to enlist bankers to act as regulators. But the banks gained little if anything by monitoring or reporting violations. There was virtually no case when somebody didn't know when a bank was doing something grossly wrong. But nobody had an incentive to do anything about it. They got it right in trying to get bankers involved in the monitoring. They went wrong in failing to create an incentive for the bankers to monitor and to reveal what they knew.

SERGIO DE LA CUADRA: I have a doubt about your conclusion in reference to the methodology. You utilize the successful experience of these cartels. From there your inference is that it could work well again but with a lot of smaller cartels that will be overlapping and competing. That is different from what you observed. You observed one cartel that was very stable. Can you infer from that, that if you have many smaller cartels competing among themselves, they also are going to be very stable?

CHARLES CALOMIRIS: I left out some things that I will now enlist in my defense. In each of these states there were other banking systems in existence. The organization of banking in the pre–Civil War period was unusual. States tended to create overlapping systems of banks every time they wanted to set up new banks.

For example, in Indiana there were two different chartering systems for banks, only one of which was insured. In Ohio there were four different chartering systems for banks, only one of which was insured.

In other words, I think there is a lot of historical evidence that these systems actually did face competition.

The way I would rephrase your question is, did the success of these systems depend in some way on the rents that they got from being noncompetitive? I don't think so.

MARVIN GOODFRIEND: I want to change the subject a little bit and try to tie together some things that have gone on here today. I want to take off from Phil Brock's introductory paper and then present a few thoughts for integrating it with the course of the day's discussion.

The issue that I think we are discussing here, at least insofar as it pertains to Chile, is what ought to be a government's policy to protect deposits in a country that is small and is a single political jurisdictional unit as opposed to Texas within a big free-trade zone, both of which are subject to significant terms-of-trade shocks. The issue is really about the protection against potential systemwide insolvencies within that region as opposed to pure liquidity problems.

There are three ways that you can provide protection against idiosyncratic national terms-of-trade shocks. The first one is that individuals deposit their funds in Chile and then all around the world. Everybody has 100 bank accounts. That's obviously inefficient.

There are two other ways.

You can have domestic Chilean banks branching internationally and let the citizens in Chile deposit in the Chilean bank and get the benefits of diverse assets held indirectly on their behalf.

A third way is to have foreign bank branches in Chile accept deposits in Chile, providing diversification and protection against idiosyncratic Chilean terms-of-trade shocks that way.

What finally clicked in my head and probably is obvious to other people around the table is that the best policy for the problem at hand is not being implemented. I have been trying to figure out why it isn't being implemented. Apparently it is because Chile has capital outflow controls which make it infeasible to do any of those three things legally.

What do I have in mind? Let's consider a domestic Chilean bank that wants to hold international assets to back some of its deposits. For every dollar that it accepted in deposit, since Chile is a small part of the world, the bank would have to take, let's say, ninety cents of that and put it overseas as part of the diversification of a given stock of assets that it had on its books.

Apparently there is a major policy impediment to doing this in a small sovereign economy like Chile's. As opposed to Texas, Chile can block the sort of capital outflow that is necessary to produce that diversification.

Why could capital export controls be popular in a small country? Some people think that controls can enhance the degree of capital formation in the country, but of course they have a perverse effect. You are not going to get outsiders to invest if they think they will never get their capital out.

To my mind there are two other explanations that make more sense. One might be the belief that persistent capital outflows generate unfavorable terms-of-trade movements. There might also be some concern that the induced exchange into depreciation might be inflationary. I must add that I don't think either of these views is a good argument for capital controls.

The point is that banking policy is tied up directly with capital controls in a small country like Chile. This is what makes Chile's situation different from that of Texas, which is in a trade union where it can't impose capital controls.

In a way we are really looking at a second best policy problem.

PHILIP BROCK: Let me continue along those lines. I had three questions before today, during today, and after all of this discussion. One of them is the title of the conference: "If Texas Were Chile," what kind of difference does this make? One of the senses I got, and I didn't think I would be feeling this way, is that Texas may not in fact be that much different from Chile. There hasn't been interstate banking between Texas and the rest of the United States. There may be political reasons why that hasn't happened. There are certainly political reasons why Chileans can't take their capital out of their country.

When I first set this seminar up, I was thinking, well, Texas is part of the United States, so there is no problem. But even within the United States the fact that Texas is a separate unit has implications for banking.

With regard to talking about banking, usually we don't really think about specifying a certain type of economy. We typically have a closed economy in mind that experiences some technology shocks or something like that. The nice things about commodity-exporting economies are that you can identify what the shock is; they make good experiments; and the shocks tend to be quite large sometimes.

So the question is, does being a Texas really differ much from being a Chile? That is one topic I would like any of your thoughts on.

A point I was about to raise, Marvin, when you were talking is that in Chile right now the pension funds that were set up in 1981 are now approaching 90 percent of GDP.

Is that right?

SERGIO DE LA CUADRA: Not yet. When they mature, they will approach that. Now they are 30 percent, and they are only nine years old.

PHILIP BROCK: So in nine years pension funds have grown to be 30 percent of GDP. But pension funds can't invest in the New York Stock Exchange. They can only invest in Chile. As you were saying, there are laws that keep Chileans from taking their funds out of the country.

I think that restrictions on external diversification may be very important to issues of financial risk and regulation.

The other topic which I mentioned at the start is the information-gathering aspects of these different systems that we are talking about. What is the appropriate role for the government in terms of collecting and evaluating information? In a commodity-exporting economy where there will be large shocks, how does that information-gathering capability correspond to the ability of the government to shut down or to recapitalize banks?

I welcome your final thoughts on that.

A third topic concerns the political considerations. We know they are a problem with any banking system in a closed economy, little technology shocks or not.

In an economy where there is going to be one big shock that hits everyone, everyone can say, well, it's not my fault; it's this terms-of-trade shock. So there is tremendous pressure for political intervention then.

In an economy that is going to face an economywide shock at some point, is there anything that can be done to make it harder to adopt a political bailout than some other solution such as the one the Chileans are trying to promote through their law?

Those three topics—diversification, information gathering and political considerations—if you have final thoughts on them, that would help to tie up what we have been talking about today.

JERRY JENKINS: With respect to diversification, there are certainly U.S. corporations not based in Texas that have deposits in Texas, and there are Texans with stock ownership in publicly traded corporations that are based outside Texas. To the extent that the gross state product, if you will, of Texas comprises activities and investments of non-Texas corporations that exceed considerably the contributions of non-Chilean corporations to that country's economic base, then identical exogenous shocks to the two economies should be expected to have quite different realized, or effective shocks experienced by their populations. And this would be so even if the Texas banking system is in all respects identical to Chile's and even if the rapidity and magnitude of changes in the price of oil are identical to those of copper.

On the assumption that such financial diversification across territorial boundaries was much greater among individual Texans than among Chileans, irrespective of their banking institutions, I approached this day with a short answer to the implicit question of the seminar: If Texas were Chile, the negative consequences experienced by Texans from any given exogenous shock would be considerably more negative than they are. I leave this seminar still thinking that, but also thinking that if Texas were Texas but with Chile's new bank legislation, exogenous shocks would have less negative effects for Texans than they do.

To say more than this with confidence requires country data that are at least as substantial as those which Charlie Calomiris provides in his paper for states within a country. Ideally, information on exogenous shocks would allow greater disaggregation from that on effective shocks (the endogenous results of exogenous shocks) than is allowed even by Charlie's data set. Then, of course, the kind of analysis that Charlie provides and Peter Diamond's comments suggest would be possible internationally. In the absence of such information and analysis, our own judgments and those of government officials cannot be expected to be much better informed than by the papers and proceedings of this seminar. One would hope that a few thousand government officials throughout the world will spend at least a day of their time with the book that results from this seminar. One also hopes that the United States might import some banking legislation from Chile.

ROBERT BARTELL: I would like to follow up on the questions of what kind of diversification makes sense as a way of reducing risk in the banking system, and whether that risk is going to be there just because you have insurance of accounts?

It seemed to me when we were talking about competing cartels, just the term suggested an inconsistency. I don't know how you have competing cartels. It would seem to me the logical extension of the idea is that you have very large nationwide or international branch banking systems, and those are how you get diversification. This doesn't require any cartel system; it just requires that you have relatively few banks because they have to operate over fairly wide areas and that operation is difficult if banks are relatively small.

When I say relatively few, if you total the banks, S&Ls, and credit unions of the United States, you have in excess of 20,000 banking units. I don't know how you characterize that other than, it's a lot. A little could be something like 500. A little could be like most other countries around the world, five to twenty.

If you have international diversification, and you had somewhere between 100 and 200 international banks that were well diversified, and you had some kind of international financial crisis, you are still going to end up with a kind of implicit insurance.

Surely if you have nationwide branch banks and relatively few of them—that could be 100 or 500 in the United States—you are still going to have implicit insurance because the government simply isn't going to allow a very large bank, especially one that is operating in a number of states, to fail.

I think if you go back to the situation where your deposit insurance is set up to take care of those institutions that fall by the wayside a few at a time and then you have a major economic disruption, you get socialized insurance. That is what we have in the United States, and I assume that is what you had in Chile.

And what's wrong with it? So the taxpayers are going to pay maybe $100 billion or maybe $200 billion, for the S&L failures, but that money goes back to taxpayers. It is just a different group of taxpayers. It's the people who have been getting something like 100 basis points over the average rate throughout the country on CDs in Texas the last couple of years and it's the people who got loans and didn't have to pay them back. So it isn't money that is lost; it is just redistributed.

CHARLES CALOMIRIS: I thought the first half of what you said was, Wouldn't it be nice if we could have an international system of branch banks? which I agreed with. I thought what you were getting at there was that you might not need deposit insurance at all in such a world. I think that might be right and that the answer to why we don't see this has to do with political jurisdictional problems.

I thought the second half of your comment was something on the order of, In establishing these coalitions, as long as you allow branch banking there are still going to be some banks that are very large; when they fail, even if it is less likely because they are branching banks and large, the government still is going to step in.

My response to that is that it may be right, and I think it is unfortunate if it is. The experience from the examples of coalitions that we know of—I rely on David Pope's Australian example, Bordo and Schwartz's other cross-country comparisons, and my own studies of these antebellum cartels—indicates that the events in which that sort of bailout will be necessary don't occur, or at least occur so infrequently that even if there is this problem, the expected social losses that result from it are very small.

Even if you believe that governments just can't say no, self-regulating coalitions still may be the best way to go.

SERGIO DE LA CUADRA: Before the lender of last resort was created in Chile, the banks operated with very high capital. On average it was 25 percent of deposits. After the central bank creation in 1924, leverage started increasing gradually, and in 1960 it was fixed at the very high level of leverage that we have now, 5 percent instead of the old 25 percent.

PHILIP BROCK: It went from 4-to-1 to 20-to-1?

SERGIO DE LA CUADRA: First it was raised to 10 and then to 20.

In a study I made about Chilean recessions I found in the period between 1913 and 1983 twelve recessions in my country. Of these twelve recessions, eleven of them could be explained by a sharp drop in the terms of trade. All eleven drops in the terms of trade were associated with a sharp decline in the rate of growth in the United States, and just one sharp decline in the rate of growth in the United States didn't produce a sharp drop in our terms of trade. So we are very correlated with the American economy.

These are large fluctuations. We are not just talking about a 2 or 3 percent change in the terms of trade; we are talking about 20 percent or 30 percent. This produced a systemic instability in the banking system.

I agree with one of the points that has been mentioned several times during this discussion today. Our capital requirement in Chile, although it is adjusted by risk, and so forth, is still very low, in my opinion.

KENNETH SCOTT: I think Bob has suggested a sort of Alfred E. Neuman approach: Why worry? This is all just kind of an efficient transfer mechanism, taxpayers to depositors. There are some winners, some losers, but no social loss.

(Laughter.)

Leaving apart the somewhat perverse nature of that transfer from a welfare standpoint, I think there are quite probably some rather significant social losses that it might be interesting to try to estimate. One social loss is the wasted resources invested in projects that are simply going to decay and be scrapped. I think there is a fair amount of real resource waste now littering the Texas landscape and elsewhere.

There are also the allocation and other costs of raising government revenues. For the government to raise a dollar through taxation and then pay the dollar back is not a costless process. I think there is some literature on it. I am no keeper of that literature, but my recollection is that the order of magnitude is something like 25 percent by some estimates—all of which suggests a rather large order of social losses. It is not just a costless transfer operation that we are witnessing.

If the concern is with payment disruption, if that is really what is the larger concern in all of this, why not just simply institute a requirement (which it seems to me the Chilean system may have approximated in a rather indirect way) to full collateralization of all transaction accounts, of all payments accounts?

If you have a requirement that the bank must fully collateralize those with marketable securities or with government securities, depending on which way you want to structure it, then there is no payment system disruption. The insurance system can still be in place to make sure that payments go through while you are mustering and liquidating the collateral pool, but it would seem to me as if it ought to be achievable at a lot less cost than, say, $100 billion.

PETER DIAMOND: Two points on that: First, as we have seen, having a marketable asset doesn't mean having a stable value even over rather short periods of time.

Second, I wonder at the success of a government in restricting transaction accounts to fully collateralized accounts, given the presence of computers and the genius of people who like to get around rules like that. It is fine to say you like a system like that. I don't know whether in fact you would end up with a system that didn't have it even though we wanted it, as we saw with the end run with NOW accounts.

KENNETH SCOTT: On your point, if you are talking about collateralization with marketable securities, by definition I have the trading data whereby I can ascertain the variances and covariances and I can mathematically calculate the appropriate degree of over-collateralization with respect to whatever time interval I think is appropriate between taking a reading that shows insolvency and acting upon it.

The second point that you made was the end run. You would at least have the advantage of having quite explicitly denominated an insured transaction account. If there was also a substitute, an alternative or near-money uninsured transaction account, they presumably would be priced at different rates, and they would compete with each other.

PETER DIAMOND: If consumer protection is the issue, then certainly making both kinds of accounts available takes care of the problem. If the issue is the point you started with, which is preservation of the transaction medium, then this doesn't do it. If you give people a choice and lots of people choose the uninsured one, you haven't preserved the system.

KENNETH SCOTT: You may have made more credible the distinction between an insured and a truly uninsured liability. If it is believed to be truly uninsured, then people can price for the risk. It seems to me you lessen the probability of the bailout case and the political plausibility of the bailout case.

PETER DIAMOND: It is the externalities of the collapse of the transaction system which don't get addressed.

KENNETH SCOTT: It could not fully collapse if you had the insured payments structure.

PETER DIAMOND: It would depend on what the American public ended up putting their money into. If you believe the Minsky hypothesis, give us a little while without a collapse, then the whole system will evolve in the wrong way.

KENNETH SCOTT: Do I believe that? I guess I don't.

ROBERT BARTELL: I agree with Ken that there are obviously some social costs in transferring money from taxpayers to depositors, but I disagree with his comment about all of the assets in Texas that wouldn't have been there had there not been a poor deposit insurance system.

I think you have to realize that those assets were created in Texas because of an economic boom, and it wasn't just Texas institutions that overinvested in Texas and it wasn't just banks and it wasn't just insured institutions; it was insurance companies and a number of other organizations as well that invested in Texas real estate and in loans to energy companies and did so in an economic environment in which regulators would have said it was a safe investment.

The point I tried to make this morning is that you have an exogenous shock and all of a sudden you have a tremendous destruction of asset values throughout the economy. That is the sort of thing that an insurance system can't deal with.

KENNETH SCOTT: Simply put, I would argue that you would have empty buildings on the Texas landscape but you would have fewer of them because you had not only an exogenous shock, but you also had an incentive structure that made it rational for management to make negative present-value investments. If you had eliminated that, then a lot of those things would simply never have been invested in.

ROBERT BARTELL: Our question is how much is a lot. I am arguing that you can overstate the "a lot" and come up with a system that would get rid of the "a lot" but not get rid of the ones that were there because of the fact that the economy said that that was the proper thing to do.

KENNETH SCOTT: There would still be real losses, yes.

ROBERT BARTELL: There were 250,000 jobs lost in Houston in a period of about three years. Those 250,000 people had come there relatively recently, and it wasn't very hard to move away. So on the face of it you have maybe 250,000 housing units that were excess. Were those 250,000 excess units there because of the fact that banks and savings and loans and insurance companies and whoever else bought the mortgages made a mistake? In hindsight, yes.

KENNETH SCOTT: I don't want to use the hindsight evaluation. Taking it *ex ante*, it seems to me you had investment that was rational and you had investment that was distorted by this incentive structure. It is only the latter that you would correct by correcting the incentive structure. Is that trivial? The magnitude of the losses that are being suffered implies to me that it is not trivial. It wasn't limited to the Texas oil patch or something like that. It occurred elsewhere.

ROBERT BARTELL: We are talking about insurance systems and whether you need a deposit insurance system. What I was suggesting is that if you do away with the deposit insurance system, you may do away with the behavior of banks that yields irrational outcomes, but unless you can protect the economy from these external shocks, you are still going to have bank failures and the government is going to have a predisposition to move in and try to prevent losses to depositors.

The thrust of my comments earlier is that even if you have very well-diversified banks and a very few of them, if you have an external shock that causes one or more to fail, the government is going to step in, and you are going to have some kind of a social sharing of the cost of failure.

KENNETH SCOTT: I return to an earlier theme. There are two issues. Economic volatility is going to produce losses. There are going to be expectations that are not realized and there are going to be losses. Maybe the magnitude is reducible by diversification and so on. But at some level there are still going to be those losses.

Given that, there are two questions: Who is going to bear them, and how are they going to be minimized? The first question very much relates to the second question. If they are borne by the government, they are not going to be minimized; they are going to be exacerbated.

PHILIP BROCK: This never got brought up today, but the Chilean collapse ended with a real estate boom also. That is, after Chile's terms of trade began to fall in 1980, there was a big boom in real estate investment, investment in shopping centers and property, expensive homes, and so on—very much similar to the situation in

Texas. For some reason or other we haven't brought that point out today, but there is that similarity across the two economies.

SALVADOR VALDÉS: I wanted to comment on this payment system discussion. The first thing I want to say is that I agree with Ken that, if that is a problem, one should approach it directly and go toward collateralization of transaction accounts. I don't think that is very easy to evade. For example, in Chile any transaction-related medium of payment must be authorized by the central bank. I understand that to some extent that does work.

What strikes me as expensive is to have 100 percent collateral on all transaction accounts. That is a lot of money. A more reasonable alternative might be to have a 10 percent deductible for transaction deposits smaller than, say, one times capital, a 50 percent deductible for transaction deposits that are greater than one but less than two times capital, and then a 100 percent deductible for transaction deposits that exceed two times capital. That is a cheaper way to achieve a similar end. That is what has been done in the Chilean banking law.

Why I think that this is important is that we must go back and evaluate Charlie's proposition of the overlapping coinsurance groups of banks. It seems to me that if we really want to protect the payment system, we must consider if one of these groups fails, because that can happen, what is the effect on the payments system? Basically you have reproduced the same problem at a higher level. Say the central bank is called forth to lend. But how can it distinguish a solvency problem from a liquidity problem? What if the group was following a risky investment strategy, counting on central bank assistance?

I don't know what your view is on that, but that is a critical point. I understand that the old clearinghouses did solve the problem because there was one clearinghouse. So all transactions, or most transactions, within a town or within a state, or whatever, were under the same treatment, so payments could continue within that area. The discount on clearinghouse paper took care of the insolvency risk.

If you have overlapping groups, you will not have that characteristic, which is essential to keep up the payments system, unless the central bank accepts moral hazard against itself.

CHARLES CALOMIRIS: This gets back to a point that Peter raised. I am describing that analogy in terms of a group in which there is just mutual-liability coinsurance and there are two scenarios, branching or unit banking. Let me just use his description of my argument, which I think is a little better, and it is the one I made in the first article.

You could just have group-contingent fees, or if you like, penalties, as he described, on a bank when a member of its group fails. You can prevent an illiquidity crisis by having the government involved. In a unit banking setup where you would have to have a lot of these different groups, the kind of problem that you are worried about could be solved by having a sort of amalgam of a private monitoring arrangement that is incentive-compatible through penalties and some form of ultimate government backing. That is also possible.

So there are ways to set up this system so that you can get an amalgam of private monitoring and ultimate lender-of-last-resort backing too. I think in a full statewide branching system that wouldn't even be necessary.

SALVADOR VALDÉS: One question on that last assertion. You say it would not be necessary. That means that big branching banks would never fail, which is absurd.

CHARLES CALOMIRIS: If you had three or four groups, each group operating at the level of the entire United States, group collapse would not be an event I would worry about. I would not design a system primarily to deal with the potential for those events.

MARVIN GOODFRIEND: I want to echo what Charlie was saying. If we really are talking about insurance, we should distinguish between pooling of risks and aggregate shocks. I think we can improve our system very much even if we are only focusing our attention on improving risk pooling, for example, by removing prohibitions on branching within the United States.

Then we can consider separately what we should do with regard to aggregate shocks. Aggregate shocks are a different story. It seems to me it is useful to keep them separate. In the case of aggregate shocks it is hard to believe the government is going to sit by and do nothing. There is going to be some tax and transfer scheme that will be in place at the discretion of government. One hopes we won't get that shock if we manage our macroeconomy right. But I think that is a separate issue from getting the best risk-pooling arrangements, which I believe ought to be the main issue, in improving the functioning of what we call deposit insurance.

6

Philip L. Brock

The Macroeconomic Consequences of Loan-Loss Rollovers

An important theme that emerges from this volume's case studies is the fiscal management of banks' loan losses following a large external shock to an economy. If financial claims against domestic assets increase in riskiness as a result of an external shock, a problem of underinvestment in the economy may occur while those claims are being resolved. Foreigners who might otherwise lend to the economy will not do so if their financial claims are placed in the same risk category as other existing claims. In this setting, fiscal management of loan losses in the financial system may involve granting loan guarantees to foreign lenders that permit the financing of new projects while failed banks and firms are being recapitalized or liquidated.[1]

Although government loan guarantees in the aftermath of an external shock encourage foreigners to lend, this chapter will explore the possibility that these loan guarantees may also distort an economy's macroeconomic adjustment by permitting the postponement of the liquidation process. For example, the failure to close banks quickly was singled out by Sergio de la Cuadra and Salvador Valdés (Chapter 2) as the dominant macroeconomic problem distorting the adjustment of the Chilean economy in 1981 and 1982. Paul Horvitz (Chapter 3) also emphasized political unwillingness to shut down insolvent savings and loans institutions in Texas as a major element in the magnification of the costs of the financial collapse in Texas. Charles Calomiris (Chapter 5) presented related evidence that bank liquidations during the 1920s took significantly longer in states with mandatory deposit insurance (for example, over six years in Nebraska and North Dakota) than in states with voluntary insurance (less than four years on average).

Standard analyses of the problems associated with regulatory forbearance stress the risk-taking incentives faced by any individual undercapitalized or insolvent bank that cause delays in the closure process to raise the government's expected costs of intervention (see, for example, Kane, 1989). According to this line of reasoning, as long as tight regulation of a bank's asset portfolio constrains a bank's risk-taking ability, a government should be unconcerned about delays in the closure of any individual insolvent bank, since the rollover of loan losses, by itself, will not raise the present value of the government's liability.

The thesis of this chapter, however, is that the preceding analysis of the loan-loss rollover of a single bank may be incorrect when aggregated to an entire economy. In the aftermath of a large external shock, the initial existence of government deposit guarantees may commit a government to buy the assets of many failed banks, rather than just the assets of a single bank. If the government's liability associated with the deposit guarantees is large enough, the government will be placed in the position of acting as a market maker who must sooner or later buy private sector assets at a price that exceeds the purchase price offered by any private agent.

If the government fails to intervene immediately in the financial system following the external shock, the price of banks' assets will fall, at most, to a level that just eliminates the net worth of the banks, since the government will buy the banks' assets for an amount equal to the value of insured deposits. If this floor on the price of assets (such as commercial real estate) exceeds a market-clearing price, then the introduction of foreign loan guarantees may induce the economy to produce more of those assets as part of an intertemporal price speculation against the government. Such an inducement to produce more assets will be especially strong if the private sector can finance the new investment entirely with government-guaranteed external borrowing. In such circumstances, the foreign loan guarantees will cause the government to extend its commitment to buy assets at a high price and to sell them back at a low price—beyond the initial commitment associated with domestic deposit insurance guarantees.

When the government finally does decide to intervene in the financial system, there will be a period in which the price of assets (such as real estate) must fall as the government sells the assets back to the private sector. The lower price, in turn, will eliminate the incentive to produce the assets, thereby generating net disinvestment by the private sector. Investment booms in the period between an external shock and a financial collapse can therefore be viewed as a logical consequence of the implicit subsidy to capital formation that is created by government delays in bank closures in conjunction with loan guarantees to foreign lenders.

The remainder of the chapter emphasizes, first, in a formal analytical setting, the intertemporal shifting of investment expenditure that may occur when a government provides foreign loan guarantees at the same time that it is acting as a temporary market maker for the private sector's assets. The chapter then examines three case studies—Chile, Texas, and the United States in the 1830s—to provide some historical examples of the macroeconomic consequences of delays in the closure of insolvent financial institutions. The analytical model is helpful, although not indispensable, for reading the case studies.

The Model

Although there have been a number of attempts to model the incentives for excessive risk taking created by mispriced government deposit guarantees at the individual bank level, there have been few attempts to model the effect of these guarantees at a macroeconomic level. The model of this chapter focuses solely on the problem of loan-loss rollovers in a setting with government guarantees on foreign lending to an economy and with no uncertainty regarding the future evolution of the economy or the date at which the government will terminate the rollover of loan losses.

In general terms the model draws on the insight of Merton (1977, 1978) that deposit insurance is a third-party loan guarantee whose characteristics are equivalent to those of a put option written on the assets backing the deposits. The model will assume that the government has granted third-party loan guarantees on all capital investment, so that the economy operates as if a put option had been written on the value of its capital stock.

The model I consider has a representative agent who produces a manufactured good, a nontraded good, and a primary commodity that is exported. The agent consumes both the manufactured good (C^m) and the nontraded good (C^n) and produces the three goods using labor (L), land (T), structures (S), and equipment (E) as factors of production. In particular, I will assume that manufacturing production requires equipment, nontraded production requires structures, and primary commodity production requires land.[2]

At any point in time, the agent's output is represented as follows: $F(E,L^m) + pH(S,L^n) + \tau G(T,L^x)$, where $F(\cdot,\cdot)$, $H(\cdot,\cdot)$, and $G(\cdot,\cdot)$ are standard constant-returns-to-scale production functions, p is the relative price of nontraded goods in terms of the manufactured good (whose price is normalized to unity), and τ (the economy's terms of trade) is the price of the primary export commodity in terms of the manufactured good.

Equipment is assumed to be internationally traded at a price that, like manufactured output, is normalized to unity. Structures are assumed to be nontraded internationally, with investment in structures (I^s) requiring nontraded output. The economy's capital account is assumed to be open, with foreign borrowing and lending taking place at an exogenously given world real interest rate (r). Consequently, at any point in time, the change in the economy's net foreign debt (b, where b is the stock of the economy's net foreign debt) is the following:

$$-\dot{b} = F(E,L^m) + \tau G(T,L^x) - rb - C^m - I^e \qquad (1)$$

where I^e is investment in equipment. Similarly, the market-clearing condition for the nontraded good requires that production equal nontraded consumption plus investment in structures:

$$H(S,L^n) = C^n + I^s \qquad (2)$$

Equipment is assumed to depreciate at a rate δ^e and structures at a rate δ^s so that the changes in the stocks of equipment and structures at any point in time obey the following constraints:

$$\dot{E} = I^e - \delta^e E \qquad (3)$$

$$\dot{S} = I^s - \delta^s S \qquad (4)$$

At time $t = 0$, the representative agent formulates a consumption plan, investment plan, and labor allocation plan to maximize the following discounted sum of utility:

$$\int_0^\infty U(C^m,C^n)e^{-\sigma t}\,dt \qquad (5)$$

where the agent's discount rate (σ) is assumed to be equal to the world real interest rate (r).

The essence of the agent's solution to the maximization problem is captured by two equations. The first equation, which describes the accumulation of structures, combines Equations 2 and 4:

$$\dot{S} = H(S,L^n) - C^n - \delta^s S \qquad (6)$$

The second equation is a no-arbitrage pricing equation and reflects the fact that, on the margin, the agent must be indifferent toward earning either a return r on foreign assets or earning the rental rate on structures [$r^s(p)$], corrected for depreciation, plus any capital gains ($\dot{p}$) on the value of structures:

$$\dot{p} = -r^s(p) + (r + \delta^s)p \qquad (7)$$

The solution to Equations 6 and 7 can be portrayed graphically by using as reference curves the sets of points where $\dot{S} = 0$ and $\dot{p} = 0$. Relative to these reference curves, an economy will evolve so that $\dot{S}$ and $\dot{p}$ will generally not equal zero. In fact, it can be shown that the optimal solution to the agent's problem will follow the trajectory JA or $J'A$ (known as a saddlepath trajectory) in Figure 6.1, depending on whether the stock of structures is initially below or above its long-run level (point A).

When the stock of structures is below its long-run level, the high price of structures encourages investment in structures, thereby gradually driving the price of structures down to the long-run level $\bar{p}$. Conversely, when there is an oversupply of structures, their low price encourages net disinvestment (when the level of gross investment falls short of depreciation on structures), thereby gradually raising the price of structures toward the long-run level $\bar{p}$.

By now comparing two economies that are identical in all respects except that the second economy faces a lower price for its export commodity, one can show that the second economy's adjustment path will be given by KK' rather than by JJ', so that in long-run equilibrium the second economy's capital stock will be lower than that of the first. Such two-economy comparisons are often used to gain some insight into the effects of a decline in an economy's terms of trade. Although this form of comparison is never likely to be precisely true, since agents in any single economy may be able to buy insurance or self-insure against such terms-of-trade declines, the comparison still proves useful in many cases (suggesting that terms-of-trade insurance is typically incomplete against large declines in the terms of trade).

Consequently, if an economy is initially at point A, with a stock of structures whose value is $\bar{p}S_0$, an uninsured decline in the terms of

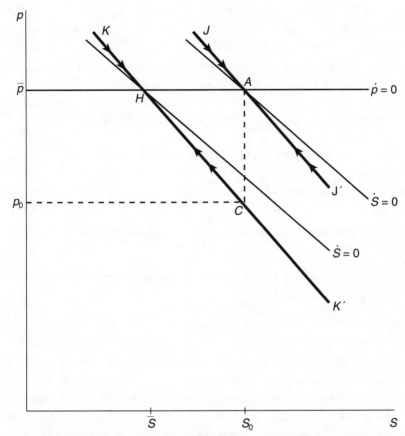

When the stock of structures is below its long-run level (S_0), a high price of structures encourages investment so that a gradual accumulation of structures accompanies a declining price along the adjustment path *JA*. Conversely, an excess supply of structures produces a low price of structures that encourages net disinvestment along the adjustment path *J'A*. An unanticipated decline in the terms of trade shifts the long-run equilibrium from point *A* to point *H* and shifts the adjustment path down to *KK'*. The price of structures falls to p_0, thereby creating the market incentives to disinvest in structures along the adjustment path *CH*.

Figure 6.1 Adjustment to an Unanticipated Terms-of-Trade Decline in a Primary Commodity-exporting Economy

trade will cause the price of structures to fall to p_0, thereby generating a capital loss equal to the area of rectangle $\bar{p}ACp_0$. After the capital loss has been borne by the economy, the stock of structures will decline along the saddlepath from point C to point H. Along this adjustment path the price of structures at any time t can be expressed (by integrating Equation 7) as the following discounted sum of future rental rates on structures, where the discount rate is the international interest rate plus the rate of depreciation:

$$p(t) = \int_t^\infty [r^s(p_v)]e^{-(r+\delta^s)(v-t)}\, dv. \tag{8}$$

The expression for the price of structures given in Equation 8 along the saddle path will be particularly useful for comparison with the price of structures in the presence of government guarantees.

Adjustment with Government Guarantees on the Price of Structures

Suppose that, in contrast to the previous example, the government has written third-party loan guarantees on foreign loans to the economy that have been collateralized by the economy's capital stock. These guarantees act like put options written by the government on the capital stock. Figure 6.2 is drawn under the assumption that the decline in the terms of trade at time $t = 0$ will produce the same backward shift in the adjustment path as in Figure 6.1 (from JJ' to KK') but that the government will be liable, through its loan guarantees, for the capital loss represented by the area of rectangle p_1BCp_0.[3] As a consequence of the government's guarantee, the agent's loss is limited to the area of the rectangle $\bar{p}ABp_1$.[4]

If, at the time of the terms-of-trade decline, the government immediately purchases the stock of structures at the price p_1 from the agent (thus requiring the agent to exercise the put option), the government will be able to resell the structures at the market price p_0, thereby incurring the loss $(p_1 - p_0)S_0$.[5] If the government intervenes at time $t = 0$ (the moment in which the agent's equity

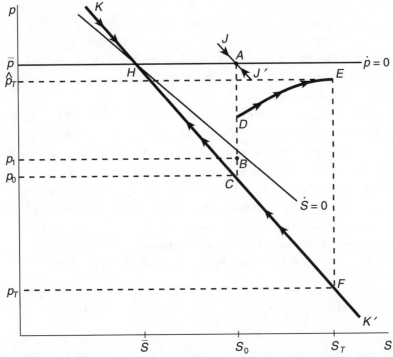

Following an unanticipated terms-of-trade decline, the private sector's capital loss, in the presence of a government's third-party loan guarantee, is the area of rectangle $\bar{p}ABP_1$. The government's liability is the area of rectangle p_1BCP_0. Immediate payment by the government of its liability permits an adjustment of the economy to take place along the saddle path from point C to point H, exactly as in Figure 6.1. Delayed payment by the government causes its liability to grow to the size of rectangle $\hat{p}_T EF p_T$ at time T.

Between time $t=0$ and $t=T$, the price and quantity of structures follow the adjustment path from point D to point E. At time T, the government buys the structures from the agent at price $\hat{p}_T$ and then resells the structures at the market-clearing price p_T, thereby transferring the amount $(\hat{p}_T - p_T)S_T$ to the agent. Following the government's transfer, the economy follows the saddlepath from point F to point H.

Any delay by the government in liquidating the stock of structures acquired at time $t=T$ will induce a transitory rightward shift of the $\dot{S}=0$ locus, thereby temporarily raising the price of structures above the competitive saddlepath price.

Figure 6.2 Macroeconomic Consequences of Loan-Loss Rollovers

participation has been wiped out by the terms-of-trade decline) to "buy high" and "sell low," the government's action will place the economy on the saddlepath at point C. At this point the stock of structures will contract in exactly the same manner as occurs in Figure 6.1 in the absence of a government put option on the capital stock.

If, at the time of the terms-of-trade decline, the government decides to *delay* its purchase of the stock of structures until time $t = T$, the price of structures will decline at most to p_1, since the representative agent understands that the government is a willing buyer of the capital stock at a price that leaves the representative agent with no equity.

Given the government's delay and the agent's loss of equity, the agent has an incentive to invest in more structures, provided that the agent can persuade the government to furnish third-party loan guarantees to new lenders. If the government agrees to guarantee the repayment of all foreign borrowing, the agent will be given the means, as well as the incentive, to exploit the government's delay in the payment of its initial put options. In formal terms, the price of structures before the government's payment of the loan guarantees at time $t = T$ will be given by the following expression:

$$t \leq T \quad p(t) = \int_{t}^{\infty} [r^s(p_v)]e^{-(r+\delta^s)(v-t)}\, dv + (\hat{p}_T - p_T)e^{-r(T-t)} \qquad (9)$$

It is the second term on the right side of Equation 9 that causes the price of structures to exceed the price, given by Equation 8, that would occur in the absence of the government's policy. The second term in Equation 9 is the present value of the government's put option per unit of structures, which, at time $t = T$, is simply $\hat{p}_T - p_T$.

Given the government's policy to move the expiration date of the loan guarantees to time $t = T$, the price of structures starts out above p_1 and then rises over time, in accordance with the price dynamics given by Equation 7. During the period prior to the termination of the loan guarantees, the price of structures will asymptotically approach its long-run equilibrium level $\bar{p}$ from below. If, as in Figure 6.2, the adjustment path DE lies above the $\dot{S}=0$ locus, the accumulation of capital will produce a slowly expanding nontraded sector and slowly contracting manufacturing and export sectors prior to the sharp drop of the relative price of nontradables at the time of the termination of the loan guarantees. If the adjustment path starts out below the $\dot{S}=0$ locus, the agent will initially undertake net disinvestment, but at a slower rate than would have occurred along the saddle path KK'.

Along the adjustment path DE in Figure 6.2 the representative agent is producing structures for a single buyer: the government. The government is willing to pay more for the structures than the private sector, since the private sector's best offer is a price located on the saddlepath KK' (which is always below the path DE). At the time of the intervention, the government will buy the stock of structures at the price $\hat{p}_T$. Failure to do so would involve a default on the agent's foreign borrowings. Following the government's intervention at time $t = T$, the government resells the stock of structures at the next best offer, the competitive price p_T, thereby placing the economy at point F on the saddlepath. The cost to the government of paying the loan guarantees at time $t = T$ is the area of rectangle $\hat{p}_T EFp_T$.[6]

Figure 6.2 assumes that both the purchase and the resale of structures by the government take place instantaneously at time $t = T$, thereby generating the downward jump in the price of structures from $\hat{p}_T$ to p_T. If the resale of the structures taken over by the government does not occur instantaneously, then there will be a period during which the government's temporary demand for structures (as a broker) will act to support the price of structures. The government's temporary demand for structures will appear in the model as a shift term (G) affecting the accumulation of structures: $\dot{S} = C^n + \delta^s S + G$.

Failure to liquidate the structures purchased by the government will shift the $\dot{S} = 0$ locus in Figure 6.2 to the right, thereby temporarily raising the price of structures above the price p_T on the saddlepath. As the government liquidates the assets it has taken over, the price will fall to a market-clearing level on the saddlepath.[7] Delays in liquidation, just like delays in the termination of loan-loss rollovers, will artificially maintain the price of structures above market-clearing levels, thereby postponing the economy's eventual adjustment to a lower stock of structures.

A comparison of Figure 6.2 with figures in Abel (1982) and Brock

(1988) indicates that the loan guarantee policy produces an investment response strikingly similar to that produced by a temporary investment subsidy. With a temporary investment subsidy, a government subsidizes the purchase price of uninstalled capital. With a loan guarantee policy for firms that are bankrupt but still operating, a government creates an above-market-clearing floor on the sale price of installed capital. Both policies cause firms to shift investment expenditure into the time period that the policies are in effect in order to maximize the value of the subsidies. With an investment subsidy the fiscal costs are paid up front by the government, whereas with loan guarantees the fiscal costs are paid only upon the expiration of the guarantees.

It is worth emphasizing that the costs of loan guarantees in this model do not arise from risk considerations, as in Merton's (1977, 1978) applications of option-pricing methods to loan guarantees. Standard use of option-pricing methods for determining the cost of governmental loan guarantees requires twin assumptions that the value of an economy's assets evolves exogenously over time and that there are no net changes in the stock of guaranteed debt. In this model, however, it is precisely the endogenous market price of assets and the elastic supply of foreign loans that cause loan guarantees to be costly to the government, even in the absence of risk-taking behavior by the agent.

The Cases of Chile and Texas

There are occasional historical episodes in which a large-scale rollover of loan losses can be readily identified. Chile during the early 1980s and Texas during the mid-1980s are two of these episodes that this volume has considered. In both episodes the negative external shocks of higher real interest rates and lower primary commodity prices should have produced, with well-functioning markets, declines in housing and commercial real estate prices. The negative external shocks, however, were severe enough to cause the insolvency of many banks and savings and loans institutions, so that government deposit guarantees, in conjunction with a failure to close the insolvent institutions, altered the economies' normal market response to an external shock.

As already noted by de la Cuadra and Valdés (Chapter 2) and Horvitz (Chapter 3), the initial response of the Chilean and Texan economies to declines in the price of their primary commodity exports (coupled with a rise in world interest rates) was a period of construction boom before a financial collapse in the two economies. In the Chilean case, a sharp fall in the price of copper in mid-1980, in conjunction with a subsequent increase in world real interest rates, preceded massive foreign borrowing in 1981 and 1982 (amounting to 15 percent of gross domestic product in 1981 and 9 percent of GDP in 1982), which permitted the construction boom to occur. In June 1982 the Chilean government began the payment of its implicit put option on banks' assets, a payment whose size the World Bank (1989) has estimated at about 19 percent of Chile's GDP. The mechanics of the payment between 1982 and 1984 included the creation of a preferential exchange rate for dollar debts, central bank purchase of nonperforming bank loans plus subsidies for the write-down of other bank debts, and the state-subsidized financial restructuring of the economy's largest banks and firms. The reprivatization of the assets in the nationalized sector (known as the "odd" sector in Chile) did not begin until late 1984 and took two years to complete.

Figure 6.3 presents time paths for the price of copper and Chile's real exchange rate, where the real exchange rate is used as a proxy for the price of structures in Chile.[8] Figure 6.3 shows two sharp drops in the Chilean real exchange rate: The first occurred between mid-1982 and early 1983, reflecting the initial intervention in the financial system; the second occurred between late 1984 and early 1986 as the government reprivatized the nationalized assets at market-clearing prices.[9] The series of steps taken by the Chilean authorities amounted to a purchase of assets from Chilean depositors and foreign lenders at a high implicit price (equal to the value of Chilean deposits and foreign loans funding those assets), followed by the delayed sale of the assets at a much lower market-clearing

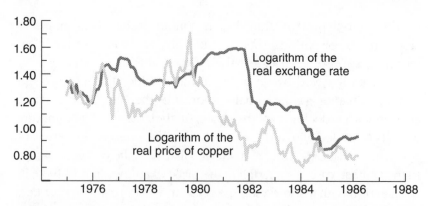

Figure 6.3 Chile's Real Exchange Rate and the Price of Copper, 1975–1987 **Source**: Banco Central de Chile, *Indicaderos económicos y sociales, 1960–1988* (Santiago, 1989).

price. The size of the government's payment associated with its implicit put option corresponds to the rectangle $p_T EF p_T$ in Figure 6.2, whereas the size of the government's payment if it had promptly intervened in early 1981 would have corresponded to the area of rectangle $p_1 BC p_0$.

In the case of Texas, the real exchange rate in Dallas had appreciated sharply between 1978 and 1981 in response to higher oil prices.[10] During the long decline of oil prices between 1981 and 1986, Dallas embarked on a construction boom that sustained a further upward movement in the city's real exchange rate and caused one analysis (*Economist*, 1988) to comment that "Dallas probably outdid any city in absurd overbuilding (much of it financed by reckless thrift lending)." Between the beginning of 1987 and July 1988, 133 Texas banks were closed by the FDIC and many savings and loans were also liquidated (Short and Gunther, 1989). But by waiting until 1987 to begin the large-scale closing of financial institutions and by allowing financial institutions to borrow heavily from outside the state, the government implicitly agreed to purchase additional shopping centers and office buildings at a price exceeding any offer that would be made by the private sector.

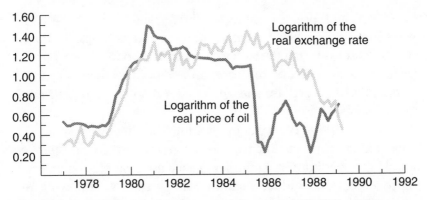

Figure 6.4 Dallas's Real Exchange Rate and the Price of Oil, 1977–1989 **Sources**: U.S. Department of Energy, Energy Information Administration, *Monthly Energy Review*, January 1977–March 1990; U.S. Department of Labor, Bureau of Labor Statistics, *CPI Detailed Report*, January 1977–March, 1990.

The sharp decline in Dallas's real exchange rate (shown in Figure 6.4), which took place between 1987 and 1990, reflects, in part, the termination of the government's put option on the assets financed by banks and savings and loans. The operations of the FDIC with regard to the stock of assets acquired by the government in its Texas bank liquidations paralleled those of the Chilean government: The FDIC purchased assets at a high implicit price from Texas depositors and out-of-state lenders and then sold them back to the private sector at the much lower market-clearing price.[11]

The Case of the United States: 1837–1839

The Chilean and Texas bank collapses have much in common with a bank collapse that occurred 150 years earlier in the United States. The U.S. financial Panic of 1837 was precipitated by a sharp decline in the price of cotton that was connected to a monetary contraction by the Bank of England. The Panic of 1837 left many firms and banks, including the newly privatized United States Bank of Pennsylvania (the successor to the Second Bank of the United States) insolvent. Between 1837 and 1839 Nicholas Biddle, the president of the United

States Bank and former president of the Second Bank of the United States from 1823 to 1836, was able to engineer a large-scale rollover of loan losses through the sale in the London bond market of new securities guaranteed by the bank. In addition, the bank began to monopolize the purchase and sale of cotton, in an attempt to raise cotton prices.[12]

The resumption of capital inflows into the United States in 1838 permitted a temporary recovery of economic activity and the renewal of expenditure by a number of state governments on internal improvements, including canal-building projects. Following an overly good cotton harvest in 1839 (from the standpoint of the United States Bank), the price of cotton collapsed, bringing down the bank and much of the U.S. banking system.

Figure 6.5 indicates two sharp declines in the U.S. real exchange rate.[13] The first decline and the Panic of 1837 occurred simultaneously, shortly after the price of cotton collapsed. This decline was primarily produced by a sharp depreciation of the U.S. exchange rate that was reversed by the beginning of 1838 as the United States

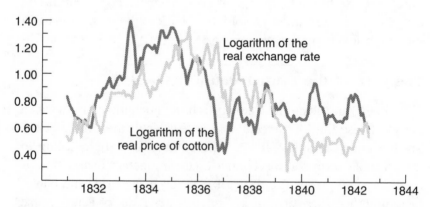

Figure 6.5 The U.S. Real Exchange Rate and the Price of Cotton, 1831–1843 **Source**: Smith and Cole (1935), Gayer, Rostow, and Schwartz (1953), and Donnell (1872).

regained access to foreign capital inflows. The second decline took place following the 1839 bank collapse. At this time there was a stable exchange rate, so the decline reflects a large drop in the U.S. price level that was closely connected to a decline in asset prices. For example, according to Warren and Pearson (1933: 343), the assessed per capita value of real estate in New York City fell by 40 percent, from $859 in 1836 to $513 in 1842.

In contrast to the Chilean and Texan cases, the U.S. Treasury was not compelled to bail out domestic depositors or the foreign lenders involved in the bank collapse.[14] In effect, the United States Bank had issued third-party loan guarantees—whose credibility rested on the strong prior record of Nicholas Biddle—to domestic and foreign investors and the bank could not honor them.

Foreign Loan Guarantees and Bank Closures

The preceding three examples of financial collapse all involved loan guarantees to external lenders of the domestic banking systems. The credibility of those loan guarantees ultimately depended on the size of the fiscal resources backing the guarantees. In both the United States and Chile, foreign lenders cut off their supply of new loans when the loan guarantees lost their credibility, thereby precipitating sharp declines in the U.S. real exchange rate between November 1839 and March 1840 and in the Chilean real exchange rate between June 1982 and January 1983. In Texas, on the other hand, the guarantee of the United States government to out-of-state lenders was strong enough that the supply of external funds was never cut off.[15] As a result, the sharp decline in Dallas's real exchange rate only took place in 1988 following the widespread closure of financial institutions.

These examples suggest that the stronger the lender of last resort to a banking system, the greater will be the ability of the banking system to attract external funds in the aftermath of an external shock. To the extent that these funds help to smooth the adjustment of the economy to the shock, a strong lender of last resort will aid the economy. But to the extent that the external funds permit borrowing to finance a temporary construction boom, a strong lender of last resort may ultimately hurt an economy.

These examples also indicate that when government loan guarantees have general equilibrium effects on asset prices, *ex ante* estimates of the cost of bank closures that ignore the downward jump in asset prices at the termination of the government's implicit put option will underestimate the cost of the closures.

Finally, although analyses of the problems associated with regulatory forbearance usually stress the microeconomic risk-taking incentives created by a government's failure to close undercapitalized or insolvent banks, the findings of this chapter regarding the investment-subsidy effects of government loan guarantees suggest that well-functioning and speedy closure mechanisms for banks are of critical importance to bank regulators, even if regulators can control excessive risk taking by financially distressed banks. The concluding chapter of this volume will return to the central role played by bank closure rules in conjunction with other prudential regulation for the design of legislation and the implementation of sound bank supervisory practices.

7

Philip L. Brock

Conclusion

This volume was inspired by a wave of bank failures and financial collapses that took place in the 1980s across a wide geographical range of economies whose distinguishing characteristic was a dependence on primary commodity exports at a time of falling commodity prices. The concentration of the volume on primary commodity-exporting economies has permitted a sharp focus on the key elements of banking reform, because commodity-exporting economies are more frequently subject to external shocks that can destabilize a financial system than are other economies. It may even be possible to improve banking legislation in other, more stable, economies by studying the performance of past and present banking regulations in commodity-exporting economies. With that idea as a backdrop, this concluding chapter summarizes some of the findings of the volume and explores some of the parallels between the 1986 Chilean banking law and the 1838 New York State free-banking law.

The Causes of Financial Instability in Primary Commodity-Exporting Economies

External causes. Walter Bagehot's *Lombard Street* (1873) was the first systematic treatment of the causes of financial crises. Concerning the real shocks that can cause financial distress, Bagehot (Chapter 6) wrote, "The most common, and by far the most important, case where the depression in one trade causes depression in all others, is that of depressed agriculture." Although Bagehot's judgment on the importance of agriculture may no longer hold true for many industrialized countries, fluctuations in primary commodity prices continue to be the most important cause of booms and recessions in many economies whose exports are concentrated in primary commodities.[1]

With regard to the specific examples of Chile and Texas, Chile's financial collapse in 1983 came at the end of a steep, eighteen-month decline in the price of copper. Texas's financial collapse came in 1987, following the sharp decline in the price of oil in 1986. In both economies the decline in the price of the mineral export produced a decline in property values, but only after an intervening period of construction boom before the financial collapses.

Internal causes. Despite the important role played by external declines in commodity prices in the bank collapses of Chile and Texas (as well as in the Farm Belt states of the 1920s), the chapters in this volume show that lax government regulation during periods preceding the declines permitted banks to undertake overly risky investments and to continue operating after they had become insolvent. As Paul Horvitz emphasized, the losses associated with the failure of the government to close insolvent financial institutions in Texas were probably larger than the original losses associated with the rise in real interest rates and fall in the price of oil.

One overarching theme of the discussion at the Texas-Chile seminar on which this volume is based was the nature of the economic and political forces that push governments into bailing out failing banks and providing regulatory forbearance that allows insolvent banks to continue operating. There are three commonly cited reasons for this behavior. One is the fear of bank runs, or the contagion effect. Peter Diamond, in his comments on Paul Horvitz's paper, drew attention to the continued relevance of the contagion effect: The 1985 run on banks in Ohio was the result of worry about the Ohio deposit guarantee fund rather than the banks themselves.

A second reason for government forbearance and bailouts is the need to protect the payments mechanism. This reason was cited by the authors of the new Chilean banking legislation to justify the incorporation of measures such as 100-percent marginal reserve requirements on demand deposit balances that are more than 2.5 times bank equity. Peter Diamond and Ken Scott each expressed reservations about the unquestioning acceptance of this reason, since historical examples—such as the 1907 New York banking crisis and the Irish bank strikes—show that alternative methods of payment spring up quickly (although at some cost) when normal payment channels are disrupted.

A third reason is the political pressure to bail out depositors and other bank lenders. This pressure can be quite strong and extends beyond banks to government bailouts of large firms, such as Chrysler and Lockheed.

In general, if governments can credibly precommit not to bail out failing banks, free banking (in the restrictive sense of free entry and exit, rather than competitive currency issue) is a feasible way to structure the banking industry. If governments cannot credibly precommit to avoid bailing out failing banks, there are two common outcomes, as noted by Gary Gorton. The stable outcome occurs when the government restricts entry into banking, creates some monopoly profits, and insures deposits. This regulatory approach creates a positive charter value for banks, so that deposit insurance generally does not create incentives for excessive risk taking.[2]

The unstable outcome occurs when bank charter values are

diluted, fiscal oversight of banks is lax, and explicit or implicit deposit insurance exists. In such an environment, banks have the incentive and the implicit authorization to make risky loans and to roll over loan losses, while at the same time regulators and politicians drag their feet on reform measures. In this unstable situation bad investments are made (involving a real resource cost typically associated with empty office buildings, shopping centers, and houses), and there are large deadweight losses associated with the collection of tax revenue to pay for the bailout. This second set of conditions characterized the financial environments in Chile and Texas before their bank collapses.

Managing the Costs of Deposit Guarantees

If a government cannot credibly commit itself to avoid bailing out failing banks (a view taken by most of the participants at the seminar), the government has given a third-party loan guarantee to bank depositors that is equivalent to a put option written on the assets of the bank. Since this implicit or explicit deposit guarantee is valuable to banks, one possible solution to the government's regulatory problem would be to price the guarantee correctly. As Merrick and Saunders (1985) and others have noted, however, the practical implementation of fair pricing requires that government regulators have accurate and constantly updated information on each bank's risk. The greater the mismeasurement of risk, the less attractive is a risk-based deposit insurance premium as a way of correcting the risk-taking incentives created by the government's guarantee.

When deposit insurance cannot be priced continuously and correctly, there are two ways to manage the costs associated with the risk taking that results from the government's third-party loan guarantee: (1) impose a set of financial controls that pay for the costs of the guarantee by "repressing" the financial system or (2) institute better financial regulations for the monitoring and closing of banks. These contrasting approaches are discussed in the following subsections.

Financial repression. The term *financial repression* is associated with the work of McKinnon (1973) on banking systems in developing countries. The term refers to the web of reserve requirements, interest rate ceilings, and credit controls that many governments have imposed on their domestic banking systems. The origins of financial repression have generally been attributed to a government's need to finance an ongoing, open fiscal deficit (see, for example, McKinnon and Mathieson, 1981, and Brock, 1989) or to a political desire to channel bank credit toward targeted borrowers. A third reason for financial repression, which has received far less attention than the other two reasons, is to finance the contingent loan guarantee arising from deposit insurance. When international real interest rates rise or commodity prices fall, the resulting decline in the value of bank assets may require a government to engineer a large transfer to the banking system in order to keep banks solvent. If the treasury of a government does not have the funds to make such a transfer, the task falls to the central bank.

In the United States the savings and loan crisis of the 1980s began in the mid-1960s with a rise in interest rates that threatened the solvency of many savings and loan institutions (whose asset portfolios consisted of fixed-rate long-term mortgages). Mayer (1982) has documented that the Congress and the administration forced the Federal Reserve to impose interest rate restrictions (Regulation Q ceilings) on bank deposits rather than deal directly with the transfer of resources to the savings and loan institutions. Although the interest rate restrictions permitted the savings and loan industry to remain solvent (at least until the restrictions were phased out in the early 1980s), the interest rate policy was an implicit tax on small depositors, which was used to finance the payment of the guarantee associated with deposit insurance. That is, the interest rate restrictions transferred wealth directly from depositors to the owners of savings and loan institutions in a way that avoided the scrutiny of the formal budgetary process.

There are abundant examples of financial repression originating in the financing of contingent insurance guarantees in developing countries. For instance, Chile suffered a collapse of its savings and loan industry in 1975, as discussed in Chapter 2. The financing of the bailout (about 8 percent of gross domestic product) did not involve money from the Treasury; rather, a portion of the financing involved an explicit capital levy on depositors. The other portion of the bailout was financed by an inflationary expansion of the central bank's domestic credit in conjunction with a policy of high reserve requirements. Similarly, the solution to Argentina's 1982 bank crisis—the freezing of bank deposits and deposit rates while hyperinflating—transferred the resources of about 11–13 percent of gross domestic product from depositors to borrowers, as reported by Lüders (1991).

Financial repression associated with the payment of a government's deposit guarantee arbitrarily imposes implicit taxes on depositors, whether those taxes are the result of interest rating ceilings, high reserve requirements, or short-lived hyperinflations. Although these implicit taxes keep the financing of the guarantee out of the treasury, they do not solve, and they may even exacerbate, the problems of excessive risk taking caused by the guarantee. In addition such arbitrary taxes may, over time, be as effective as the other two sources of financial repression in stifling financial intermediation.

Better financial regulation. Are there better solutions to the problems associated with government deposit guarantees than the use of financial repression to finance them? The chapters in this volume indicate that better financial regulation can indeed reduce the problems associated with loan-loss rollover and moral hazard in the presence of government deposit guarantees. Paul Horvitz, in response to comments on his paper (Chapter 3), claimed correctly that we have known the key elements of better financial regulation for a long time: They are bank capital, monitoring, and closure policy.[3] One important goal of this volume was to move from general guidelines concerning bank regulation to the details of that regulation. Including the chapter by Guillermo Ramírez and Francisco Rosende on the 1986 Chilean banking law and the translated text of the law in the appendix was one way of providing those details. A second way was to provide the transcript of the discussion of the seminar's participants on these regulatory details. The following sections summarize some of the specific insights gained from both the seminar and this volume with regard to closure, monitoring, bank capital, and other regulatory policies.

Closure policy. Closure policy is the Achilles' heel of any explicit or implicit governmental deposit insurance commitment. The inability to close failing banks permits bank equity holders to engage in loan-loss rollover and risky lending practices, thereby bidding deposits away from other institutions and transmitting incentives for risky lending to the rest of the financial system.

Both political and technical reasons explain why closure policy is such a thorny issue for bank regulation. Politically, allowing a bank to fail will not only incur the wrath of noninsured lenders to the bank but will also go against the interests of politicians who depend on bank owners for political support. The problem for reformers of banking legislation is to create *ex ante* agreements that make it difficult *ex post* to renege on the "no bailout" position.

In his comments on the Ramírez and Rosende chapter, Ken Scott made a number of suggestions concerning measures to prevent political bailouts of banks. At the constitutional level the legislative ability to override prohibitions against bank bailouts could require super-majority votes. At the legislative level one could implement a procedure like the Gramm-Rudman deficit-reduction law, where a waiver of the law requires a 60-percent vote in the U.S. Senate rather than a simple majority.

Scott also suggested explicitly building into the insurance fund law some form of *ex post* levy on other banks to pay for any one bank's losses. Such a move would create a group that would act as a counterlobby to any one bank's request for regulatory forbearance in the face of solvency problems. As both Gary Gorton and Charles Calomiris noted, Scott's proposal was similar to the way that nineteenth-century clearinghouses actually operated in the United States. Although none of these proposals would guarantee solutions other than the political bailout, Scott suggested that they would improve the odds.

As Scott's examples demonstrate, the main challenge regarding the reform of closure policy is the creation of well-defined and credible rules for closure. The lack of credible closure rules creates a discretionary environment in which regulatory forbearance allows banks to continue operating long after they have become insolvent. A discretionary environment also permits the costs of intervention to be financed in capricious ways, so that small banks and small depositors tend to bear proportionately more of the costs than large banks and large depositors.[4]

The new Chilean banking law devotes about twelve single-spaced pages (out of forty) to the precise specification of alternative closure and recapitalization mechanisms for banks in Chile (see Appendix I, Title XV, Articles 116–150, and Appendix II, Title III, Articles 19–23). The recapitalization mechanisms include voluntary recapitalization by a bank's owners, interbank loans that turn into preferred stock if the borrowing bank does not regain solvency, and a recapitalization process that turns a fraction of a bank's noninsured liabilities into preferred stock (so that domestic depositors and foreign lenders are given a "haircut").

The new banking law has been used twice already to recapitalize banks. In the first instance, during 1988, the superintendent of banks forced the Banco del Pacífico to increase its loan-loss provisions by 60 percent against bad loans. Banco del Pacífico obtained the funds in the form of subordinated debt from another bank. Under the new law the subordinated debt would have been converted into capital if Banco del Pacífico had not been able to pay it off. In January 1989 another bank purchased and recapitalized the Banco del Pacífico in accordance with the requirements of the new law.

In the second instance the superintendent intervened in Banco Nacional in May 1989 after discovering hidden losses that approached 100 percent of the bank's capital. Following the intervention, Banco Nacional was sold to another bank for about 5 percent of its preintervention book value.

Even given the initial success of the new law in closing or recapitalizing two banks, Sergio de la Cuadra and Salvador Valdés expressed some frustration at the failure to incorporate into the law a proposed provision that would have required all uninsured depositors to lose 5 percent of their deposits in the case of a government bailout of a bank. The idea of the proposal was to create some cost for a political rescue of a bank. Guillermo Ramírez explained that such a proposal had been seriously considered but government lawyers had decided that it violated the property rights of depositors.[5]

Monitoring policy. In contrast to the political problems of bank closure, the technical problems stem from difficulties in monitoring the true net worth of banks. The ability to monitor the net worth of banks is closely related to the quality of information the government receives and to the quality of the inspectors employed by the government. In explaining the magnitude of the bank crises in Chile and Texas, respectively, de la Cuadra and Valdés and Horvitz emphasized the disastrous impact of poorly trained bank inspectors. Ken Scott raised the point, however, that as long as bankers have incentives to engage in overly risky activity (from the regulators' point of view), even well-trained bank inspectors may not be able to prevent all such activity.

A number of writers, including Benston and colleagues (1986), have suggested a potential role for subordinated debt as a way to complement the government's monitoring ability by creating incentives for the private assessment of risk. Empirical evidence in both the United States (Avery, Belton, and Goldberg, 1988) and Chile (Valdés and Lomakin, 1988) suggests, however, that subordinated debt holders behave as if a government guarantee extends to them as well as to depositors. The various discussions during the day of the seminar on the topic of subordinated debt led toward the conclusion that without a credible closure policy, subordinated debt holders cannot be counted on to help monitor the risk-taking activity of banks.

Charles Calomiris took a somewhat controversial position by advocating the creation of self-regulating bank cartels (see the discussion of the chapter by Calomiris). One advantage of self-regulating cartels is the enhanced ability of cartel members to monitor one another's actions. A disadvantage is the potential for collusive price setting, a potential that Calomiris suggested could be eliminated by antitrust policy. While agreeing with Calomiris that banks may be superior to government inspectors as bank examiners, Peter Diamond suggested a variation on Calomiris's proposal that would scrap the idea of bank cartels but still require banks to be examiners of other banks, with an appropriately constructed set of incentives to ensure careful monitoring.

Salvador Valdés brought out the point that bank cartels in Chile had to be severely curtailed by the government after 1983. Before 1983, bank holding companies (known in Chile as economic groups) were able to create shell companies so fast that the Superintendency of Banks could never correctly assess the net worth of the holding companies. Ex post facto, it is clear that several of the large holding companies were allowed to operate for at least eighteen months in a state of insolvency. The relevant point is that the existence of large bank holding companies may increase the costs of monitoring, especially when the economic environment deteriorates enough to cause a substantial reduction in the net worth of the holding companies.

The 1986 Chilean banking law has made some significant changes in the bank-monitoring process in Chile. First, the bank secrecy law was changed to allow authorized private risk-rating firms access to privileged bank information (see Appendix I, Title II, Article 20). In addition, the superintendent of banks and the pension funds issue their own assessments of the riskiness of each bank.

Second, the superintendent requires all banks to rate the quality of all loans above a certain size according to risk. The superintendent receives this information monthly and can compare risk ratings given by different banks to the same company. Third, the banking law places strict limits on the amount a bank can lend to other companies in the same holding company.

As Sergio de la Cuadra pointed out, however, the proliferation of holding companies in Chile has created substantial coordination problems among various supervisory agencies. For example, the risk-rating firms and superintendent of banks are only permitted to judge the riskiness of banks, but bank-holding companies can reshuffle assets and liabilities in ways that cause the banks' riskiness to provide an incorrect measurement of the true risk of the conglomerate. This regulatory problem has also surfaced in the United States in the form of a 1990 federal appeals court ruling that the Texas-based MCorp bank holding company was not responsible for the losses of any of its bank subsidiaries, even though the 1956 Bank Holding Company Act requires holding companies to ensure the capital adequacy of their bank subsidiaries.

Bank capital policy. During the discussion at the seminar the issue of the "appropriate" debt/equity ratio for banks in commodity-exporting economies kept resurfacing. During the 1920s Chilean banks operated with debt/equity ratios of 4:1, while U.S. Farm Belt states operated with ratios of about 10:1. During the 1970s Chilean banks operated with debt/equity ratios of 20:1, much the same as U.S. banks. The 1988 capital adequacy standards of the Basle accords (which originated in the Bank for International Settlements) require that all large banks in industrialized countries meet a debt/equity ratio of 12.5:1 by 1993.

One problem with capital adequacy standards is the fact that more capital, by itself, will not reduce incentives to take on risk. Indeed, one can argue that legislating higher capital standards may actually force under-capitalized banks into riskier activities in an attempt to meet those higher standards.

The new Chilean banking law contains two types of capital requirements. The first type is a risk-adjusted capital requirement of 5 percent of the bank's liabilities. The provisions for riskiness are based on the risk ratings received by the banks. The 5 percent capital requirement is in addition to the risk provisions. The second type of capital is a 100 percent marginal reserve requirement against all demand deposits that exceed 2.5 times the bank's equity.

In addition, all other liabilities of banks are potentially convertible into preferred bank stock (through recapitalization agreements) should the bank sustain losses that exceed the risk-adjusted equity requirements. This is one form of equity that may never be used if the Chilean government always resorts to political intervention to rescue depositors of failed banks.

In general, it appears that risk-adjusted capital requirements can complement a bank regulatory system with well-defined closure rules and adequate monitoring of bank risk. Without good closure and monitoring policies, however, raising bank capital requirements may be almost meaningless.

Foreign banks. An initial bias of mine and of some other seminar participants was to assume that opening a domestic financial market to foreign banks would tend to stabilize an economy. As we found out, the matter is not that simple. In comments following the Horvitz chapter, Sergio de la Cuadra noted that in the past fifteen years the increased presence of foreign banks in Chile had forced domestic banks to be more competitive and to offer better services than before. It is not clear, however, that foreign banks are willing to place more capital at stake in any market than the subsidiary's own stake.

Furthermore, during the early 1980s, twenty-eight out of thirty banks operating in Uruguay were branches of foreign banks. During the economic crisis in Uruguay all the foreign branches of banks suffered large losses in their loan portfolios. By threatening not to renew any loans in Uruguay, the banks were able to force the Uruguayan central bank to purchase the bad loan portfolio at par value. As Salvador Valdés remarked, there is a large difference for a small country between diversifying its assets and its liabilities. The liabilities receive local deposit insurance so that no risk reduction is achieved, even though the banks are foreign.

The important lesson from Chile's and Uruguay's experiences is that a small country must have a closure, monitoring, and bank capital policy that can be applied equally well and credibly to foreign banks as well as to domestic banks.

Deregulating asset and liability powers. In the discussion following Paul Horvitz's paper, Ken Scott and Horvitz had a useful interchange on the consequences of bank deregulation for bank behavior. In brief, banks can always take on more risk, even when they are fairly closely regulated. For example, they can issue fixed rate mortgages at low interest rates, thereby taking a bet on the downward future movement of interest rates. Deregulation of asset powers simply offers bankers more ways to take on risk.

Deregulation of liability powers is potentially much more damaging. In Chile, deregulation of liability powers meant that banks could become heavily indebted to foreign banks in a very short period of time and use those funds for speculative investment projects (for ultimate sale to the government). In the United States, deregulation of liability powers meant that banks and savings and loans in Texas (and elsewhere in the United States) had access to almost unlimited dollar amounts of brokered deposits, provided that they paid a high enough premium for the deposits.

It is the latter type of liability deregulation, rather than the asset power deregulation, that has the potential to create enormous financial and economic problems in a short period of time. Consequently, as long as government guarantees on the banking system permit the rollover of loan losses and encourage excessive risk taking, governments need to monitor foreign (or out-of-state) borrowing very closely.

The Chilean Banking Law and Free-Banking Legislation in the United States

As discussed in Chapter 6, the origins of the Chilean banking law of 1986 have much in common with the origins of the Free-Banking Era (1838–1863) in the United States. In both economies external commodity price shocks, in conjunction with a two-year period of loan-loss rollovers, produced a financial collapse and subsequent severe economic depression. New York's free-banking law, which was passed in 1838, became a widely copied model of state bank regulation in the period before the Civil War (and was also the model for the 1863 National Bank Act). By 1860, free-banking statutes had been adopted in Michigan, Georgia, Alabama, New Jersey,

Illinois, Massachusetts, Ohio, Vermont, Connecticut, Indiana, Tennessee, Wisconsin, Florida, Louisiana, Iowa, and Pennsylvania.

Free-banking laws featured two important provisions: First, all bank notes were subject to a 100 percent reserve requirement, since the notes had to be secured by authorized collateral (usually state bonds or certain types of mortgages), and second, state governments gave no insurance guarantee to note holders or depositors. As recent research has shown, actual losses to note holders under free-banking were very small, since bank deposits were treated as a form of subordinated debt.[6]

The 100 percent reserve requirement. Free banking and the 1986 Chilean bank law share the notable feature that demandable (and other short-term) debt is subject to a 100-percent marginal reserve requirement. Such a requirement has been advocated by well-known economists such as Henry Simons, Irving Fisher, and Milton Friedman. The U.S. Congress even considered adopting such a provision in 1935. The arguments in favor of a 100 percent reserve requirement have generally stressed the importance of separating the provision of liquidity by banks from the provision of credit through bank loans.[7]

An even more important role of a 100 percent reserve requirement on short-term bank liabilities may, however, be the information content of such reserves to the superintendent of banks. For example, in New York's 1838 free-banking law (Articles 4 and 11, Appendix III of this volume) note holders who failed to receive payment from a bank could file a complaint with the state comptroller. If the bank did not provide payment within ten days, the comptroller had the right to liquidate the bank.

In the Chilean banking law (Title X, Appendix I of this volume), if a bank has a deficit in the provision of the 100 percent marginal reserve requirement on deposits demandable within thirty days, it must inform the superintendent of banks. If the deficit lasts more than fifteen days, the board of directors of the bank must present a recapitalization proposal to the superintendent.

Under Chile's 1986 banking law, banks that are in financial trouble are prevented by the reserve requirement regulation from using short-term borrowing to finance ongoing operations. In effect, the 100 percent reserve requirement forces banks in trouble to apply for emergency loans from the discount window of the central bank sooner than they would have in the absence of the requirement. In that regard, it is worth emphasizing that Chile's 100 percent reserve requirement applies only to marginal deposits that exceed 2.5 times the amount of bank equity, so that the information content of the requirement is clearly connected to marginal changes in short-term debt.

Deposit insurance funds. In the aftermath of a financial collapse, governments have two common reactions with respect to deposit insurance funds: (1) they set up such a fund if none existed before the collapse, or (2) they attempt to restrict the government's insurance obligations if a fund existed before the collapse. The first reaction characterized the 1933 U.S. deposit insurance legislation, the 1977–1980 Spanish legislation establishing and refining a "*fondo de garantía de depósitos bancarios*," and the creation of similar deposit guarantee funds in Venezuela and Colombia in 1985 and 1986.[8] The second reaction characterized the 1975 Chilean decision to retract deposit guarantees following the collapse of the savings and loan industry, the 1988 Brazilian law banning the bailout of failed banks with public funds following several large bank failures, and a number of U.S. congressional and Treasury proposals to limit deposit insurance coverage following the 1987–1989 Texas financial collapse.

Either reaction has tended historically to set up unfunded deposit guarantees. In the first case the insurance funds do not use risk-based premiums and do not collect actuarially fair premiums. The premiums tend to be too low before a banking crisis and are imposed, *ex post facto*, at too high a rate on healthy banks following a crisis. In other words, deposit insurance funds exhibit characteristics that lead them to "repress" a financial system by first encouraging overly risky behavior and then imposing arbitrary capital levies on the surviving well-run banks in the aftermath of a financial crisis. In Chapter 5 Charles Calomiris documented those perverse aspects of deposit insurance before and during the Farm Belt banking crisis of the 1920s.

In the second case government statements limiting deposit insurance are not, by themselves, credible. The Chilean government found that the lack of well-defined closure mechanisms for banks created irresistible pressures for a bank bailout in the 1981–1983 bank collapse. Similarly, the Costa Rican central bank was forced to bail out large, noninsured finance companies in 1988 despite repeated pledges that it would not intervene in those firms (see Chapter 1 of this volume).

Neither the New York free-banking law nor the 1986 Chilean banking law includes a deposit insurance fund. Under both laws short-term demandable debt is effectively insured by the assets that banks hold as collateral against that debt.[9] As discussed in Chapter 4, the Chilean banking law insures 90 percent of all small deposits (those that sum to less than $2,000 per natural person within the entire banking system) but does not levy a premium on banks to pay for an insurance fund (see Title XV, Articles 141–150, Appendix I of this volume). In each law explicit closure mechanisms are set up to impose the majority of the costs of bank failure on the creditors of the bank rather than to allow a deposit insurance fund discretion in financing bank liquidations.

Beyond Deposit Guarantees

There are times when external circumstances cause an existing set of bank regulations to generate a deposit guarantee that is too expensive for a government to fund. The change in external circumstances may be caused by an increase in the volatility of commodity prices or world interest rates, or it may be caused by changes in an economy's structure of production (as occurred in Chile in the 1970s following the dismantling of tariff protection). Whatever the cause, if asset prices become more volatile and bank charter values become diluted, deposit guarantees will permit loan-loss rollover and encourage risk-taking behavior on the part of banks.

When the deposit guarantee becomes too expensive, a government can either repress a financial system with a set of restrictions that allows banking authorities to control risk taking, or a government can take measures to allow greater freedom of banking in conjunction with measures to ensure the timely closure of failing banks. Free-banking, self-regulating bank cartels and Chile's bank law offer different ways of reducing government control over the lending activities of banks while at the same time lowering the cost of any government guarantee on the banks.

The Chilean banking legislation provides an instructive modern example of banking legislation that includes a complete guarantee for demand deposits, partial insurance for small time deposit holders, reform of bank secrecy laws and the establishment of bank risk-rating agencies, risk-adjusted capital requirements, and closure rule reform. Advocacy of these measures can be found in sources such as Benston and colleagues (1986) and Merrick and Saunders (1985). The Chilean contribution has been to take these ideas for regulatory reform and turn them into a working body of legislation and regulation.

Neither the Chilean authors of the studies for this volume nor their commentators and other seminar participants maintain any illusions that the new Chilean banking law has eliminated incentives for excessive risk taking by banks and the possibility of political bailouts of banks. The Chilean legislation does, however, improve the odds that failing banks will be promptly recapitalized or closed.

As the volume's chapters and discussion have repeatedly emphasized, well-functioning closure mechanisms for banks involve much more than public pronouncements that only certain deposits are insured by the state. Well-functioning closure mechanisms involve a careful delineation of the legal property rights of bank creditors and debtors, rules regarding procedural issues during the closure process, monitoring mechanisms that put the closure process into motion with a minimum of regulatory discretion, and political will. Failure to create and enforce closure mechanisms that sustain a competitive banking system inevitably produces an alternative outcome—such as financial repression, the creation of a banking oligopoly, or a *de facto* or *de jure* nationalization of the banking system—that misallocates an economy's resources and may retard economic growth.

If Texas Were Chile

This volume has approached the issue of banking reform from a comparative and historical perspective, guided by the following implicit questions: What difference does national sovereignty make for the financial stability of a small economy that is open to the rest of the world? How does one create and implement a credible and nondiscretionary set of monitoring and closure processes for financial institutions? How does national sovereignty affect the process of banking reform? As should be clear to readers of this volume, these are questions for which there are no simple and narrow answers. The following general answer, however, emerges from a careful reading of the chapters, and the accompanying discussion of the chapters, in this volume.

If Texas *were* Chile, there would be no Federal Deposit Insurance Corporation, no Federal Savings and Loan Insurance Corporation, no Resolution Trust Corporation for bailing out its financial system. And, as illustrated in this volume (at pages 184–85, for example), Texas's prospects as a sovereign country for diversifying risk would be inherently more problematic than its potential for interstate diversification of risk within the United States. Despite these advantages of statehood within a larger political union, it appears possible that the Texas economy would be stronger today had its financial system been as fully exposed to the exogenous shocks of the 1980s as was Chile's. Such exposure might have created pressure for a sovereign Texas to reform its financial system. Chileans have already undertaken fundamental banking reform with their 1986 banking law; Texans still wait for Washington.[10]

Appendix I

Extracts from the General Banking Law of Chile, Titles II, X, and XV
Decree with Force of Law No. 252
(Including the modifications introduced by
Law No. 18,576 of November 27, 1986,
Law No. 18,707 of May 19, 1988,
and Law No. 18,818 of August 1, 1989)

[Translators' note: The English translation of these extracts from the Chilean banking law was made by Y. Barahona, P. Barahona, and the editor. Creating a readable translation of the law was the primary goal of the translators. Consequently, the translation should not be viewed as a legal document.]

Title II

Concerning Fiscal Oversight

Article 19.–The institutions subject to fiscal oversight by the Superintendency must keep their books, forms, mail, documents, and file cards for a period of ten years. The Superintendent may authorize the elimination of part of this file before this period or ask to keep some documents for a longer period. He may also authorize the institutions to keep microfiches or microfilms of these documents instead of the originals.

The ten-year period will be counted from the date of the last record done on the document or the date it was issued, whichever is relevant.

Under no circumstances can an institution destroy books or instruments that have a direct or indirect relation with a pending business or litigation.

The Superintendent may authorize the banks to return canceled checks to depositors.

Article 20.–Any deposit or investment received by the banks is subject to bank confidentiality. Accordingly, no information relative to these operations can be provided by the banks unless requested by a customer or someone authorized by him or his legal representative. Breakers of the above rule will be sentenced to minor imprisonment with minimum to medium degree.

Other operations are confidential and banks can only reveal them to those who show legitimate interest, provided that such revelation will not adversely affect the client. However, in order to evaluate its financial position, the bank can give detailed information concerning its operations to specialized firms. These specialized firms, which must be approved and registered by the Superintendency, are subject to the confidentiality rules established above.

In any event, banks can reveal their financial operations, in general terms, for statistical purposes or when it is on behalf of the public interest, provided that it is approved by the Superintendency.

The civil and military courts, when conducting an investigation, can request information relative to specific operations that are closely related to the issues being investigated, including investments, deposits, and other operations carried out by any of the parties involved in the trial if necessary.

Title X, Article 78, 80 *bis*, and 81

Concerning Required Reserves and the Maximum Limit of Deposits and Liabilities of the Commercial Banks

Article 78.–All commercial banks and the State Bank of Chile (*Banco del Estado de Chile*) should maintain as a reserve:

1. for their sight deposits, 10 percent

2. for their time deposits, 4 percent

For this purpose sight deposits or liabilities will be those whose payment can be legally required in a period less than thirty days. Ones that can be paid in thirty or more days will be considered time deposits or liabilities.

The reserve ratios for the deposits, established in numbers (1) and (2) of this article, can be modified by the Central Bank of Chile (*Banco Central de Chile*) according to the authority conferred by its organic law. Under no circumstances can the Central Bank fix rates lower than the ones established in this article.

Article 80 *bis*.–To the extent that a bank's demand liabilities— including checking accounts, the rest of the deposits and liabilities at sight that a bank receives, and the amounts allocated to pay demand liabilities that are incurred as part of the bank's financial operations— exceed the bank's paid-in capital and reserves by two and a half times, this excess must be maintained as vault cash or in a technical reserve consisting of deposits in the Central Bank of Chile or in documents issued by this institution or Treasury Services (*Servicio de*

Tesorerías), that will mature in no more than ninety days. The documents in the Central Bank of Chile will be redeemed by the central bank for the value of the principal plus interest payments and readjustments calculated to the date of their redemption when the bank with title to the documents requires these funds for any of the situations anticipated in the second and third paragraphs of Title XV.

For the purpose of this article:

a. Demand deposits and liabilities are those in which payment can be legally required unconditionally, immediately or in less than thirty days, as well as time deposits and liabilities that are within ten days of maturity.

b. The loans received by the bank from others will always be considered conditional obligations.

The deposits and liabilities affected by this article's norms that exceed the amount indicated in the first clause will not be subject to the reserve obligation foreseen in Article 78; neither will the quantities that the bank maintains in the Central Bank of Chile for required reserves help to establish the technical reserve.

The titles to the technical reserve will not be subject to lien. Neither the deposits that the bank has made in the Central Bank of Chile nor the documents that the bank has acquired in meeting the requirements of this article can be seized or made the object of precautionary measures.

If a bank has a deficit in meeting the reserve requirement established in this article, the manager must inform the Superintendent on the working day following the one in which the deficit happened, and also indicate the adjustment measures he will take. The bank, in this case, will incur a fine that will be calculated by applying to each daily deficit the maximum conventional interest rate for nonreadjustable operations, while the deficit is maintained. If the deficit does not last more than three working days and as long as the institution has not incurred another deficit in the same calendar month, the Superintendent may decide not to apply the fine.

If the deficit lasts more than fifteen days, the board of directors must present a recapitalization proposal as foreseen in Article 119, although the presentation of such a proposal will not affect the Superintendent's authority to designate a provisional administrator for the company or to decide on its liquidation.

Article 81.–The deposits and liabilities of a commercial bank with third parties cannot exceed twenty times the bank's paid-in capital and reserves. Infractions to this rule will be punished with a fine equivalent to two per thousand over the excess of the deposits and liabilities for each day that they are maintained.

The proportion to which the first clause refers may be decreased by the Superintendent, with the approval of the President (*Presidente de la República*), by as much as fifty percent.

Title XV

Concerning the Measures to Regularize a Bank's Situation and Its Forced Liquidation

First Paragraph
Concerning Preventive Capitalization

Article 116.–When something occurs in a bank that endangers the bank's financial situation and that the board of directors does not normalize in thirty days, the bank's administration will proceed as directed in this article.

The board of directors must call a Stockholders Meeting by the fifth working day of the expiration of the term noted in the previous clause. The meeting must be held within the following thirty working days, and the stockholders will have to determine the capital increase necessary for the bank's normal performance. The meeting will note the term, form, conditions, methods, and amount of the shares whose issue must have prior approval of the Superintendency. Rejection of the conditions for calling the meeting must be for a good reason.

If the Stockholders Meeting rejects the capital increase as proposed or, if it is approved, and it is not completed in the established amount of time, or if the Superintendency does not approve the meeting's conditions proposed by the board of directors, the bank cannot increase the total amount of its loans nor can it make investments of any kind, except in documents given out by the Central Bank of Chile.

It will be presumed that there have been acts that put the financial situation of a bank in danger when:

a. The bank's deposits and obligations exceed by twenty times its paid-in capital and reserves as of January 1 of the year in question, after correcting for inflation during the intervening period and after deducting the losses for which no provisions have been made. The losses for which no provisions have been made are the ones that the Superintendency has defined in general terms for financial institutions. This presumption will not be applied if the excess has been due to a simple increase in deposits and liabilities, in which case the bank will be subject to the fine indicated in Article 81.

b. Nonprovisioned losses that appear from two consecutive financial statements are defined to be those that, if the proportional increase of those losses were maintained in the following six months, the deposits and obligations of a bank would exceed twenty times the bank's paid-in capital and reserves, as defined in letter (a).

Second Paragraph
Concerning Insolvency and the
Recapitalization Proposal

Article 117.–A bank can only be declared in bankruptcy when it is in voluntary liquidation.

Article 118.–If a bank stops paying an obligation, the manager will immediately inform the Superintendent, who has to determine whether the institution's solvency will survive and, otherwise, to take the corresponding measures according to the law. This rule does not prejudice the right of the affected creditor to go directly to the Superintendency.

Article 119.–When a bank faces solvency problems that prevent it from paying its obligations on time, the board of directors must present a recapitalization proposal (*proposiciones de convenio*) to its creditors, with the exception of preferential creditors and those who hold deposits, liabilities or other obligations at sight to which Article 80 *bis* refers.

It will be presumed, in any case, that a bank faces solvency problems that prevent it from paying its obligations on time when:

a. The value of its assets less provisions, after deducting losses not covered by provisions, and subtracting its legally contracted liabilities, is equal to or less than 40 percent of the bank's paid-in capital and reserves as of January 1 of the year in question, after adjusting for inflation during the intervening period.

It will be the Superintendent's task to establish, through general guidelines, the disposition and characteristics of the assets and liabilities that must be considered for this calculation. For the identification of the nonprovisioned losses that must be deducted from the bank's capital, the last part of letter (a) of Article 116 will be used.

b. There is a repeated violation of the financial administrative guidelines imposed by the Central Bank of Chile for emergency loans of more than fifteen days or for the renewal of those already given. In these cases, it will be presumed that the financial institution has a permanent liquidity problem.

There will be a repeated violation when the financial administrative guidelines imposed by the Central Bank of Chile, in the cases noted in this letter, are violated twice with the same loan.

Article 120.–The recapitalization proposal can deal with:

1. the total or partial capitalization of loans
2. the extension of nonpreferential debt maturities
3. remission of part of the debt
4. any other legal method with respect to debt payment

The recapitalization proposal must be the same for all the creditors to whom it will be applied and the approved proposal cannot contain, in any case, different norms for different credits.

The financial institution will present the recapitalization proposal to the creditors and will maintain in all of its offices a list of those who must decide on the proposal. The list will contain the value of each credit balance, taking into account the settlement of the principal plus interest payments and readjustments. The list can only be shown to the creditors with the right to vote on the recapitalization proposal. Notices will be published in the *Official Gazette* (*Diario Oficial*) and, on the next working day, in a newspaper of national circulation indicating the circumstances surrounding the recapitalization proposal, the date of the presentation, a copy of the proposal, and a reference to the creditors list.

Once the proposal is published the Central Bank of Chile, after being asked by the financial institution and after being given a favorable report from the Superintendency on the proposal, will surrender the amounts necessary for the payment of the deposits and obligations not considered in the recapitalization proposal, to the extent that the institution's available funds are not enough for that matter.

From the date of the presentation of the recapitalization proposal and during the period in which the creditors have not made a decision about the proposal, the institution will not be required to repay deposits and other obligations that are not noted in Article 80 *bis*, second clause, letter (a).

The deposits and liabilities on credit referred to in the same disposition will be considered as sight obligations when their expiration takes place within the ten days after the date the bank presents the recapitalization proposal. In any case, if, at the moment of making the recapitalization proposal to the creditors, the bank has not completed the obligations imposed in the first clause of this article, it will only be paid the deposits and other obligations referred to in the second clause, letter (a), of Article 80 *bis*, whose expiration has taken place within the ten days following the date of failure to fulfill those obligations. The Superintendency will determine that date.

The sight deposits that the bank receives in the period indicated in the fifth clause will not be affected by the suspension of payment and should be kept in a separate account.

Article 121.–The creditors whose credits appear in the list referred to in the previous article will have the right to vote concerning the recapitalization proposal, as will those whose credits are recognized by the entity before the initiation of the vote. Any disagreement caused by including noncreditors in the list or by omitting those that were qualified as creditors, or by incorrectly stating the amount of a credit, will be resolved by the Superintendency no later than the second day preceding the termination of the voting period.

All creditors residing in a foreign country, besides being included in the list, will be notified by telex, cable, or any other equivalent means, addressed to the domicile registered with the institution.

Within the fifteen-day term from the date of publication in the *Official Gazette*, referenced in the previous article, the creditors will have the right to vote on the recapitalization proposal, for which purpose they must vote in the bank's offices expressly indicated for that matter. The voting must be made in the presence of and under the scrutiny practiced by a public notary or other legal official. The recapitalization proposal will be accepted if it is approved by creditors that represent the majority of the bank's total liabilities with the right to vote, with the estimation of the value of the liabilities in accordance with the preceding article.

The Superintendency will dictate the norms by which the vote will be governed and will resolve administratively any matter that comes out while the discussion, voting, acceptance, or rejection is taking place.

The resolutions dictated by the Superintendency in virtue of this article cannot be overruled by any other authority, provided that the resolutions concern the validity of the recapitalization agreement.

If the recapitalization proposal made by the board of directors is rejected, the board within the next three days shall submit to the same creditors another proposal based on reducing the bank's deposits and obligations to third parties to fourteen times its paid-in capital and reserves, by capitalizing the relevant credits. In the case of a *financiera* the reduction will be to ten times its paid-in capital and reserves. The new proposal must be published in the *Official Gazette* and in a newspaper of national circulation according to the norms of Article 20. If this new proposal is rejected, the procedures of Article 127 take effect.

The norms of the Bankruptcy Law (*Ley de Quiebras*) are not applicable to the recapitalization proposals which are treated by this article.

Article 122.–In the situations considered by this paragraph, the board of directors will take bids on the mortgage portfolio of credits subject to Title XII. Other public or private institutions can participate in the bidding, as long as they agree to pay the letters of credit corresponding to the respective portfolio, subject to a proper accounting of those credits and obligations.

If the offers received are equivalent to or higher than the amounts agreed upon for payment to the rest of the creditors in the recapitalization proposal, the board of directors will transfer the respective assets to the acquiring institution. In that case, the value of the letters of credit will be reduced by the percentage offered and the acquiring institution will pay up to that amount. This acquisition will be recorded in the *Official Gazette*. The institution will proceed to reseal the mortgage titles, with the corresponding percentage reduction, when they are presented for collection.

The bidding should be called so as to be completed no more than ninety days after the recapitalization proposal and, if none of the offers received is equal to or higher than the amount asked, the board of directors must reject it. If there is no offer, a new bidding will be called so that it is completed within ninety days after the first one.

If the first bidding is rejected because of the reasons indicated in the previous clause or if in the second bidding there are no bidders, or if those that bid do not bid the amount asked in the recapitalization proposal, the stipulations of the recapitalization proposal will then apply to the holders of the letters of credit issued in relation to the mortgage portfolio.

The payment of the letters of credit to the creditors will be suspended until the mortgage portfolio is transferred or those creditors agree to the terms of the recapitalization proposal or to the results of the liquidation. The money received from the mortgage debtors in this period must be given to the bank acquiring the assets.

Article 123.–When the mortgage credits of Title XII are transferred, in compliance with the dispositions of this Title, the acquiring bank will take charge of the total or partial payment of the letters of credit, subject to a proper accounting of those credits and obligations. The rest of the creditors of the bank, in liquidation or not, cannot oppose this transfer. The acquirer will have all the rights, guarantees, and privileges inherent or attached to the acquired credits.

The transfer will consist of a public document, complemented by a list of the ceded credits, which must be made official. The list will contain the debtors' names and the original amounts of the credits and the data of the mortgage inscriptions.

The Conservators of Real Estate (*Conservadores de Bienes Raíces*) must note the transfer of these credits in the margin of the respective mortgage documents, as required by the ceding or the acquiring party, in order to document the change.

Solely for information purposes, the bank will publish in the *Official Gazette* and in a newspaper of national circulation a notice concerning the transfer of the mortgage record, indicating the date of the contract and the Notary where the transfer was made.

The Notary and the Conservators of Real Estate can only charge the standard fixed rate for the proceedings referred to in this article, without proportional overcharge.

Article 124.–In the case that the recapitalization agreement is approved and the institution, as a result of the recapitalization proposal's stipulations, has to give out shares in payment to the creditors, the board of directors, as the representative of the stockholders, will give out the shares whose summary will be inscribed and published in accordance with Article 28.

The issued shares will be given to the creditors pro rata for the capitalized part of their credits.

When the shares are issued, the stockholders' commission will be called to elect a new board of directors.

When, as a result of a recapitalization proposal, new bank shares are issued, these new shares will be priced according to the value that results from dividing the bank's capital by the number of subscribed and paid-in shares, provided that the bank's capital is positive according to the procedure of Article 119(a).

The stockholders that receive shares as a result of a recapitalization proposal will have the right to require the bank to repurchase these shares pro rata at book value with the bank's annual operating profits, after the bank deducts the amount of dividends that would have been paid to these same stockholders. This right must be exercised within ninety days after the approval of the agreement and, if not exercised, the stockholder will lose this right during the following year. The bank must redistribute the shares so acquired among the holders of shares before the recapitalization proposal, without penalty and pro rata according to the number of shares they possess. The norms applied in this paragraph only apply when there still exist shares that were issued before the recapitalization proposal.

Any natural or juridical foreign person who was a creditor in foreign currency, and who receives shares as a result of the capitalization process to which this article refers, will be able to require that this operation fall under the norms of Decree Law No. 600 of 1974 (The Foreign Investment Code) and its modifications.

Article 125.–For the matter of the capitalization of credits noted in this Title, the limitations and prohibitions concerning the acquisition of shares contained in this or other legal texts do not apply.

Any share acquired as a result of the authorization contained in this article must be divested (*enajenada*) within a three year's term from the date of the capitalization. If the holders of these shares are the National Government (*Fisco*) or the Central Bank of Chile, those shares will not have the right to vote in the election of directors, unless they have been already divested.

Article 126.–Any bank that considers itself affected by any resolution of the Superintendency concerning its financial situation or solvency problems, in accordance with the general or specific norms contained in the fourth clause of Article 116 and the second clause of Article 119, may ask the Superintendency for reconsideration of that resolution, attaching evidence to justify the reconsideration.

The reconsideration will refer to the general quality of the bank's assets and must be done within five working days from the date of the Superintendency's announcement. The Superintendency must make a decision concerning the reconsideration within fifteen days from the date at which all evidence is presented.

In order to reject the reconsideration, partially or totally, the Superintendency must proceed with the approval of the Executive Committee of the Central Bank of Chile.

During the period in which the request for reconsideration has not been resolved, the thirty-day term established in the first clause of Article 116 will be suspended.

Third Paragraph
Concerning Forced Liquidation

Article 127.–If the Superintendent decides that a bank is not sufficiently solvent to continue in operation, or that the security of its depositors or other creditors requires the bank's liquidation, or if the recapitalization proposals have been rejected, it will proceed to revoke the authorization for the bank's existence and will declare the bank to be in forced liquidation, subject to a favorable decision by the Executive Committee of the Central Bank of Chile.

The resolution dictated by the Superintendent for the forced liquidation will also contain the designation of the liquidator, unless the Superintendent assumes direct responsibility for the liquidation. The Superintendent should base his findings of insufficient solvency or lack of security for the depositors or creditors on data coming from financial statements and other information available to the Superintendency.

Article 128.–When the Superintendent is put in charge of the forced liquidation of a bank, he can delegate all or some of his powers to one or more representatives.

The liquidator will have a three-year position and will have the powers, duties, and responsibilities that the law establishes for stock company liquidators. The term of the liquidation can be renewed for successive periods of no longer than a year by resolution of the Superintendent. In the case of a renewal the liquidator must first publish a statement concerning the progress of the liquidation in a newspaper of national circulation.

Article 129.–Once the forced liquidation of a bank is declared, then the checking deposits and the other deposits at sight that the bank has received, the obligations at sight that the bank has contracted in its financial operations, and the time deposits and liabilities referred to in the second clause, letter (a), of Article 80 *bis*, will be paid from the bank's vault cash and from funds deposited in the Central Bank of

Chile or invested in documents of technical reserve referred to in Article 80 *bis*. These norms take precedence over the procedures of payment and the limitations that rule the process of forced liquidation. For the matters contemplated in this article, it is presumed that all the vault cash of the institution will be used for the payments with which this article deals.

If these funds are not enough, the liquidator will have to proceed with as much diligence and urgency as possible to make these payments and, for that purpose, he can divest the rest of the bank's assets. The Central Bank of Chile will have to give him the necessary funds to pay creditors for the obligations noted in this article. For this purpose the Central Bank of Chile can, at its own discretion, acquire some of the bank's assets or make loans to the liquidator. The loans that the Central Bank of Chile gives in order to fulfill this obligation, or the one noted in Article 120, will have precedence over the loans of any other creditor.

The liquidator can transfer the checking accounts and other deposits at sight to another bank, which will be put in charge of the operation of those accounts and of the payment of the deposits as a legal successor to the bank in liquidation.

If, after the date the recapitalization proposal is made or the forced liquidation is announced, a creditor of the bank for obligations not considered in Article 80 *bis* has received the payment or a partial or total compensation for his credit balances, the creditor will lose the right to receive payment for his sight balances until he agrees not to contest the amount of the compensation for his credit balances.

Article 130.–The liquidator is especially required to:

a. Make a detailed list of all the creditors not included in the previous Article, indicating the amount and nature of the credit balances that they have, which will be kept in all the offices of the institution and can only be shown to those that are creditors of the liquidation.

Notices will be published in the *Official Gazette* and in a newspaper of national circulation, calling on the depositors and other creditors to go to the bank to acknowledge their credits. The content of the list can be contested within thirty days of publication in the *Official Gazette* in front of the Civil Judge of Letters (*Juez de Letras en lo Civil*) that has jurisdiction over the location of the bank in liquidation.

The definitive list will constitute the recognition of the creditors with the right to collect the corresponding assessments.

b. Make an annual report concerning the bank's management to the stockholders and creditors of the bank and give the final financial statement as established in the Stock Companies Law.

For the purpose of the distribution of funds to the creditors of the liquidated bank, the amount due that appears in the list referred to in letter (a) will be augmented as follows:

1. Those accounts in which there was a price-level-linked readjustment to the principal or payment of interest, or both, will continue to draw the readjustments and interest payments according to the account's stipulations.

2. Those accounts that do not draw readjustments or interest payments or stop drawing them because their term is finished, will get current interest rates for nonreadjustable operations.

Article 131.–The liquidator should proceed with the mortgage credits subject to Title XII as contemplated in Articles 122 and 123.

The bidding that is needed should be called so that it can be resolved within ninety days following the date in which the firm's liquidation starts. If the received offers imply that the acquiring party is responsible for the payment of the letters of credit for an amount less than 90 percent of their nominal value, the liquidator should call the holders of those letters to a vote to determine whether they accept the purchase offer or whether they wish to wait for the results of the liquidation. The offer will be accepted if it has the favorable votes of the creditors that represent the absolute majority of the nonredeemed value of the letters of credit. For this purpose, the liquidator will publish notices in the *Official Gazette* and in a newspaper of national circulation, in conformity with the third, fourth, and fifth clauses of Article 121.

If no one attends the bidding specified by this Article, a new bidding will be called to take place within ninety days of the first one. In this bidding the norms noted in the previous clause will be applied.

Article 132.–Once the forced liquidation of a bank is announced by the Superintendency, actions currently undertaken by the bank will be frozen and prior obligations of the bank will remain in force.

Article 133.–The order to liquidate a bank will produce the immediate liquidation of all the existing credits against the bank, without prejudice to the specific rules established in Article 131 for the letters of credits.

While there are available funds, the liquidator can, after putting aside the resources for the liquidation expenses, make payments to the preferred creditors and distribute the rest among the common creditors, proportionally to the amount of their credits.

If for any reason the bank's obligations cannot be paid, they will be covered *pro rata*, without prejudice to the legal preferences.

When a creditor is at the same time a debtor of the bank, compensation will take place at the same time as the respective distribution of funds to other creditors, up to the amount of the credit, provided that the other legal requisites are fulfilled. Other compensation will not take place during the liquidation process.

The Superintendent will turn over the proceeds from the liquidation to the stockholders when all the credits from the depositors and other creditors are paid and once the liquidation expenses are covered.

Article 134.–In the resolution ordering the forced liquidation of a bank, the Superintendent can authorize the firm to continue the operation of its checking accounts or the receipt of other deposits at sight. These funds will be kept in a separate account and will not be subject to the limitations imposed in the previous article.

Article 135.–When a bank that is in liquidation has divested all of its assets or a substantial part of them to another financial institution, that transfer can be done through the notarization of a public document in which the transferred goods are indicated globally, by their amount and lot, as they appear on the balance sheets used in the banks. The same notary will officially record the inventory of those goods. After notarization, the delivery of the goods and the corresponding guarantees and additional concessions will operate legally and will not require endorsement, notification, or inscription. Nevertheless, the transfer of the ownership of real estate and of motorized vehicles requires an inscription. The acquirer can exercise the rights of the transferor without having to prove the transfer, provided that the acquirer has the title to the real estate or motor vehicle with the name of the transferor who has made the inscription to the public document referred to in this clause.

If credits guaranteed with a mortgage are ceded, the Conservators of Real Estate will have to note the transfer of these credits on the margin of the respective mortgage inscriptions, at the request of the transferor and acquirer, with the sole purpose being that of updating the official record where the list of credits appears.

For the purpose of this article, the substantial part of the assets of a bank is that part which corresponds to at least a third of the accounting value of the bank's assets.

Solely for information purposes, the bank must publish information about the transfer in the *Official Gazette* and in a newspaper of national circulation, indicating the date of the document and the location of the Notary's office.

Article 136.–The dispositions of this Title will not be applicable if a financial institution has temporarily suspended its operations or the payment of its obligations because of a legal employees' strike or some other major reason that prevents it from functioning properly.

Fourth Paragraph
Concerning the Capitalization of a Bank by the Financial System

Article 137.–If a bank is in any of the circumstances described in Articles 116 or 119 or is subject to temporary administration, it can arrange a loan for a two-year term with another bank. If, subsequent to the loan, there is a creditors recapitalization proposal, the loan will be paid after the guaranteed credits have been paid.

The conditions of these loans should be determined in a Stockholders Meeting of both institutions and have the authorization of the Superintendency.

No bank can concede credits of this nature for an amount greater than 25 percent of its paid-in capital and reserves.

This loan will be computed as capital of the borrowing company for the purpose of the margins established by law. The lending institution can impose upon the debtor company the obligations, limitations, and prohibitions referred to in letter (d) of Article 17 of Law No. 18,045.

The loan referred to above can only be repaid if the debtor company is duly capitalized according to this law without the noted loan.

If the loan is not repaid within the two-year term, it can be used for the following purposes:

a. To be capitalized if a merger occurs between the borrowing company and the lending institution.

b. To retire a capital increase authorized by the lending institution, but only if the issued shares are subscribed to by a third party. The conditions for financing the shares will be decided between the bank that capitalizes the credit and its subscribers. These shares cannot be purchased on credit by the persons entitled, directly or indirectly, to the property or activities of the bank that capitalizes the credit.

c. To subscribe and pay for an increase in the bank's capital. In that case, the shares should be divested in a secondary formal market within 180 days of the date of the capitalization, unless they were distributed between the stockholders according to general norms. If no bidder attends the first auction, the auction should be repeated each calendar month.

The share purchasers must fulfill the terms of Article 65, No. 18. The Stockholders Meeting that is necessary to comply with this Article must have the quorum noted in Article 61 of Law No. 18,046.

These loans cannot be made by the State Bank of Chile, banks under provincial administration, or banks that have common stockholders who, directly or indirectly, control the majority of the bank's shares.

Fifth Paragraph
Crimes Related to Forced Liquidation

Article 138.–When a bank is declared in forced liquidation, the following constitute fraudulent acts:

1. if the bank had recognized nonexistent debts

2. if the bank had divested property to the prejudice of its creditors

3. if the bank had employed in its business activities the goods received in the payment of a custody deposit or of a trust fund

4. if, based on the knowledge of the declaration of the forced liquidation of the bank and without the authorization of the liquidator, its administrators had taken any act of administration or disposition of goods in prejudice to the creditors

5. if, within fifteen days preceding the declaration of forced liquidation, the bank had paid a creditor in prejudice to others anticipating the expiration of an obligation

6. if the books or documents of the bank or other supporting papers had been hidden, altered, falsified, or made useless

7. if, within sixty days preceding the declaration of the forced liquidation date, the bank had paid interest on deposits on credit or savings accounts with rates considerably higher than

the average in force in similar institutions, or if it had sold some of its assets at prices obviously lower than the market price, or used other harmful methods in order to get funds

8. if, within a year preceding the date of the declaration of the forced liquidation, the bank had infringed many times on the credit margins referred to in Article 84, Nos. 1, 2, and 4 or those margins that govern the concession of guarantees, or had done any act with the purpose of hindering, misleading, or evading the inspection of the Superintendency, including those acts noted in Article 26 *bis*

9. if contracts or other kinds of agreements had been signed in prejudice to the bank's proprietorship, with natural or juridical persons referred to in Article 84, No. 2

10. if, during the ninety days preceding the declaration of the forced liquidation, the bank had incurred a deficit in meeting the obligations imposed by Article 80 *bis*

11. if, in general, the bank had undertaken an operation fraudulently that diminished its assets or increased its liabilities

The crime of fraud established in this article is one that will be prosecuted publicly.

Article 139.–The directors, managers, or other people that have participated in the direction or administration of the bank will be considered authors of the crime referred to in the previous article and they will receive the minor imprisonment penalty in its medium to maximum degree when, in the performance of their jobs, they had executed any of the acts or had incurred any of the omissions previously noted, or when they had authorized those acts or omissions, without prejudice to the civil responsibility that may affect them.

The application of the previous clause does not exclude the application of the rules in Articles 14 to 17 of the Penal Code.

If the acts committed in this Article would have a higher penalty under the Penal Code than this Article, the higher penalty will be applied.

Article 140.–When any of the presumptions established in Article 138 can be formed, the Superintendency, or the National Defense Council upon the Superintendency's request, will inform the criminal judge of the declaration of forced liquidation and the circumstances that could constitute the crime. With this evidence, the judge will start to draw up an indictment in order to investigate whether the administrators of the company or any other person or persons are responsible for the state crime.

The Superintendency or the National Defense Council will appear as part of the trial with the corresponding rights of litigants, without the need to formalize the charge. Proceeding that way, they will ask for the evidence needed for the liquidation proceedings and for the arrest of the responsible parties, when this measure applies. At any time, they can, as well, look at documents of the trial.

Sixth Paragraph
Concerning the Government's Guarantee

Article 141.–The Government's guarantees are given to the obligations coming from deposits and liabilities, through savings accounts or bearer documents, issued by banks and financial companies. That guarantee will apply only to natural persons and will cover 90 percent of the amount of the obligation.

The set of deposits and liabilities protected by this guarantee that a creditor has in a financial company will be considered as a single obligation for the purpose of this paragraph.

Article 142.–No one can be the beneficiary of this guarantee in the same institution or in all the financial system for obligations greater than 120 UFs in each calendar year.[1]

Article 143.–If the document where the deposit or liability subject to guarantee is in the name of more than one natural person, the payment of the guarantee will be understood as made to each person in proportion to the total number of persons, independent of any agreement between them. Any juridical person that appears in a document is excluded from the guarantee.

When a guaranteed obligation appears in a document, it will be presumed that the endorsements were done later than the date of the suspension of payments by the financial institution and that the guaranteed person is the first beneficiary, unless the endorsee has registered the endorsement in the respective institution.

Article 144.–If the payment of an obligation on credit has to be done within the system foreseen in Article 80 *bis*, that obligation will not be considered for the purposes of this paragraph.

Article 145.–The guarantee and the obligations that comprise the guarantee will be put in force by resolution of the Superintendency when a recapitalization proposal is approved according to the second paragraph of this Title or when a financial institution is declared in forced liquidation. In the first case, the payment will be done by the Superintendency and in the second case by the liquidator.

Article 146.–The scope of the guarantee comprises all the obligations referred to in Article 141 that have been contracted by the financial institution, but only in the percentage noted in that Article and with the limitation established by Article 142.

Article 147.–Payments of the guarantee will take into consideration the amount of the original capital obligation or the last renewal and the readjustments and interest that have accrued since the payment date.

Article 148.–In order to receive the payment of the guarantee, the guarantee's beneficiary must renounce any claims on the remainder of the obligation or the part of it that originated with the payment. If the beneficiary rejects the payment of the guarantee, he will still have his rights to recover the balance in the recapitalization proceedings or in the liquidation.

Article 149.–Once the guarantee is paid, the Government will be subrogated only by the operation of the law covering the rights of the beneficiary of the guarantee.

Article 150.–A beneficiary of the guarantee, who at the same time is a debtor of the affected financial institution, will have the amount of the debt charged against his credit balance, unless he gives proper warning concerning the amount of coverage to which he is entitled by the guarantee.

Appendix II

The Organic Law of the Superintendency of Banks and Financial Institutions of Chile
Decree Law No. 1,097
(Including the modifications introduced by
Law No. 18,576, of November 27, 1986,
Law No. 18,707, of May 19, 1988,
and Law No. 18,818, of August 1, 1989)

[Translators' note: This law was translated by Y. Barahona, P. Barahona, and the editor. The caveat attached to the translation of Appendix I also applies to the translation of this appendix.]

Title I

Concerning the Superintendency of Banks and Financial Institutions

Article 1.–The Superintendency of Banks and Financial Institutions is an independent institution with juridical personality of unlimited duration that will be ruled by the present law and will be related to the Government through the Treasury Department (*Ministerio de Hacienda*).

Its location will be in the city of Santiago and, notwithstanding its function as a public law institution, it will not be considered a member of the National Organic Administration (*Administración Orgánica del Estado*). The special or general norms that are dictated for the public sector will not be applied to it and, as a consequence, the Superintendency and its personnel will be ruled by the norms of the private sector, without prejudice to what is established in Article 5.

Article 2.–The Superintendency of Banks and Financial Institutions is concerned with the inspection of the Central Bank, the State Bank (*Banco del Estado*), banking companies of any kind, and financial companies when their control is not given by law to another institution.

The Superintendency will be in charge of the inspection of the companies that issue credit cards or the operation of any other similar system.

The people who perform that function on a regular basis and who evade the Superintendency's inspection will be punished as established in Article 34 of the General Law of Banks.

The Superintendency will also be in charge of the exclusive inspection of the societies referred to in Numbers 11 *bis*, letter (b), and 15 *bis* of Article 83 of the General Law of Banks, even for the registration of the stocks issued by the societies, and will also dictate the general norms that must be followed in their operations.

Article 3.–An employee with the title of Superintendent of Banks and Financial Institutions will be the head of the Superintendency. The Superintendent will be designated by the President and will be considered official head for legal purposes.

The prohibitions and incompatibilities that affect the members of the Executive Board of the Central Bank (*Comité Ejecutivo del Banco Central*) will also affect the Superintendent. He will not be allowed to ask for credit from the inspected entities, except for what corresponds to him as a member of a social security fund.

Article 4.–The Superintendent will be replaced by the Intendent in case of vacancy, absence or incapacity. If there are many Intendents, the replacement will be done in the order of precedence that the Superintendent decides.

The prohibitions, disabilities, and incompatibilities established in the previous article for the Superintendent will also affect the Intendents.

Article 5.–The personnel of the Superintendency will be chosen by the Superintendent, who will designate one or more Intendents and the employees, inspectors, special agents, and other people that, in his judgment, he needs to use; and he will determine their obligations and duties.

The Superintendent can formalize contracts for rendering services on fee for the execution of specific labors. These contractors will not have, in any case, the legal standing of employees nor be able to contribute to the pension fund of the personnel.

The Superintendent will have a very wide freedom to designate and remove personnel, with complete independence of any other authority. For these purposes, and especially for those of termination of the working contract, all the personnel of the Superintendency are the exclusive responsibility of the Superintendent.

The President (*Presidente de la República*), within the next four months, will dictate the rest of the labor rules to which the personnel are subject.

Whatever is not foreseen in this decree law or in the Personnel Statute (*Estatuto del Personal*) referred to in the previous clause will be ruled by the Administrative Statute (*Estatuto Administrativo*) as a supplemental legislation.

Article 6.–The personnel of the Superintendency cannot ask for credits in the banking and financial companies subject to the Superintendency's inspection nor get goods from those companies without previous written permission of the Superintendent. The personnel cannot receive money or goods, as a present or for any reason, directly or indirectly from those companies or from the owners or employees.

Whoever violates the prohibition established in this Article as well as everybody else involved will be subjected to the fines that the law advises for bribery.

Article 7.–It is forbidden to any employee, representative, agent, or person that works in the Superintendency to reveal any detail of the issued reports, or to give to strangers any information about business or any situation that he learns about while he was working in the Superintendency. If this prohibition is violated, he will incur the fine noted in Articles 246 and 247 of the Penal Code (*Código Penal*).

Article 8.–The resources for the functioning of the Superintendency will come from the inspected institutions.

The fee that corresponds to each institution will be paid every semester and it will be one six-thousandth of the average of its assets in the previous semester, as they appear in the general balance sheet that this organization presents.

The calculation of the assets that determine the fee that each institution has to pay will not include the goods and items that may be excluded in the opinion of the Superintendent.

The fee has to be paid within ten days following the required date.

Article 9.–The Superintendent will put together the funds which the inspected institutions must contribute to maintain the Superintendency and will deposit them in the State Bank. From that account he will draw the money he needs for the proper functioning of the Superintendency.

Article 10.–The Superintendent will have the legal, judicial, and extrajudicial representation of the Superintendency and can execute the acts and formalize the contracts necessary or convenient for the fulfillment of the Superintendent's purposes and, within those powers, can freely make the acquisition and the disposal (*enajenación*) of the Superintendency's property.

However, for the acquisition and disposal of real estate, the approval of the President of the Monetary Board (*Presidente del Consejo Monetario*) will be needed.

The Superintendent can delegate some of his powers to the Intendents or other employees of the Superintendency and for special cases he can delegate to third parties.

The Superintendent must report and can bring charges for the crimes that he discovers while acting as an inspector in any of the companies under his vigilance. In addition, he can ask for the intervention of the National Defense Council (*Consejo de Defensa del Estado*) for the exercise and maintenance of the penal and civil actions that proceed. In these cases he will not have to give warning.

Article 11.–The Superintendency will be subject to the inspection of the General National Comptroller (*Contraloría General de la República*) exclusively in what concerns the examination of the Superintendency's expenses.

Title II
Concerning Fiscal Oversight

Article 12.–It will be the Superintendent's responsibility to ensure that the inspected institutions fulfill the laws, regulations, statutes, and other dispositions that rule these institutions and to make the best possible inspection over all their operations and businesses.

The inspection responsibilities also include the application or interpretation of the laws, regulations, and other norms that rule the monitored companies.

For the indicated matters, the Superintendent can control without any restriction and in any way, all the businesses, goods, books, accounts, archives, documents, and correspondence of those institutions and ask the managers and personnel for all the facts and explanations that he thinks are necessary for his information about an institution's situation, its resources, the way its businesses are administrated, the performance of its official representative, the degree of security and prudence used to invest its funds, and, in general, any other thing that should be explained.

He can also give instructions and adopt measures to correct the deficiencies that he observes and, in general, those he thinks are necessary to protect the depositors or other creditors and the public interest.

Within his powers, the Superintendent can ask for a rectification or correction of the accounting value of the investments of the inspected institutions when he decides that this value is not the real one. Concerning the resolutions dictated in virtue of this clause, the Superintendent can enforce them within ten days after they are communicated, applying the procedure established in Article 21 for other matters. However, for the purpose of the application of the system for monetary correction of the Rent Interest Law (*Ley de Impuestos a la Renta*) the standard valorization will be considered as indicated in Article 41 of the mentioned law; nevertheless, the director of the Internal Revenue Service (*Servicio de Impuestos Internos*) can establish that the value determined by the Superintendent should be used.

The Superintendent can exercise the powers given by this law from the beginning of the organization of an inspected institution until its liquidation is over.

Article 13.–For the purpose indicated in the previous article, the Superintendent, personally or through his inspectors or special agents, will visit the institutions under his supervision as often as he wishes.

The Superintendent will also visit periodically the Mint of Chile (*Casa de Moneda de Chile*) and will check the material used for the printing of the bills and the coining of money of the Central Bank and its printing, circulation, and custody.

In the inspections that the Superintendency makes, the Superintendency can integrate its own personnel with the personnel of the visited company.

Article 13 *bis*.–In spite of what was established in Article 7 and without prejudice to the rules concerning banking secrecy contained in Article 20 of the General Law of Banks (*Ley General de Bancos*), the Superintendency must give information about the inspected entities to the Finance Minister (*Ministro de Hacienda*), to the Monetary Board, and to the Executive Committee of the Central Bank of Chile.

The Superintendency will also let the public know, at least three times a year, information about the placements, investments, and other assets of the inspected institutions and their classification and evaluation according to the pace of their recovery, and it is necessary that this information be given for all the monitored entities. The Superintendency can also, through general instructions, require that those companies give information to the public on a regular or occasional basis about the same matters.

For the sole purpose of allowing a regular evaluation of the financial institutions by specialized firms that demonstrate a genuine interest, the Superintendency should let them know about the list of debtors of the bank, the settlement of the bank's obligations, and the guarantees have been made. The previous actions will only proceed when the Superintendency has approved the inscription of the specialized firms in a special record that will be opened for the matters contemplated in this clause and in the second clause of Article 20 of the General Law of Banks. The Superintendency will also maintain permanent and updated information about this matter to be used by the financial institutions under its supervision. The persons that get this information cannot reveal its content to third parties and, if so, they will incur the penalty of minor imprisonment in its minimum and medium degree.

Without prejudice to the previous paragraph, the Superintendency should ask the banks to make available for the public a list that contains information about the debtors that owe the banks 3 percent or more of their paid-in capital and reserves, according to the general norms that the Executive Committee of the Central Bank of Chile dictates.

In any case, the banks and financial institutions should fulfill the obligation established in Article 9 of the Law No. 18,045 about Stock Markets (*Mercado de Valores*), regardless of whether its shares are or are not registered in the Stock Records (*Registro de Valores*). In case this obligation is not fulfilled, the Superintendency can provide that information.

Article 14.–The Superintendent will fix general rules concerning the presentation of the balance sheets of the inspected institutions and the way in which they should do their accounting, making sure that the application of those norms helps to show the real situation of the company.

Article 15.–The Superintendent can ask the institutions under his supervision for any information, document, or book that, in his judgment, is necessary for inspection or statistics.

He must ask for the presentation of statements concerning the financial situation of the institutions at least four times a year. When soliciting the general balance sheets, the Superintendent will determine the date to which they will refer; this date will be prior to the date of that notification. The notification should also include the term within which the document must be presented. The statement will be published within the ten days following its delivery, in one of the newspapers of the city where the institution has its central office.

Together with the publication of the general balance sheets referred to in this article, the Superintendency can ask that the inspected institutions publish the data that, in his judgment, are necessary for the public's information. The distributed norms about this matter should be of general application.

The balance sheets of the institutions inspected by the Superintendency should be reported by an external auditing company. It will not be necessary for the stockholders of an institution to designate account inspectors. The auditors will send copies of their report with all the appendices to the Superintendency and the financial institution will publish it together with the balance sheet.

The Superintendency can require, any number of times, at any time in the year, from the inspected institution, balance sheets referring to certain dates of the calendar year, which must be verified by the external auditors that the Superintendency designates.

These balance sheets will be made according to the general or particular norms that the Superintendent notes, especially with respect to the allowances or punishments that he thinks are the correct ones and that will produce real effects for the application of the dispositions that rule the inspected institutions.

Article 16.–Following an inspection, the manager of an inspected institution or the person in charge will inform the board of directors or the corresponding directive body at the next meeting about all communications received from the Superintendent. In addition, a record of the manager's report will be placed in the minutes of the meeting.

Upon the request of the Superintendent, all communications from the Superintendent will be inserted completely in the minutes.

Article 17.–The Superintendent and his inspectors, representatives, or special agents will have the authority to call any person to testify, under oath, about any fact that might be relevant for the elucidation of any operation of the inspected institution or the behavior of its personnel.

Article 18.–Without prejudice to the authority that this law gives to the Superintendency, this institution will have, with respect to the inspected institutions, the same authority that the laws give to the Superintendency of Stock and Securities (*Superintendencia de Valores y Seguros*).

The Superintendency will have, with respect to the external auditors with which the inspected institutions make contracts, the same authority that the Organic Law of the Superintendency of Stocks and Securities and the Stock Companies Law (*Ley de Sociedades Anónimas*) confers to those oversight institutions.

Title III
Concerning Penalities

Article 19.–The institutions under the inspection of the Superintendency that incur any violation of the law that rules them, their organic laws, their statutes, or the orders legally given by the Superintendent, that do not have noted a special sanction, can be warned, censured, or convicted with a fine of up to an equivalent of 5,000 UFs. In the case of repeated violations of the same kind, a fine of up to five times the normal maximum amount can be applied.

In the same way, the Superintendency can warn, censure, or fine the directors, managers, and personnel in general that are responsible for the violations up to an amount equivalent to 1,000 UFs. The fine will be communicated to the violator and to the general manager of the company.

Likewise, the board of directors must notify stockholders in the next Stockholders Meeting about the penalties against the company or its personnel.

Article 19 *bis*.–When an inspected institution presents a state of financial instability or deficient administration, the Superintendent can impose totally or partially and for the maximum term of six months, renewable once for the same period, one or more of the following prohibitions:

1. the granting of new credits to any natural or juridical person entitled, directly or through third parties, to the property or negotiation of the institution

2. the renewal of any credit for more than thirty days

3. the raising or limiting of the guarantees of outstanding credits

4. the acquisition or divestiture of corporate property or intangible assets that correspond to the institution's capital assets or to its financial investments

5. the divestiture of documents from loans and discounts

6. the granting of credits without guarantee

7. the formalization of certain events, contracts, or conventions or the renewal of those in force with the people noted in (1)

8. the granting of new loans or acquisition of financial investments if the growth of the loans and financial investments, compared with the previous month, is greater than the change in the value of the UF in the same period[1]

9. the granting of new powers that permit any of the events noted in the previous numbers

It will be presumed, in any case, that a company has financial instability or deficient administration when:

a. it is in any of the circumstances described in Articles 116 or 119[2] that put its financial situation into jeopardy or that permit the estimation of solvency problems

b. three or more financial statements show losses that on average exceed 10 percent of the initial paid-in capital and reserves during the same calendar year

c. it has asked for urgent financing from the Central Bank of Chile in three or more months of the same calendar year

d. it has paid to the public interest rates that exceed by 20 percent or more the average of the financial institutions of the same kind, in three or more months of the same calendar year

e. it has conferred credits to people related, directly or through third parties, to the property or management of the company, giving better terms, interest rates, or guarantees, than those given to others in similar operations; or it has given credit to related people for an amount greater than its paid-in capital and reserves

f. it has formalized contracts for rendering services or acquisitions or divestiture of assets of any kind to persons related, directly or through third parties, to its property or management, and that had been objected to by the Superintendency, either before or after its formalization

g. the external auditors of the company have doubts about the administration or the stability of the company

Without prejudice to what is established in Article 20, the directors, managers, administrators, or representatives will be punished with minor imprisonment in its maximum degree if they decide, execute, or ask somebody to execute any of the forbidden acts of this Article without a written authorization from the Superintendency.

During the time period referred to in this article, the renewal or resignation of the directors of the institution or the resignation or expiration of the contracts of its managers, administrators, or representatives will not have any effect if those events were not authorized by the Superintendent.

If, during that same period a Stockholders Meeting is called in order to increase the capital of the institution, to merge it, or to sell its assets, the Superintendent can modify the length of the notification term and the number of notices that must be published announcing the meeting.

Article 20.–The directors, administrators, managers, representatives, or employees of an inspected institution that approves or executes operations that are not authorized by law, by statutes, or by the norms dictated by the Superintendency, will be liable with their own goods and assets for the losses that those operations cause to the company.

Article 21.–All the fines that the law establishes and that the Superintendency applies will be imposed administratively by the Superintendent to the infractor and will have to be paid within ten days from the time that the resolution is communicated. The people affected can appeal in front of the Court of Appeals that corresponds to the company's address unless it has an office in Santiago, in which case the Court of Appeals of Santiago will be applicable. The appeal should be made within ten days from the payment of the fine, provided that the payment has been made within the initial ten-day term. The Court will have access to the Superintendent for six days and, once having given notice to the accused, the Court will pronounce judgment within thirty days, without further recourse.

It will also be possible to appeal, subject to the same procedure, the resolutions of the Superintendency that impose the prohibitions or limitations contained in Article 19 *bis*; that designate a temporary administrator, or renew that designation; or that revoke the authorization for the institution's existence or that call for the forced liquidation of the institution. In these cases the appeals should be presented within the ten days following the date of the communication of the resolution and should be agreed to by the majority of the directors of the affected company, even if their functions have been suspended or terminated because of the appealed resolution. The effects of the resolution will not be suspended because the appeal is presented nor can the Court resolve any measure with that purpose while the appeal is pending.

Article 21 *bis*.–The fines that the Superintendency applies will expire in a three-year term from the date the act is over or the sanctioned omission is over.

This term will be six years if there was fraud in the act and this will be presumed when false declaration was given to the Superintendency concerning the committed act.

The time given for the application of the fines will be suspended when the Superintendency starts the investigation that determines the respective fine.

Article 22.–The product of the fines applied to the institutions inspected by the Superintendency will be of fiscal benefit. The Superintendent will discharge periodically in the National Government Treasury (*Tesorería Fiscal*) the fines not appealed and those in which the affected had lost the appeal by executorship judgment (*sentencia ejecutoriada*). While the claim is pending, the amounts collected by fines will be kept in a special account in the State Bank, from which the Superintendency will draw to make the corresponding devolution in case the appeal is accepted.

Article 23.–If an inspected institution has incurred repeated infractions or fines, failed to fulfill the orders legally given by the Superintendent, or had a role in any serious event that put the economy's economic stability in danger, the Superintendent can designate a representative inspector who will have the rights noted for that effect and, especially, the Superintendent will also delegate the right of suspending any agreement of the board of directors or of the attorneys of the institution.

Under the same circumstances, the Superintendent can, with the agreement of the Executive Committee of the Central Bank of Chile, designate a temporary administrator to the institution, who will have all the authority that the law and the statutes give to the board of directors and to the manager, regardless of whether the Superintendent has or has not designated the representative inspector.

The designation of the representative inspector and the temporary administrator cannot be longer than one year; without prejudice, the appointments can be renewed by well-founded decisions as many times as the Superintendent thinks is needed.

The temporary administrator will have the duties and will be subject to the responsibilities of the stock company's directors.

By well-founded resolution in situations that occur before the designation of the temporary administrator and only within the first year of this administration, the Superintendent can suspend the application of the margins foreseen in the General Law of Banks to the financial institution where that measure was applied or to those that had given them credits. However, the Superintendent cannot suspend the obligations established by Article 80 *bis* of the General Law of Banks.

Article 23 *bis*.–In the case that the Superintendent has designated a temporary administrator or liquidator for an inspected institution, he can hire professionals to take charge of the initiation of the judicial actions that will establish the penal and civil responsibilities of the administrators, executives, and other people that, in any position, have been involved in the respective company. Likewise, he can hire professionals to defend in court the people that are participating or have participated in the temporary administration or liquidation of the company, if necessary.

Appendix III

The 1838 New York State Free-Banking Law
Titles 1–12, 18–29, 33
Laws of the State of New York passed
at the Sixty-first Session
of the Legislature,
begun and held at the city of Albany.
Chapter 260
An act to authorize
the business of banking
Passed April 18, 1838

The People of the State of New-York, represented in Senate and Assembly, do enact as follows:

1.–The comptroller is hereby authorized and required to cause to be engraved and printed in the best manner to guard against counterfeiting, such quantity of circulating notes, in the similitude of bank notes in blank, of the different denominations authorized to be issued by the incorporated banks of this state, as he may from time to time deem necessary to carry into effect the provisions of this act, and of such form as he may prescribe. Such blank circulating notes shall be countersigned, numbered and registered in proper books to be provided and kept for that purpose in the office of said comptroller, under his direction, by such person or persons as the said comptroller shall appoint for that purpose, so that each denomination of circulating notes shall all be of the same similitude and bear the uniform signature of such register, or one of such registers.

2.–Whenever any person or association of persons formed for the purpose of banking under the provisions of this act, shall legally transfer to the comptroller any portion of the public debt now created or hereafter to be created by the United States or by this State, or such other States of the United States as shall be approved by the comptroller, such person or association of persons shall be entitled to receive from the comptroller an equal amount of such circulating notes, of different denominations, registered and countersigned as aforesaid; but such public debt shall in all cases be, or be made to be, equal to a stock of the state producing five per cent per annum; and it shall not be lawful for the comptroller to take any stock at a rate above its par value.

3.–Such person or association of persons are hereby authorized, after having executed and signed such circulating notes in the manner required by law to make them obligatory promissory notes payable on demand, at the place of business within this state, of such person or association, to loan and circulate the same as money, according to the ordinary course of banking business as regulated by the laws and usages of this state.

4.–In case the maker or makers of any such circulating note, countersigned and registered as aforesaid, shall at any time hereafter, on lawful demand during the usual hours of business, between the hours of ten and three o'clock, at the place where such note is payable, fail or refuse to redeem such note in the lawful money of the United States, the holder of such note making such demand may cause the same to be protested for non-payment by a notary public, under his seal of office in the usual manner; and the comptroller on receiving and filing in his office such protest, shall forthwith give notice in writing to the maker or makers of such note to pay the same; and if he or they shall omit to do so for ten days after such notice, the comptroller shall immediately thereupon, (unless he shall be satisfied that there is a good and legal defence against the payment of such note or notes,) give notice in the state paper that all the circulating notes issued by such person or association will be redeemed out of the trust funds in his hands for that purpose; and it shall be lawful for the comptroller to apply the said trust funds belonging to the maker or makers of such protested notes, to the payment and redemption of such notes, with costs of protest, and to adopt such measures for the payment of all such circulating notes put in circulation by the maker or makers of such protested notes, pursuant to the provisions of this act, as will, in his opinion, most effectually prevent loss to the holders thereof.

5.–The comptroller may give to any person or association of persons so transferring stock in pursuance of the provisions of this act, powers of attorney to receive interest or dividends thereon, which such person or association may receive and apply to their own use; but such powers may be revoked upon such person or association failing to redeem the circulating notes so issued, or whenever, in the opinion of the comptroller, the principal of such stock shall become an insufficient security; and the said comptroller, upon the application of the owner or owners of such transferred stock in trust, may, in his discretion, change or transfer the same for other stocks of the kinds before specified in this act, or may re-transfer the said stocks, or any part thereof, or the mortgages, or any of them hereinafter mentioned and provided for, upon receiving and cancelling an equal amount of such circulating notes delivered by him to such person or association, in such manner that the circulating notes shall always be secured in full either by stocks or by stocks and mortgages, as in this act provided.

6.–The bills or notes so to be countersigned, and the payment of which shall be so secured by the transfer of public stocks, shall be stamped on their face, "Secured by the pledge of public stocks."

7.–Instead of transferring public stocks as aforesaid to secure the whole amount of such bills or notes, it shall be lawful for such person or association of persons, in case they shall so elect before receiving any of the said bills or notes, to secure the payment of one half of the whole amount so to be issued, by transferring to the comptroller bonds and mortgages upon real estate, bearing at least six per cent interest of this state, payable annually or semi-annually; in which case all such bills or notes issued by the said person or association of persons, shall be stamped on their face, "Secured by pledge of public stocks and real estate."

8.–Such mortgages shall be only upon improved, productive, unincumbered lands within this state, worth independently of any buildings thereon, at least double the amount for which they shall be so mortgaged; and the comptroller shall prescribe such regulations for ascertaining the title and the value of such lands as he may deem necessary; and such mortgages shall be payable within such time as the comptroller may direct.

9.–The comptroller may, in his discretion, reassign the said bonds and mortgages, or any of them, to the person or association who transferred the same, on receiving other approved bonds and mortgages of equal amount; and when any sum of the principal of the bonds and mortgages transferred to the comptroller shall be paid to him, he shall notify the person or association that transferred the bonds and mortgages of such payment, and may pay the same to such person or association on receiving other approved bonds and mortgages of equal amount.

10.–The person or association of persons assigning such bonds and mortgages to the comptroller, may receive the annual interest to accrue thereon, unless default shall be made in paying the bills or notes to be countersigned as aforesaid, or unless in the opinion of the comptroller the bonds and mortgages or stocks so pledged shall become an insufficient security for the payment of such bills or notes.

11.–In case such person or association of persons shall fail or refuse to pay such bills or notes on demand in the manner specified in the fourth section of this act, the comptroller, after the ten days' notice therein mentioned, may proceed to sell at public auction the public stocks so pledged or the bonds and mortgages so assigned, or any or either of them, and out of the proceeds of such sale shall pay and cancel the said bills or notes, default in paying which shall have been made as aforesaid; but nothing in this act contained shall be considered as implying any pledge on the part of the state for the payment of said bills or notes beyond the proper application of the securities pledged to the comptroller for their redemption.

12.–The public debt and bonds and mortgages to be deposited with the comptroller by any such person or association, shall be held by him exclusively for the redemption of the bills or notes of such person or association put in circulation as money, until the same are paid. . . .

18.–Such association shall have power to carry on the business of banking, by discounting bills, notes and other evidences of debt; by receiving deposites; by buying and selling gold and silver bullion, foreign coins and bills of exchange, in the manner specified in their articles of association for the purposes authorized by this act; by loaning money on real and personal security; and by exercising such incidental powers as shall be necessary to carry on such business; to choose one of their number as president of such association, and to appoint a cashier, and such other officers and agents as their business may require, and to remove such president, cashier, officers and agents at pleasure, and appoint others in their place.

19.–The shares of said association shall be deemed personal property, and shall be transferable on the books of the association in such manner as may be agreed on in the articles of association; and every person becoming a shareholder by such transfer shall, in proportion to his shares, succeed to all the rights and liabilities of prior shareholders: and no change shall be made in the articles of association by which the rights, remedies or security of its existing creditors shall be weakened or impaired. Such association shall not be dissolved by the death or insanity of any of the shareholders therein.

20.–It shall be lawful for any association of persons organized under this act, by their articles of association, to provide for an increase of their capital and of the number of the associates, from time to time as they may think proper.

21.–Contracts made by any such association, and all notes and bills by them issued and put in circulation as money, shall be signed by the president or vice-president and cashier thereof; and all suits, actions and proceedings brought or prosecuted by or on behalf of such association, may be brought or prosecuted in the name of the president thereof; and no such suit, action or proceeding shall abate by reason of death, resignation or removal from office of such president, but may be continued and prosecuted according to such rules as the courts of law and equity may direct, in the name of his successor in office, who shall exercise the powers, enjoy the rights, and discharge the duties of his predecessor.

22.–All persons having demands against any such association may maintain actions against the president thereof; which suits or actions shall not abate by reason of the death, resignation or removal from office of such president, but may be continued and prosecuted to judgment against his successor; and all judgments and decrees obtained or rendered against such president for any debt or liability of such association shall be enforced only against the joint property of the association, and which property shall be liable to be taken and sold by execution under any such judgment or decree.

23.–No shareholder of any such association shall be liable in his individual capacity for any contract, debt or engagement of such association, unless the articles of association by him signed shall have declared that the shareholder shall be so liable.

24.–It shall be lawful for such association to purchase, hold and convey real estate for the following purposes:

1. Such as shall be necessary for its immediate accommodation in the convenient transaction of its business; or

2. Such as shall be mortgaged to it in good faith, by way of security for loans made by, or moneys due to, such association; or

3. Such as shall be conveyed to it in satisfaction of debts previously contracted in the course of its dealings; or

4. Such as it shall purchase at sales under judgments, decrees or mortgages held by such association.

The said association shall not purchase, hold or convey real estate in any other case or for any other purpose; and all conveyances of such real estate shall be made to the president, or such other officer as shall be indicated for that purpose in the articles of association; and which president or officer, and his successors, from time to time may sell, assign and convey the same, free from any claim thereon, against any of the shareholders, or any person claiming under them.

25.–Upon the application of creditors or shareholders of any such association, whose debts or shares shall amount to one thousand dollars, and stating facts, verified by affidavit, the chancellor may, in his discretion, order a strict examination to be made by one of the masters of his court, of all the affairs of such association, for the purpose of ascertaining the safety of its investments, and the prudence of its management; and the result of every such examination, together with the opinion of the master and of the chancellor thereon, shall be published in such manner as the chancellor shall direct, who shall make such order in respect to the expenses of such examination and publication as he may deem proper.

26.–Such association shall, on the first Mondays of January and July in every year after having commenced the business of banking as prescribed by this act, make out and transmit to the comptroller, in the form to be provided by him, a full statement of the affairs of the association, verified by the oaths of the president or cashier, which statement shall contain,

1. The amount of the capital stock paid in according to the provisions of this act or secured to be paid;

2. The value of the real estate of the association; specifying what portion is occupied by the association as necessary to the transaction of its business;

3. The shares of stock held by such association whether absolutely or as collateral security; specifying each kind and description of stock, and the number and value of the shares of each;

4. The amount of debts due to the association; specifying such as are due from moneyed or other corporations or associations; and also specifying the amount secured by bond and mortgage or judgment; and the amount which ought to be included in the computation of losses;

5. The amount of debts due by such association; specifying such as are payable on demand, and such as are due to moneyed or other corporations or associations;

6. The amount of claims against the association not acknowledged by it as debts;

7. The amount of notes, bills or other evidences of debt issued by such association;

8. The amount of the losses of the association; specifying whether charged on its capital or profits, since its last preceding statement, and of its dividends declared and made during the same period;

9. The average amount in each month during the preceding six months of the debts due to and from the association; the average amount of specie possessed by the same during each month, and the amount of bills and notes issued by such association and put in circulation as money, and outstanding against the association, on the first day of each of the preceding six months;

10. The average amount in each month during the preceding six months due to the association, from all the shareholders in the association, also the greatest amount due to the association in each of the said preceding six months, from all the shareholders in such association;

11. The amount which the capital of the said association has been increased during the preceding six months, if there shall have been any increase of the said capital; and the names of any persons or any persons who may have become parties to the said articles of association, or may have withdrawn therefrom since the last report.

It shall be the duty of the comptroller to cause the statement required to be made by this section, to be published in a newspaper printed in the county where the place of business of such association is situated, and in the state paper; the expense of which shall be paid by such association.

27.–If such association shall neglect to make out and transmit the statement required in the last preceding section, for one month beyond the period when the same is required to be made, or shall violate any of the provisions of this act, such association may be proceeded against and dissolved by the court of chancery, in the same manner as any moneyed corporation may be proceeded against and dissolved.

28.–If any portion of the original capital of any such association shall be withdrawn for any purpose whatever whilst any debts of the association remain unsatisfied, no dividends or profits on the shares of the capital stock of the association shall thereafter be made, until the deficit of capital shall have been made good, either by subscription of the shareholders, or out of the subsequently accruing profit of the association; and if it shall appear that any such dividends have been made, it shall be the duty of the chancellor to make the necessary orders and decrees for closing the affairs of the association, and distributing its property and effects among its creditors and shareholders.

29.–Such association shall be liable to pay the holder of every bill or note put in circulation as money, the payment of which shall have been demanded and refused, damages for non-payment thereof, in lieu of interest, at and after the rate of fourteen per cent per annum, from the time of such refusal until the payment of such evidence of debt, and the damages thereon. . . .

33.–No association of persons authorized to carry on the business of banking under this act, shall at any time, for the space of twenty days, have on hand at their place of business, less than twelve and a half per cent in specie, on the amount of the bills or notes in circulation as money.

Notes and References

1. Philip L. Brock, "Introduction"

Notes

1. The information in these summaries was taken from various issues of the *Latin American Weekly Report* between 1980 and 1988. Another excellent source of information on banking problems in Latin America is Morris (1990). Vittas and Cortés Douglas (1992) contains case studies on the banking collapses in Malaysia and Norway. The World Bank (1989) provides additional thumbnail sketches of banking problems during the 1980s in Bangladesh, Ghana, Greece, Guinea, Kenya, Korea, Kuwait, Madagascar, Nepal, Pakistan, Philippines, Spain, Sri Lanka, Tanzania, Thailand, and Turkey, and several countries in West Africa.

2. During 1859 discussion in the chamber of deputies of Chile's national congress relied upon the laws of Massachusetts and New York for guidelines regarding the issue of bank notes as a proportion of bank capital (Sesiones del Congreso Nacional, Camara de Diputados, August 4, 1859). Shibusawa (1910: 490–95) discusses the trip to the United States of a Japanese delegation in 1870 to study the American system of bank regulation and the subsequent influence of the National Bank Act on the framing of the Japanese national bank law.

3. This way of expressing the intent of the volume owes an intellectual debt to Daniel J. Boorstin's introduction to *An American Primer* (Boorstin, 1966).

4. The 1986 revision to the Chilean banking law was initiated by Hernán Büchi,

who was superintendent of banks from May 1984 to February 1985 before being appointed finance minister. Guillermo Ramírez succeeded Büchi as superintendent of banks in March 1985, a position that he held until the beginning of 1990. See Rosende (1986) for a discussion of some of the intellectual underpinnings of the new law.

5. Richard Webb's plane from Lima was forced to return to the airport an hour after its departure because of mechanical difficulties. His comments, which were faxed to the seminar, are included in this volume.

References

Benston, George J., Robert A. Eisenbeis, Paul M. Horvitz, Edward J. Kane, and George G. Kaufman. 1986. *Perspectives on Safe and Sound Banking: Past, Present, and Future.* Cambridge, Mass.: MIT Press.

Bernanke, Ben, and Mark Gertler. 1989. "Agency Costs, Net Worth, and Business Fluctuations." *American Economic Review* 79 (March): 14–31.

Boorstin, Daniel J. 1968. *An American Primer.* New York: New American Library.

Calomiris, Charles, and Charles Kahn. 1991. "The Role of Demandable Debt in Structuring Optimal Banking Arrangements." *American Economic Review* 81 (June): 497–513.

Morris, Felipe. 1990. "Latin America's Banking Systems in the 1980s: A Cross-Country Comparison." World Bank Discussion Paper no. 81. Washington, D.C.: The World Bank.

Rosende, Francisco R. 1986. "Institucionalidad financiera y estabilidad económica." *Cuadernos de economía* 23 (April): 77–100.

Shibusawa, Baron Yeiichi. 1910. "The Development of Banking in Japan." In Count Shigenobu Okuma, *Fifty Years of New Japan.* London: Smith, Elder, & Co.

Townsend, Robert M. 1990. *Financial Structure and Economic Organization.* Cambridge, Mass.: Basil Blackwell.

Vittas, Dmitri, and Hernán Cortés Douglas. 1992. *Financial Regulation: Changing the Rules of the Game.* Washington, D.C.: The World Bank.

Williamson, Stephen D. 1987. "Financial Intermediation, Business Failures, and Real Business Cycles." *Journal of Political Economy* 95 (December): 1196–216.

World Bank. 1989. *World Development Report 1989.* New York: Oxford University Press.

2.   Sergio de la Cuadra, Salvador Valdés, "Myths and Facts about Financial Liberalization in Chile: 1974–1983."

Notes

1. Arellano (1983) asserts that "liberalization of credit controls . . . generated a spiral of increases in asset prices and interest rates, and of intermediation, because business groups used bank credit to buy assets."

2. On the tenth of each month the daily value of the unit is fixed for the next thirty or thirty-one days, according to the inflation rate measured by the CPI in the previous month.

3. Although many individual savings and loans were controlled by large, profit-oriented construction companies, the financial entities themselves, by law, had to be nonprofit organizations.

4. This promise was repeated publicly by the finance minister in March 1975.

5. Authors such as Jeftanovic (1976) assign the demise of SINAP to the extension of the minimum maturity of requirement for indexing that took place on August 1, 1974. That hypothesis is contradicted by the huge increase in deposits at SINAP for five more months after that date.

6. In fact, this difference was so strong in Chile in the 1970s that some authors have concluded that the only important type of moral hazard is self-lending by business groups. See Tagle (1988): xix.

7. In the Chilean case we know that the Vial group did not develop consolidated information until mid-1981, when it found it was bankrupt. This is common in fast-growing business groups.

8. See *Ercilla* (Chilean newsweekly), no. 2161 (December 29–January 4, 1977).

9. It was set at 100 *unidades tributarias mensuales*, which amounted to 175 *unidades de fomento* (UF), where the latter are units of account widely used in Chilean credit operations whose movement is determined by the variation in CPI of the preceding month.

10. See *Qué pasa* (Chilean newsweekly), no. 354 (January 26, 1978), which interviewed Francisco Fluxá. Banco Osorno asked for a U.S. $10 million bridging loan until a hypothetical new foreign partner invested in Banco Osorno shares.

11. Alvaro Berdón, interviewed in *Ercilla*, no. 2164 (January 19–25, 1977). The economists at ODEPLAN were the most consistent opponents of the state supervision school.

12. It is unlikely that they realized that the result of this policy would have been a bank cartel, which would have regulated its members.

13. The best reference is Errázuriz (1982).

14. This preoccupation is probably well-founded. For a bank, liquidation usually means very large losses; as the bank ceases to be a viable concern, debtors become more laggardly in their payments because the capital value of their reputation as good payers disappears.

15. Such an alternative has been introduced in Chile, albeit ten years too late, by the 1986 and 1989 banking law reforms. The need for special bankruptcy procedures for banks has been proposed by new advances in banking theory that have heavily influenced the current Chilean banking law.

16. *Ercilla*, no. 2167 (February 9–15, 1977): 21.

17. *Ercilla*, no. 2333 (April 16–22, 1979): 22.

18. See Larraín (1979), who became the superintendent of banks at the behest of the state supervision school. He simply asserts that "if a bank fails, it must reduce depositor faith in other banks."

19. *Hoy* (Chilean newsweekly), no. 32 (January 4–10, 1978): 27.

20. For example, for the year that ended in December 1979, the auditors required

provisions of 0.70 percent of Banco de Chile's loans, 2.40 percent of Banco Español's loans, 0.68 percent of Banco Austral's loans, 0.43 percent of Banco de Concepción's loans, 0.15 percent of Banco de Santiago's loans, and 0.69 percent of BHC's loans.

21. Published in Circular no. 1686 (June 19, 1980).

22. They were bancos Español, de Talca, de Linares, de Fomento del Bío-Bío and financieras Cash, De Capitales, and Del Sur, and Compañía General Financiera.

23. Circular no. 1764 (December 14, 1981).

24. The real growth rates in loans from banks and *financieras* were 76 percent in 1977; 53.6 percent in 1978; 31.9 percent in 1979; 45.9 percent in 1980; and 17.8 percent in 1981. The ratio of loans to GDP rose from 16.6 percent in 1977 to 50.4 percent in 1981. See Held (1989).

25. *Información financiera*, Superintendencia de Bancos e Instituciones Financieras (May 1988). There was a change in definitions, as 60 percent of C loans were provisioned in 1988.

26. The book value of equity-assets ratio of U.S. banks was, in 1980, 3.69 percent for the seventeen international banks, 4.12% for the domestic banks with more than U.S. $5 billion in assets, and 6.77 percent for the domestic banks with assets between U.S. $300 million and U.S. $1 billion. See Talley, S., Federal Reserve Board of Governors Staff Study no. 122 (February 1983).

27. Held (1989) has proposed an alternative method of estimation of the volume of unrealized loan losses, which we think is flawed. He starts by taking the average elasticity of the real volume of bank loans to GDP for developing countries, which is 2.7. He multiplies this elasticity by two, and then assumes that the maximum volume of healthy loans in 1980 can be estimated by applying this elasticity to the 1978 size of bank loans. The excess is taken as comprising bad loans. This procedure is flawed because it ignores the fact that Chile underwent both a domestic financial liberalization and an opening to international capital inflows, which the average developing coutry did not do. In addition, the initial size of the Chilean banking sector was very small, so the procedure ignores the importance of the initial portion of bad loans and of the level of real interest rates.

28. For an interesting debate on the appropriateness of the fixed exchange rate policy, see Corbo (1985) and Edwards (1988).

29. Because of heavy speculation in sugar futures, expectations of devaluation were further fueled by the failure of a large sugar-refining company in May 1981.

30. The perspectives of "conservatives" and "optimists" provided in the text is obviously oversimplified. Other views included the hope that the value of the U.S. dollar would stop rising against the yen and deutsche mark. A dollar appreciation inflicted losses on Chile because most of its foreign debt was denominated in dollars, while only a third of its exports went to the United States. In addition, many investors remembered well the 1960–1962 Chilean attempt to fix the exchange rate, and its abandonment in the middle of a balance-of-payments crisis in which the government bailed out most dollar debtors.

31. See *Hoy*, no. 145 (May 1980), in which the "Cruzat-Larraín Empire" is denounced. Also see Dahse (1979).

32. Bidders were required to offer a 20 percent down payment, plus quarterly installments over the next two years at CPI variation plus 8 percent annual interest rate. Although these terms were below market rates, their financial conditions were used by the government to claim that a high price had been paid.

33. Gálvez and Tybout (1985) provide evidence in support of better management techniques as a third possible reason for member firms of business groups being more successful than similar independent companies.

34. This is equivalent to an equity/assets ratio between 0.33 and 0.25. The main holding companies of the two big groups and their largest subsidiaries had an equity/assets ratio near 0.50. In a straight two-level hierarchical structure the consolidated ratio is the product of both, or approximately 0.25.

35. This practice was known as "back-to-back lending." The net result is that the effective capital base of the banking system is smaller than a case-by-case analysis would suggest. In the most favorable case, in which the loan to the other business group is secured by a lien on real assets that can be inspected by the superintendency, the practice still allows business groups to sidestep the rule that bank capital must be supplied in cash or securities approved by the superintendent.

36. Some argued that this practice was the result of collusion among the large Chilean business groups. This argument is incorrect because evading regulation is privately profitable in an atomistic market as well.

37. The minimum denomination for commercial paper had been set in 1977 in 350 UF.

References

Acevedo, Julio. 1983. "Evolución del sistema financiero en 1982." *Información financiera* (Superintendencia de Bancos e Instituciones Financieras) (January): 5–15.

Acevedo, Julio, and Guillermo Ramírez. 1983. *Información financiera* (Superintendencia de Bancos e Instituciones Financieras) (March).

Arellano, José Pablo. 1983. "De la liberalización a la intervención: El mercado de capitales en Chile: 1974–1983." *Colección estudios CIEPLAN*, no. 11 (December): 5–50.

Barandarián, Edgardo. 1983. *La crisis financiera chilena*. Centro de Estudios Públicos Working Paper no. 6 (October). Santiago.

Bosch, A. M., A. Emhart, and M. Giudice. 1986. "Concentración de créditos en deudores vinculados a la propiedad o gestión de las instituciones financieras." *Información financiera* (Superintendencia de Bancos e Instituciones Financieras) (August).

Corbo, Vittorio. 1985. "Reforms and Macroeconomic Adjustment in Chile during 1974–1984." *World Development* (August): 893–916.

Dahse, Fernando. 1979. *Mapa de la extrema riqueza*. Santiago: Editorial aconcagua.

de la Cuadra, S., and S. Valdés. 1989. Myths and Facts about Instability in Financial Liberalization in Chile: 1974–1983. Instituto de Economía Universidad Católica de Chile, Santiago. Draft.

Díaz-Alejandro, C. 1985. "Good Bye Financial Repression, Hello Financial Crash." *Journal of Development Economics* 19, 1: 1–24.

Edwards, Sebastian. 1985. "Stabilization with Liberalization: An Evaluation of Ten Years of Chile's Experiment with Free Market Policies, 1973–1983." *Economic Development and Cultural Change*, no. 1 (January): 223–54.

————. 1988. "Monetarismo en Chile, 1973–1983: Algunos dilemas económicos." In *Del auge a la crisis de 1982*, ed F. Morandé and K. Schmidt-Hebbel. Santiago: ILADES.

Errázuriz, Hernán Felipe. 1982. "Evolución de la legislación bancaria y financiera 1973–81." In *Legislación económica chilena y de comerco internacional*. Santiago: Banco Central de Chile.

Eyzaguirre, Nicholás. 1988. "La deuda interna chilena: 1975–1985." In *Deuda interna y estabilidad financiera*. Vol. 2. Ed. C. Massad and R. Zahler. Proyecto ECLAC/77/021. Buenos Aires: Grupo editor Latinoamericano.

Ffrench-Davis, Ricardo. 1973. *Políticas económicas en Chile 1952–1970*. Santiago: Ediciones Nueva Universidad, Universidad Católica de Chile.

Gálvez, J., and J. Tybout. 1985. "Microeconomic Adjustments in Chile during 1977–81: The Importance of Being a Grupo." *World Development* 13, no. 8: 969–94.

Gorton, Gary. 1985. "Clearinghouses and the Origin of Central Banking in the United States." *The Journal of Economic History* XLV, no. 2 (June).

Harberger, Arnold. 1984. "La crisis cambiaria chilena de 1982." *Cuadernos de economía* (August): 123–136.

————. 1985. "Lessons for Debtor Country Managers and Policy Makers." In *International Debt and the Developing Countries*, ed. G. W. Smith and J. Cuddington. Washington, D.C.: The World Bank.

Held, Günther. 1989. "Regulación y supervisión de la banca en la experiencia de liberalización financiera en Chile (1974–1988)." Working Paper IC/R 758, May 3. Santiago: Economic Commission for Latin America and the Caribbean.

Herring, R., and P. Vankudre. 1985. "The Moral Hazard Constraint on the Pricing of Deposit Insurance." *Brookings Discussion Papers in International Economics*, no. 40 (November).

Jeftanovic, Pedro. 1976. "La evolución del SINAP durante 1974–76." In *Comentarios sobre la situación económica*, 2d semestre, Taller de Coyuntura, Departamento de Economía, Universidad de Chile.

Larraín, Mauricio. 1979. "Regulación financiera y riesgo." *Boletín mensual* (Banco Central de Chile) 622 (December): 5–32.

Lüders, Rolf. 1978. *Hoy* 35 (January 25–31).

————. 1985. "La razón de ser de la intervención del 13 de Enero." *Economía y sociedad*.

————. 1988. Latin American Contrasts: Capital Markets and Development in Argentina and Chile. Universidad Católica de Chile (May). Draft.

Marcus, Alan. 1984. "Deregulation and Bank Financial Policy." *Journal of Banking and Finance* 8 (December): 557.

Mayer, Thomas. 1965. "A Graduated Deposit Insurance Plan." *Review of Economics and Statistics* 47 (February): 114–116.

McCarthy, Ian. 1980. "Deposit Insurance: Theory and Practice." *IMF Staff Papers* 27 (September): 578.

McKinnon, Ronald. 1988. *Financial Liberalization and Economic Development: A Reassessment of Interest-Rate Policies in Asia and Latin America.* International Center for Economic Growth Occasional Paper no. 6. San Francisco: ICS Press.

Meigs, J. 1984. "Regulatory Aspects of the World Debt Problem." *Cato Journal* 4 (Spring/Summer): 105.

Merton, Robert. 1977. "An Analytic Derivation of the Cost of Deposit Insurance and Loan Guarantees." *Journal of Banking and Finance* 1 (June): 3.

Ramos, Joseph. 1988. "Auge y caída de los mercados de capitales en Chile: 1975–1983." In *Del auge a la crisis de 1982*, ed. F. Morandé and K. Schmidt-Hebbel. Santiago: ILADES.

Schmidt-Hebbel, Klaus. 1988. "Consumo e inversión en Chile (1974–1982): Una interpretación real del boom." In *Del auge a la crisis de 1982*, ed. F. Morandé and K. Schmidt-Hebbel. Santiago: ILADES.

Tagle, Arturo. 1988. "Control de operaciones bancarias con conglomerados de empresas relacionadas." *Información financiera* (Superintendencia de Bancos e Instituciones Financieras) (July).

Tapia, Daniel. 1977. *Ercilla* no. 2164 (January 19–25).

Undurraga, Sergio. 1974. "Política de desarrollo de un mercado de capitales moderno y eficiente para Chile." In *Estudios monetarios III* (Banco Central de Chile) (July): 41–63.

Valdés, Salvador. 1989. "Orígenes de la crisis de la deuda: ¿Nos sobreendeudamos o nos prestaron en exceso?" *Estudios públicos*, no. 33 (Summer): 135–174.

Gary Gorton, "Comment"

References

Bernanke, Ben. 1983. "Nonmonetary Effects of the Financial Crisis in the Propagation of the Great Depression." *American Economic Review* 73 (June): 257–76.

Kane, Edward J. 1989. "The High Cost of Incompletely Funding the FSLIC's Shortage of Explicit Capital." *Journal of Economic Perspectives* 3 (Fall): 31–47.

3. Paul M. Horvitz, "The Causes of Texas Bank and Thrift Failures"

Notes

An earlier treatment of this topic can be found in Horvitz (1990).

1. It turns out that *failure* is a rather difficult term to define precisely. Most banks

that fail in an economic sense do not simply close their doors and disappear—they are often merged into a healthy institution, recapitalized, or sold to a new owner with financial assistance from the federal deposit insurer (FDIC or FSLIC), sometimes without being put into receivership. It should be noted that banks are not subject to the usual bankruptcy laws—see Campbell and Glenn (1984). I will count as failures all those institutions that are put into receivership or receive government assistance. In nearly all these cases the stockholders of the failed institution are wiped out, though in some cases they may (as in corporate bankruptcy) receive some securities that ultimately turn out to have real value (First Pennsylvania Bank is the best example of that). I will distinguish failure from *insolvency*, by which we mean an excess of liabilities over assets (negative net worth). Differing concepts of insolvency are possible depending on whether the assets are valued on the basis of market values or in accordance with generally accepted accounting principles or so-called regulatory accounting principles.

2. This experience led many to believe that the well-diversified Dallas economy was immune to economic problems associated with the energy business and may have led to a continuation of real estate construction long after such activity had virtually closed down in Houston.

3. See Arnold (1986).

4. There is some evidence that stock savings and loans are more aggressive and risk-prone than mutuals, but the differences are not great. For analysis of that evidence, see Brigham and Pettit (1969), Hester (1968), and Kohers and Simpson (1984). The earlier studies were accurately summarized by the conclusion of Jones and Pettit (1974) that "there is relatively little difference between mutual and stock deposit institutions in terms of either their objectives or the ability to emplement efficiently these objectives." None of these studies, however, deals with the reactions of management and owners to financial crisis.

5. A recent study compared the cost to FSLIC of resolving failed federal and state-chartered savings and loans. These costs (in millions) since 1980 were as follows:

	1980–1982	1983–1985	1986–1988
State	$ 540	$1,219	$27,263
Federal	1,188	821	10,405

See *Savings Institutions* (May 1989): 9.

6. Texas law delegates to the state savings and loan commissioner complete discretion to issue rules governing loans and investments. During the relevant time period, there were no limits on the percentage of assets used for loans secured by first liens on commercial real estate, raw land, or personal property (up to 100 percent of appraised value). Up to 10 percent of assets can be invested in service corporations (which can then borrow) that can make direct real estate investments. A recent study cites Texas, California, Arizona, and Florida as the "four states [that] probably have the most liberal laws." See Strunk and Case (1988): 84.

7. It is interesting to note that construction employment was higher in 1986 than in 1981.

8. See *Savings Institutions* (1989): 25.

9. A recent study of the causes of bank failures by the Office of the Comptroller of the Currency put heavy weight on aggressive growth. In interviews with the CEOs of healthy banks in troubled economic regions, "these bankers emphasized profitability and conservative lending, even at the expense of growth. Each of the bankers interviewed pointed to the overly aggressive pursuit of growth . . . as a major weakness in the troubled banks in their areas." See Office of the Comptroller of the Currency (1988): 15–16.

10. This discussion draws on Jacobe (1987).

11. These results were reported in a speech by James Barth, chief economist of the Office of Thrift Supervision before a U.S. League of Savings Institutions Conference, August 22, 1989. Barth indicated that the 205 failures represented a total cost to FSLIC of $32 billion, of which no more than $3 billion could be attributed to fraud. Barth noted that "fraud and insider abuse exacerbated the problem but it's wrong to say fraud was rampant."

12. For most of our post–World War II experience, of course, the profit margins of financial institutions were protected by regulatory ceilings on deposit interest rates—Regulation Q. There is no doubt that the elimination of such ceilings has made the banking business much more competitive and difficult and has reduced the franchise value of the bank charter (see Furlong and Keeley (1987).

13. Corporate demand deposits are not totally free, since the rational corporate treasurer expects the bank to provide services that involve operating costs to the bank. Nevertheless, most commercial banks view demand deposits as their most profitable source of funds.

14. This is offset to some extent by the fact that the noninterest operating costs of commercial banks tend to be higher than those of thrifts (because of the need to service high-activity corporate checking accounts), and thrifts have historically had a higher volume of low-cost passbook savings accounts.

15. See Clair and Gunther (1987).

16. The Federal Home Loan Bank Board and the comptroller of the currency issued proposed regulations in 1989 that assert their authority and intention to take action against institutions that are marginally solvent on a book basis.

17. The FDIC and the Federal Home Loan Bank Board made a concerted effort during this time to outlaw the money brokerage business. Their efforts were misguided because money brokers contribute to economic efficiency by moving funds to where they are most valuable. They put together large numbers of small accounts and divide large accounts into insurable amounts. They do this cheaply by taking advantage of the falling costs of computer power and communications. A bank can do this for itself by setting up a money desk and calling large depositors directly, although that might be more expensive. The problem, of course, is not in the generation of funds but in what the acquiring institutions do with the funds. In any case, the courts ultimately ruled against the agencies' efforts to consider such deposits as uninsured.

18. It is difficult for a savings and loan to enter the commercial lending business on a sound and profitable basis. After all, the best customers already have

commercial banking relationships. The thrift entering this market is likely to attract those who have been turned down by the commercial banks. Those thrifts that were sensitive to this problem and moved gradually as they slowly built up experience have generated profits from commercial lending. Those that attempted to grow a large portfolio quickly almost invariably suffered losses.

19. This is not exactly correct—weak banks have had to pay more for deposits than strong banks, but the differences are measured in tens of basis points rather than the hundreds that the differences in credit quality would require in the absence of deposit insurance.

20. Some economists, particularly Kane, emphasize the moral hazard problem caused by our current system of fixed rate deposit insurance, whereby all banks pay the same premium. That provides a subsidy to riskier banks and may lead some banks to take greater risks in order to obtain that subsidy. If this behavior is common, then deposit insurance could be responsible for increasing the *number* of failures and not just their cost; if deposit insurance allows insolvent banks to stay in business and provide competition for solvent banks, that increased competition may increase the number of failures. There is little doubt that if all the insolvent thrifts in Texas had been closed when they became insolvent, the profit margins of the remaining banks and thrifts would have been significantly better.

21. See Barth, Bartholomew, Edwards, and Labich (1989).

22. The recent FIRREA legislation represents strong congressional response by removing the independence of the Federal Home Loan Bank Board, making it a bureau of the Treasury, and, further, stripping away responsibility of the FHLBB for FSLIC and operation of the Federal Home Loan Banks. Some government agencies have performed poorly in the past, but it is hard to find another example of an agency basically abolished in response to poor performance.

23. That phrase was used by Federal Reserve Chairman Arthur Burns in a speech to the American Bankers' Association in 1974.

24. See Horvitz (1980): 645–59.

25. The largest case of bank failure handled by the FDIC involves Continental Illinois. That bank had assets of about $40 billion and will ultimately cost the FDIC between $1 billion and $2 billion, or less than five cents per dollar. That is approximately the cost of First City and First Republic. One of the largest failures in the past was Franklin National Bank of New York, on which the FDIC recovered all of its initial outlay (with interest).

26. It should be noted that as problems arose with commercial banks in Texas, the banking agencies had too few examiners in place to maintain their schedules. The FDIC and the OCC responded to that shortage by temporarily assigning many examiners from around the country to examine Texas banks. At this time economic conditions in the rest of the country (other than the Farm Belt, with its relatively small banks) were favorable, so the examiners could be spared.

27. Ultimately, Gray went around the administration by moving the examination force to the district banks. The Home Loan Banks were not subject to civil service

salary restrictions or to federal manpower constraints, so a substantial improvement in the capability of the examination staff was possible.

28. Note that the action by Bank Board chairman Gray in moving the examiners to the district banks removed this artificial separation between examiners and supervisors. The top supervisory officials of the banks now have both examination and supervisory personnel reporting to them.

29. These data are discussed in White (forthcoming).

References

Arnold, Jasper. 1986. "Assessing Capital Risk: You Can't Be Too Conservative." *Harvard Business Review*, no. 64 (September).

Barth, James R. 1989. Speech to a U.S. League of Savings Institutions Conference, August 22.

Barth, James R., Philip F. Bartholomew, Donald C. Edwards, and Carol J. Labich. 1989. "The Causes of Thrift Failures." In *Bank Structure and Competition*. Chicago: Federal Reserve Bank.

Brigham, Eugene, and R. Richardson Pettit. 1969. "Effects of Structure on Performance in the Savings and Loan Industry." In *Study of the Savings and Loan Industry*, ed. Irwin Friend. Washington, D.C.: U.S. Government Printing Office.

Brumbaugh, Dan. 1988. *Thrifts under Seige*. Cambridge, Mass.: Ballinger.

Campbell, Tim, and David Glenn. 1984. "Deposit Insurance in a Deregulated Environment." *Journal of Finance*, no. 39 (July): 775–87.

Carron, Andrew S. 1982. *The Plight of the Thrift Institutions*. Washington, D.C.: The Brookings Institution.

Christian, James. 1989. "U.S. Tax Policy Shares Some Blame for FSLIC's Woes." *Savings Institutions* (June).

Clair, Robert T., and Jeffery W. Gunther. 1987. "Problem Loans and the Profitability of Eleventh District Commercial Banks in 1986." *Economic Review*. (Federal Reserve Bank of Dallas) (November).

Furlong, Frederick T., and Michael Keeley. 1987. "Bank Capital, Regulation, and Asset Risk." *Economic Review* (Federal Reserve Bank of San Francisco) (Spring).

Hector, Gary. 1988. *Breaking the Bank: The Decline of BankAmerica*. Boston: Little, Brown.

Hester, Donald D. 1968. *Stock and Mutual Associations in the Savings and Loan Industry*. Washington, D.C.: Federal Home Loan Bank Board.

Horvitz, Paul M. 1975. "Failures of Large Banks: Implications for Banking Supervision and Deposit Insurance." *Journal of Financial and Quantitative Analysis*, no. 10 (November): 589–601.

———. 1980. "A Reconsideration of the Role of Bank Examination." *Journal of Money, Credit and Banking*, no. 12 (November): 654–59.

———. 1990. "The Collapse of the Texas Thrift Industry." In *Restructuring the American Financial System*, ed. George G. Kaufman. Boston: Kluwer Academic Publishers.

Jacobe, Dennis. 1987. "Money Market." *Savings Institutions* (October).

Jones, Lawrence, and R. Richard Pettit. 1974. *The Role and Viability of Mutual Banks.* Philadelphia: Rodney L. White Center for Financial Research.

Kane, Edward J. 1989. *The S&L Insurance Mess: How Did It Happen?* Washington, D.C.: The Urban Institute Press.

Kohers, Theodore, and W. Gary Simpson. 1984. "Ownership Form, Regulator Status and Performance in the Savings and Loan Industry." *Review of Business and Economic Research*, no. 20 (Fall):63–75.

Office of the Comptroller of the Currency. 1988. *Bank Failures.* Washington, D.C.: June.

Savings Institutions. 1989. "U.S. Tax Policy Shares Some Blame for FSLIC's Woes." (June): 25.

Singer, Mark. 1985. *Funny Money.* New York: Knopf.

Strunk, Norman, and Fred Case. 1988. *Where Deregulation Went Wrong.* Chicago: U.S. League of Savings Institutions.

Weinstein, Bernard L., and Harold T. Gross. 1986. The Texas Economy in Transition: Causes, Implications and Policy Responses. Southern Methodist University. Mimeo.

———. 1988. The Texas Economic Rebound. Southern Methodist University. Mimeo.

White, Lawrence J. "The Problems of the FSLIC: A Policy Maker's View." *Contemporary Policy Issues*, forthcoming.

Zweig, Philip L. 1985. *Belly Up: The Collapse of the Penn Square Bank.* New York: Crown Publishers.

4. Guillermo Ramírez and Francisco Rosende, "Responding to Collapse: Chilean Banking Legislation after 1983"

Notes

1. A description and summary of the main economic policy steps taken to rehabilitate the financial sector are found in *Información financiera*, Superintendencia de Bancos e Instituciones Financieras (March 1985).

2. See the paper by Sergio de la Cuadra and Salvador Valdés in Chapter 2 of this volume for an in-depth analysis of the preventive measures the Superintendency of Banks did take.

3. On this point see Rosende and Vergara (1986).

4. This hypothesis is formally examined for the Argentine case in Fernandez (1983).

5. See the article by de la Cuadra and Valdés in this volume for a detailed discussion of the 1980 measures. Since 1980, SIB has been perfecting its asset

portfolio rating system in accordance with expected risk. Information is gathered for this purpose every four months. This supervision process currently covers 94 percent of all loans and the comptrolling institution reviews the ratings conducted by field inspectors once or twice a year according to the nature of the financial institution concerned. In addition, trade-related credit, consumer loans, and the housing mortgage portfolio are also rated by special methods.

6. *Bis* denotes an addition to a law that has been inserted between two pre-existing articles.

7. There are at present five bank-rating firms. The system began operating in 1989, and the firms' first opinions of the banking system were published in March 1989. A joint commission composed of members from public and private organizations has also been operating since 1985, under Decree Law 3,500. It is known as *Comision de Riesgo* (Risk-Ranking Commission), and its object is to prepare a public ranking of risk involved in capital market instruments, including notes issued by banks for purchase by Pension Funds (AFP).

8. This issue was raised initially in de la Cuadra, Valdés, and Wisecarver (1988).

9. *Proyecto de modificaciones a la ley general de bancos* (1989): 6.

10. *Proyecto de modificaciones a la ley general de bancos* (1989): 7.

11. On this issue, see Sanchez-Carlero (1981).

12. On this issue, see White (1983) and Gorton (1985).

13. State aid to sectors affected by unforeseeable shocks for which the firms involved cannot be held responsible—such as the recent cyanide scare in the Chilean fruit sector—is not inconsistent with full application of the provisions of this law, although the value of banks' assets is thereby indirectly enhanced and government aid is thus channeled to the banks.

14. For this reason the law contemplates a state guarantee on time deposits up to about U.S. $2,000.

15. On the evolution of money demand in the Chilean business cycle, see Matte and Rojas (1988).

16. Precisely for that reason the banking law of 1986 allowed Chilean banks to go into investment banking by acting as holding companies for a number of subsidiaries devoted to stock intermediation, mutual fund management, bank leasing, and financial services. A significant number of such organizations are operating today.

17. The notion of spread, as used here, is broad and covers all interest rates charged on all financial assets, together with the cost of all liabilities, including demand deposits and net worth.

18. According to recent estimates by the Superintendency of Banks, in March 1989 the average economic worth of the financial system was 9.7 percent higher than capital and reserves, that is, a net worth coverage coefficient of 109.7 In 1988 banks' after-tax surpluses amounted to 20.8 percent of banks' capital and reserves. About 68 percent are ordinary resources, the balance being special revenues, including operations with foreign debt notes, the benefits from which amounted to 6.3 percent of capital and reserves.

References

de la Cuadra, Sergio, Salvador Valdés, and Daniel Wisecarver. 1988. Supervisión bancaria: Anticipatión de problemas y alternativas de acción. A study commissioned by the Central Bank of Chile and the Superintendency of Banks. Mimeo (August).

Fernandez, R., "La crisis financiera argentina 1980–1982." *Desarollo económico* no. 12 (June): 79–97.

Gorton, Gary. 1985. "Banking Theory and Free Banking History: A Review Essay." *Journal of Monetary Economics* 16: 267–76.

Matte, R., and Rojas, P. 1988. *Evolución de mercado financiero y una estimación de la demanda por dinero en Chile*. Document no. 33, Serie de estudios economicos. Santiago: Banco Central de Chile.

Proyecto de modificaciones a la ley general de bancos. 1989. Chilean government working document, final version (June).

Rosende, Francisco, and R. Vergara. 1986. "Opciones de política para el sector financiero." *Cuadernos de económia* 70 (December): 373–97.

Sanchez-Carlero, F. 1981. "El fondo de garantía de depositos bancarios." *Revista de derecho bancario y bursátil* (January–March): 35–36.

Superintendencia de Bancos e Instituciones Financieras. 1985. *Información financiera* (March).

White, Eugene N. 1985. *The Regulation and Reform of the American Banking System, 1920–1929*. Princeton, N.J.: Princeton University Press.

5. Charles W. Calomiris, "Do 'Vulnerable' Economies Need Deposit Insurance? Lessons from U.S. Agriculture in the 1920s"

Notes

This paper was prepared for the Sequoia Institute Conference on Financial Risk and Financial Regulation in Commodity Exporting Economies. The author thanks Herbert Baer, George Benston, Philip L. Brock, Douglas Evanoff, Kenneth Kuttner, Larry Schweikart, Lawrence J. White, participants in the Conference on Financial Risk and Financial Regulation; and seminar participants at the Wharton School of Finance, Rutgers University, the University of Illinois at Urbana-Champaign, the University of Michigan, Queens University, and the University of Western Ontario, for helpful comments. Eric Klusman provided excellent technical assistance.

1. Recent research shows that banks perform unique roles in corporate finance (James 1987; Lummer and McConnell, 1989; Gilson, Kose, and Lang, 1990; Hoshi, Kashyap, and Scharfstein, 1990).

2. For a discussion of the behavior of Southern branching banks during the Panic of 1837 and the Panic of 1857, see Calomiris and Schweikart (1991).

3. There will still be a need for a properly designed monetary authority and lender of last resort to manage the money supply, but this issue is separate from the question of insuring banks.

4. Any government transfer program must be financed somehow, and this fact gives rise to additional costs. Raising revenue, either through direct taxation or money creation, can have important adverse allocative consequences. Indeed, as McKinnon (1973, 1988) and others (see Fry, 1988, for a review) point out, in less-developed economies, the need to raise revenue often places a disproportionate burden on the banking system. Reserve requirements and mandated loan subsidies are among the methods to tax financial intermediaries. The ease of enforcing these taxes and their indirect nature presumably have made them a desirable means of raising funds for governments with little power to impose or enforce direct taxation. That governments in less-developed economies need to rely on banks as a source of finance may limit the ability of the government to bail out banks. I return to this point in the concluding section of the paper.

5. As White (1983) has shown, these points are related. Banks wishing to locate in rural areas were more likely to choose a state charter, presumably because of the less restrictive provisions for making loans on agricultural real estate.

6. The sector-specific crisis of the 1920s was followed by the general depression of the early 1930s. The dust storms of 1934–1935 kept agriculture from sharing in the general recovery of 1933–1937. These factors combined to produce a period of agricultural depression that lasted at least fifteen years.

7. Alston (1983: 886).

8. Foreclosure data are provided in Table 5.3. These data are not identical to those reported in Alston (1983) for two reasons. First, 1928 rather than 1930 is used as a bench mark for the number of farms operating from 1926 to 1930. Second, and more important, Alston only subtracted "croppers" from the total number of farms to estimate the number of farms at risk of foreclosure; my estimates subtract all farms operated by tenants, not only croppers. This alternative definition is meant to identify more clearly the relevant population of farmers subject to foreclosure risk, assuming that tenant-run farms are typically owned by individuals who operate their own farms as well.

9. It is also important to note that the extent of the threat to the financial survival of farms and farm lenders from a given decline in income or wealth depends in a nonlinear fashion on the rapidity of the decline and its persistence. Two consecutive years of drastic price and income reductions may produce far more bankruptcies than a similar one-year decline amidst intervening good years or a similar overall decline spread over a longer period. This fact is especially true when a rapid decline follows a boom period—farm leverage, having first been increased by borrowing during the boom, becomes further increased by reductions in farm values during the bust, precisely at a time when the cash flow necessary to meet debt service requirements is reduced. For evidence on the importance of such nonlinearities see Rucker and Alston (1987).

10. See Goldenweiser et al. (1932: Vol. 5, 205–207).

11. See, for example, the discussion of large urban bank reactions to deposit insurance in cities such as Chicago and Philadelphia in White (1983: 191–97).

12. Specifically, in Oklahoma and Kansas interest rates were limited to 3 percent; in Texas, deposits bearing any interest would be exempt from insurance; in Mississippi and South Dakota interest rates were limited to 4 and 5 percent, respectively; and in North Dakota and Washington interest rate limits were set by the Guarantee Boards. Summary tables of these and other regulations are provided in White (1983: 210–11) and Calomiris (1989: 18).

13. Evidence of this phenomenon can be found in numerous historical studies of the operations of bankers under deposit insurance. For example, see Robb (1921).

14. In Oklahoma and Kansas, trusts were not admitted to the insured system. This action further discouraged large urban banks from joining.

15. Oklahoma's first bank failure, that of the Columbia Bank and Trust, was a clear case of speculative expansion through loans to the oil firms owned by the banker W. L. Norton. For details, see Robb (1921: 50–53).

16. See Fenstermaker et al. (1984) and Schweikart (1987).

17. The data in Table 5.10 are end-of-year, unlike the other tables, which are end-of-June. Thus, the peak in Table 5.10 occurs in 1919 rather than 1920.

18. For the forty-eight contiguous states the correlation between the ratio of capital to assets and the average size of banks is strongly negative. For state-chartered banks the correlation in 1920 is -0.47 (significantly different from zero at the 99-percent confidence level); for national banks the correlation in 1920 is -0.43 (significant at the 97-percent confidence level).

19. See FDIC (1956: 55–58).

20. Some of the exceptionally high banking growth in these states reflects favorable economic fundamentals. As Table 5.1 shows, livestock prices rose rapidly in the late 1920s relative to grain prices; thus livestock-dependent states like Wyoming, Idaho, and Arizona should have seen more banking recovery. In regression results that follow, I control for economic environment to isolate the role of regulatory regimes in promoting banking growth.

21. Lee Alston has suggested to me that the increased use of automobiles may also have permitted greater bank consolidation by reducing the need for banks to be located in thinly populated areas.

22. The reduced riskiness of branch, as opposed to unit, banks is established in the third section of this chapter, where I show that branching banks were less likely to fail during the 1920s than unit banks. See also Cartinhour (1931), Doti and Schweikart (1991: Chapter 3), and White (1983: 218–19).

23. According to the Federal Reserve Board of Governors (1926), Wyoming is an exceptional case in that it allowed statewide branch banking, but no banks opened branches during the 1920s. The Federal Reserve seems to be in error on this point. Maeda (1990) argues that the substantial presence of bank chains in Wyoming provides *prima facie* evidence that branches were prohibited. While state law implicitly allowed branches (see Board of Governors, 1925), existing unit bankers

seem to have lobbied state regulators successfully to prevent branching (see Woods, 1985: 102–104). This gave Wyoming a particularly vulnerable nondiversified unit banking system. As Woods (1985: 101) point out, banking outside of major cities was confined mainly to very small banks organized in rural areas to provide financing for expansion to local groups of insider entrepreneurs. Of Wyoming's 113 state banks in 1920, thirty-one had a deposit base of under $100,000 (see Woods, 1985: 96).

24. In Georgia, one of the largest banks in the state, operating thirty branches, failed. According to Cartinhour (1931: 307), the cause of this failure was "poor management."

25. This included, but was not limited to, banks owned by holding companies. The Federal Reserve's agents used their own judgment in determining whether banks under a single holding company operated under centralized control. While they attempted to provide an exhaustive survey of bank practices, sometimes the agents found that "neither the power to exercise such control nor the amount of control actually exercised [could] be determined." See Board of Governors (December 1929: 766).

26. Data on failures of chain banks have not been collected in a consistent or thorough manner, but evidence reported in Chapman (1934) as well as other examples of the collapse of large chains indicates that unit banks belonging to chains were not insulated from shocks as were branch banks. The failure rates of branching banks are discussed in the third section of this chapter.

27. Thies and Gerlowski (1989) provide a detailed discussion of the Oklahoma experience and describe regression results showing that insured state systems had a 0.7 percent higher propensity to fail on average than uninsured state-chartered systems for the period 1921–1929. A separate regression for national banks found no significant difference for national banks in the insured states. Although the authors control for "time, region, and urbanization" (specific results and explanation of data are not provided), this is insufficient to capture differences across states in fundamental disturbances.

28. The distinction between failures and suspensions is empirically important. Their incidences often differed greatly, and the fraction of suspended banks that reopened differed across states and chartering systems. A cross-sectional analysis of these differences remains a topic for future research. Thies and Gerlowski (1989) seem to have used suspensions as their measure of bank failures.

29. See FDIC (1956: 69).

30. These are calculated using the banks in existence immediately before the period of failure as the denominator in the calculation. (As noted in Table 5.15, insured banks sought to avoid rising assessments by converting to national charters.) This methodology avoids the exaggeration of failure rates, due to voluntary exit by banks, that arises when the average number of banks in existence over the whole period is used as the denominator. With either measure there is an adverse selection problem to consider in measuring failure rates of different systems within the same state. Early failures in the insured system could lead

insured banks that are healthy to exit to the other available systems and thereby raise the subsequent observed failure rates for national and uninsured state banks. Observed differences in failure propensity would thus provide all the more evidence of greater riskiness of insured banks. Empirical evidence, however, indicates that the movement of banks from one system to another did not have an important effect on bank failure rates. For example, compare failure rates for national and state banks reported in Table 5.20 for the periods 1921–1924 and 1925–1929 for Kansas, Mississippi, North Dakota, Oklahoma, and Texas—all states with a substantial rate of conversion from state to national charters. In two cases (Mississippi and Oklahoma), national bank failure rates fell in the later period; in the other three cases, they rose slightly.

31. Weighted least squares is the appropriate regression technique in circumstances where aggregate failure rates are compared across different samples. To control for truncation bias in the regressions, I used the log of the odds ratio—the log of $p/(1-p)$—as the dependent variable, where p is the probability of failing, measured by the proportion of banks failing. For a more complete description of the weighted-least-squares technique and its applicability to this case, see Maddala (1984: 28–30).

32. The variations with which I experimented included the following: whether to include Mississippi with the other compulsory-insurance states (given its stricter entry requirements, discussed below); whether to pool national- and state-chartered banks, estimate them separately, or allow their coefficients to differ within a pooled regression; whether to include the ratio of capital to assets and the average size of banks in the regressions; and whether to use commercial failures, real-estate loans, and land price declines, by themselves, or interacted with farm-population proportion and bank real estate loan holdings, as control variables.

33. See also American Bankers' Association (1933), Calomiris (1989), and Thies and Gerlowski (1989). The impossibility of separating unincorporated and incorporated state bank failures in Texas and Washington makes a similar comparison impossible for those states. Also, the small number of uninsured banks in Texas and the short duration of insurance in Washington make such comparisons less interesting.

34. American Bankers' Association (1933: 22) and Robb (1921: 165–70) argue that Mississippi maintained exceptionally high standards for admission of new banks. For example, ABA (1933) writes that "the banking authorities in Mississippi had full discretion in the matter of granting new charters and used it liberally in refusing permission for unneeded banks or to unqualified promoters to open new institutions."

35. For sources see Data Appendix.

36. For a discussion of the costliness of these delays in liquidating savings and loans see Barth et al. (1989).

37. U.S. House of Representatives (1930, 1: 462).

38. Georgia is not part of this group because it prohibited new branch banking only in August 1927.

39. See Chapman and Westerfield (1942: 126–30).

40. Note that I am not arguing that insurance systems should allow voluntary exit. I would argue, however, that since none of the insurance systems succeeded in providing payments system protection, voluntary insurance was superior to compulsory insurance in the 1920s because it engendered less loss.

41. Branching not only leads to a more stable banking system, but it also increases the ability of banks to meet the banking needs of peripheral areas. Using current county-level data from the United States, Evanoff (1988) shows that branch banks provide a far superior means of servicing remote areas than unit banks. If one holds demographic factors constant, one finds that branching increases the number of banking offices per square mile by 65 percent.

42. Ideally, such a system would allow branching as well. In the absence of freedom to branch, the large number of unit banks creates a problem, as noted in Calomiris (1989). For mutual guarantee systems to be effective they must be small enough to make interbank monitoring worthwhile to individual banks. Systems of hundreds of mutually liable banks provide trivially small marginal gains to monitoring the behavior of another bank. An alternative would be separate smaller groups of mutually liable unit banks. A second problem that arises in either the branching or unit banking versions of the mutual-guarantee system is the potential for banks to abuse their self-regulatory power to inhibit competition. To prevent this, the government should create more than one group of banks, and define group membership in a manner than encourages intergroup competition. For example, in a unit-banking mutual-guarantee system (where local monopolies may arise) groups should overlap geographically.

References

Alston, Lee J. 1983. "Farm Foreclosures in the United States during the Interwar Period." *Journal of Economic History* 43 (December).

American Bankers Association. 1933. *The Guaranty of Bank Deposits*. New York: ABA.

Balke, Nathan S., and Robert J. Gordon. 1989. "The Estimation of Prewar Gross National Product: Methodology and New Evidence." *Journal of Political Economy* 97 (February).

Bankers Encyclopedia Co. *The Bankers Encyclopedia*. New York: Bankers Encyclopedia Co. Semi-annual.

Barth, James R., Philip F. Bartholomew, and Carol J. Labich. 1989. "Moral Hazard and the Thrift Crisis: An Analysis of 1988 Resolutions." Research Paper no. 160. Washington, D.C.: Federal Home Loan Bank Board (May).

Bernanke, Ben S. 1983. "Nonmonetary Effects of the Financial Crisis in the Propagation of the Great Depression." *American Economic Review* 73 (June).

Board of Governors of the Federal Reserve System. 1924. "Branch Banking in the United States." *Federal Reserve Bulletin* (December).

———. 1925. "State Laws Relating to Branch Banking." *Federal Reserve Bulletin* (March).

————. 1926. "Branch Banking in the United States." *Federal Reserve Bulletin* (June).

————. 1927. "McFadden Bill Now Law." *Federal Reserve Bulletin* (March).

————. 1929. "Branch Banking Developments June 30, 1928." *Federal Reserve Bulletin* (February).

————. 1929. "Branch and Chain Banking Developments: 1929." *Federal Reserve Bulletin* (December).

————. 1937. "Changes in the Number of National and State Banks During 1921–1936." *Federal Reserve Bulletin* (November).

————. 1943. *Banking and Monetary Statistics.* Washington, D.C.: Federal Reserve Board.

————. 1959. *All Bank Statistics.* Washington, D.C.: Federal Reserve Board.

Bordo, Michael D., and Anna J. Schwartz. 1989. The Performance and Stability of Banking Systems under "Self-Regulation": Theory and Evidence. Rutgers University. Unpublished manuscript.

Brewer, Elijah, III. 1991. "The Impact of Deposit Insurance on S&L Shareholders' Risk/Return Trade-offs." Working Paper WP-91-18. Chicago: Federal Reserve Bank of Chicago.

Brock, Philip L. 1988. The Transmission of Terms of Trade Shocks in Latin America. Durham, N.C.: Duke University, Unpublished manuscript.

Calomiris, Charles W. 1989. "Deposit Insurance: Lessons from the Record." *Economic Perspectives.* (Federal Reserve Bank of Chicago) (May/June).

Calomiris, Charles W. and Gary Gorton. 1991. "The Origins of Banking Panics: Models, Facts, and Bank Regulation." In *Financial Markets and Financial Crises*, ed. R. Glenn Hubbard. Chicago: University of Chicago Press.

Calomiris, Charles W., R. Glenn Hubbard, and James H. Stock. 1986. "The Farm Debt Crisis and Public Policy." Brookings Papers on Economic Activity 2. Washington, D.C.: Brookings Institution.

Calomiris, Charles W., and Charles M. Kahn. 1991. "The Role of Demandable Debt in Structuring Optimal Banking Arrangements." *American Economic Review* (June).

————. 1989. Interbank Monitoring as Seignorage Sharing: The Suffolk System. Northwestern University. Unpublished manuscript.

Calomiris, Charles W., and Larry Schweikart. 1991. "The Panic of 1857: Origins, Transmission, and Containment." *Journal of Economic History* (December).

Cannon, James G. 1910. *Clearing Houses.* Washington, D.C.: U.S. Government Printing Office.

Cartinhour, Gaines T. 1931. *Branch, Group, and Chain Banking.* New York: Macmillan.

Chapman, John M. 1934. *Concentration of Banking.* New York: Columbia University Press.

Chapman, John M., and Ray B. Westerfield. 1942. *Branch Banking: Its Historical and Theoretical Position in America and Abroad.* New York: Harper and Brothers.

Clifton, Ivery D., and William D. Crowley, Jr. 1973. "Farm Real Estate Historical Series Data: 1850–1970." U.S. Department of Agriculture, Economic Research Service (June).

Comptroller of the Currency. Various years. *Annual Report*. Washington, D.C.: U.S. Government Printing Office.

Cooke, Thorton. 1910. "The Insurance of Bank Deposits in the West." 1910. In *State Banks and Trust Companies*, ed. George E. Barnett. Washington, D.C.

Doti, Lynne Pierson, and Larry Schweikart. 1991. *Banking in the American West from Gold Rush to Deregulation*. Norman: University of Oklahoma Press.

Evanoff, Douglas D. 1988. "Branch Banking and Service Accessibility." *Journal of Money, Credit and Banking* 20 (May).

Federal Deposit Insurance Corporation. 1956. *Annual Report*. Washington, D.C.: FDIC.

Fenstermaker, J. Van, J. E. Filer, and R. S. Herren. 1984. "Money Statistics of New England, 1785–1837." *Journal of Economic History* (June).

Fry, Maxwell. 1988. *Money, Interest, and Banking in Economic Development*. Baltimore: Johns Hopkins University Press.

Gilson, Stuart C., John Kose, and Larry H. P. Lang. 1990. "Troubled Debt Restructurings." *Journal of Financial Economics* (October).

Goldenweiser, E. A., et al. 1932. *Bank Suspensions in the United States, 1892–1931*. Material prepared for the information of the Federal Reserve System by the Federal Reserve Committee on Branch, Group, and Chain Banking.

Gorton, Gary. 1985. "Clearing Houses and the Origin of Central Banking in the U.S." *Journal of Economic History* (June).

———. 1989. Self-Regulating Banking Coalitions. The Wharton School. Unpublished manuscript.

Hoshi, Takeo, Anil Kashyap, and David Scharfstein. 1990. "The Role of Banks in Reducing the Costs of Financial Distress in Japan." *Journal of Financial Economics* (September).

James, Christopher. 1987. "Some Evidence on the Uniqueness of Bank Loans." *Journal of Financial Economics* (October).

Kane, Edward J. 1988. How Incentive-incompatible Deposit-insurance Funds Fail. Ohio State University. Unpublished manuscript.

Leven, Maurice. 1925. *Income in the Various States: Its Sources and Distribution, 1919, 1920, and 1921*. New York: Columbia University Press.

Lummer, Scott L., and John J. McConnell. 1989. "Further Evidence on the Bank Lending Process and the Capital-Market Response to Bank Loan Agreements." *Journal of Financial Economics* (January).

Maddala, G.S. 1984. *Limited-dependent and Qualitative Variables in Econometrics*. London: Cambridge University Press.

Maeda, Eiji. 1990. Wyoming's Failure to Develop Branch Banking. Unpublished manuscript.

McKinnon, Ronald I. 1973. *Money and Capital in Economic Development*. Washington, D.C.: Brookings Institution.

———. 1988. "Financial Liberalization and Economic Development: A Reassessment of Interest-Rate Policies in Asia and Latin America." International Center for Economic Growth Occasional Paper no. 6. San Francisco: ICS Press.

Merton, Robert C. 1977. "Analytical Derivation of the Cost of Deposit Insurance and Loan Guarantees: An Application of Modern Option Pricing Theory." *Journal of Banking and Finance* (June).

Robb, Thomas B. 1921. *The Guaranty of Bank Deposits.* New York: Houghton-Mifflin.

Romer, Christina D. 1989. "The Prewar Business Cycle Reconsidered: New Estimates of Gross National Product, 1869–1908." *Journal of Political Economy* 97 (February).

Rucker, Randal R., and Lee J. Alston. 1987. "Farm Failures and Government Intervention: A Case Study of the 1930s." *American Economic Review* 77 (September).

Schweikart, Larry. 1987. *Banking in the American South.* Baton Rouge: Louisiana State University.

Stauber, B. R. 1931. "The Farm Real Estate Situation." U.S. Department of Agriculture, Circular no. 209, Washington, D.C.: USDA.

Stock, James H. 1984. "Real Estate Mortgages, Foreclosures, and Midwestern Agrarian Unrest, 1865–1920." *Journal of Economic History* 43 (March).

Strauss, Frederick, and Louis H. Bean. 1940. "Gross Farm Income and Indices of Farm Production and Prices in the United States, 1869–1937." U.S. Department of Agriculture Technical Bulletin no. 703 (December). Washington, D.C.: USDA.

Thies, Clifford F., and Daniel A. Gerlowski. 1989. "Deposit Insurance: A History of Failure," *Cato Journal* 8 (Winter).

U.S. Department of Commerce. Various years. *Statistical Abstract of the United States.* Washington, D.C.: U.S. Government Printing Office.

————. 1927. *United States Census of Agriculture, 1925.* Washington, D.C.: U.S. Government Printing Office.

————. 1932. *Fifteenth Census of the United States.* Washington, D.C.: U.S. Government Printing Office.

U.S. House of Representatives. 1930. "Branch, Chain, and Group Banking." Hearings before the Committee on Banking and Currency, 71st Congress, Second Session.

White, Eugene N. 1982. "The Political Economy of Bank Regulation." *Journal of Economic History* (March).

————. 1983. *The Regulation and Reform of the American Banking System, 1900–1929.* Princeton: Princeton University Press.

————. 1985. "The Merger Movement in Banking, 1919–1933." *Journal of Economic History* 45 (June).

Woods, L. Milton. 1985. *Sometimes the Books Froze: Wyoming's Economy and Its Banks.* Boulder: University of Colorado Press.

Richard Webb: "Comment"

Reference

World Bank. 1988. *World Development Report 1988.* New York: Oxford University Press.

6. Philip L. Brock, "The Macroeconomic Consequences of Loan-Loss Rollovers"

Notes

1. For example, the International Monetary Fund, through its Compensatory and Contingency Financing Facility, assists member countries who face external shocks. Loans are given senior claim for repayment and must be repaid within five years. James (1989) analyzes the underinvestment problem at the level of a bank's financing decisions.

2. Brock (1992a) develops an alternative model of government loan guarantees that relies on a single aggregate capital stock, rather than on a disaggregated capital stock of structures and equipment.

3. To focus attention on the incentives created by the timing of the government's payment of its liability, the model abstracts from distortions normally created by tax collection by assuming that the government can finance the liability with nondistorting taxes.

4. Figure 6.2 is drawn so that the adjustment path is the same for both immediate payment of the guarantee and delayed payment of the guarantee. In fact, delayed payment of the guarantee creates a real cost that lowers the agent's wealth, thereby shifting the adjustment path associated with delayed payment to the left of the adjustment path associated with immediate payment of the guarantee. To simplify Figure 6.2, this negative wealth effect has been suppressed.

5. In the context of a world with deposit guarantees, such an action corresponds to a closure of the financial system that leaves the value of deposits intact so that depositors can then repurchase the structures at the lower, market-clearing price. In such a scenario, the government essentially buys the structures at a high price from depositors and sells the structures back at a low price.

6. At point A in Figure 6.2 (prior to the external shock), it can be shown that the value of consumption is equal to the annuity value of income from the stock of capital net of foreign debt plus the stream of labor income and rental income on land: $C^m + \bar{p}C^n = r(E + \bar{p}S - b) + wL + r^T T$, where w is the real wage (measured in terms of the importable) and r^T is the rental rate on land.

Following the external shock, $E_0 + p_0 S_0 < b_0$ at point C, thereby placing the put option "in the money." At point B in Figure 6.2, the value of the stock of physical capital equals the value of the guaranteed debt, $E_1 + p_1 S_0 = b_0$. Along the adjustment path $DE, p_t S_t + E_t > b_t$ and $\dot{p}_t S_t + p_t \dot{S}_t + \dot{E}_t < \dot{b}_t$. At time $T, p_T S_T + E_T = b_T$ and $\int_T^\infty [C_t^m + p_t C_t^n] e^{-r(t-T)} = \int_T^\infty [w_t L + r_t^T T] e^{-r(t-T)}$. This terminal condition, together with the requirement that the postintervention price lie on the saddlepath, pins down the endpoint of the trajectory DE (by determining the size of the jump in the relative price of nontradables that must take place at time T) and is analogous to conditions employed by Abel (1982: Figure 3) and Brock (1988: Figure 2) in connection with the analysis of temporary investment subsidies. One of the important determinants of the starting point of the adjustment path *DE* is the responsiveness of nontraded consumption to changes in the relative price of nontraded goods (determined in part by the intertemporal elasticity of substitution in consumption) since, holding other things constant, a greater willingness to reduce nontraded consumption in response to a higher relative price of nontraded goods permits more investment and a higher rate of capital accumulation for any given relative price of nontraded goods.

It is the general equilibrium determination of the relative price of nontradables that may make it difficult, in practice, to know whether a solvency problem exists in an economy following a large external shock, since the existence of an explicit or implicit government guarantee will cushion the initial fall in the value of an economy's capital stock. Indeed, the value of the capital stock will exceed the value of the guaranteed debt prior to the termination of the government's guarantee, as illustrated by the adjustment path *DE* in Figure 6.2. See Brock (1992b) for a more technical treatment of these issues and for an analysis of the behavior of an economy in which the government operates with a guarantee fund rather than with a policy to pre-announce a date at which the government's guarantee expires.

7. Delays in the liquidation of structures create wealth effects that alter nontraded consumption expenditure and shift the saddlepath to the left. See note 3.

8. The real exchange rate for Chile is the ratio of the corrected Chilean consumer price index divided by Chile's exchange rate and the U.S. producer price index. The real price of copper in Figure 6.3 is the average monthly spot price on the London Metal Exchange divided by the U.S. producer price index.

Movements in real exchange rates are also often used as proxies for movements in the price of nontraded consumption goods relative to a basket of traded goods. In this chapter's model, the price of structures (p) and the relative price of nontraded consumption goods (p) are identical.

9. The first drop in Chile's real exchange rate was also accompanied by a decision to devalue the nominal exchange rate and to permit real wages to decline (eliminating an indexation mechanism).

10. The real exchange rate for Dallas is the ratio of that city's consumer price index divided by the all-urban consumer price index for the United States. The real price of oil is the actual U.S. domestic average price divided by the producer price index.

11. In the case of Texas, provisions of the 1981 Economic Recovery Tax Act permitting investors to write off about 40 percent of their investment in real estate projects in the first five years of the project interacted with the incentives created by the government's failure to close insolvent financial institutions. The 1986 Tax Reform Act, by reducing the five-year tax write-off from 40 percent to about 18 percent, interacted with the sharp oil price decline to trigger the government's intervention in Texas's financial institutions.

12. There are numerous references to this episode. For example, Gayer, Rostow, and Schwartz (1953, 1: 287) contains the following passage:

It appeared to Biddle that the country could only be rescued, in the first place, by persuading the London money market to absorb more American securities in liquidation of the most pressing obligations, and secondly, by extending sufficient credit to American planters and cotton factors to enable them to hold their stocks for a rise in the price of cotton. As it developed the two policies were but aspects of a single grandiose operation.

Detailed description of the mechanisms employed by Biddle for the rollover of loan losses can be found in Smith (1953). See also Temin (1969).

13. The U.S. real exchange rate is the ratio of the U.S. wholesale price index (taken from Smith and Cole, 1935) divided by the U.S./British exchange rate (taken from Smith and Cole, 1935) and the British wholesale price index (taken from Gayer, Rostow, and Schwartz, 1953). The price of cotton is the Liverpool price for Upland cotton (taken from Donnell, 1872).

14. Congressional support for federal assumption of state debts was defeated in 1843 (Ratchford, 1941).

15. The Federal Home Loan Bank Board did, however, attempt to restrict the flow of out-of-state loans to Texas, as discussed by White (1991, 126–28). In April 1984 the bank board enacted a set of regulations that limited the value of brokered deposits from any single source to $100,000. In June 1984 a Federal District Court judge issued an injunction against the enforcement of the regulations, and in January 1985 the U.S. Court of Appeals ruled against the bank board. Thus, the one attempt to limit loan losses in Texas by restricting external funding to Texas banks and savings and loan institutions was overruled, thereby delaying and worsening the financial collapse.

References

Abel, Andrew B. 1982. "Dynamic Effects of Permanent and Temporary Tax Policies in a *q* Model of Investment." *Journal of Monetary Economics* 9: 353–73.

Brock, Philip L. 1988. "Investment, the Current Account, and the Relative Price of Non-Traded Goods in a Small Open Economy." *Journal of International Economics* 24: 235–53.

———. 1992a. "External Shocks and Financial Collapse: Foreign Loan Guarantees and Intertemporal Substitution of Investment in Texas and Chile." *American Economic Review* 82.

———. 1992b. Government Insurance Fund Crises: The Role of Intertemporal Substitution in Investment. Unpublished working paper, Department of Economics, University of Washington, Seattle.

Donnell, E. J. 1872. *Chronological and Statistical History of Cotton*. New York: James Sutton and Co.

Economist, The. 1988. "Waiting for the Texan Sunrise." (October 8): 75–76.

Gayer, Arthur D., W. W. Rostow, and Anna Jacobson Schwartz. 1953. *The Growth and Fluctuation of the British Economy: 1790–1850*. Oxford: Clarendon Press.

James, Christopher. 1989. "Off-Balance Sheet Activities and the Underinvestment Problem in Banking." *Journal of Accounting, Auditing and Finance* 4: 111–24.

Kane, Edward J. 1989. "The High Cost of Incompletely Funding the FSLIC's Shortage of Explicit Capital." *The Journal of Economic Perspectives* 3 (Fall): 31–47.

Merton, Robert C. 1977. "An Analytic Derivation of the Cost of Deposit Insurance and Loan Guarantees." *Journal of Banking and Finance* 1: 3–11.

———. 1978. "On the Cost of Deposit Insurance When There Are Surveillance Costs." *Journal of Business* 51: 439–52.

Ratchford, B. U. 1941. *American State Debts*. Durham, N.C.: Duke University Press.

Short, Genie D., and Jeffery W. Gunther. 1989. "The Texas Thrift Situation: Implications for the Texas Financial Industry." *Financial Industry Studies* (Federal Reserve Bank of Dallas) (October): 1–18.

Smith, Walter B. 1953. *Economic Aspects of the Second Bank of the United States*. Cambridge, Mass.: Harvard University Press.

Smith, Walter B., and Arthur H. Cole. 1935. *Fluctuations in American Business, 1790–1860*. Cambridge, Mass.: Harvard University Press.

Temin, Peter. 1969. *The Jacksonian Economy*. New York: Norton.

Warren, George F., and Frank A. Pearson. 1933. *Prices*. New York: John Wiley and Sons.

White, Lawrence J. 1991. *The S & L Debacle: Public Policy Lessons for Bank and Thrift Regulation*. New York: Oxford University Press.

World Bank. 1989. *World Development Report 1989*. New York: Oxford University Press.

7. Philip L. Brock, "Conclusion"

Notes

1. For example, Cortés Douglas and de la Cuadra (1984), Cortés Douglas (1989), and Lagos (1988) have all documented the close connection between movements in Chile's terms of trade and movements in output. Cortés Douglas and de la Cuadra show that ten out of twelve recessions in Chile since 1926 have been accompanied by a deterioration in Chile's terms of trade. The relatively recent literature on the "Dutch Disease," such as the volume by Neary and van Wijnbergen (1986), has also confirmed the strong link between commodity price movements and aggregate economic performance in commodity-exporting economies.

2. Even under this regulatory approach, large shocks to asset portfolios will cause banks to switch from risk-averse to risk-loving behavior. See Marcus (1984) for the influence of positive bank charter value on bank portfolio choice.

3. In addition to Horvitz's verbal comments, see his insightful analysis on the role of bank examination regulations in Horvitz (1980).

4. Large banks are often considered "too big to fail," so everyone, including equity holders, is bailed out. Large depositors can usually avoid deposit interest rate ceilings by capital flight out of the banking system and possibly out of the country.

5. Ramírez explained that if a bank turned out to be solvent after a government take-over, the expropriation of a fraction of depositors' funds would be unconstitutional.

6. See Rolnick and Weber (1983, 1984) and Rockoff (1975) for calculations of the losses to note holders under free-banking.

7. Statements supporting 100-percent reserve banking can be found in Simons (1936), Fisher (1935), and Friedman (1948). See Fisher for a discussion of the bills presented to Congress for the purpose of creating a 100-percent reserve banking system.

8. See Sánchez Calero (1981) for a detailed analysis of the creation and evolution of the Spanish deposit guarantee fund between 1977 and 1980. The cases of Colombia and Venezuela are discussed in Chapter 1 of this volume.

9. The Chilean constitution bans the central bank from offering deposit guarantees. According to Article 129 of the Chilean banking law, during a bank's liquidation central bank loans used to pay demand depositors and other short-term creditors have preference over the claims of any other creditor.

10. I wish to thank Jerry Jenkins for numerous invaluable suggestions made between the outset of the Texas-Chile project in October 1988 and the publication of this volume, as well as for the many hundreds of hours he has spent working to improve the volume's contents.

References

Avery, Robert B., Terrence M. Belton, and Michael A. Goldberg. 1988. "Market Discipline in Regulating Bank Risk: New Evidence from the Capital Markets." *Journal of Money, Credit and Banking* 20 (November): 597–610.

Bagehot, Walter. 1873. *Lombard Street: A Description of the Money Market*. London: Kegan Paul, Trench, & Co.

Benston, George J., Robert A. Eisenbeis, Paul M. Horvitz, Edward J. Kane, and George G. Kaufman. 1986. *Perspectives on Safe and Sound Banking: Past, Present, and Future*. Cambridge, Mass.: MIT Press.

Brock, Philip L. 1989. "Reserve Requirements and the Inflation Tax." *Journal of Money, Credit and Banking* 21 (February): 106–21.

Cortés Douglas, Hernán. 1989. "Lessons of the Past: The Role of External Shocks in Chilean Recessions, 1926–1982." In *Latin American Debt and Adjustment: External Shocks and Macroeconomic Policies*, ed. Philip L. Brock, Michael B. Connolly, and Claudio González-Vega. New York: Praeger.

Cortés Douglas, Hernán, and Sergio de la Cuadra. 1984. *Recesiones económicas, crisis cambiarias y ciclos inflacionarios en Chile, 1926–1982*. Santiago: Instituto de Economía, Pontificia Universidad Católica de Chile.

Fisher, Irving. 1935. *100% Money*. New York: The Adelphi Company.

Friedman, Milton. 1948. "A Monetary and Fiscal Framework for Economic Stability." *American Economic Review* 38 (June): 245–64.

Horvitz, Paul. 1980. "A Reconsideration of the Role of Bank Examination." *Journal of Money, Credit and Banking* 12 (November): 654–59.

Lagos, Luis Felipe. 1988. "El efecto de los shocks externos sobre el producto: Un análisis para la economía chilena." *Cuadernos de economía* 25 (August): 215–28.

Lüders, Rolf J. 1991. "Latin American Contrast: Capital Markets and Development in

Chile and Argentina." In *Capital Markets and Development*, ed. Steven H. Hanke and Alan Walters. San Francisco: ICS Press.

Marcus, Alan J. 1984. "Deregulation and Bank Financial Policy." *Journal of Banking and Finance* 8: 557–65.

Mayer, Thomas. 1982. "A Case Study of Federal Reserve Policymaking: Regulation Q in 1966." *Journal of Monetary Economics* 10 (September): 259–71.

McKinnon, Ronald I. 1973. *Money and Capital in Economic Development*. Washington, D.C.: Brookings Institution.

McKinnon, Ronald I., and Donald J. Mathieson. 1981. "How to Manage a Repressed Economy." *Essays in International Finance*, no. 145, International Finance Section, Department of Economics, Princeton University, Princeton, New Jersey.

Merrick, John J. Jr., and Anthony Saunders. 1985. "Bank Regulation and Monetary Policy." *Journal of Money, Credit and Banking* 17 (November): 2, 691–717.

Neary, J. Peter, and Sweder van Wijnbergen. 1986. *Natural Resources and the Macroeconomy*. Cambridge, Mass.: MIT Press.

Rockoff, Hugh. 1975. *The Free Banking Era: A Re-Examination*. New York: Arno Press.

Rolnick, Arthur J., and Warren E. Weber. 1983. "New Evidence on the Free Banking Era." *American Economic Review* 73 (December): 1080–91.

———. 1984. "The Causes of Free Bank Failures: A Detailed Examination." *Journal of Monetary Economics* 14 (November): 267–92.

Sánchez Calero, Fernando. 1981. "El fondo de garantía de depósitos bancarios." *Revista de derecho bancario y bursátil* (January-March): 11–77.

Simons, Henry. 1936. "Rules versus Authorities in Monetary Policy." *Journal of Political Economy* 44 (February): 1–30.

Valdés, Salvador, and Alexandra Lomakin. 1988. "Percepción sobre la garantía estatal a los depósitos durante 1987 en Chile." *Cuadernos de economía* 75 (August): 229–46.

Appendix I

Translator's Note

1. One UF is worth approximately U.S. $16.50.

Appendix II

Translator's Notes

1. The daily value of the UF is based on the previous month's consumer price index, and serves as a unit of constant purchasing power.

2. This reference is understood to refer to Articles 116 or 119 of the General Law of Banks.

Contributors

Philip L. Brock is a member of the Department of Economics at the University of Washington, Seattle. His previous work on the Chilean financial collapse, as well as his contributions as author and coeditor of *Latin American Debt and Adjustment: External Shocks and Macroeconomic Policies* (New York: Praeger, 1989), reflect the research interests that he brings to this book. His work as adviser to the central bank of the Dominican Republic also influenced the choice of materials for this volume.

Salvador Valdés is currently a member of the faculty of Economics and Business Administration of the Catholic University of Chile. His doctoral dissertation (MIT, 1986) on the Chilean banking collapse as well as his ongoing research on banking regulation has contributed to his work for this volume.

Sergio de la Cuadra is a former minister of finance and president of the central bank of Chile. He is currently a private consultant and member of the faculty of Economics and Business Administration of the Catholic University of Chile.

Gary Gorton is a member of the faculty at the Wharton School of Business (University of Pennsylvania). Among his numerous publications, his "Clearinghouses and the Origin of Central Banking in the U.S.," *Journal of Economic History* (June 1985) may be the most appropriate background reference to his lead commentary for this volume.

Paul M. Horvitz, a former research director for the U.S. Federal Deposit Insurance Corporation (1967–1977), is presently the Judge James A. Elkins Professor of Banking and Finance at the University of Houston. He coauthored the widely cited book, *Safe and Sound Banking* (MIT Press, 1986).

Peter Diamond is a member of the faculty at the Massachusetts Institute of Technology's Department of Economics. His earlier work on models for overlapping generations played an important part in the development of recent general equilibrium models with banks. His more recent work on stochastic credit in search equilibrium reflects his interest in the basic theoretical problems connected with the efficient functioning of financial markets.

Guillermo Ramírez presided over the reprivatization of banks in Chile and was the superintendent of banks for that country's government at the time of the Texas-Chile seminar. He is currently employed as a private consultant.

Francisco Rosende wrote a number of influential articles that helped to shape the current Chilean banking legislation. At the time of the Texas-Chile seminar, he was director of studies of the Central Bank of Chile. He is currently a member of the faculty of Economics and Business Administration of the Catholic University of Chile.

Kenneth E. Scott is a member of the Law School faculty at Stanford University and is a senior research fellow at the Hoover Institution. He has written extensively on legal regulation of corporate structures and financial institutions and serves as a member of the Financial Institutions Committee for the State Bar Association of California.

Charles W. Calomiris is a member of the Finance Department of the University of Illinois at Urbana-Champaign and is affiliated with the National Bureau of Economic Research. Of his numerous publications on banking history and theory, perhaps the most useful as background to his chapter in this volume is "Deposit Insurance: Lessons from the Record," *Economic Perspectives* 13 (May 1989): 10–30.

Richard Webb is well known as an academic, both as a professor at Princeton and as a researcher at the World Bank, for his long-standing work on the association between economic growth and income distribution. He also worked at the central bank of Peru for a number of years, including service as president between 1980 and 1985.

Seminar Participants

Robert Bartell, East Tennessee State University
Alan Batchelder, A.I.D.
John Boyd, University of Minnesota
Philip L. Brock, University of Washington
C. Stuart Callison, A.I.D.
Charles W. Calomiris, University of Illinois and National Bureau
  of Economic Research
John Chang, A.I.D.
Ed Costello, A.I.D.
Carolin Crabbe, A.I.D.
Sergio de la Cuadra, Catholic University of Chile
Peter Diamond, Massachusetts Institute of Technology
James Fox, A.I.D.
Sandra Frydman, A.I.D.
Claudio González-Vega, Ohio State University
Marvin Goodfriend, University of Chicago
Gary Gorton, Wharton School of Business
Brian Hannon, A.I.D.
Patrick Honohan, World Bank
Paul M. Horvitz, University of Houston
Jerry Jenkins, Sequoia Institute
Fred Kirschstein, A.I.D.
Donald Mathieson, International Monetary Fund
Guillermo Ramírez, superintendent of banks (former), Chile
Kenneth E. Scott, Stanford University Law School and Hoover Institution
Richard Sines, A.I.D.
Salvador Valdés, Catholic University of Chile
Neal Zank, A.I.D.

ACADEMIC ADVISERS

The services of the following academic advisers to the Sequoia Seminar Series have distinguished the series and its publications:

Robert H. Bates
  Political Economy Center
  Duke University

Brigitte Berger
  Department of Sociology
  Boston University

Peter Berger
  Director,
  Institute for the Study of
    Economic Culture
  Boston University

Richard M. Bird
  Department of Economics
  University of Toronto

L. E. Birdzell, Jr.
  Coauthor,
  How the West Grew Rich

Philip L. Brock
  Department of Economics
  University of Washington

William O. Chittick
  Director,
  Center for Global
    Policy Studies
  University of Georgia

Hernando de Soto
  President,
  Institute for Liberty
    and Democracy
  Lima, Peru

Robert Higgs
  Department of Business
  Seattle University

Douglass C. North
  Director,
  The Center in
    Political Economy
  Washington University

Elinor Ostrom
  Codirector,
  Workshop in Political
    Theory and Policy Analysis
  Indiana University

Han S. Park
  Director,
  Development Studies
  Sequoia Institute

John P. Powelson
  Department of Economics
  University of Colorado

Lawrence H. White
  Department of Economics
  University of Georgia

Index